THE MIDDLING SORTS

THE MIDDLING SORTS

EXPLORATIONS IN THE HISTORY OF THE AMERICAN MIDDLE CLASS

Edited by
Burton J. Bledstein
and
Robert D. Johnston

ROUTLEDGE
NEW YORK   LONDON

Published in 2001 by
Routledge
29 West 35th Street
New York, NY 10001

Published in Great Britain by
Routledge
11 New Fetter Lane
London EC4P 4EE

Routledge is an imprint of the Taylor & Francis Group.
Copyright © 2001 by Routledge

Printed in the United States of America on acid-free paper.

2   4   6   8   0   9   7   5   3   1

Library of Congress Cataloging-in-Publication Data
The middling sorts: explorations in the history of the american middle class/
edited by Burton J. Bledstein and Robert D. Johnston.
p. cm.
Includes bibliographical references and index.
ISBN 0-415-92641-6—ISBN 0-415-92642-4 (pbk.)
1. Middle class—United States—History—19th century.
2. Middle class—United States—History—20th century.
I. Bledstein, Burton J.   II. Johnston, Robert D.
HT690.U6 M475 2001
305.5'5'0973—dc21   00-044639

Contents

Acknowledgments

We wish primarily to thank each other for sticking together over the long haul, as well as our families for allowing that to happen. Deirdre Mullane brought us on board at Routledge and provided both the wisdom and the prodding we needed to work on the book, and Brendan O'Malley offered the support necessary for its completion. Lisa Vecchione was terrific at facilitating the production of the book, while Adam Bohannon supplied the graceful design. Carrie Lane gave incisive commentary on the essays, Michael Jo helped with tasks in the completion of the manuscript, and Aaron Sachs proffered superb editorial advice. Above all, the authors offered not just important intellectual contributions, but also plenty of wisdom—and patience.

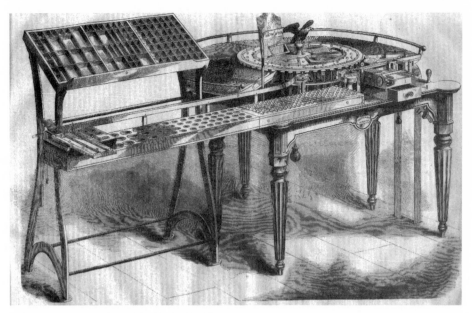

Alden's Type-Setting and Type-Distributing Machine. SCIENTIFIC AMERICAN, VOL. 14, NO. 2,
JANUARY 7, 1866, 23.

Sam Clemens, Apprentice Printer. COURTESY OF MARK TWAIN
PROJECT, BANCROFT LIBRARY.

Introduction: Storytellers to the Middle Class

BURTON J. BLEDSTEIN

Continually we hear reference to the "middle class" in our daily lives. Indeed, in the twentieth century, a large body of Americans—a majority in most polling data since the 1930s—have identified themselves as somewhere in the middle of the class structure, neither rich nor poor, neither upper nor lower, closer to being typical than not, striving to be in the center—the middle. But who are these characters, and what makes them middle class?[1]

The questions are provocative, interesting, and significant. At a minimum, many scholars agree that the middle class for the last three centuries has been elusive to investigation and slippery to define. As G. D. H. Cole expressed it,

> The concept of the middle class is exceedingly elusive, by whatever route one approaches it. Clearly membership of the middle class, or classes, [is] not simply a matter of income, either absolutely or of relative income within a particular social structure. Nor is it exclusively a matter of the nature and source of the income received, or of profession or calling. Nor again is it exclusively a matter of education, or of manners; for no definition based on these will avail to mark off one part of the middle classes from the upper class or another from the working class.[2]

Scholarly exploration has before it a promising field. Where, then, should we begin?

One obvious place is common observation, better known as common sense. From a practical perspective, for instance, most Americans who self-consciously identify as middle class appear to be savvy about what they perceive to be the advantages. Stories abound both in the popular media and in casual discussion about former radicals who once crusaded to trash the "hegemonic" system turning out to be stock brokers, advertising executives, corporate lawyers, government civil servants—even tenured professors. The attractions of the so-called American Dream, even among those who claim to heap contempt on it, look irresistibly positive in a long list of potential benefits.[3] These include personal financial security, an opportunity to accumulate assets, access to good schools and increasingly higher levels of education, skilled work in upwardly mobile careers, a safe environment in which to live and raise a family, health insurance, material possessions to make life more convenient and comfortable, room for personal adventure, self-expression, and a spiritual life.

Furthermore, systematic evidence supporting such commonsense observations indicates that the ambitions to achieve these benefits cut across income levels, except at the extremes. The same conclusion applies across occupational identities, political affiliations, and national origins. The middling is broad—*too* broad and amorphous, the critics say. Scholars have also recently found that the middle classes in minority communities—African American, Latino, Asian—have been growing significantly in the last generation in terms of numbers as well as self-consciousness, advocacy of interest, and political expression.

Common sense, however, may be common nonsense. The phenomenon we need to pin down may look, talk, and walk like the middle class—shop at the same stores, go to the same schools, enter the same professions, work out at the same clubs, patronize the same doctors, purchase the same commodities, aspire to the same lifestyle. But is this spectacle merely transparent, an easy myth for consumers and politicians looking at differences? Is middle-class social identity merely material and transient, especially in comparison to supposedly more primal cultural identities, a wallpaper covering divergences in values and attitudes that are, beneath the surface, inestimable and profound?

For instance, does an African American middle class today—although it pretty much dresses, talks, and lives like everyone else—differ more in values and lifestyle than it shares with a Mexican American middle class? Thinking historically: A century ago, did a Jewish American middle class differ more than it shared with an Anglo-American middle class? More generally, is the "whiteness"—currently in vogue in public discussion—such an absolute gulf that nonwhite and white middle classes can never feel for each other except cosmetically? Also, how exclusive are other social identities, especially gender? Does a middle-class professional woman share more and have deeper ties and understandings with her husband in the suburbs—whatever the arguments between them—than with a working-class minority woman in the inner city? When push comes to shove, which identities count the most?[4]

Given the stubborn nature of the problem, it is important to recognize by way of introduction that the most significant social and political controversies in the last third of the twentieth century appear to have revolved less around the desirability of ends generally considered to be "middle class" than around the mixed policy of means to achieve them. Which does the job best: specifically government entitlements, regulation, and protections (against discrimination, for instance), or marketplace "efficiencies"? The debate about means has certainly been robust and politically charged. Yet the responses have not been easy to categorize. Ironically in this recent period, unionization to achieve a higher standard of living prospered in elite service and wealthy entertainment sectors—airline pilots, professional athletes—and among selective white-collar professions while declining significantly in the traditional manufacturing industries.

From the historian's perspective, the turns in this story about the appearance of social class identities—the why, how, and when people identified with the middle—are intriguing. They number among the most important in the field of American history. One place to begin a deeper and more sustained exploration of these issues is with the primary blocks of the story— the nuances and shifting meanings of vocabulary. For instance, do the "Middle Ranks" in the seventeenth century connect easily to the modern middle class? Why the difference in reference between the "Middling Classes" in the first half of the nineteenth century and the middle class today? Simply put, what did people mean when they represented themselves as middle class? For three centuries people have been representing and drawing references to the social and class conditions of the middling sorts in a variety of phrases that themselves need sorting out. First we will put the words in place. Then we can hear from two consummate storytellers who made large audiences of middle-class readers, and even in a real sense taught them to speak.

First the story, then the storytellers, and finally the historians who have attempted to interpret both.

"Middling Sorts, Middle Classes"

In the seventeenth century, reference began to be made to a social grouping called the *Middling* or *Middle Rank*, also known as the *Middle Order*, *Estate*, *Degree*, *Standing*, *Station*, or *Strata*. The world of social ranks differed from the later one of social classes. First, ranks were determined by birth and taken to be a given in the cosmic ordering of the social structure. To transgress the cosmic geography was synonymous with original sin. For instance, the fictional Robinson Crusoe, the ambitious son of a family of middling fortune, cautioned himself against "rash and immoderate Desire of rising faster than the Nature of the thing admitted" lest he be cast down into "Deepest Guelph of human Misery." Marooned on an island prison in solitary confinement, the incarcerated Crusoe had plenty of reason to reflect upon and time to respond to what had gone wrong.[5]

Second, ranks were brimming with visible codes indicating who someone was and where he or she fit in the overall social scheme. In this early period, there was one major division in the social structure, between the Gentry that included all levels of nobility, and the Commons and Common Sorts. Within the Gentry, for instance, the lesser nobility below Peerage were arranged into baronets, knights, esquires, and gentlemen. Gentry were important because of who they were. Across the great gulf everyone else belonged in the Commons and were only recognized for how and where they fit in the service of the Gentry-centered system. Commoners, who often had no name in documents beyond a functional identity—carpenter or goodwife, for instance—were perceived in derogatory connotations as mediocre, second-rate, unmannered, crude, and mean: mean as average and mean as cheap.

Robinson Crusoe described himself as belonging to the "upper Degree of low Life." He was well-informed about the divisions in the "low Life" population: the *Yeoman* and *Tenant Farmers* (owners or renters of property), *Tradesmen* and *Merchants* (creditors and debtors of goods), and *Artisans* and *Mechanics* (apprenticed to acquire skills). In the "lower Degree of low Life" below lived the *Common Sorts*, laborers without assets, property, or means of improving themselves who were often contemptuously referred to as boorish, barbarous, rude, illiterate, possibly "thieves, pickpockets, low-cheats and dirty sots"—in other words, a "rabble."

Manners, attire, learning, and occupational activity were like bulletin boards announcing the visual appearance of the order of things in this stratified, hierarchic, often nasty social world. Typical of a woman of her genteel standing, the well-born Elizabeth Drinker in 1797 easily identified the station of a visitor in an observation in her diary: "A Woman was here yesterday dressed very fine in but a middling way, gold ear-bobs, white french dress, and a Vail on, she had a young girl with her who made, partly, the same appearance." Slurs regarding common sorts—common woman, common herd, common criminal—lived long after official designations of rank fell from favor. In the vernacular of nineteenth-century Americanisms "common doings," which first meant plain food in contrast to dainties, now described "persons, actions, or things in general of an inferior kind."[6]

The reference to "middling sorts" in the eighteenth century pointed to a development within the dual classifications of rank. "Sorts" was a more neutral category than rank or station, reflecting changing realities. Middling sorts were separating themselves in the "low Life" from the boorish common sorts. In 1709 Daniel Defoe referred to "the middle sort who live well"—a positive evaluation.[7] Subsequent descriptions in the eighteenth and early nineteenth centuries expanded upon Defoe's hopeful inferences: "honest, sober men who mind their own business," "the better kind of people," "orderly and industrious," the center of the wealth and intelligence of a nation. Improving, industrious, and useful were terms this group began using to characterize itself against gentility.[8] Based on his own modest yeoman background in Connecticut, Noah Webster in his monumental dictionary removed any negative inference—mediocre, mean, low life—from the definition of middling sort: "about equally distant from the extremes; moderate."[9]

The middling sorts could not count on the privileges and patronage conferred by the State. Moreover, they lacked the genteel character, education, and manners of the learned upper strata. What distinguished their existence was a shaky independence in the precarious marketplace. Life was a "business" to them, with specific goals to achieve: the accumulation of sufficient property to support a family, a competence in old age, reasonable health and longevity. A young man was estimated to take about forty years to reach the foundations of middling status. Morbidity was the enemy, time the friend, navigating a stormy economy the trial, persistence the test. Caught in the middle, between great and small, the powerful and the anonymous, the dissolute above and the wretched below—the middling sorts tossed around on a sea of risk.

Initially the social designation of *better-middling-lower* "Sorts" appearing in the eighteenth century stood for a weakening of hierarchic social distinctions and a transition away from the more formalized authority of and deference to the classifications of "Rank." Ranks were determined by birth (well-born), education (learned), manners (codes of conduct), and to a less visible degree wealth (landed rents). Different ranks, at least conceptually, were neither in competition nor in conflict, representing the essence of structure, order, and place—a fit calling—unlike the more mobile and open system of class designations a century later. In the authority system of rank at the upper end, how one lived mattered, not what one did. Sorts represented a relatively neutral representation meant to defuse growing resentments, between "rich" and "poor," the "big bugs" and "small fry." Ben Franklin, for one, who like many parvenus aspired to become a gentleman, spoke for the "poor" (tradesman) in this context. Social groupings were in flux, and the middling sorts of average farmers, traders, and artisans were best known for their lack of noble attributes, including civilized manners, generosity, and high principles.

Franklin gave advice and instruction to the middling sorts. James Guild lived it, an example of an ambitious young man in the late eighteenth century carefully watching his social flanks in the treacherous social economy. An "illiterate" (meaning not "learned") Vermont peddler turned schoolmaster, self-taught painter of portraits, and tutor of penmanship, Guild gave an inestimable description of his unstable social position together with the limitations of his skills and training. With an uncommon eloquence as he groped with uncertain forms of spelling, grammar, diction, and words, he was attempting to place an identity:

Now I begin to learn human nature. I find people are not always what they seem to be. I have been traveling (said I to myself) this two or three years, but my busnefs [business] was such that I thought it was a mean calling, for it was neither good for society nor beneficial to any one only to gratify the eye. I find by experience if a man thinks he is something and puts him self forward he will be something. I don't mean he must put himself forward by crowding himself into company but despising those who haunt the grog shop or the gambling table, and act with an independent manner and face the rich proud and haughty, with the same ease and politeness of manner as though you belonged to the same class. I had formerly accustomed myself to refrain as much as possible in conversing with big canisters. Neither would I associate with the mean, but with the middle class I used to make myself free. I find I need not confine myself to either but conform myself to the class I am in. When I am in the first stile of people, there I would put on my polish as it ware & I began find I had a difficult task to please Evry one, and there is often many young starts who if they could would run me lower than themselves.[10]

Guild was positioned on the cusp of change between a fixed system of ranks and a materializing dynamic relationship between classes. The Middling Sorts increasingly assumed the name Middle Classes in the first half of the nineteenth century. The primacy of the economy and wealth were determining perceptions of social relationships. Young men such as the itinerant peddler Guild, for instance, were becoming aware that however bad one's manners, however "illiterate," or lacking the generosity of gentlemen, personal aspiration, status, and success were intrinsically tied to occupational and familial positioning among competitive audiences. In 1782 Crévecoeur observed that it was the economy that made the difference in the decision to come to America:

> The rich stay in Europe, it is only the middling and poor that emigrate. It is no wonder that the European who has lived here a few years is desirous to remain; Europe with all its pomp is not to be compared to this continent for men of middle stations or laborers. . . .
> I do not mean that every one who comes will grow rich in a little time; no, but he may procure an easy, decent maintenance by his industry.

In 1786–1787, Alexander Hamilton in the *Federalist Papers* similarly took note of "a distinction of interest between the opulent land-holder and the middling farmer."[11]

The idea of social class in the later eighteenth and early nineteenth centuries was historically revolutionary. It is a revolution we have yet to understand very well, or even to work through. In the beginning were the middle classes, the lightning rod, the matrix, the context in which the working classes beginning around the 1830s would in many ways eventually define and fashion themselves. The idea of ranks was increasingly out of touch with the changing realities of the lives of ordinary people. Social class—the "Middle Classes"—was an idea whose time had come. First, ranks differed in absolute kind, not in degree, and the essential relationship between them was external, as represented in spatial metaphors. There was a "geography" of ranks.

Classes, on the other hand, were made, not given. As industrialism expanded they differed more in degree than in absolute kind and were time-bound over the course of movement or mobility in a personal history. Knowing people by their "careers" over an extended time surpassed knowing them by the fixed features of "character." Conceptually speaking, the student must look toward a history, not a geography, of classes. A vocabulary emerged to reflect the flexibility of class thinking—upper, middle, lower, and the coalitions of combinations (lower-middle, upper-middle, middle-middle)—all serving to direct attention to the degrees of hyphenated variety and fluidity *within* as well as between class structures. Class thinking created temporal opportunity to make small but real moves upward but also downward, often accruing over more than one generation.

Neither self-contained nor static, classes were expansive. The potential for conflict, competition, and struggle, especially, within class identities as well as between them, was endless. In the historical context, the conundrum became who, when, why, under what circumstances, and how were the lines drawn along the continuum between upper and lower, between rich and poor, between refinement, respectability, and shabbiness? In the setting of ranks, the wanna-be aspiring gentleman or gentle lady could never become a real gentleman or lady, however clever their style or careful their observance of detail. Even under favorable circumstances, when gentility sold its badges of honor and refinement to the lower sorts for needed cash, the middling classes were snubbed as upstarts or, worse, as impostors, charlatans, pettifoggers, mountebanks, frauds, humbugs, quacks. Jeopardized elites and besieged learned professions commonly spoke such rhetoric.[12]

The storyteller in Mark Twain had a field day with this new role-playing in class society. The "confidence man" as a type appeared in America in the 1840s. Twain built his humor on the incongruities magnified by exaggeration between human pretentiousness and commonplace vernacular realities in the era he together with Charles Dudley Warner named the Gilded Age. He called his brand of humor "stretchers"—an apt description for his own experience with social class. In the context of class thinking, the burden of proof shifted to whom a person was claiming to be. For instance, when the "greenhorn" in the nineteenth century bought a new suit, starched collar,

Stetson, watch and fob and presented a self in a photograph sent back to the old country; began using toothpaste instead of ashes or employed toothpicks and not a pocket knife; could afford to eat meat every day; mastered the rudiments of American slang; signed checks against a bank account; moved from a common laborer's job to the career of a clerk; furnished his home from a store—could he not legitimately feel that he belonged somewhere on the rungs of the ladder of the middle classes? In a sense all class identities became a matter of economic and emotional confidence—a kind of confidence game—based on resources and credit. Within social ranks people had known who they were from the beginning. Within social classes they calculated over time who they wanted to be at the end.[13]

Class thinking introduced other novelties. In the 1820s a "middling interest" of mechanics rose as a political constituency inside the bastion of Federalist Boston. Its well-publicized platform centered on debtor and property tax relief, housing reform, and distributing power more equitably in city government. "Middling Interest" quickly entered the vocabulary as a recognized Americanism, defined by John Russell Bartlett as the "middle class of people." Contemporary Bostonians patronized a bank named the "Middle Interest," and a Connecticut newspaper editorialized: "Men of the *middling interest* class are now the best off. Men who have done a safe or small business are now the richest....They have felt they belonged to the *middling interest*, and have resolved to stay there, and not cope with the rich."[14] A nineteen-year-old Bostonian, Ralph Waldo Emerson, was less generous. In 1822 he called the middling interest insurgency "an ill-managed, poor-spirited party" that "promises little good to our civil welfare." The resentment displayed by this Harvard-educated schoolmaster was visible. He divided society into three great classes:

> First, the aristocracy of wealth & talents; next, the great multitude of mechanics & merchants and the good sort of people who are for the most part content to be governed without aspiring to have a share of power; lastly, the lowest order of day laborers & outcasts of every description, including schoolmasters.

The Brahmin was feeling sorry for his threadbare social self. Subsequently he spent a professional lifetime—in the ministry, in the literary marketplace, on the lecture circuit, and as an apostle of culture—reconfiguring and secularizing that self.[15]

Class thinking in the nineteenth century was innovative in several significant ways. First, foreshadowed in the phrase "*middling interest class*," middle class was in the process of taking the form of an adjective, pointing to the shift from plural—middle classes—to singular in the second half of the century. Becoming middle class was increasingly a way of doing things, a display of selective *characteristics*, a delimiting agent, a matter of discerning emphasis and attention rather than the demonstration of an undivided whole character. One could enter the middle class piecemeal, through discriminating practices: in family activities, child-rearing procedures, gender relations, techniques of worship, work habits, labor relations, education and health methods, recreation routines, and personal as well as domestic consumption patterns.[16] Within families, for instance, this made for differences of opinion and controversy, especially regarding such primal matters as policies toward children and money. The proliferation of diaries by ordinary people, both male and female, in the nineteenth century provides an especially good source of evidence. With greater personal ambition and aspiration for higher standards of living and a better life than one's parents, the social world of class thinking was becoming more complex and less easy to read on the surface than it had been in the eighteenth-century world.

Two contemporary developments in the 1830s and the 1840s set the scene for storytellers to the middle classes. Factories, machinery, canals, and railroads were assuming a more prominent position in the accelerating production of the economy, in textiles, shoes, paper, machinery, and domestic appliances. Activists among the laboring classes were drawing a line between their interests and those of the middling ones by claiming that only laboring classes and working classes were "producers," makers of value and rightful owners of the increased wealth. As commodity producers they were the industrious and useful classes, while the middle classes of vendors, distributors, retailers, and entrepreneurs of capital were parasites and speculators.[17] While this strategy served to make laborers aware of a working-class status, it failed to succeed as an argument adequately representing the roles of the middle classes in the economy. Ultimately the rhetoric became increasingly ideological and removed from the realities of a modern economy. Only at the extremes did a description of manual versus nonmanual occupations divide "working" classes from middle ones. The effective difference to contemporaries was between drudgery or mindless hard labor and mindful work directed by an intelligence.[18]

As the working classes were becoming aware of a difference of interests, the middle classes simultaneously were maturing to an awareness of their distinctive identity in a service economy. Generally speaking, prior to the 1830s, the middling sorts provided necessary goods and services to the nobility and upper sorts. Now with structural developments in the domestic economy—especially in transportation, graded roads, canals, steamships, and railroads—they began to cultivate their own audiences. These audiences had to be made in a marketplace of patrons, by clergymen like Henry Ward Beecher as well as by merchants in shops. Beecher, for instance, installed a massive organ in Plymouth Church in Brooklyn to build up an audience, and became a national advertising spokesman for Pear's Soap.[19] Goods did not sell and move themselves; services were required to explain, promote, and distribute them.

For instance, in the Preface to *The Mother's Book* (1831), Lydia Maria Child wrote:

> When I wrote the 'Frugal Housewife,' some booksellers declined publishing it, on account of the great variety of cookery books already in the market. I was perfectly aware of this circumstance; but among them all, I did not know of one suited to the wants of the middling class in our own country. I believed such a book was needed; and the sale of more than six thousand copies in one year has proved that I was right in my conjecture.[20]

The book, its 1828 title changed from "Frugal Housewife: Dedicated to Those Who are Not Ashamed of Economy" to "The American Frugal Housewife . . ." in 1832, went through thirty-two editions in as many years and could be found both in frontier sod houses and Eastern cottages. Child, who identified her father as a "mechanic," strenuously identified with the middle classes—whom she targeted as the dominant reading audience for her self-help guides like *The Family Nurse* (1837), a companion volume to the "American Frugal Housewife." To Mrs. Shaw, a well-to-do woman correspondent, Child wrote in a revealing manner:

> I smiled to see you class yourself and Mrs. Barrow, and Mr. Curtis, with the *middling* class. Certainly none of you have aristocratic airs, but all of you have luxurious habits, and are unaccustomed to wait upon yourselves. If you were to find yourselves suddenly in the surroundings of the middle class, you would be like fishes out of water.[21]

Two vehicles were central to the expanding awareness of middle-class audiences. First, by means of new technologies for the production and distribution of cheap print, everyday casual reading among the middling sorts accelerated rapidly in the United States, more so than in other Western countries. Among the first great audiences made among the middle classes was the reading audience. The distribution of cheap accessible print influenced attitudes, played on perceptions, and created a shared or common opinion more quickly and effectively than did either oral media or classical learning.[22]

Buying a guidebook, manual, handbook, or book of reference in order to function—*by the book*—became a necessity of everyday activity for the middling classes. Handy "information" gave people unprecedented flexibility and options not found in earlier forms of "instruction" books. A "traveler" or "tourist," for instance, purchased a steamship and railway guide with the latest maps, including the important details about the urban centers and corridors along the route. A "house keeper" consulted a manual when acquiring new appliances and organizing a household in which the kitchen was no longer sovereign. According to Sergeant Larson, "the fact that I was not educated stood in my way, and for hard work I was considered too small." Joining the army was his break, and when the Civil War broke out he was required to learn the fundamentals of cavalry tactics quickly without the peacetime luxury of trial and error:

> The great trouble with me was that I was uneducated. I could not even read except small and common words. Bigger words I had to spell over and over, and by comparison with other words in the sentence, gather the meaning. . . . I had to dive into the "Blue Book" [Articles of War] and the Cavalry Tactics at once, and they contained a great many large words which I had never heard before, as they were not in general use even among solders, no verbal instructions being given except in Tactics. . . .
>
> I learned to read in those books, tedious as it was in the beginning. After I had made some progress in reading and getting to understand it, I became interested and continued to read and study military law and tactics whenever I had an opportunity, and later on I found that the knowledge obtained, came in all right.[23]

Likewise, the young man who went West first purchased a guidebook to equip him for the trip and direct his passage. The accuracy of these guidebooks could bear serious consequences. "Emigrants" in the Donner party in 1846 ran into tragedy, for instance, because the book and maps they were following steered them wrong.[24]

A related development regarding the new reading audience was an expanding number of personal documents about experience: letters, journals, diaries, memoirs, and accounts. They reflected the unprecedented confidence that the middling classes were placing in the importance of the promise and opportunities of their personal lives. A previously unchronicled and semieducated strata of men and women, about whom it had once been assumed that nothing of importance ever happened, began in large numbers leaving visible tracks for the record. Among them was the youthful and ambitious printer's devil Sam Clemens—alias the storytelling river pilot Mark Twain.

"The Advantage of Being 'Middle Class'": Two Storytellers

Poor, pitiful business, this being a middling sort, a melancholy—even suicidal—Mark Twain referred to his own hapless career in San Francisco in 1865, after his earlier ambitions for a fit calling seemed to be crumbling.[25] His father died when he was twelve years old. As was commonly the practice of orphaned youth from middling families in the period, he went into the workplace to learn a trade and help support himself and his family, first as an apprentice printer and subsequently as a riverboat pilot, miner, clerk to the secretary of the Territory of Nevada, speculator, and newspaper reporter. In the 1840s middling-class youth began being more concerned with the track of an occupational career than with the well-born signs of "character" required by a fit calling. Twain observed that he had no character but could have a prospering career as a "low humorist." After he left home at age fourteen he traveled extensively, eventually joining thousands of middling young men in the years after the Gold Rush in California. He meant both to "make his pile" and "see the elephant"—meaning to face up to the realities of life where hard experience met expectations of getting ahead and aspirations for a better material future. Seeing the elephant was acquiring the self-knowledge to know when to take the profit and cut the losses, when to cut out for a different territory.

The future seemed dark for this unsettled thirty-year-old, who had been kicking around from industry to industry for more than a dozen years. As he gained knowledge in the context of his evangelical nurture, he reasoned that he was God's fool, not merely his own, and God could afford to take risks. Struggling on for two more years, Twain wagered on a local frog with which he jumped to national recognition. While establishing a name as a California newspaper humorist, he wrote a successful travel commentary and took to the lecture circuit, where his droll wit became a favorite. From an initial viewing of a photograph, he aggressively courted a well-to-do girl and married into a family with substantial resources.[26]

Sam's status was middling. It included basic learning, a working-class youth, an itinerant career, self-professed ambition, and self-education in the value and significance of money. His successful father-in-law knew a good investment in intellectual property to be among Sam's assets and liabilities. Twain became a newspaper editor in Buffalo with family resources, and then a full-time writer and publisher in Hartford. With the text for *Roughing It* drawn liberally on his Overland Trail and California mining experiences (1872), the river boy became a prospering writer in popular demand. He had made a "competency," a long-standing middling value, and could have retired comfortable if not wealthy in the 1870s, a gilded product of the Gilded Age. But the writing engine in Mark Twain steamed on, racing to the top of its form in the 1880s with *Life on the Mississippi* (1882), *The Adventures of Huckleberry Finn* (1885) and *The Connecticut Yankee in King Arthur's Court* (1889).

Poor pitiful business indeed, this chasing a career versus relying for credit and credibility on one's good character. The "fool" in Twain (and his ever-present evangelical mother in the fictional form of maiden aunts) did question whether the gilding of this young man's life stemmed from the deceptive attractions of fool's gold from the California-Nevada hills. Twain himself did not disagree. His humor corresponded to his own life, which stretched from local riverboat tyke to global traveler.

For his entire working life, Twain was a traveling man in every sense.

Born in 1835, he grew up in the 1840s in Hannibal, a Midwestern river town near St. Louis before that thriving city was eclipsed by Chicago. The river town had become a hub of transportation, river industry, and the railroad. The working people Sam Clemens knew in Hannibal and then Keokuk were struggling to make a decent living and shelter themselves against the vicissitudes of life, the routine failures of precarious business cycles, the perceived predatory interests of the "big bugs," and the consequences following the untimely deaths of parental breadgivers.[27] Moving around the country with an impeccable ear for the ordinary person's vernacular slang and literature, Twain capitalized on the evolving experiences, interests, and opportunities of the sorts familiar to him. A career that catapulted upward within a few years drew continually upon deeper readings below the surface of his youthful experience with the middling folks from whom he had come.

Twain's audience chose to be amused into respectability rather than sermonized into refinement. He characterized his expanding readership in visceral terms as the "belly and member" crowd, descendants of the Middling Sorts from the eighteenth century and the Middling Classes from the first half of the nineteenth. By means of an army of subscription salesmen canvassing the nation for mail orders, he built the first great popular mass reading audience for an individual writer in the nineteenth century. Early on Twain had mastered the distribution of his personal image for promotion. He projected his bushy appearance and penetrating stare—unlike carefully coiffed and controlled Victorians—to instant recognition among an audience desiring modern goods and services, including solid value at affordable prices. It was in his audience that the former working miner (who hated physical work) found the real thing, in an exposed vein of self-made readers lacking the flourishes of higher learning and educated aesthetics.[28]

Many elite observers remained without a clue regarding Twain's success among the middling classes. Others were dismissive of the low taste and popular vulgarity of the new audience of readers. The highbrow spectators were conscious of fearing what the future held, even before the occurrence of large-scale foreign immigration to the United States. For example, E. L. Godkin, for one, editor of the *Nation*, expressed his mistrust: "The cultivated class we have with us, but the class next below do not know quite what to make of us, and are suspicious and hostile."[29] In 1896, William James panned the solidly middling Chautauqua audience as relentless "tepidity," an audience of "more women and less beauty . . . more voices and less sweetness . . . than I ever thought possible":

> I went in curiosity for a day, I stayed for a week, held spell-bound by the charm and ease of everything, by the middle-class paradise, without a sin, without a victim, without a blot, without a tear. . . . I have learned a lot, but I'm glad to get into something less blameless but

more admiration-worthy. The flash of a pistol, a dagger, or a devilish eye, anything to break the unlovely level of 10,000 good people—a crime, murder, rape, elopement, anything would do. . . . Even an Armenian massacre, whether to be killer or killed, would seem an agreeable change from the blamelessness of Chautauqua as she lies soaking year and after in her lakeside sun and showers.[30]

Even Theodore Dreiser, closer to the rawness of the urban everyday than most, came down hard on Sister Carrie. Her first encounter with the reader was "as a fair example of the middle American class—two generations removed from the immigrant." Possessed of a rudimentary mind, "books were beyond her interest—knowledge a sealed book." In bodily graces she was "crude": her hands "ineffectual," her feet flat.

And yet she was interested in her charms, quick to understand the keener pleasures of life, ambitious to gain in material things. A half-equipped little knight, she was, venturing to reconnoiter the mysterious city and dreaming wild dreams of some vague, far-off supremacy, which should make it prey and subject—the proper penitent, groveling at a woman's slipper.[31]

"Why is it," asked George Ade—a Dreiser contemporary and fellow migrant from the Indiana hinterland—that "the middle class has a monopoly of the real enjoyment in Chicago?" Ade, son of a part-time farmer and clerk, had migrated to the "Great City" in 1890 to work as a cub reporter writing the daily weather story for the *Chicago Morning News*. Mark Twain, a frequent visitor to Chicago, admired Ade's prose and recognized in him his own reading audience now one generation removed to the city. Ade was appreciative of Twain's support and influence "when I was doing the first of my realistic little yarns."[32]

Ade observed more than the atmospherics. Quickly his droll vignettes describing the middling strata of people filling up the public spaces in the city became the substance of his "fables in slang," which, although not reaching the heights of Twain, gained worldwide visibility. Never before had anyone taken such close notice of the quirky, whimsical, irreverent, and personable public mannerisms of the rapidly growing social segment in the city "not held down by the arbitrary laws governing that mysterious part of the community known as society." Who were these people, whom Ade labeled neither rich nor poor, who were between civilized and crude, who worked with hands and brain?[33]

Ade observed with the journalist's camera-eye. These folk were "young workingmen and their tittering girls, clerks in new straw hats and unmistakably summer clothes, tired husbands and smiling wives"—all streaming aboard the lake steamer for music and dance on an evening's cheap excursion. Or the family during the summer heat sitting on the front stoop indulging in a pitcher of ice cream while father indecently discarded his tight dress coat and choking collar and smoked "either pipe or Cigar without scandalizing anyone." Or the boarders patronizing the street concerts of Italian musicians, or the two shadowy figures making out on a bench in the public park with the woman pillowing her head suggestively, "on the man's shoulder...either asleep or contented" —a "shocking fact" to society.[34]

Ade's crowd also included brash Artie and Sister Mae, for whom the hard work of talking a good game was the way of getting ahead. And it included all the ironic reversals and satirical consequences happening to those hapless folks who took too seriously traditional pieties, moralism, and public proprieties. Ade highlighted the points of difference between "learning and learning how." The learned now lost out to the smart, and the respectably naive "began to find out things"—for instance, the two young people who after exchanging photographs and credentials wooed by correspondence and married, and in housekeeping realized as a child arrived that "she was a case of Ambrosia and Nectar and he was plain old Ham and Spinach." Ade pondered the social question with "the Caddy who hurt his head while thinking." The Caddy admired his father, who, although he worked in a lumber yard, knew "all about the Silver Question and how J. Pierpont Morgan done up a Free People on the bond issue." Moreover, the Caddy's father was too serious a man "to hammer a Ball from one Red Flag to another." Why then, the Caddy wondered,

> was it that his Father, a really Great Man, had to shove Lumber all day and could seldom get one Dollar to rub against another, while these superficial Johnnies who played Golf all the Time had Money to Throw at the Birds. The more he Thought the more his Head ached. Moral: *Don't Try to Account for Anything*.[35]

Never the sentimentalist or burlesque playwright, Ade told stories of neither melodramatic success nor conspicuous failure. A keen observer of the ironic twist in commonplace life, he focused a prose eye on the middling sorts who were sufficiently vulnerable to the foibles, foolishness, and stupidity of their own aspirations to pay a high price for the unintended consequence of their own agency. Appreciative of the "caustic mirth" and frank sarcasm without the slightest cynicism in Ade's topics— ambition, financial interest, youthful sexuality, marriage, leisure, work, family, religion—William Dean Howells observed, "You are not asked to be interested in any one because he is in any way out of the common, but because he is every way in the common. Mr. Ade would not think of explaining or apologizing or at all accounting for the company he invites you to keep."[36]

In the porous occupational boundaries of immigrant Chicago, Ade observed the nascent middle classes on the streets. Sidewalk merchants and penny speculators thrived peddling their cheap and discounted wares. In "a city where manual labor has always commanded a fair remuneration the broad-shouldered immigrant prefers to take his chances hawking collar-buttons. He would rather make 25 cents a day and be in 'business' than work for $1.50 a day."[37] Contemporaneous with Ade, social commentators such as Joseph Jacobs writing on "The Middle American" and John Spargo on "Contemporary Socialism" also recognized that predictions of monopolistic capitalism and big business crowding small-unit middling sorts of producers, jobbers, and retailers out of existence were unfounded both in the experiential record and in the numbers.[38] In the proliferation of his columns, short stories, books, and essays, Ade documented the practices of this expanding population. These urban middling sorts remained largely invisible both to the educated professionals and to the working-class union advocates of class as a noun who preferred a two-class structure, the classes or society and the masses, the refined and the rough.

In the popular genre of Twain's writings, Ade's work was descriptive and entertaining. However, the class analysis embedded in the verbal snapshots, incidents, and vignettes was creative. First, in the modern industrial, polyglot context of city streets and urban life, Ade employed the notion of "middle class" and "class" itself as an adjective—a social and hyphenated phenomena characterizing and differentiating specific observable practices and activities. The storyteller Ade was immersed within events; he was not an omniscient observer. Implicitly he discarded social class as a noun—Bourgeoisie, Proletariat—a metaphysical entity communicated through an idealized consciousness driven by relentless teleological imperatives such as economic individualism in a bourgeoisie or economic solidarity in a proletariat. Consciousness—as William James was explaining for individual psychology during this period—was not a metaphysical essence but an excited comprehension embedded in the senses and feelings of the material world and aroused when the situation presented itself by the need to motivate oneself to act in events. Intuitively Ade applied this notion to a social grouping like the middle class with which people chose to identify in degree and relative to their changing resources, opportunities, and priorities.

Ade approached class in a permeable and flexible manner, through specific practices based on observations about how his crowd spent time and money and made and experienced value. Class as adjectival modifier—limiting, qualifying, specifying, not standing alone—made the parts of a group, the many roles it played, greater than the sum of a whole represented in an artificial noun. Middle-class careers, child-rearing practices, health concerns, educational aspirations, family matters, money matters, ambitions for professionalization, needs for buffers against insecurities—all cut across ethnicities, nationalities, religions, races, genders, and regions. Identifying with middle-class activities was less an assimilating process than a hyphenating and splitting one. Disparate people in a heterogeneous population, commonly from different places, backgrounds, cultures, and economic circumstances, could both play numerous roles and retain an original identity while sharing in the common practice of specific values.

As a participant-observer, Ade was aware that choosing selectively to participate in one or more lifestyle practices characterized as class practices depended on material resources available for budgeting. Family income was a necessary component, although not a sufficient one. A lack of class conflict, or even consciousness, indicated to these observers generally that access to such resources was perceived to be within reach—if not immediately, then perhaps over more than one generation. Ade's stories detailed the reasons for these assumptions. The business of urban street vendors, jobbers, small retailers, noncorporate professionals, and even labor organizations was to react quickly by making goods and services available, often by cutting prices and extending credit, especially in hard times. These actions functioned to cut slack in the system, making it relatively spongy and recession-proof by cultivating new avenues for cheaper distribution of excess production and inventory. The emblematic banner displayed on the Maxwell Street market visited by George Ade was, "We cheat you fair." Perhaps this slogan best summed up modern class relationships.

What George Ade understood most fundamentally was that realistic expectations and accomplishments, rather than disappointments and defeats, nurtured a mindfulness of class identities, middling as well as working. There was evidence that standards of living in staples was rising in the first decades of the twentieth century, even at the lesser end of the social scales. Beyond the reach of big business, the middling folk made the street economy work in a place like Chicago, thereby both raising working people's expectations and mitigating desperation. The testimony of immigrant families to urban America was a supporting witness. The line between working classes and the middle, both in neighborhoods and at work, was often fuzzy and in flux, tempered by ethnicity, nationality, and religion. The more enduring friction in the early twentieth century, even with knowledge about the events at Haymarket and Pullman, was less between classes than between generations within families, as well as between workers.[20]

The Disadvantage of Being "Middle Class" in Twentieth-Century Historiography

The purpose of this volume is to begin sorting out the middling sorts, to begin thinking about the middle classes in fresh idioms. "Middle class" appears to be one of those categories that academics, commentators, journalists, and ordinary people have continually needed to invoke and shape to their own purposes. However, the discussion has tended to cut so close to the identity of those looking at the subject—present company included—

that the distancing of a participant-observer has been difficult to sustain. In this final section several major models of historiographic interpretation are reviewed in order to locate our current understanding and look toward new investigations.[39]

In the century after George Ade, few followed up on the significance of what he perceived regarding the experiences of a class variously labeled lower middle class and petit bourgeois. Ade fell into obscurity except as a local Chicago journalist-humorist and Midwestern regionalist, his insights dormant. *Elusive* remains the word that perhaps best describes historiographic interpretations of the middle class in American history. In the twentieth century many interpretations of social class have preferred a vertical two-class model: an upper middle class or bourgeoisie (privileged, individualistic, materialistic) and a lower working class or proletariat (poor, communal, principled).

To be in the middle has meant to be ephemeral, unstable, living a dream on one hand and fearful of falling and failure on the other. In a recent essay "stalking" was the phrased used, as if it were a prey or quarry to corner and cage, an unruly beast. Indeed, an excessive amount of caricature, stereotype, and cultural allusion has punctuated the discussion. Vachel Lindsay, a poet and critic in the early part of the century, for instance, displayed a typical contempt for the "middlebrow": "Our democratic dream has been a middle-class aspiration built on a bog of toil-soddened minds. The piles beneath the castes of our near-democratic arts were rotting for lack of folk-imagination. The Man with the Hoe has no spark in his brain."[40]

The usage of "middlebrow" presumed unimaginative, linear, dull. Declares the OED in a citation from 1925: "It consists of people who are hoping that some day they will get used to the stuff they ought to like."

In the context of these cultural attitudes, we should ask: Where has the historiography fallen short? First, "objective" indices in measuring the boundaries of class have been less than conclusive and persuasive. *Income*, for instance, has not been a useful indicator of class other than for the primary purposes of government, specifically taxation and welfare. Commonly hidden, misstated, or unstated, individual income has easily been obscured by immediate family income and larger family networks, by the unpaid contributions of housekeeping wives and mothers, by the contributions of child labor, and by any number of other strategems. With the explosion of self-help manuals after the 1840s, sweat equity created substantial intangible forms of income. Ownership of small working-class bungalows was income-producing. In Chicago in the early twentieth century, inner-city working classes and Catholics in their parishes often bought real estate, while the better off in the city rented apartments. The indications are suggestive that informal street economies in George Ade's Chicago may well have been larger and more deeply penetrating than was the formal economy. In those economies, made up by the junk dealers and market vendors, saloon keepers and entrepreneurial bootblacks, Ade identified the proto-middle classes.[41]

As an "objective" measure, *occupation* has faired no better than income. Job titles and descriptions as well as census categories, for example, have been notoriously misleading or slow to be revised. Clerking in most establishments in the 1890s referred to a different set of duties and skills compared to the 1840s, although the job classification persisted. Euphemisms such as sanitary engineer, administrative assistant, and project coordinator glorified the commonplace tasks of janitor, typist, and secretary, only serving to magnify the perception of a century-long trend toward the professionalization of work and the automation of mechanical tasks. White collar as an occupational category appeared only in the twentieth century, together with blue collar.[42] Either in the workplace or at home through much of the nineteenth century, there were few jobs that did not dirty a collar and dress. Staying clean was hard for everyone to do and was thus an imperfect marker of class identity.[43]

Second, the dominant interpretative plots in twentieth-century historiography have by and large lost their persuasion. Among the strategies of interpretation, two influential models particularly merit discussion: the Liberal and the Marxian.

The Liberal model commonly traced a developmental scheme between the Old Middle Class in the nineteenth century and New Middle Class in the twentieth. The "old" were identified as small self-reliant property owners and independent mechanics, artisans, farmers, and tradesmen, the "new" as social engineers, efficiency experts, and white-collar organization men. Yet the presumptions of the model are problematic: not only the evolutionary pattern of development from "island communities" to corporate society, but even the ideal types inhabiting this social universe.[44]

On the one hand it turns out that the old middle class of independent small proprietors, tradesmen, farmers, and entrepreneurs with "honest callings" were not as independent, resourceful, self-made, frugal, and producer-minded as once presumed. State-sponsored services, including the construction of expensive infrastructure and an elaborate public communications system, played a significant role in the material fortunes of this middle stratum. Partisan politics, associations and churches, and the cheap services of labor—including wives, apprentices, servants, slaves, and especially young men and women—served their interests. Recent investigations suggest that these very *old* middling types cultivated the fundamentals of a *new* "service" economy centered in towns and cities, resting on investment and depending on marketing, distribution, and the consumption of goods and services.[45]

On the other hand, characterizations of the new middle class of white-collar clerks and sales types, together with managers and professionals, appear just as vulnerable to critique. Literary allusions of other-directed and alienated dupes smiling in the "personality" marketplace triumphed in the 1950s and later in popular jeremiads by sociologists such as David Riesman, C. Wright Mills, William Whyte, and Will Herberg and philosophers and critics such as Norbert Wiener, Jacques Ellul, Herbert Marcuse, Philip Rieff, Peter Berger, and Christopher Lasch.[46] The images embodied in books of the period—white collar, lonely crowd, organization man, therapeutic society, one-dimensional man, homeless mind, culture of narcissism—projected an enfeebled conforming group without a politics, an organizational mass without a soul, a consensual class that in the sentiment of Mills worked to deny the reality of classes themselves. *Life Magazine* became the visual embodiment of a feel-good "nebbish" American dream.[47]

The model served contemporary cultural criticism, both from the perspective of Mills's left-liberal views and Riesman's right-liberal views. White-collar workers have not displayed any greater anxiety or sense of alienation than did their predecessors, or their more independent contemporaries. To assume that white-collar consumption patterns—the good life—were "compensatory" in support of a regimented dream factory was excessively reductive. A contemporary colleague of Mills's, Richard Hofstadter, passionately beat up on his dystopian vision:

> You have somehow managed to get into your portrait of the white collar man a great deal of your own personal nightmare. . . . Look at . . . the words you apply to the white collar man: living out in slow misery his yearning for the quick climb, pushed by forces, pulled, acted upon but does not act, never talks back, never takes a stand, in a frantic hurry, paralyzed with fear, morally defenseless, impotent as a group, open to the focused onslaught of manufactured loyalties, turns to his leisure frenziedly, bored at work, restless at play, standardized loser, must practice prompt repression of resentment and aggression, etc.

Hofstadter discreetly concluded in his letter that he did not "totally reject this," but there must be "something else even in white collar life." Based on his own historical knowledge and liberal persuasion he felt that there was considerably more at play than institutional loyalty.[48] The "new" corporation harbored a significant number of free-wheeling types who learned the game, did it their own way, and worked to further their interests. In the last two decades of the twentieth century, the rapid growth of the communications industry has presented a dramatic example of such flexibility. Corporate America has appeared immeasurably more disciplined, standardized, efficient, and profitable in its flow charts and annual reports than historical evidence, ethnographic observation, and labor relations have supported. No one knows this better than Wall Street.

The last generation of academic studies has achieved new results in explorations of race and gender. Yet explorations of class have lagged, arguably because of the persistence of the two-class model of explanation.[49] Take as an example the cultural model of "bourgeois" refinement versus middling rough prominent in the literature. Recent depictions of refinement in a nineteenth-century Anglo-American middle class have emphasized its professions of "sincerity," parlor sentimentality, and secluded domesticity. The women in this fashionable group appeared more than a little fragile moving through the porcelain-like passages of their higher civilization. Male "roughing it" was the alter ego of genteel refinement. These brash sorts were ambitious individuals speculating on get-rich-quick schemes, gambling on the main chance and celebrity, betting on the marketplace while supported at home by overburdened housewives and dependent families.[50]

It is difficult to locate here ordinary middling-class youths like Mark Twain and the thousands, male and female, with comparable histories who have deposited traces of their lives and careers in our archives. These youths were neither low nor high status, neither poor nor rich, neither uneducated nor well-educated, neither permanently working class nor advantaged, neither desperate nor pursuing "castles in the air." These middling boys have been sighted in the documents starting out as mechanics, craftsmen, and tradesmen and eventually reaching modest success in professions such as journalism, the book trades, and the law; taking time out for the adventure and risk of "seeing the elephant" in California; playing early baseball in amateur and professional leagues; chasing fires with friends in urban fire departments. The girls in turn began leaving home for factory work and schoolteaching, female friendship, and marriage opportunities in growing towns and cities and on the frontier.[51]

These life histories, however, do not fit easily into the current historiographic schemes. Among the reasons is that no investigation of the history of the middle classes can go forward and break new ground without addressing the assumptions of the Marxian model that continues to color our thinking about class. Karl Marx, at the beginning of class analysis in the mid-nineteenth century, moved the eighteenth-century usage of "class" beyond a mere collectivity of any sort to an economic connection—groups in relationship to the means of production based on private ownership, a labor market, and the appropriation of surplus value. His foundational ideas were class "formation" and class "consciousness."[52]

Marx defined the formation of social classes in terms of structural relationships between economic interests, originally landlords, capitalists, and laborers. Classes developed from the historical context of the traditional ranks and estates. What is interesting is that characteristics of ranks and estates persisted in the formation process of Marxian social classes. Yes, ranks and estates were inherited and givens, while classes were made in a historical process. Yes, ranks fit together in a harmonious system, while classes by means of a fixed historical dialectic clashed in competition, conflict, and war. While there were differences, however, the similarities were just as striking. The two dominant social classes to which all others were compelled by forces to gravitate toward were the bourgeoisie and the proletariat. Like ranks and estates, each matured into a monolithic entity—a single proper noun. To focus on the external struggle, each disciplined or eliminated internal friction or disloyalty. On the one hand, as the formation of the grande bourgeoisie matured, the financiers assumed absolute control from the top and measured all activity by aggrandizing profits on the bottom line. On the other hand, the proletariat, reduced to the exploitation of wage-slavery by being deprived of the value of its labor, responded in kind with an integrated organization. The meanings of "formation" included both the structured process of becoming formed as well as the structured formations within a military-like order.

What counted as class formation for Marx was fixed in the relative material positions of the dominant classes. The bourgeoisie as the employer class was acquisitive and myopically absorbed in the accumulation of its own commodity comfort. The laboring proletariat, being thoroughly stripped of humanity and deprived of livelihood, became a mere extension of the new machines. Neither the grande bourgeoisie nor the proletariat were in the middle of anything.[53] Marx's class message was therefore: Join the big leagues—sign up—or be crushed. Like pests and archaic survivals, the middle classes—with their fluidity, divisiveness, and expansive internal categories on the ladder between upper and lower—were yesterday's rejects. Marx wrote in *The Communist Manifesto*:

> The lower strata of the middle class—the small tradespeople, shopkeepers, and retired tradesmen generally, the handicraftsmen and peasants—all these sink gradually into the proletariat, partly because their diminutive capital does not suffice for the scale on which Modern Industry is carried on, and is swamped in the competition with the large capitalists, partly because their specialized skill is rendered worthless by new methods of production.

Like ranks and estates, Marxian social classes were integrated, incorporating, and exclusive. By way of contrast, the obsolete middle classes were independent, expanding, and inclusive. Inevitably, as Marx put it, standing "between the workman on the one hand and the capitalist and the landlord on the other," the middle classes would find themselves in the wrong place at the wrong time. They became "a burden weighing heavily on the working base" while serving to increase the "power of the upper ten thousands."[54]

Bigness and a well-defined adversarial material position in the social order were the preconditions for the "consciousness" required by effective political action in Marxian class analysis. As Marx clarified the position in the *Eighteenth Brumaire of Louis Bonaparte*, no room existed for third parties, dissenting factions, or less than total commitment.

> Insofar as millions of families live under economic conditions of existence that separate their mode of life, their interests and their culture from those of other classes, and put them in hostile opposition to the latter, they form a class. Insofar as there is merely a local interconnection among those small-holding peasants, and the identity of their interests begets no community, no national bond and no political organization among them, they do not form a class.[55]

It followed that the multiplying interests of the middle classes, the mobile personal alliances, changing occupational fortunes, and shifting career affiliations dictated against a group consciousness or politics. Accordingly, historians from the left such as Dorothy Ross have argued that the languages of middle-class awareness have worked to deny the reality of classes themselves, that the majority of Americans are living a myth of liberalism by imagining that the United States has been "exceptional," lacking the conditions for class struggle.[56]

Despite the attractiveness of the analytic structures of the Marxian concept of social class, a series of assumptions missed the mark, historically speaking. Contrary to assumption, it was not the case that every job or occupation in the class structure existed only in one class rather than including multiple and changing identifications.[57] Nor was it the case that working people would be cut down to absolute impoverishment with downturns in the business cycle. The expansion of gross national product in industrial and postindustrial economies has not been a zero-sum game in which winners could be lined up against losers in a system of double-entry bookkeeping. A multitude of factors were at play. Ironically, the cost of labor in commodity production diminished while professional services became more labor intensive and expensive.

It is not a stretch to conclude that the Marxian model has lacked the heuristic value to support a robust research agenda for studies of class in the United States.[58] For instance, few if any working-class communities and labor movements in American history ever met Marx's high standard for class consciousness or even class formation, rooted as so many were in working-class areas and ethnoreligious, urban, and mixed commercial neighborhoods. Working people burdened with memories of tyrannical, corrupt regimes in countries from which they fled commonly cast suspicion on the designs of labor leaders in the United States as well as corporate managers and politicians.[59]

Moreover, among the unintended consequences of history the twentieth century witnessed were dramatic growth in the size and depth of the middle classes in the United States, in part a result of demographic trends in global and domestic industrial immigration, in global displacement of refugees during wars, and political instability in colonial and Third World nations. These displaced middling sorts were not a "bourgeoisie." As a result, at the turn of the millennium few Americans, including academics and intellectuals, currently speak the language of class "consciousness." The middle has turned out to be the most persistent and enduring among all the social classes—apparently not to the disadvantage of the many who participate in it.

An exploration of the subject of the middling sorts by means of clues, nuance, and connections extracted from empirical research is thus now more compelling than ever. In *The Making of the English Working Class*, E. P. Thompson set out to rescue "the poor stockinger, the Luddite cropper, the 'obsolete' hand-loom weaver . . . from the enormous condescension of posterity." He largely succeeded, first by moving beyond Marxist reductionism of class to economic "forces" and the "industrial revolution." Second, he privileged the common experience of ordinary people as agents who made events happen. Thompson assisted us in understanding the emotional logic behind the rioting crowds disciplined by an eighteenth-century "moral economy." The middle classes remained largely invisible in Thompson's studies. Nevertheless, he made the historian's narrative point of view necessary to the process of discovery, beyond the rationalist conceits of liberal sociology and the economic fundamentalism of dogmatic Marxism.[60]

The essays that follow are all drawn from original work based on archival research. They represent only a beginning in the possibilities for studies of the middle classes. An editor's introduction prefaces each section. Section I, "Middling Sorts for the New Nation," looks at the changes occurring in lifestyles, habits of thought, and patterns and practices in the economy in the early years of the nineteenth century. Section II, "Morality and Markets in the Nineteenth Century," explores how the products of morality—fancywork, children's books—cultivated early marketplaces among middle-class audiences. Section III, "The Cultural Uses of the Spirit," examines a series of interfaces between religion and culture in the middle and later nineteenth century: the audience for Henry Ward Beecher, changes in congregational music, and the success of Chautauqua. Section IV, "The Middle Is Material," demonstrates the significance of photography and material culture for perceptions of the public realm as standards of living rose in the later nineteenth and early twentieth centuries. Section V, "Business Careers in Modern Times," investigates previously neglected trends in the business world regarding local economies, corporate careers, and the Realtor's role in home ownership. Section VI, "The Politics of Race and Community," exposes the affiliations between race, suburbanization, and community activism in the twentieth century. Section VII, "Why Class Continues to

Count," closes the volume by returning to theoretical considerations in class analysis in the context of current historiography.

At the end of the day, we all must answer to the "so what" question—who cares about the middle classes, anyway? For one, those who care about the working classes put understanding at risk by not taking an interest in the history of the middle classes, since these histories are intrinsically related. For another, the passionate concerns with race, gender, and crimes against humanity can only benefit by a deeper understanding of the complexity of the history of the middle classes. Who cares? Most all of us who live middle-class lives, whatever else we are or wish to be.

MIDDLING SORTS
FOR THE NEW NATION

Patent-Office Department. SCIENTIFIC AMERICAN, VOL. 7, SEPTEMBER 20, 1851, 4.

In the first section, two noted historians discuss the increasing visibility of the "middling sorts" and then the "middle interest" and "middle classes" in the later eighteenth and early nineteenth centuries. Both historians describe changing perspectives on class boundaries, Joyce Appleby in the context of politics and social mores in the generation following the American Revolution, and Bruce Laurie in relation to the commercial economy in the 1820s and 1830s. Even in this early period, Appleby and Laurie show, there emerged features of the middle classes recognizable to us today.

Appleby characterizes the glass as half full for the common folk living in the shadow of privilege and rank before 1820. Landowning and wealth, office holding, the familiar status distinctions of "family, taste, literacy, and access to knowledge"—all were becoming more equitable and homogenous, except for African Americans. Appleby concludes that "the rent in the social fabric opened up for people who were ready to walk through it." Two dynamics were at work. One, by "inheriting the Revolution" and campaigning against the grip of Federalist elitism and deference, Jeffersonian Democracy leveled the political and social playing field upward toward respectability and refinement. Two, ambitious individuals embraced a free market economy that opened careers to talent (not birth) and improved standards of living. Gaining a "competency" favored greater personal self confidence. Appleby's middling sorts were rebellious, breakers of bounds, and defiant against the unearned entitlement and preferments granted the "well born." They were contemptuous of the specter of privileged stations conspiring against unlettered middling upstarts and parvenus. However, like many revolutionary classes caught up in momentous events, they knew better what they resented and whom they despised than what they stood for in its own terms. They shared a common enemy more than a common direction, and often failed to perceive their own elitism and concentration of economic power in the growing commercial expansion of their liberal society.

Bruce Laurie picks up the story at this point, after 1820. He focuses on the economic concerns of "middle interest" mechanics and craftsman, an increasingly self-conscious group carving out its own space and articulating its own values. Laurie's working and producing small businessmen were more typical and numerous than the celebrated contemporary entrepreneurs and "self-made" men. The struggling mechanic's glass was half full. Knocked about by the money economy, toiling to gain a toehold in capital markets, small businessmen continually found themselves in precarious circumstances. Failure rates for small businesses were high in a volatile economy. Start-up money was not easily found from conventional banking and credit sources. Bi-employment and movement between employer and employee status were common. "Whoever said," Laurie asks, "that being in the middle was easy?"

He concludes, first, that neither a straight line nor a single pattern tracked upward from petty producer to capitalist, and second, that despite predictions of their inevitable demise these small employers persisted, in part by means of equity grown through sweat. They were not afraid to work, they were not averse to risk. Moreover, their economic responses proved to be flexible and nimble, not easily fitting into a pattern of polarized occupational categories recently accepted by historians such as Stuart Blumin: a manual working class versus a nonmanual professional class.

Laurie draws a compelling picture of liminal men and their largely invisible strategies designed for survival and eventual success in an economy that mixed personal and impersonal market practices. These men shifted with the business cycles; they were neither unambiguously for capitalism and competition nor against it. Nor were they capitalists "in the rough" or obsolete craftsmen. They both made do and got ahead by raising capital through the formation of casual connections: with family, former owners, fraternal connections, clients and vendors, and their own workers. They entangled themselves in social webs of obligation, reciprocity, and responsibility. They found room to maneuver in territory unfamiliar to the "big bugs," and they sharpened an awareness that endured among struggling and aspiring middle-class families attempting to build up, usually from nothing, some assets and security.

Visiting America in the 1830s, Alexis de Tocqueville observed in his diary the relevance of what many of his aristocratic acquaintances in Philadelphia and Baltimore were beginning to accept—the political and cultural presence of the middle classes: "There is one thing that America demonstrates invincibly of which I was hitherto doubtful. . . . This is that the middle classes are capable of governing a state. I don't know if they would come off honourably from really difficult political situations, but they are adequate for the ordinary conduct of society, despite their petty passions, their incomplete education, their vulgar manners. Clearly they can supply practical intelligence, and that is sufficient."[1]

The broad outlines of this group would become very familiar to the experience of many, possibly a majority of, Americans in later generations. Whether by ideology or familiarity, historians have not been sufficiently attuned to the pliance and hustle of this many-sided group.

The Social Consequences
of American Revolutionary Ideals
in the Early Republic

JOYCE APPLEBY

In *Memoirs of a New England Village Choir*, Samuel Gilman depicts the rough waters of social change that very nearly capsized his youthful hometown. The unlikely site of this turmoil was the meeting-house balcony from which the church choir held forth every Sunday. Far from soothing the savage breast, the liturgical music along with its performance and performers promoted a succession of disruptive wrangles. Cast as a gentle satire, Gilman's story offers a shrewd analysis of the seismic shaking of the old colonial social structure. Although the traditional European hierarchy, with its chasm between the gentry and ordinary folk, had never been successfully transplanted to the American colonies, the model of a society ordered by status had exercised considerable influence, its forms of dress and address the dominant ones in the colonial era. Challenging these, the Revolution had introduced a political philosophy subversive to distinctions based upon birth, confusing local mores in ways that *Memoirs of a New England Village Choir* neatly captures.

Gilman's story begins when the longtime director, Gilman himself, departed to resettle in Maine, leaving the choir so upset that, the following Sunday, "not an individual ventured to appear in the singing seats."[1] Thus does Gilman beguilingly introduce the principal plotting element of his and America's new storyline: the volitional character of participation. Choristers could freely choose to mount the stairs to the octagonal pews above the lectern, or they could refrain from singing by remaining downstairs with the congregation, or they could not come to church at all, and each option was exercised by various singers over the ensuing seven years of discord. Like the United States as a whole, Gilman's New England village found itself buffeted by free choice, changing standards, and a highly mobile population.

Knowing how to "set the tune" was the only essential qualification for the position of choir director. Charles Williams, a shoemaker's apprentice with great musical talents, could certainly set the tune, but diffidence immobilized him, so the choir members sought out a different young man to lead them, a newcomer from rural New Hampshire who had recently moved to the village to study with the local doctor. Despite some difficulty controlling his pitch pipe, the doctor's apprentice served the choir well enough until he, too, departed to set up practice in one of the country's new settlements.

Meanwhile, young Williams had "increased in years, skill, and confidence" — in short, lost his diffidence. His willingness to lead the choir infused new life into the whole vocal company. The church bought a large supply of the latest edition of "Village Harmony," and the choir swelled to fifty members. Williams's personal triumph as choir leader proved, however, to be the choir's undoing. So offensive became the idea of someone with Willliams's talents becoming a shoemaker that the villagers came up with the money to send him to Harvard.[2]

At this juncture, Gilman assumes the duties of director as a stopgap measure, only to find himself embroiled with a young academy preceptor who had joined the choir while courting a local woman. Exuding the poise of an out-of-town sophisticate, the preceptor called one morning for "Old Hundred," a tune that only the most venerable vocalists could remember. This was but a foretaste of his campaign to get the village choir to follow "a new and purer taste for sacred music" by eschewing all American tunes in favor of "the slow, grand, and simple airs" that their forefathers had sung.[3] This imperious demand tore the choir asunder, as devotees of the fashionable new atavism battled those deeply attached to the choir's accustomed "animated" style. Now came into play the choir members' weapon of not coming to church at all. "Pew after pew became deserted," Gilman recounts, "until we found that we were singing, and Mr. Welby preaching almost to naked walls," except for the few families of fashionable pretensions who saw something "aristocratical" in the modish return to "Old Hundred." The director stood alone in the choir stall until four octogenarians, "laurelled old men," all veterans of the War for Independence, "tottered up the stairs one Sabbath morning . . . and took their places in the seats left vacant by their degenerate grandsons."[4]

Saved by this timely intervention, the singing continued, but the choir fell apart. Gilman himself went off to college. When a matron of the village offered her services for the duration of the emergency, the ladies of the choir returned. The resolution of this latest crisis only set the stage for a deeper, more lacerating quarrel. The matron-director, "who knew not, or affected not to know the squeamishness respecting rank," invited Mary Wentworth, who was employed as a maid in the village, to the front seat so as to capitalize on her gorgeous voice. Worse was to come for those who were squeamish "respecting rank." The new director, laid low by illness one Sunday, asked Wentworth to direct. The distaff side of the choir then deserted their musical posts en masse, leaving the shunned servant to sing with the sole support of the pastor, an obligation that she turned into a stunning demonstration of "the whole blazing extent of her musical powers." Forthwith the men returned to the balcony, and the choir briefly recovered some of its former volume, only to run afoul of the male choristers' effort to get rid of the new director, in order "to emancipate themselves from the mortifying dominion of a woman."5

Fascinated by the confusion that democratic rhetoric had wrought on older ways of thinking, Gilman rehearsed all the questions about status that were bedeviling his generation. Why, he pondered, had the villagers recoiled at the thought of the talented Charles Williams following in his father's shoemaking trade? Europeans, he ruminated, claimed that all Americans were plebeians. A Harvard-educated Unitarian minister himself, Gilman concluded that Americans had chosen to "draw arbitrary lines of distinction between different professions." More important than family, wealth, or even education, he felt, were "vocations." New livelihoods carried an invitation to the sons and daughters of rural America to join the sprawling middle class of teachers, clerks, preachers, proprietors, lawyers, and physicians. This explained why "certain sets of persons do somehow contrive to obtain an ascendancy in every town and village," but, as Gilman conceded, the whole subject was extremely unsettled, "the Mass is fermenting," and only time would reveal its logic.6 This ferment would bubble up throughout Gilman's story of changing music directors, for he had adroitly chosen to include all of the elements of social structuring—sex, rank, religion, merit, mobility, and ambition. Only the question of race failed to make an appearance in the New England village, even though it moved the entire social system of Gilman's adopted home in South Carolina, where he served as the pastor of the Charleston Second Congregational Church.

Appealing to British standards, the academy preceptor demonstrated that emulating English aristocratic ways still had appeal and could be promoted through the simple mechanism of singing "Old Hundred" with "a conscious superiority in taste." Yet the villagers accepted the upward mobility of the talented shoemaker's son and the New Hampshire farm boy studying medicine. The men supported the singing privileges of a servant, but rejected a woman as choir director, while the female choristers could not so easily abandon considerations of rank.

Mary Wentworth's brief authority had outraged the female choir members, even though her position as a domestic worker was glossed over by the euphemism, "help." Gilman hailed this novel circumlocution because it admitted into the mind "a sense of independence and a hope of rising in the world," which Wentworth in fact did by leaving town to become a teacher. "Help" did not carry with it the stamp of dependency of "servant," Gilman noted. Less charitably, he called the farmer's son studying medicine "an uncouth personage," but, once his education was completed, he nonetheless went off to a new settlement to enjoy the status of a doctor. Gilman's village choir struggled to maintain an equilibrium while being assailed by a succession of surprises as unexpected as they were unwelcome.

The egalitarian spirit promoted by the Revolution might have remained a patriotic sentiment had not the rush to new lands, the religious revivals, and the prosperity that brought the accoutrements of refinement to an ever-widening circle of families strengthened the hand of those who longed for comprehensive social change. Seeking to expand rather than limit the ambit of popular government, they sought to eliminate the traces of a deferential society. The protracted battles between the Federalists and their Jeffersonian challengers had thoroughly politicized the very notion of social superiority. Those who found the jumbling of social place unsettling put up stiff resistance to translation of political values to social norms, but other forces conspired to promote parity among white American men. The abundance of public land for sale opened up farm ownership to the majority of those maturing in the first decades of the nineteenth century. The revitalization of American Protestantism through the revivals of the "Second Great Awakening" undermined old religious hierarchies. At the same time, an expanding commercial inventory of commodities—adding convenience, comfort, and beauty to everyday life—released a pervasive yearning for refinement and its handmaiden, respectability.

It is difficult to taxonomize the American social structure of the early nineteenth century using the stock categories of class analysis, unless one wishes to rely upon income and wealth distribution independent of their social meaning. Yet it would also be a mistake to label this period as one moving toward egalitarian social norms *tout court*. Not only were there distinctive regional patterns of social structure, but the democratization of ambition, which undermined a fixed system of status, fueled new forms of differentiation. Neither the assertiveness of servants nor the homogenization of dress forced a redistribution of income. American's reputation for equality of condition was relative and earned through comparison. Landownership and wealth distribution were much more equitable in the United States than in any other country. Looking at the nation as a whole, very nearly half of the free white men in 1798 owned property, with the top 10 percent controlling almost half of all wealth.[7] Colonial habits of deference had been a casualty of the Revolutionary War; notional acceptance of equality was a badge of patriotism, but more enduringly, Americans who succeeded in establishing a competence on farms, in trade, or through the new array of urban professions began to shape a new social order around their interpretation of American virtues.

After 1800, a very large rent in the social fabric opened up for those ready to walk through it. The justification of independence had offered an explicit defense of political rights, and the Jeffersonians quickly linked democratic governance with equality of respect. Manners, forms, and idle gossip were all drawn into the political battles between the Federalists and Jeffersonians that persisted into the 1820s. Looking back on those days, Martin Van Buren considered the key difference between him and the Federalist patrons of New York to have been his "faith in the capacity of the masses of the people of our Country to govern themselves, and in their general integrity in the exercise of that function."[8]

Talk of an egalitarian society disencumbered of privilege and rank forced the defenders of tradition to become Cassandras, declaiming on the troubles to be visited upon Americans if they abandoned ancient wisdom about public order. A dispute over the Order of Cincinnati—provoked when a group of continental army officers formed a society for themselves and their descendants—sounded an early warning that ordinary Americans would oppose any national institutions based on hereditary distinctions. The outcry startled George Washington and seemed sufficient in John Marshall's eyes to argue for the Order's disbandment. Seven years later, John Adams's campaign to find a suitably majestic salutation for the president ended in a rout when the consensus supported henceforth addressing the nation's chief executive as "Mr. President." Reading Mary Wollstonecraft, Adams exploded with anger at her expectation that the French Revolution would effect lasting change: "And does this foolish woman expect to get rid of an aristocracy?" "God Almighty has decreed in the creation of human nature an eternal aristocracy among men," he scribbled in the margins of his book, adding that "the world is, always has been, and ever will be governed by it."[9]

In these tempests in a teapot can be read the leaves of America's social future. What neither Adams nor Wollstonecraft could have imagined was that expanded opportunities in politics and commerce, along with changing sensibilities in religion, would soon blur the distinctions of family, dress, taste, literacy, and access to knowledge—the work horses of social differentiation. Shrewd about the political import of social messages, Jefferson rejected the formality that intimidated ordinary people. At the White House, he frequently opened the door himself, receiving guests in his lounging jacket. Diplomatic protocol at state dinners yielded to the simple dictum, "those next to the dining room go in first." Even more significant, at his receptions Jefferson replaced Washington's stiff bow from a dais for the fraternal handshake at ground level. The new custom communicated parity and warmth. As a greeting proper only between men, it also signaled a masculine camaraderie that excluded women, to whom one might still bow.

The spirit of high Federalism continued to flourish in many places after 1800. Northern cities became sites of what can now be seen as rear-guard actions against the emerging social ethic. John Pickering, the son of arch-federalist Timothy Pickering, worried about the Americans' corruption of the English language, quoting with approval an article in the *Edinburgh Review*, which appealed to "men of birth and education" to do something about the American idioms that grated on English ears. "America has thrown off the yoke of the British nation," Pickering's British authority acknowledged, "but she would do well for some time, to take the laws of composition from the Addisons, the Swifts and the Robertsons of her ancient sovereign." Slowly these conservatives came to realize that "mysterious energies" were acting upon American society in utterly radical ways. By the time of Jefferson's second election they had given up hope that they could bring Americans back to their senses and conceded that for their country "the sunlit world of peace and order and prosperity it had so recently known under Washington" would not return.[10]

The rambunctious politics of the 1790s brought disillusionment to cultural nationalists like Noah Webster, Charles Brockden Brown, Samuel Latham Mitchell, and David Ramsay. They had expected the free institutions of America to promote literature, science, and scholarship; their nationalist fervor had been nourished by fantasies of American greatness in areas marked out by the high civilization of metropolitan Europe. Despite the Federalists' vigor as journalists and their election to state office through the 1820s, the party died a slow death once ordinary people ceased to defer to their social superiors. As the Federalists painfully learned, maintaining social ranks required consent from below. Looking back to her childhood in a New England village, Eliza Lee described the great influence of the pastor before "any sectarians had invaded our parishes." Taking a less nostalgic view, Catharine Sedgwick contrasted the Stockbridge pastors' three-cornered beaver hat of her youth with Henry Ward Beecher's "Cavalier" hat: "the first formal, elaborate fixed; the last easy, comfortable, flexible, and assuming nothing superior to the mass."[11] It was exactly these relaxed ways that concerned Dolly Madison, who arranged for the composition "Hail to the Chief" to be played at state receptions to rouse people to appropriate respect when her husband, the president, entered the room.

With varying degrees of intensity, champions of an open society battled the defenders of old ways. At risk were the old markers of wealth, style, and family now attacked as irrelevant to a democratic ethic founded upon equality of respect and an appreciation of individual merit. Distinctions, whether linked to the economic notion of class or left to float as shared preferences in attitudes and behavior, only work when most men and women recognize them and seek to perpetuate them in their public performances and through the lessons they pass on to their children. The well-defined ranks of gentry, middling folk, and poor increasingly lost credibility in a world with few strongholds for the gentry to command, and new opportunities to stir ambitions throughout the "fermenting mass." Without a consensus, the ideal of a structured society slowly faded, leaving a welter of organizing principles to vie for public affirmation. Deeply offended by the crass self-assertion of common folk, the Federalist elite increasingly turned their refinement into an end in itself, strengthening their ties with the English world from whence they took their values. In New York and Philadelphia, rising real estate prices sustained the wealth of clusters of intermarrying families of the colonial upper class.[12] Disappointed by politics and the lack of American distinction in the arts, the Federalists became the country's first cultural critics. Their laments, however, were those of a spurned elite, dispossessed of its admiring following. Men and women in various social settings began examining once-shared values, questioning American indebtedness to British tastes, the status of women, the connection of piety to respectability, and whether the continuation of slavery undercut the Republic's claim to the high ground staked out in the Declaration of Independence.

Foreign visitors puzzled over the displays of undifferentiated sociability in the United States and attributed them to American politics. Ludwig Gall thought that politicians had to be ultra-democratic: "In the six months before the election of 1820 the governor of Pennsylvania did his own shopping, appearing in the market with basket on arm. When there was a public auction," he continued, "his business took him there"—and this twenty years before the "log cabin" campaign of 1840. The Scottish traveler James Flint, giving the relationship of manners and politics a more extended critique, decided that universal suffrage and frequent elections strengthened the bonds of American society: "the candidates having no boroughs to be treated with in the wholesale way, and the constituents being too numerous, and coming too often in the way, to admit of their being bought over, expectants are obliged to depend on their popularity, and do not find it their interest to repulse any one." "It is only from these causes," he explained, that he could "account for the affability of manners which are almost universal." In contrast to Britain, "where neighbors do not know the names of persons who live in adjoining houses," an American, even in new settlements, will know "almost any person, within ten miles of him." "The symptoms of republican equality are visible in all the members of the community," Flint claimed, for America was not "divided or formed into classes by the distinctions of title and rank, neither does political party seem to form such a complete separation amongst men, and the unequal distribution of property operates much less." Hence, he concluded, the individuals who compose American society "are less mutually repellent to one another . . . and the distinctions formed here are of a more natural kind, such as those . . . that proceed from the sympathies of human nature."[13]

In legal theory, of course, all the autonomous and independent white men, who in common law had command over their wives, children, servants, and slaves, should have secured order in their domains. In practice, free young men and women sometimes struck out on their own; death regularly broke up families; slaves liberated themselves; and of course not all householders were up to assuming their supervisory responsibilities. Prospering in the early nineteenth-century economy often required movement—on to new land, toward urban opportunity, into new types of ventures.

The migration of men and families onto the frontier exemplifies this point. The availability of public land for private purchase rapidly increased the number of property owners. While many of them became dirt-poor farmers, they had made it to the right side of the critical divide between independence and dependency, probably the most salient of all social markers in an America that was still 80 percent rural. Their status as the heads of their own farming families enabled thousands of young men and women to replicate the world of their parents. Morris Birkbeck, writing for his English compatriots, felt that it was almost impossible to convey the American love of movement. Imagine, he wrote of his 1815 visit, the numerous stages, light wagons, and horseback riders and "you have before you a scene of bustle and business, extending over a space of three hundred miles, which is truly wonderful."[14] People not only moved out; they sometimes moved up as they moved out. This very mobility eroded expectations of enduring status and scrambled the social codes inherited from a Europeanized colonial world. The mobility of young adults leaving the place of their birth, the mobility of talent searching for its optimal rewards, or the mobility of cash and credit chasing after innovation worked against fixed statuses just as, somewhat paradoxically, prosperity made it possible for many more people to mimic the consuming tastes of the old colonial gentry. When annual sales of western land vaulted from a hundred thousand acres in the 1790s to five times that number after Jefferson's election, new farms multiplied at a rate that had not been duplicated since the original settlements.[15] Meanwhile, in older sections, farmer-artisans found new profits in the growing demand for clocks, implements, and furniture. As with so many other developments in the West, these new mores bounced back East, opening communities to new ways to value themselves, their neighbors, and their servants, as Gilman's Village Choir memoir so charmingly showed.

The frontier had a different impact on America's enslaved population. What was a white man's great chance often brought misery to African

Americans because the fifty-year cotton boom that began in 1793 lashed slavery to the planters' rising profits and promoted a thriving domestic slave trade to boot. Slave sales separated hundreds of thousands of African Americans from their homes and families on what had been the relatively stable plantations of Virginia and Maryland. On the southern frontier, the harshest working conditions on the continent existed. Occasions for forming new black communities to replace the ones left behind in Virginia or Maryland rarely materialized. Economic developments fixed the status of slavery more firmly than ever before, and the rhetoric of American opportunity, largely produced in the North, rang hollow for this full fifth of the nation's population.

Nor was white mobility always upward. Bankruptcy was a common fact of life, given the fragility of the country's credit system and the foolhardiness of nascent entrepreneurs. Overspeculation brought the highest flyers down while abrupt financial downturns like Jefferson's embargo or the War of 1812 exposed all borrowers to sharp reversals of fortune. New land undercut the value of old, especially in the northern frontiers of Vermont and Maine, though the intensification of garden cultivation around cities helped offset this trend. Popular lore had it that American wealth was never successfully passed down through three generations. John Chambers gave voice to this view when he told his children, "I have yet to see wealth pass by descent beyond the third generation, but I have seen & see every day the second generation who has squandered the labours of their predecessors."[16] Echoing Chambers, Ebenezer Thomas remarked upon how unusual it was that the family of the Providence East India merchant John Brown "has increased in wealth through three generations—a circumstance which I do not recollect to have occurred before, as it has been almost a universal practice, for the children to squander what the father accumulates." Even the enormous fortune amassed by the assiduous town developer William Cooper melted away before his heirs could lay claim to it.[17]

Egalitarian rhetoric, mobility, and the absence of great and enduring fortunes tended to promote a social homogeneity in which Americans began to take pride. The prominent Baltimore journalist Hezekiah Niles regularly told his readers that a man had more honor being descended from a line of mechanics like himself than from royalty. Even American landholdings seemed relatively uniform in comparison with European norms. Benjamin Latrobe, who was reared abroad, described George Washington's Mount Vernon as pleasant and modest, the country estate of someone in England, he calculated, who would have an income of 500–600 pounds a year. Martha Washington, who he thought had retained "the strong remains of considerable beauty," had "no affectation of superiority in the slightest degree, but acts completely in the character of the mistress of the house of a respectable and opulent country gentleman." At that time, George Washington ranked as one of the wealthiest men in the United States.[18]

A further homogenizing force were the names this generation gave to its children. Young adults eschewed their parents' habit of looking for names in the Bible, few calling their children Ichabod, Ebenezer, Sylvester, Eleazar, Ephraim, Jehudi, Alphaeus, Elnathan, Begalel, Ezekiel, Jedidiah, Zebulon, Eliphelet, Lo-ammi, Hezekiah, Adoniram, Seled, Jabez, Erastus, Zadok, Asahel, Arphaxad, Zephaniah, Shubael, Zacchaeus, Zebadiah, Azariah, Amariah, or Kemuel, all names that they had carried. The expression, "every Tom, Dick, and Harry" could only have meaning after this cohort left a progeny named not for Biblical figures, but instead for the Georges, Thomases, Richards, Johns, and Jameses of the revolutionary leadership.[19]

American homogeneity extended spatially as well. Accustomed to the dramatic differences in rural and urban life at home, foreign travelers repeatedly expressed amazement at the sophistication of farming people. Crossing the Allegheny Mountains, Birkbeck reported that what was "most at variance with English notions of the American people, is the urbanity and civilization that prevail in situations remote from large cities," where people "have not for a moment lost sight of the manners of polished life." Americans, he claimed, "are strangers to rural simplicity: the embarrassed air of an awkward rustic, so frequent in England, is rarely seen in the United States." He went on to say that this was doubtless "the effect of political equality, the consciousness of which accompanies all their intercourse, and may be supposed to operate most powerfully on the manners of the lowest class." Gall found that country wagoners dressed much like city folk. Flint was impressed that farmers "who own but small properties, keep one horse gigs," which their "ladies drive dexterously."[20]

Women, children, and blacks could be assigned a fixed place in society because they were easily identified. The case became more complicated with white men. Unwilling to claim prestige through sartorial distinction, many upper-class men dressed negligently, adopting a kind of social camouflage that foreigners found perplexing. As knee breeches and buckled pumps gave way to long pants and laced shoes, the male body carried fewer signs to be read for social status, especially as the expanding ranks of clerks and storekeepers added to the number of men in conventional town garb. Close attention to clean linen and proper style became a matter of importance to those aspiring to move up. Interlopers—men like James Guild, a Yankee farmer turned peddler and calligrapher—invested in clothes to win respect from strangers. He became furious when the stratagem failed.[21]

In nineteenth-century America, the behavior of servants loomed large in daily life, for almost every household, down to the poorest farm, had one or more. To be really poor was to live without a servant. Lydia Sigourney, in one of her many didactic writings for young women, warned them of the scarcity of good household help and, like foreigners, linked the shortage to American political mores: "In our state of society, where equality so visibly prevails...servants faithful, and thoroughly trained in their several departments, are not always to be found." White servants wreaked the most havoc on traditional social arrangements in America. Their aversion to the social stigma of dependency manifested itself in what Flint declared a genuine Americanism—the new rubric of "help" that Gilman had praised. Remarking on the reluctance of young women to go into house service, Flint recalled hearing from a Philadelphia manufacturer that he had no difficulty finding "females to be employed in his work-shop; but a girl for housework he could not procure for less than twice the manufacturing wages." He also noted that throughout the West agricultural laborers were never called servants, but always "hired hands." When manufacturing jobs came to New England, young women voted with their feet, rarely going "out to service" when they could do factory work. Mary Ann Morris Cooper, James Fenimore Cooper's sister-in-law, crowed in her diary when she succeeded in finding a girl "free from Yankee dignity and ideas of Liberty," which she labeled "insolence only."[22]

If servants resisted a servile attitude, ordinary farmers in New England disdained the efforts of their superiors to dictate taste in matters of architecture and landscaping. Upper-class reformers longed to preserve rustic scenes from some imagined idyllic past when simple cottages festooned with roses and bordered with verdant fields and orchards dotted the countryside. Instead, the farmers, who often carried on trades in their garages, poured their profits into outbuildings that sprawled awkwardly across the landscape.[23] Secure in their property rights, these enterprising husbandmen ignored the lofty prescriptions for rural beauty.

The dethroning of older, invidious social distinctions opened the way for new standards, and many successful Americans wrote about their country as the locus for exchanges of talents and riches. Productive, inventive individuals were presented as powerful nodes of attention and admiration, their lives serving as models of innovation in a society losing all desire to replicate past ways of doing things. This functional, future-oriented social blueprint replaced the older picture of communities unified around a stable social order. The personal qualities of intelligence, honesty, commitment, and enterprise became more relevant to the function of society.

Intelligence was the word that contemporaries used to characterize those who succeeded in their midst, but it took a specific kind of intelligence to pry open opportunities in the United States. The demand for those who could read, write, calculate, and speak was higher than the supply; the commercial opportunities dependent upon literacy far outstripped the educational capacities of what remained a primitive schooling system. Moreover, fitting into the beckoning commercial world involved a willingness to move where the jobs were. Those who prospered from these changes were the disciplined, hardworking sons and daughters of farm families who tailored their talents to society's demands. Because there were thousands of able young people to fill the positions of a developing society, the old filters of social distinction became useless. Employers no longer needed to rely upon the old system of sponsored promotion; the fit between talent and task could be made as quickly as young people found their ways to opportunity. Lying in the future was the industrial order with its hierarchies of workers and owners, blue collars and white collars, wage earners and managers. "A pattern of informal leniency," it has been noted, marked even factory relations, until Irish and French-Canadian mill workers arrived in great numbers in the 1840s.[24] American-born artisans tended to go to other skilled jobs, leaving unskilled work for the new arrivals. With such upward mobility for native-born, white Americans, it was difficult to institutionalize a strong class consciousness. However, invidious distinctions of foreign birth soon joined that of race.

For a significant proportion of the population, being saved was an even more potent differentiator than intelligence. The three decades of successful evangelizing across the hamlets, villages, towns, and cities of the United States pushed humility, charity, and faith to the forefront of public consciousness. Commitment to the true Christian life exercised a powerful hold upon hundreds of thousands of Americans, encouraging them to rework their old selves into new and better ones. The conversion experience released enough reforming energy from those touched by the revivals—probably a quarter of the population—to reshape American public life. Intensely personal, the revivals succeeded in replacing the ceremonialism of American churches with the unabashed emotionalism of the Baptists and Methodists, leaving those converted with a heightened sense of the difference between the saved and the unsaved, the spiritually alive and spiritually dead, distinctions that further challenged the old hierarchies.

Methodists, Baptists, and Presbyterians, like the Quakers, announced their new devotion by spurning fancy clothes, lavish entertainment, and slaves. They kept a strict watch over their members' public behavior. Displaying their religious convictions in their dress, evangelical Christians often provoked reactions from the less religious. Julia Tevis, a bride travelling West with her husband, a Methodist circuit rider, was humiliated when a farmer refused them the conventional hospitality of the road. So unexpected was this, she explained, that its denial had to be taken as an insult. Sensing her distress, the son of the house explained, "It's the broad brim and straight coat that made him do it. . . . You see, we're going to have a dancing party tonight."[25] Censorious, the revivalists stirred the ire of those with more relaxed standards or none at all.

Because the revivalists successfully challenged the religious hegemony of the Anglican and Congregational churches, the "Second Great Awakening" contributed to both the social homogenization and democratization of American society. Its social ideals complemented the republican equality spread by the Jeffersonians. And it attracted the same kind of critics. Arthur Singleton, a New England travel writer, sketched in acid a camp meeting he visited in Kentucky: "the ministers are a species of without-method Methodists; happy compounds of illiterateness and fanaticism. . . . With most of these apostles, the text is but a pitching of the tone to the nasality," he continued, "for, altho they name a text when they commence, that is commonly the last you hear of it." Christiana Tillson gave a similarly sharp appraisal of the Methodist circuit riders who visited her frontier Illinois settlement once a month, "singing and ranting." "If preachers had come among the people meekly, and with an earnest desire to do a good to the souls of men—however weak and ignorant they might have been—I could have respected their effort . . . but their whole manner evinced so much arrogance and self display and such unblushing impudence as to repel me."[26]

In the end, those who cherished the learned Christian tradition yielded to the success of the revivalists and imitated their style. In turn, the revivalists learned to accommodate the new tastes that were surfacing among their members. Timothy Flint, a New Englander turned champion of the West, analyzed the revivals' social power when he explained:

> The ambitious and wealthy are there, because in this region opinion is all-powerful; and they are there, either to extend their influence, or that their absence may not be noted to diminish it. Aspirants for office are there, to electioneer, and gain popularity. Vast numbers are there from simple curiosity, merely to enjoy a spectacle. The young and the beautiful are there, with mixed motives, which it were best not severely to scrutinize.[27]

Their parishioners' pursuit of refinement was a snare for the evangelical preachers, appearing as a diversion to the pious life, but it could be interpreted as offering the road to respectability that preserved good family morals.

The buoyancy of the early national economy put money in pockets that had formerly carried stones, apples, string, and scraps of paper. Refinement, once closely associated with the style of a royal court, became an integral part of the aspirations of ordinary men and women in the first decades of the nineteenth century. Where earlier gentility had been the quest of those in the upper reaches of colonial society (one thinks of George Washington laboriously copying injunctions from English etiquette books), the early nineteenth century witnessed a popular surge toward the elusive goals of good manners and refined taste. Linoleum floors, stenciled furniture, pianos—even painted barns and walled-off bedrooms—announced a more genteel, capacious way of life. Country stores expanded their inventories in response to the demands of country folk, stocking more and more household comforts and decorative items.[28]

Fashion, too, began to encourage a more honest, direct, and simple presentation of self. Elihu Shepard remembered well his shock at finding his teacher, "the morning star of fashion," unrecognizable at the beginning of the term in 1800 when "she had caused her long hair to be trimmed short like a young girl's" and had also abandoned the fashionable dress of 1798 for "comely and informal attire." He mused on the change in the times. "Gentlemen of taste laid aside their sharp-toed shoes and books, their knee and shoe buckles, their long stockings and short breeches, their long vests and ruffled shirts, their single-breasted coats and broad-brimmed cocked hats." Censored by many, the new fashions, he noted, brought "great zest and pleasure to the young." From the 1790s through the 1820s, women's fashions were simple and light, conveying a nonchalance with uncorseted waistlines and minimalist, draped skirts. Cut to permit easy movement, the dresses could also be cheaply produced.[29]

In this as in so many ways, Jefferson took the lead, renouncing powdered wigs and taking up the humble shoe lace. Possessing book learning, holding office, and having a house with more than two rooms no longer set a few people off from the great majority. The brisk circulation of news about fashion and manners brought the elements of refined living to an ever-expanding audience. As new consumer commodities found their way into homes and onto bodies, they became new social markers. Carpeting not only indicated the money and desire to purchase it, but signaled as well that those who trod on it had learned to wipe their feet. Still the rough work and long hours of ordinary laborers militated against adoption of much in the way of new home furnishings, even if their labor remained the lodestar of American patriotism—its energy, inventiveness, and intelligence furnishing the proof that the American experiment in democracy was working.

Pleasurable in themselves, the new comforts were implicated in a way of life long associated with the upper strata of society. American democratization involved two mildly contradictory developments: the elevation of all white Americans to a plateau of respect, and the extension of refined tastes to an increasing number of families that were then differentiated from the poor and the dissolute. On the one hand, most Americans exulted in their abandonment of European snobbery; at the same time many copied European forms of gracious living that enabled them to feel superior to those who did not. Having rejected most aspects of a tiered society, ordinary Americans went on to embrace the ideal of refinement, struggling to maintain an equality of respect as they responded to new distinctions. New patterns of spending were implicated in emerging social practices. Where people could afford an extra room, parlors became centers for domestic conviviality. In 1823, people could purchase from Jonas Chickering the first piano produced entirely in the United States. (The market linked patriotic chauvinism to gentility.)

Refinement involved far more than purchasing embellishments for self and home; it entailed a demanding set of avoidances—not slumping, shuffling, or gaping—along with mastering a range of skills. The popularity of etiquette books detailing courtly codes of behavior gave proof that economic success whetted the appetite for genteel self-fashioning and the careful cultivation of appearances. Handwriting became a prized accomplishment as calligraphy instructors sprang up like dandies at a cotillion. Holding short-term classes in towns up and down the eastern seaboard, itinerant teachers brought the beauty of cursive script to thousands of eager self-improvers. James Guild, a particularly raffish purveyor of refinement, claimed to have attracted forty scholars in Norfolk simply by advertising "to teach writing, and painting miniatures."[30]

New England moralists, especially faithful Federalists, feared that the western settlements would foster the same leveling tendencies that alarmed them at home: in this they were correct. Rebecca Burlend noted that every man was called "sir, however slender his pretensions to knighthood, or how long soever the time since his small-clothes were new." Women, she said, were "in like manner honoured with madam." Birkbeck found the frequent invocation of the word 'elegant' a source of amusement, as in "elegant mill, an elegant orchard—used everywhere that is inappropriate in English language."[31]

The contradiction of gentility spreading through a society proud of its democratic ways did not go unnoticed. John Chambers, a frontier political leader, excoriated "the arrogance of poor stupid wretches who founded their claims for notice, if not for distinction, upon the wealth of some ancestor or relations, or perhaps worse, upon the accidental possession of it in their own persons." Equally indignant, America's first professional architect, Benjamin Latrobe, mocked the folly of loving rank, particularly army titles: "Captains, majors, colonels and generals elbow a man out of all hopes even of this country."[32]

Although the revolutionary zeal for change stopped at the threshold of the "castle," where the master reigned supreme over his household, its transforming potential could be seen in everything from the institution of slavery to the conduct of youth. Few American women emerged to urge a redress of laws affecting property, divorce, or child custody, yet it was difficult to keep talk of freedom from spilling over the formal channels of law and spreading to informal and private areas. Little was done to change the legal restrictions affecting women's control over their lives, but the outpouring of writings, mostly from men, forced fresh thinking about women's schooling, the examples set by their mothers, and the erotic appeal of feminine incapacity.

John Neal, among the most unconventional writers of the period, wrote an inflammatory pamphlet, *The Rights of Women*, which began with the provocative statement that American women "are not free—free, in the sense that men are free, according to any definition of liberty." Whether the women of this country were slaves, Neal decided, depended upon one's definition of slavery. Referring to the fact that women voted in New Jersey, Neal explained derisively that the legislature there had settled the constitutional question "by declaring that the word 'inhabitants' meant free white males!" For his part, he resolved that if women were part of the people, they were "entitled to participate in their legislative council: and not being represented, have a right to legislate for themselves."[33]

The neglect of girls' education and their premature involvement in the frivolity attendant upon courtship bothered lots of people, but women writers were significantly more timid than male ones in treating of this subject. Mary Hunt Tyler, the strong-willed wife of playwright Royall Tyler, demurred only slightly from contemporary mores when she wrote that even if mothers must guard the complexions of their daughters, there was no reason not to let them run and enjoy themselves in full liberty for a few hours every day. Obeisant to the misogynist discourse that held likeness to a woman as the worst fate of a man, Tyler entreated mothers "to reflect upon what manner of men you will wish to see" your sons become, threatening effeminacy and pusillanimity if mothers instilled "into their tender minds the love of dress and show."[34] Thus conventional morality swiveled in a round of fears about depriving girls of their intellectual development and boys of their hopes for virility as adults.

Perhaps nothing challenged gendered prescriptions more than the issue of women's education. The vibrancy of urban culture found expression in lecture series, scientific demonstrations, and a heightened appreciation of learning. Some young women clearly benefited from these developments, even though their intellectual growth clashed with the eroticizing of frailty and innocence. Elizabeth Levick remembered attending lectures on botany with other young women at the American Philosophical Society in 1815. "This was considered a great innovation, and by not a few we were regarded," she explained, "as very strong-minded young women." Describing doubts as to "the propriety and the delicacy of our conduct," Levick went on to affirm how interesting and instructive the lectures proved to be. "I was at that time a member of the House of Industry, and growing out of these lectures a committee of us was appointed to collect herbs . . . for the poor." Other women contrasted their education with that of their parents' era, noting, as Olive Cleaveland Clarke did, that "girls were not much esteemed in those days."[32] Between the two generations, the literacy gap between women and men in most of the North was closed, though literacy for both sexes remained lower in the South.[35] More important, women's careers as missionaries, writers, preachers, and school proprietresses revealed a range of female talent that prevented closure on the subject for this first generation.

Lydia Sigourney's essays "to young ladies" reveal sharply the conflicts that inhered in a society in flux, where women could be enjoined alternately to preside gracefully in the parlor and meet stoically any eventuality. As Sigourney so perceptively saw, refinement held the key to women's intellectual development without challenging contemporary attitudes. Indeed, for the majority of middle-class women, the cultivation of conversational skills was liberating, enabling them to turn their parlors into centers of sociability. Refinement effected a number of changes in the American social scene. The successful effort to make public space safe for women—a fact oft-noted by foreigners—meant that they could move freely outside their homes. Frederick Marryat, a British officer traveling through the United States noted the "universal deference and civility shown to the women, who may in consequence travel without protection all over the United States without the least chance of annoyance or insult."[36] The goal of being refined also created an incentive for both sexes to acquire the knowledge and taste that made for lively and agreeable exchanges between them. Subtly the range of acceptable feminine qualities expanded, pushing as it did against entrenched misogynist views of women's capacities.

Sigourney asserted that the United States had produced a society in which the "the grades of rank and station" were not very clearly defined, and yet the expectation of defined social tiers continued to underpin her observations, as when she commented that "the lower classes sometimes press upon the higher." And then again she would affirm democratic values, as when she concluded that in the United States "all should be willing to pay some tax for the privilege of a government, which admits such an high degree, and wide expansion of happiness."[37] Sigourney's concept of upper-class indulgence in lower-class aspirations conveys both an openness to fundamental changes and the condescension of a social superior.

Southerners no less than northerners were affected by the tendencies of American independence to subvert the old colonial order. Indeed, the Revolution had dealt southerners two blows: it exposed the freedom-seeking zeal of enslaved men and women, and it turned slavery into a regional institution. Because many slaves ran to the British lines during the Revolutionary War, it was no longer possible to believe that they accepted their enslavement, and the response of northerners to the emancipatory spirit of the Declaration of Independence signaled the beginning of an international crusade against slavery. Forced for the first time to provide a moral defense of their now peculiar institution, southerners turned increasingly to an idealization of kith and kin, honor, and gracious living. The great divergence between rich and poor in the South fed the elite's sense of superiority, an overriding attitude that shaped the sensibilities of all southerners.

The number of *middling* families of farmers, clerks, master craftsmen, storekeepers, merchants, and professional men who formed the dominant social group in the North and West grew slowly in the South. The scramble for land and slaves on the southern frontier ended with a residue of losers whose lack of options forced migration out of the "black belt." The successful new planters then replicated the ostentation and oppression that characterized the Old South. Only in the pine barrens did poor farmers thrive, trading the comforts of settled areas for the independence of the "hillbilly."

Increasingly, southerners construed the habits of industry as nothing more than distasteful northern attributes compared to their own open, free-spending, impulsive, honor-observing ways. For their part, northerners used the rhetoric of liberty to shame the South. The list of differences grew longer, sharper, more invidious. Soon northerners and southerners thought of themselves as the carriers of opposite qualities, a tendency that in turn distorted their own self-images: the South as a resort for the vanishing virtues of aristocracy; the North as a haven of equality. In fact, the disgruntled Federalists of the North had shared many of the planters' ideas about family, hierarchy, and order, but slavery and the attitudes toward work that its presence promoted drove an unbridgeable gulf between them. The defeat of the Federalists deprived southern planters of a northern political elite that shared some of its values.

During the first decades of the nineteenth century, the rejection of European aristocratic norms and the experimentation with equality had created an alternative American tradition. Decisions made in deference to revolutionary hopes showed that political ideals could influence the terms of social life, but inequality grew gradually after the 1820s—greater in cities than in the country, in settled areas than the frontier, in southern states than northern ones. A fragile opening toward African and Native Americans deposited a deep, but narrow, vein of tolerance in the social sediment. Viewed from the outside, the United States looked like a polyglot country, noisy and chaotic with its cacophonous voices and disparate customs, but on the inside white Americans were acquiring the capacity not to see some of the people. Yale President Timothy Dwight left African Americans out of his 1805 census of New York City even though they formed a quarter of the city's workers. Blacks and Native Americans were often treated as invisible, unless they or some champion like William Apess or David Walker spoke out on their behalf. Still there were enough references to interracial possibilities to suggest that racial attitudes had not yet congealed, as when the distinguished New England biblical scholar William Jenks spoke of American character as "a mixture of Dutch phlegm, the sanguine complexion of the Englishman, French choler and vanity, Irish rapidity, German sensibility and patient industry, Negro indifference and Indian indolence." There was food, he went on to say, "for any plant whatever."[38]

Race, respectability, and refinement slowly gained momentum as the new arbiters of social place, but the affirmations of the first generation guaranteed that they would exist in tension with the tradition of natural rights, widely viewed as the nation's most distinctive characteristic. To build institutional support for sharper social distinctions in the future would require going against the grain of the values deposited by the most outspoken of the first generation. Quick to interpret their experiences as harbingers of a progressive future, they made sure that their understanding of America was expressed in politics, taught in schools, and reinforced by the churches of the disinherited. The middle class experienced its birth in this heady environment, as the heirs of the American Revolution worked out the terms of their legacy.[39]

"We Are Not Afraid to Work": Master Mechanics and the Market, Revolution in the Antebellum North

BRUCE LAURIE

When we think of the middle class, especially in the nineteenth century, we think of small business owners. These entrepreneurs were the darlings of the period roundly celebrated by European observers and hagiographic historians. But they remain one of the groups most understudied by modern historians. We really know very little about them— their intriguing economic views, their complex politics, or even whether or not they truly qualify as "middle class" in the conventional sense of the term. As we will see, they do and they do not.

Starting with Richard Hofstadter, historians have sketched several different pictures of mechanics and small employers in antebellum America. Hofstadter envisioned them as capitalists in the rough, lesser versions of greater entrepreneurs, who, from the nation's beginning embraced individualism, market competition, and profit maximization.[1] Such proprietors had more circumscribed careers in the view of Alan Dawley, who, in the spirit of Marx, depicts mechanics as an ephemeral class of petty producers. Governed by craft tradition and sustained by local customers, such employers were no match for the lusty merchant capitalism of the market revolution that swept them to the margin of the economy or wiped them off the economic map altogether. In Dawley's blunt formulation, they were "done in" by merchant capitalists. [2] A third school, closely associated with the recent debate on the market revolution, describes a more complex process of economic transformation that sundered the mechanic community into a small group of entrepreneurs, and conversely, a larger aggregate described variously as petty capitalists, small producers, and so on.[3] It may be an overstatement, however, to call this a "school" because of significant differences of emphasis and kind. In his masterful study of New York that acknowledges deepening social division between entrepreneurs and mechanics, Sean Wilentz tends to accent the entrepreneurial ambitions of the Empire City's master craftsmen.[4] Gary Kornblith, by contrast, argues that entrepreneurial sensibilities developed both more slowly and more unevenly, but triumphed in the end, as the old republicanism gave way to the new liberalism of "unregulated economic growth at the expense of social equality and the pursuit of private interest at the expense of public virtue."[5]

This essay makes two points about master craftsmen in the antebellum North that run counter to the conventional scholarly wisdom. First is the obvious but still important one that small proprietors simply did not disappear. The concentration of ownership, which is generally assumed to have displaced small producers in the course of the nineteenth century, had a stronger impact on newer industries than on older ones. Larger firms in metalwork and textiles were dominant even before the Civil War, employing most of the labor and accounting for a disproportionate share of the product. This familiar pattern, however, fit most handicrafts loosely or hardly at all, even in such a burgeoning industrial center as Philadelphia. In the 1850s, for instance, small shops with fewer than six employees in that city accounted for about a third of all establishments in printing and approximately 60 percent in building construction. While this would suggest at least some concentration of ownership, the data also show that the process was fitful and uneven. Thirty years later, in the heat of industrial transformation, the proportion of small printing houses did not change at all, and small construction companies actually increased to more than 70 percent. (It is also worth mentioning that the percentage of non-managerial employees in such shops remained constant in both cases.)

Such small establishments were even more resilient in the neighborhood trades of baking, meat preparation, and light metalwork, in which owners living above their stores served local customers.[6] This configuration of ownership takes on added significance when we recall that big urban centers like Philadelphia housed a small proportion of the entire population before the Civil War. Villages, small towns, and rural places, which claimed about 70 percent of Americans at the end of the period, offered much better environments for mechanics and independent proprietors. Whether they operated in the country or the city, small proprietors were far more typical of the nation's productive employers than were its lionized entrepreneurs.

Second, this piece takes issue with work that either envisions a linear, unmediated progression from petty producer to capitalist, with all that implies, or assumes that small employers were capitalist from the beginning. One of the more impressive works in this latter spirit, Joyce Appleby's recent essay on the popular origins of American capitalism in the late eighteenth century, merits a closer look. Having pored through some 1700 life stories of men and women in the last quarter of the eighteenth century, Appleby argues forcefully against work that treats capitalism as an external force imposed on reluctant farmers and mechanics from without by urban financiers. Local producers, she argues, far from being averse to economic transformation, subscribed to "deeply rooted values essential to the rapid and pervasive development of America's free market economy." She goes on to argue that the interplay between this disposition and "structural imperatives of market development" yielded the pervasive capitalist ethos of the early Republic.[7]

This view is not mistaken, only incomplete and one-sided. It overlooks the other side, a large group and possibly the vast majority of mechanics who doubted the values Appleby describes. It also takes the first-person accounts of farmers and mechanics to be accurate gauges of economic realities. While such sources reveal quite a bit about individual choice and personal reflection, they tell us very little or nothing at all about relationshsips with fellow producers and other actors. These must be complemented with newspaper accounts, trade manuals, records of trade associations and mechanics groups, which together leave a rounder and more comprehensive impression of the actual workings of the market and its social relationships. Such sources suggest that through the antebellum period a significant group of master mechanics remained unimpressed with classical liberalism, if by this one means the unbridled pursuit of individual economic interest. They instead received the advent of laissez-faire selectively. They welcomed the wider personal latitude that attended smaller government but did not construe its freedom to be license for unfettered pursuit of economic individualism. In the private space opened by receding government, they developed new tactics—both individual and collective—designed to contain competition in the name of sustaining personal independence and economic security. In addition, such economic tactics reflected and sustained the identity of petty proprietors as an intermediate class suspended between the working class and the established middle class. Even though at its social margins this "middling" class blended into the working class and the middle class, its core persisted as an important economic force and political presence through the nineteenth century. Mechanics of the "middling sort" were also busy men deeply involved in civic matters and fraternalism as well as state and local politics. Since it is impossible to capture the whole of their experience in this short space, however, we will focus attention on their economic affairs and refer to their politics.

Aspiring master craftsmen in the antebellum North at once faced economic opportunity and economic peril.[8] The main chance seldom appeared so close at hand for so many. In some instances, as the memoirs of Thurlow Weed, Joseph Tinker Buckingham, and other printers indicate, masters sold their businesses to favored journeymen on generous terms, sparing upstarts the need to establish themselves with suppliers, creditors, and customers.9 Others who began without such an edge could parlay membership in churches, militia units, or mechanics' institutes into business connections that fetched backers as well as buyers. Indeed, given finance capital's aversion to the handicrafts, it is difficult to see how independent producers got along at all without benefit of patrons beyond the banking community.

Lansford Wood, of Worcester, Massachusetts, certainly had his share of them. A cabinetmaker by trade, Wood developed into an all-around tradesman who would just as soon paint a railing or repair a chair as work a rough piece of hardwood into a stylish bureau. He also enjoyed an enviable location in the heart of a small, but thriving, commercial center with an upscale market sustained by Worcester's first families. The Salisburys, Lincolns, and other provincial worthies who appear in Wood's ledger meant reliable demand, prompt payment in cash, and, one imagines, credit in a pinch.10 Timing also came in to play. It was easier to set up shop before the depression of 1837, partly because of the relative affordability of land and rental space in cities and boom towns.11 Surging land prices in the 1840s thrust prime locations beyond the means of small proprietors, and not a few large ones, in land-extensive pursuits.12 The tight urban land market virtually spelled the end of the small proprietor who owned his shop; more and more of them had to rent.

Country mechanics like Wood who owned land also enjoyed readier access to the means of economic independence than their urban colleagues. Such proprietors balanced work at their crafts with farm chores, practicing what modern historians describe as bi- or dual employment. This pattern of bi-employment, which proved central to the quest for independence, has long escaped the attention of historians largely because of a shared modernist outlook that reads the specialization of function of modern times into the early nineteenth century.13 As this Weberian dynamic has it, bi-employment was an artifact of a preindustrial era destined for extinction by imperatives of evolving urbanization and market capitalism.

More recent work indicates, however, that bi-employment endured into the antebellum period.14 Rural and small-town mechanics who owned farmland shifted back and forth between field and workshop according to seasonal chores, market demands, and the state of the larder. Elihu Burritt, the self-styled "Learned Blacksmith," was not one to let his anvil or forge impede his crusades for abolitionism and world peace. Though Burritt kept a dizzying schedule of talks and lectures in the 1850s, he was both smith and farmer when at home in Worcester or New Britain, "working a little patch of corn, which will constitute the head and front of my grain for the year."[15] Burritt was a plain man who lived simply and for social reform; his garden provided some beans and grain for the dinner table, a little something for a man on the fringe of the market economy. The Lancaster County brushmaker Matthias Zahn likewise fattened a slim income from his trade by selling honey from his bees, a common source of income for village proprietors.[16]

Mechanics with larger holdings were more deeply involved in marketing farm commodities. The Dedham, Massachusetts, yeoman carpenter Isaac Whiting simultaneously ran a woodworking shop and small farm in the early national period, both with the help of his son and a hired hand, and he sometimes did maintenance work at a textile mill in which he had an interest.[17] The cord wood, maple products, and fresh-killed meat from such farms as Whiting's could produce enough income to rival money from craft work. So could pursuits more closely allied with one's calling. Lansford Wood earned at least some cash from renting his horse and wagon to local teamsters, and a larger sum still from selling paint and varnish made in his shop.[18] Lyman Wilson, a bookbinder in Milton, Pennsylvania, was even more economically versatile. He earned at least a third of his annual income from working as village postmaster and fixing guns, hauling wood and coal, and lending small sums of money.[19]

The frequency of bi-employment is in doubt for want of more studies of property ownership. Possibly—and most likely—it was in decline in older regions and widespread in newer ones on the frontier. We can be more confident that village mechanics like Wood and Wilson were more representative of their class than their urban counterparts. For the landholders among them—and those that rented farmland—the line between craft and field work remained fluid.

Whether or not a mechanic practiced bi-employment, he could not avoid being knocked about in the marketplace.[20] Several of the proprietors whose memoirs and account books are analyzed here never made it to retirement or went broke. Lansford Wood's promising furniture shop closed when he died suddenly at age 38 in 1844. The Bostonian Joseph Tinker Buckingham lost several journals before starting the (New England) *Galaxy*. Nor was he untypical.[21] Recent studies of petty proprietors in the nineteenth century in small towns and big cities depict a ghoulish economic landscape thick with the remains of small shops. Between 70 percent and 90 percent of petty businesses went under after a few years.[22] Failure was so common that even in a trade as honorable as printing, apprentices went through several bosses, moving from one to another as they went under and reemerged; Thurlow Weed learned the craft under the stewardship of at least six employers.[23] Every mechanic either went bust or knew someone who did. Many of them, like Buckingham, suffered serial reversals.

Of the forces that conspired against the master mechanic, none was so lethal as the volatile economy. All businesses—not simply the outdoor trades—went through cycles of boom and bust, marked by the busy period of spring and fall, and the slow season of winter and late summer.[24] This meant that the master who had no alternative means of employment or subsistence was especially vulnerable. Those with land probably closed their shops in the doldrums with the intent of reopening in "the season." More perilous still were the chronic slips and slumps that rippled through the national economy following the War of 1812—the panics/depressions of 1819, 1837, 1854, and 1857, as well as the quick, sharp dips in between.[25] Every downturn large and small claimed myriad shops.

Surviving hard times, however, hardly meant an easy ride. Even in times of prosperity, master mechanics struggled with torturous economic relationships that made their firms frightfully brittle. Relations with bankers took one of two forms, neither of them particularly helpful. The highly speculative "wild cat" banks of the countryside, typically fostered by Democrats, had the virtue of liberal lending practices but the liability of dubious capital and capricious policies, while urban bankers and creditors discounted their notes or refused to accept them at all.[26] Some mechanics enjoyed good relations with country bankers; most, and those in provinces, angrily assailed them as little better than thieves "wholesale robbers, and scoundrels in broadcloth," as the grumpy Pennsylvania brushmaker Matthias Zahn put it.[27]

Urban banks with Whig backers tended to be a much safer bet, but a longer shot, since they vastly preferred the more secure and remunerative outlets of urban land, national and international commerce, and marine insurance. When such banks did lend to mechanics and manufacturers, they preferred larger and more profitable ones, leaving master craftsmen in the lurch. As a result mechanics had mixed to mostly jaundiced views of bankers, who often doubled as their senior partners in the Whig Party. Whig stalwart Joseph Buckingham lined up with the Bank of the United States in its epic conflict with President Andrew Jackson, but was too much a mechanic to have much use for its silk-stocking president. Buckingham found Nicholas Biddle aloof and autocratic, and feared that his bank was too powerful and despotic for the good of the economy or its craftsmen.[28]

The New Haven, Connecticut, printer John Babcock shared Buckingham's reservations. Like tradesmen throughout the region, he lobbied lawmakers for a mechanics' bank, founded by mechanics for mechanics. Its charter, as drafted by Babcock, left very little to chance. It earmarked a "fixed proportion" of loans for "manufacturers and mechanics"; prevented "speculation in [the] embryo state of the institution" by proscribing stock transfer; and mandated that a proportion of the "directors are to be drawn from . . . manufacturers and mechanics corresponding in number" to the amount of stock held.[29] We do not know what became of Babcock's petition, only that it was part of a larger effort to establish lending institutions in the first half of the century. Mechanics' or farmers' and mechanics' banks shot up through-out the North but seem to have had only a slight impact—not nearly enough, it turned out, to muffle complaints over capital starvation.[30]

Bankers were not the sole source of capital. Though most farmers were cash-poor, prosperous staple growers and dairymen were known, even in hardscrabble New England, to take a chance on local enterprise. Farmers who were not risk averse, however, tended to distrust manufacturing.[31] So mechanics on the prowl for capital got a much more sympathetic hearing from merchants and traders. This explains the pervasive business partner-ship of mechanic and merchant in a marriage of craft know-how and capi-tal, which proved particularly common in the printing industry. When, in 1824, Joseph Buckingham pursued the dream of his own daily newspaper, he sought out a group of Boston merchants coincidentally in search of a popular voice for Daniel Webster and his "American System." Working closely with Webster, Isaac C. Pray, a self-made import/export merchant and industrial promoter, helped the fledgling publisher assemble a consor-tium of six sponsors, nearly all of whom shared Buckingham's impover-ished beginnings, along with the bad luck that had stalked his early journals and magazines.[32] Most of their firms also crashed, which reveals yet another threat to the mechanic. It was essential to cultivate ties with backers and fin-anciers who could supply start-up capital or credit in a crisis. Patrons could make mischief, however. As every newspaper publisher was keenly aware, their firms were wholly owned subsidiaries of some political interest. Pub-lishers answered to backers, who shamelessly withdrew support from sheets for breaking party discipline, as recorded by Thurlow Weed.[33] Joseph Buck-ingham flirted with his own demise in 1832 by openly embracing maritime journeymen and sympathetic master mechanics in their strike for a ten-hour day. The transgression brought down the fury of local merchant capitalists, who demanded that he retract a column criticizing their resistance to short-ening the workday. Though Buckingham refused to retreat then, three years later, when another "ten-hour" strike erupted in Boston, the voluble printer was silent.[34]

Suppliers of machinery, raw materials, or both offered another avenue of credit. Indeed, it was difficult and perhaps impossible to sustain any busi-ness without channels for equipment and supplies. Subcontractors in the finishing trades did not share this problem before the 1850s because tech-nology was still simple and raw materials were owned and distributed by contractors or merchant capitalists. Conversely, printers, bookbinders, fur-niture makers, and so on, depended directly on external sources of credit. The Boston typefounder/printer Samuel N. Dickinson maintained several customers in rural New England by supplying the latest technology, new typefaces, and paper stock on easy credit terms. He kept what appears to have been something akin to an open credit line for the provincial printer Elihu Geer and presumably for other customers as well.[35]

Geer's correspondence with Dickinson leads us to believe that customers could be nearly as treacherous as patrons. Friction between these parties, it should be said, hinged on location and timing. As late as the 1840s, rural and small-town proprietors with local customers accepted payment in kind and were usually in no hurry to settle accounts, carrying obligations for months and even years.[36] Proprietors in regional and distant trade, however, demanded quicker payment, and in cash, usually requiring settlement in full within six months.[37] Dickinson may have cut his metropolitan customers the slack typical of early market exchange.[38] When it came to distant clients however, he played by the tougher rules of long-distance trade. In the early 1840s, he sometimes agreed to payment in kind, as long as the goods in question bore some relationship to the craft, and could be sold easily.[39] He usually specified cash within a period of three to six months, and that was the rub. While he was quite prepared to carry customers in the backlands, sometimes through questionable schemes that he took some care to conceal from his banker, he also had to be a stickler for payment. His account with Geer is thick with dunning letters laced with throbbing irritation over arrears. After several warnings to Geer in 1845–1846, the Boston typefounder exploded over still another request for credit. "If this is not enough to make a man curse all business by notes or credit," he fumed, "I don't know what is."[40]

Though Dickinson was a facile man with a wry Yankee humor, this was no laughing matter. Just about a year later, in 1847, he hit a bumpy patch that began with a debilitating respiratory ailment, followed by a fire in summer that consumed part of his sprawling complex of offices and workshops. By late 1847, Dickinson was confined to a sick bed and hopelessly behind in correspondence with debtors. When the pressure of his dunning letters let up, so did remissions, and Dickinson, now weak and dying, could only watch as his business slipped away.[41]

Dickinson's run of misfortune probably started earlier, in the mid-1840s, with the emergence of new competitors following recovery from the panic of 1837. Like most mechanics with a feel for their craft, Dickinson valued competition largely in the abstract; he thought rather less of it in real life—as something to be contained or avoided. When he learned that a fellow founder was underselling him, he wrote in disgust to a customer that his rival was "an old fool, and to spite his neighbor would bite his own nose off. He does not seem to see that other founders will fall down to his prices." As if that were not bad enough, "[a]nother bad thing about it will be an opening of many doors for a host of adventurous Printers to try their hand at the business because they can get their type so much cheaper."[42] What was a mechanic to do?

Master mechanics dealt with competition through both formal and informal means. Informal activity is still quite opaque and poorly understood, but probably took several forms. Fellow tradesmen in the 1830s and

1840s agreed among themselves to refrain from raiding one another's workers, just as they had agreed earlier in the century to desist from taking on runaway apprentices.[43] Dealers in perishables and light consumer goods, who could operate outside designated market areas, probably worked out territorial agreements to prevent flooding neighborhood markets.[44] Many masters shared equipment, materials, and even customers when orders ran high and there was enough work to go around.[45]

One suspects that many more mechanics resorted to market niching, a strategy closely associated today with the recent competitive surge unleashed by deregulation since the late 1970s, but one that goes back at least to the mid-nineteenth century. The carriage-building trade in Worcester during the 1850s offers a close look at this earlier version. Worcester housed at least seven carriage-making firms in 1850, very few of which, it turns out, competed against one another. Instead, each firm either turned out standardized parts for assembly in larger shops or produced a particular model for a select clientele. Tolman & Russell hired twenty workers who made "costly and expensive carriages" on a custom basis for wealthy families nearby and perhaps as far afield as Boston; Breck & Wilder's twenty workmen, by contrast, turned out stagecoaches and omnibuses—capital goods as it were—for regional transportation companies. Farther downmarket sat Wilder's, a much smaller company that made the new "light York carriages" for the town swells. The only general producer was William Whiting, whose ten hands did work "of all descriptions" and relied heavily on repair work. During the 1850s, and possibly earlier, these core firms contracted out parts and component work to smaller, more specialized shops on the periphery of the trade. Fitch & Winn made spokes and wheels; Nathan Washburn did castings. Other firms supplied different parts for the core companies that effectively evolved into assemblers.[46]

There was no substitute, however, for formal association. This is precisely what one of Joseph Buckingham's reporters had in mind when he described the early 1830s as an age of "organization," a period in which mechanics sought the cover of institutes and associations for their own protection.[47] Mechanics' institutes are better known and need not detain us here. It is enough to observe, as Gary Kornblith has, that such groups arose in the 1790s to promote the "mechanic interest" in politics and the economy while giving vent to its generous civic spirit. As combination social clubs, trade associations, and political lobbies, institutes sponsored a range of projects including control of labor markets and adjudication of squabbles between members of craft associations. In time, however, most brought their policies closer into line with freer markets by sponsoring craft fairs with prize money for distinguished work and by launching programs designed to domesticate unruly apprentices. Not a few of them also fought the stigma attached to manual labor through galas and pageants contrived to improve the public image of the trades.[48]

Though the membership of mechanics' institutes often overlapped with those of trade associations, the two were quite different. Limited as they were to a single craft, the associations were much smaller than the institutes and more at home in urban centers, large and small. While they shared the institutes' civic and beneficial functions, associations proved far more aggressive in the economic sphere, filling the regulatory vacuum left by the institutes and by receding government, and thus meriting a closer look here.

One of the more robust trade associations in the early nineteenth century was the Boston Booksellers' Association, a group of master printers—not merchants, as the name would suggest—who came together in fall 1801 to bridle a runaway book market. As they saw it, the "want of a system in [the] business," along with the need to promote both trade solidarity and the "public interest," called for a collective response.[49] With this in mind, they drafted what a modern observer would call a code of fair competition. One rule prohibited discounts on titles published in the United States or sold in single copy to "a transient person" or retail customer; another specified a 10 percent discount on U.S. and European publications purchased by libraries, both public and private; still another established a sliding scale of discounts for volume sales. The printers agreed to abide by the code and reinforce their ranks by aggressively recruiting new members. Those found guilty of violations by an investigating committee and vote of the membership were declared foul and subject to a boycott.[50]

The Booksellers' quarterly meetings were uneventful through the opening decade of the century, indicating that its code held, if not in the city as a whole then surely among its name publishers. This commercial calm broke during the War of 1812, which saw a proliferation of new shops not affiliated with the association and decidedly more opportunistic. The Booksellers reacted in 1814 by revising its rules to reflect the harder sell of the new market. Discounts were itemized in somewhat greater detail and generally revised, sanctions were increased, and enforcement strengthened—all to no avail.[51] A year later, in 1815, a special committee blasted "undersellers" and urged fellow printers and publishers in major eastern cities to consider a "uniformity in prices, and to regulate the exchange in books."[52] Nothing came of this canvass because attention shifted from the alleged renegades in the region back to Boston. Some city printers broke ranks between 1815 and 1817, and in 1819 the panic that plunged the national economy into prolonged depression left members in dire straits and their association badly shaken. In 1820 the sudden departure of two leading firms strapped with stock that could not be dumped without violating association norms brought the crisis to a head. Noisy meetings in spring produced a compromise resolution that suspended the rules for three months to allow the unloading of inventory.

This, however, only postponed the end, which came in September when a committee charged with investigating dissolution made its report.[53] The committee acknowledged the corporate traditions of the trade by defending "honorourable concert and uniformity of practice," while conceding that "experience" revealed the difficulty of observing rules" which, "however good . . . when they govern only a part of our Profession operate injuriously to the interests of those who strictly conform to them" by chasing customers to cheaper streets. The committee insisted that the "union & harmony" of the trade had done "much public good," but, it continued, in a telling concession to the market, "the present dullness of Business—the increasing numbers engaged therein—the various encroachments of other Professions—and the desire of many of our Brethren to diminish their stocks with the least sacrifice" left no alternative. It reluctantly recommended disbanding the association in the hope "that the spirit of the Rules will be long retained and observed in all cases where practicable—more especially as respects the *retail* business."[54]

This spirit of "union & harmony" did in fact endure. No less than three years after the demise of the Boston Booksellers, erstwhile members called a meeting that sent two delegates to a regional conference of the trade in Philadelphia to discuss dealing with auctions and other pests bred by the expanding market. While nothing seems to have come of this gathering, eight years later in 1831 a new Booksellers' Association resolved that "publishers' prices should be vigorously maintained by all, under penalty of losing the trade discounts."[55] About twenty printers and publishers, some of the city's most prominent, signed this agreement, though we know very little about the development of this association or how, if at all, it differed from its Jeffersonian antecedent.

What is clear is that mechanics' groups of colonial or early national vintage operated in late antebellum times. The oldest and best known is the Carpenters' Company of the City and County of Philadelphia, founded during the 1720s and still vital in the early 1850s when it published what was the fourth (at least) edition of its price list.[56] The city's master plasterers and master masons, who seem to have organized after the 1830s, likewise published and updated price books during these years, and, one suspects, so did its printers.[57] Philadelphia's handloom weavers, specializing in fancy goods, may also have had a pricing code of some sort.[58]

But these weavers were probably exceptional. While we are only beginning to grasp the extent of self-organization among master craftsmen and should be prepared to be surprised, it appears that the "lesser" trades—shoemaking, tailoring, and so on—were simply too competitive and product lines too dynamic to sustain organization, even though tailors and shoemakers sometimes tried.[59] Groups of both types of tradesmen rose and fell in the late 1820s and early 1830s, and if any emerged thereafter, they were probably confined to the luxury trade or what masters themselves called "bespoken work." More durable, though still brittle, association came more easily to craft sectors with local or protected commodity markets and force-ful trade or corporate customs—baking and meat preparation, and the hon-orable trades of printing, building construction, shipbuilding, and the like.[60] Few were as strong as Philadelphia's venerable house carpenters, who may not have been far from the mark when they boasted in 1858 that their book of rules and prices "regulated" the trade.[61] Possibly these carpen-ters, and most organized masters in the building trades who honored price lists, worked at the high end of the market. We get this impression from a caveat at the end of the Philadelphia plasterers' book of prices, which men-tions that "work . . . highly embossed and . . . done in a strong, full, and superior manner, to be placed near the eye, may be nearly double the above prices." [62]

Such groups reached beyond cities of the eastern seaboard. Fellow tradesmen in shire towns and market centers likewise banded together to regulate markets. In the early 1854, for instance, printers in the five western counties of Massachusetts formed the Association of Editors and Printers of Western Massachusetts in Springfield. Standing committees on advertis-ing, job printing, labor, and prices drafted policies, which were approved by the organization as a whole. The committee on advertising not only devel-oped a pricing scale but also uniform standards of measurement for particu-lar kinds of copy; it also removed from the category of *pro bono* work meet-ing notices placed by a broad range of groups, wiping out a historic tendency in a stroke. The labor committee picked up where the mechanics' institutes left off in the 1820s, prohibiting employers from taking on apprentices who could not certify proper training or who were already bound out to a member office.[63]

In Worcester, not far away, master-building tradesmen combined as well. We do not quite know when organization reached these craftsmen, only that in the early 1850s several masters' associations formed a broad front that forced agreements across craft lines. When the painters met in February 1854 to consider an increase in rates, a building contractor fearful of rising costs rose to object. The painters heard him out and called a gen-eral meeting that included builders and carpenters "to justify their course, if they see fit."[64] It is impossible to tell at this juncture whether the increase went through as initially proposed or in modified form to accommodate the builders. We can be certain that such building tradesmen had a tradition of collective determination of pricing and work rules, and that they were open to negotiation with kindred crafts and callings. Equally noteworthy, a master painter who defended the rate advance observed that the "new prices would slightly enhance our profits, and enable us to give a slight advance to 'jours.'"[65]

By invoking journeymen this self-styled "Old Painter" put his finger on the most troublesome and complicated of all social relations for master mechanics. This aspect of the master's world is hardly a mystery given the voluminous literature on the antebellum labor movement in the North, which has left a good sense of the quality of class relations—at least in such moments of polarization as the ten-hour struggles of the Jackson years, the initial standouts of New England textile hands, and the great Lynn shoemakers' strike of 1860. Nonetheless, it is fair to ask what happened in between such flashpoints. It is clear that the daily regime in mechanics' shops could approach the authoritarianism of the grittiest textile mills. The memoirs of numerous journeymen-made-good tell of troubled apprenticeships served under impatient and abusive employers.[66] Masters themselves often confirm such a picture. Elihu Geer, the village publisher who made S. N. Dickinson's life so difficult, was no kinder to his employees. He simply laid down the law and turned over enforcement to his foreman, a position another publisher likened to "Captain and Commander . . . of a ship."[67] The Boston printer J. L. Homer was another hidebound individualist intolerant of unions and trade associations who took a literal view of his position as master. Homer grew red-faced in damning the ten-hour movement in 1832, and he still had not completely cooled off four years later. In a rambling jeremiad on class relations to the Massachusetts Charitable Mechanic Association in 1836, he bragged that his shop was untainted by short-hours sentiment. His journeymen put in fifteen-hour days without complaint, or they did not work at all.[68]

There is reason to believe, however, that before the 1850s or so, the social relations of the handicrafts outside of the most degraded trades fell somewhere between the clockwork system of the cotton mill and the permissiveness of the traditional shop. The uneven pace of work, coupled with the familiarity of small-scale production, the leverage exerted by skilled workmen, and the survival of shop customs (along with the creation of new ones) made for more supple labor relations. The social personality of master craftsmen could also act as a break on excessive managerialism. All but the most status-conscious mechanic straining for acceptance in higher social circles considered himself part of the fraternity of the craft. Those that did not turn over management to foremen and retreat to front offices—and most did not—continued to share workbenches with hired hands. Worker and employer socialized off the job and met in bars or churches and lodge halls.[69] Masters rewarded work well done, unusual effort, or plain loyalty with extra pay; some helped strapped employees through hard times with timely loans or credit.[70] Many lent fledging shopowners supplies and equipment.[71]

But this was not a one-way street, in which masters liberally showered benefits on supplicants in their employ. Mechanics, after all, were entangled in a web of debt, dependency, and obligation, and never quite knew when a debtor would default or a creditor come calling. The uncertainty left them dependent not only on patrons and clients, but also on their own workers, who were sometimes asked to sacrifice by taking payment in kind or going without pay at all until a crisis passed. Joseph Buckingham's workmen several times accepted pay deferrals, which allowed him to negotiate settlements with creditors that staved off the dank cell of debtor's prison.[72] They, in turn, extracted some sort of favor from their grateful boss.

This is not to turn what were essentially profit-making enterprises, hierarchically arranged, into egalitarian cooperatives. Master mechanics were no democrats when it came to the workplace, the household, or anywhere else except the polling booth, and even there only in a qualified way. All who looked forward to accumulating a competence knew they had to render the market its due. When they did indulge or propitiate journeymen or show flexibility in labor relations unknown in factories, it was not simply out of residual respect for the conventions of craftsmanship. Their fraternal spirit also derived from their unique market position vis-à-vis consumers and workers. Since mechanics typically dealt directly with customers, and not through middlemen, it was easier for them to pass on costs. Flexibility gained in product markets did not necessarily extend to subordinates in the shop because of chronically tight labor markets, as the Boston printer Josiah Loring found out. In a candid note to an anxious customer Loring despaired of filling an order "in season" because one of his best journeymen "treated him like a rascal" and " left . . . suddenly" to work for the competition.[73] Not all workmen had such leverage, but enough did as late as the mid-nineteenth century to make even rigid masters a bit more compliant. It would seem that the more skilled the workforce, the more fraternal the employer.

This combination of idealism and interest helps explain the response of masters to Boston's "ten-hour" strike in 1832. Not all masters agreed with Joseph Buckingham on the desirability of the ten-hour day or the necessity of craft organization. J. L. Homer, for one, expectedly demonized the "ten-hour" movement as a conspiracy of "foreign adventurers" adept at exciting a "turbulent spirit" in the shop.[74] Master mechanics thus divided on the question of hours in the 1830s, chiefly for two reasons. On the one hand, they accepted the popular republican argument heard again and again that overwork sapped the body and deadened the mind, killing the republican spirit. Industrial drudgery also smacked of slavery. Contrarily, for the small master and even some large ones who continued to work with their hands, it was not a simple matter of breaking for the door at 6 P.M., the quitting time "ten-hour" advocates imagined, and leaving the help to carry on. Master mechanics had to stay because they, alas, were labor, too. Few, to be sure, would have granted the ten-hour day without the compulsion of strikes or force of law; when pushed by labor, many did concede, only to be checked from the other side by merchants, who were their employers in this age of merchant capitalism. Whoever said that being in the middle was easy?

The fundamental problem was that it was getting harder, not simply to attain a competence, but to survive at all. The failure rate fluctuated through the 1840s and leapt upward in the 1850s, as ownership consolidated more rapidly even in such traditional crafts as carriage making.[75] Masters reacted in several ways. As the persistence and resurrection of trade associations would suggest, they sought stability by banding together to regulate prices. Had that effort worked across the board, the broad outlines of labor relations after 1845 would have looked very different, perhaps resembling the rough equilibrium of printing, in which two highly organized groups—employers and employees—worked out relatively stable trade-union agreements with impressive provisions for worker control.[76] The fact is, however, that very few trades sustained the printers' level of organization.

Since mechanics had precious little control over creditors or suppliers, and had great difficulty maintaining any semblance of solidarity in trade associations, they had no realistic recourse except to keep down costs by leaning on labor. Those who conceded the ten-hour day, and many in the trades did, had to bear down even harder, especially in labor-intensive shops with primitive technology. This did not go down easily. Most mechanics, after all, continued to think of themselves as masters and brothers of the craft imbued with fraternal feeling, the sense that norms of reciprocity mediated relations with employees in the shop.

Mechanics pursued this idea of reciprocity with increasing vigor in the face of sharpening social tensions with labor. They sought to harmonize the workplace through informal relations with workers and through ameliorative programs expressed in a variety of fraternal groups and political organizations.[77] They figured prominently in the Protective Union movement of the 1840s and similar economic organizations that tried to channel the class conflict of trade unionism into cooperative workshops.[78] A variant of this collaborative spirit animated innumerable fraternities, nativist and otherwise, that mushroomed in the decades immediately preceding the Civil War, from the Order of United American Mechanics to the Mechanics' Mutual Protective Association.[79] Such groups, along with their companionate parties, tried with some success to bridge the class divide by uniting employer and employee around expressive patriotism alloyed to militant Protestantism. As one of their stalwarts put it so succinctly, nativism would restore "those healthful and fraternal feelings" between the "middle and working classes."[80]

Put another way, master mechanics embodied at once the nonmanual status of the merchant cum manager and the manual status of the work man. They were liminal men personally torn by the same economic forces that rent the larger society. They retained the tradesman's pride in craft along with the widely shared axiom, rooted in Scripture and reinforced in the work of plebeian pamphleteers and political economists, that manual labor was the source of all wealth. Paeans to handwork coincided not only with its cheapening in the marketplace, but also in popular discourse. A developing middle class of retailers and professionals, as the historian Stuart Blumin has shown, took pains to distance itself from the horny-handed working class. This steady dequalification of manual labor could not help but affect mechanics.[81] "We have been so long looked upon by others as a degraded class," a small proprietor told the Massachusetts Charitable Mechanic Association in 1836, *"that many of us have finally acquiesced in the opinion and adopted the feeling."*[82]

A related source of tension and ambiguity emerged from the mechanic's strong investment in personal independence. Young mechanics just starting out who were not yet independent in an economic or political sense believed they soon would be. What, after all, was the point of diligence and frugality if not to set up on one's own and accumulate a competence? The problem here was as simple as it was glaring. No mechanic was independent, not with his need for capital, for customers, and for cooperation from his help. Some, of course, felt their dependence more strongly than others. Few gave it more candid admission than Joseph Buckingham. The volatile and righteous printer given to tirades against the patronage/clientage system that often reduced fellow tradesmen to shills for powerful and wealthy interests openly damned the "the curse of purchased dependence" in an editorial.[83] In a more private and reflective moment, he confessed in a letter to a political friend opposed by his financial backers: "I am not in *independent circumstances,* and must submit to influences from which I would most heartily be free."[84]

This scorching attack on patrons and by extension, merchant capital in general, had a wide compass. One also encounters it among the middling ranks of the countryside. Edward Jenner Carpenter was a cabinetmaker's apprentice in the shiretown of Greenfield, Massachusetts, in the 1840s. Though Greenfield had no Working Men's party, or labor press, and not much overt social conflict in the Jackson era, Carpenter and his friends nursed grievances and social resentments not unlike Buckingham's. He derisively dubbed the village upper class of merchants and lawyers "Aristocrats," or "big bugs." He seldom mentioned friends without identifying their trade, as in "Taylor the shoemaker," or the "printer boys," and was so thoroughly invested in the work of his craft that he spent holidays and off hours in his master's shop.[85] He took on the swagger of a triumphant athlete when a debate at the town literary society on "Which have done more good, Lawyers or Mechanics?" ended "in favor of the Mechanics." He could scarcely contain himself when his fellows sponsored a bigger and livelier dance than the "big bugs." [86] He was not fazed when a fair organized by the town's first families to raise funds for a cemetery never got off the ground for want of voluntary help, or that another fundraiser gotten up by the mechanics and their set drew a great crowd, because the middling sort, he told his diary, "are not afraid to work."[87]

Nor were they afraid to compete. All but the most entrepreneurial, however, much preferred to compete on their own terms. They never fully accepted the emergent credo of Smithian economics that elevated competition to a religion. Their relationship with free market capitalism wasn't so simple. It was complicated by the persistence of craft traditions and by evolving relationships with a host of interdependent players in the new economic game. Such practices as market niching and the regulatory policies of trade associations lead one to believe that even as some mechanics soared to the heights of freewheeling entrepreneurialism and others sunk to the depths of sweating system, a good number followed a different course marked by collusive action to control competition.

The evidence gathered here strongly indicates that small employers were a distinct social stratum. The question remains, though, as to whether they amounted to something more than a social layer, however spongy, between the working class and the (nonmanual) middle class. Can we consider them a social class, that is a group with a sense of its own commonalities, on the one hand, and differences with other social classes, on the other?

The privatistic activities of small employers in pursuit of market regulation strongly suggests as much. Given the thrust of recent scholarship on the middle class, however, it is fair to say that most historians would not settle for this; they would insist on stronger evidence outside of economic relations in the realm of politics. This, at least, is the implicit claim of Stuart Blumin's luminous study of the rise of the middle class in nineteenth-century American cities. In it, Blumin maintains that political movements based "explicitly on the grievances or aspirations of intermediate social classes are indeed rare in American history," because the middle class displayed class awareness rather than class consciouness. That is to say, Blumin's middle class cohered not around awareness of its own commonalities and differences with other classes but around the idea that class did not exist at all. The middle class drew "together as a social group in part through the common embrace of an ideology of social atomism."[88]

The class Blumin has in mind includes nonmanual workers of various descriptions, and not the petty proprietors covered in this essay. He treats such proprietors separately and slightly, hinting that they were too incoherent socially to form a single class or express class consciousness. He argues that they cleaved in two: one group, which remained socially plebeian, blended into the working class; the other, which rose economically, traded in craftsman's aprons for businessmen's suits, identifying themselves with the middle class. They postured as "progressive businessmen" who owed their success to the application of "science," which allowed them "to transcend the stigma associated with manual labor even while it legitimized their position as productive members of their trades."[89] Neither class faction, one assumes, hewed to independent politics.

There are several problems with this analysis, quite apart from its unconscious adherence to a conventional two-class model with no room at all for the intermediate class treated in this essay. The first is that third parties were not exceptional in the nineteenth century. As I have argued elsewhere, they were an important part of a "party system" mistakenly described as a two-party system. That no such parties, with the notable exception of the Republican, showed much staying power should not blind us to the larger pattern that saw single-issue and general reform parties pop up throughout the nineteenth century. Virtually all showed the similar social configuration of a "popular bloc," which brought together farmers and skilled workers under the leadership of petty proprietors. It is difficult to escape the conclusions that petty proprietors were emphatically political and virtually synonymous with insurgent politics.[90]

The political cast of their parties (and larger political consciousness) escapes easy categorization. Were they legitimately radical groupings out to slay the dragons of injustice or reactionary forces motivated by the classic resentments of the lower middle class? There is no escaping the rhetorical and even programmatic similarity between the popular radicalism of petty proprietors and the economic radicalism of working-class militants. Both, after all, drew heavily on the vocabulary of antebellum producerism, which assailed merchant capital as an exploitative and corrupt force, on the one hand, and identified manual work as the only legitimate source of wealth and public virtue, on the other.

Petty proprietors, however, balked at the sharp-edged class rhetoric of labor radicalism, emphatically rejecting its advocacy of trade unionism. In this sense the outlook of mechanics more closely approximated the populism that would reach fuller expression at the end of the century. And it resembled what we might consider conservative populism in another way. By the 1840s, if not earlier, third parties and fraternities embraced the venomous nativism welling up from ranks of the skilled working class that scapegoated European immigrants. This new political complexion strongly suggests that conservative populism was not, as some have argued, a modern phenomenon originating in the second half of the twentieth century.[91] It seems excessive, however, to invoke nativism as the standard for inclusion in the ranks of the populists. It is more useful to think of the politics of the mechanics sketched here as a transitional form poised between labor radicalism and populism. It was neither radical nor reactionary in the conventional sense of the terms, but combined features of each in a synthesis that showed as much resiliency as mechanics themselves.

Nor was it unambiguously pro-capitalist. Legitimate capitalists, after all, celebrated the free market and its opportunities for greater levels of capital accumulation. Such employers, to be sure, were hardly averse to the collusive forms of market regulation described here. For them, however, market regulation was a means to an end, a tactic quickly discarded when the opportunity arose. For mechanics and small employers, however, collusion was something of an end in itself, part of a larger outlook premised not so much on anti-capitalist principles as on an ethic of restraint, both individual and collective.

Samuel N. King captured this spirit quite well. A brushmaker by trade who opened a small store in downtown Philadelphia in 1837, King ran his shop for about fifteen years, then retired suddenly in 1851. When asked why he left such a lucrative business, he replied, "I know when I have enough."[92]

MORALITY AND MARKETS
IN THE NINETEENTH CENTURY

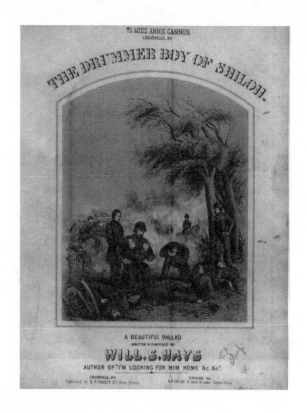

The Drummer Boy of Shiloh, by Will S. Hays (1863), American Memory, Historic American Sheet Music, 1850–1920, Library of Congress. COURTESY OF DUKE UNIVERSITY RARE BOOK, MANUSCRIPT, AND SPECIAL COLLECTIONS LIBRARY, B-1051.

Dress the Wearer. GODEY'S LADY'S BOOK, VOL. 42, NOVEMBER 1851.

Visiting America in the I830s, Alexis de Tocqueville observed that the "love of physical prosperity" was "essentially a passion of the middle classes," those persons "stimulated and circumscribed by the obscurity of their birth or the mediocrity of their fortune." Tocqueville further noticed that distinctive to democracy in America was that forbidden pleasures conventionally sought by nobility failed to satisfy the middle-class passion for physical well-being. Instead middling folk pursued a materialism that had eventually become socially respectable. A "virtuous materialism," Tocqueville characterized this pattern that was spreading upward from the middle "into the higher orders of society" and downward "into the mass of the people."[1]

Virtuous consumption not only sold well in the early nineteenth-century marketplace, but was also becoming a major force for expansion in the economy. What historians of labor have identified as the adversarial relationship between a shared "moral economy" of community and a profit-oriented "money economy" of business is problematic. We can more usefully describe the middling sorts as taking advantage of the benefits of a marketplace while perceiving few inconsistencies with encouragement for a morality of mutual association. Buyers for emblems of morality could be found everywhere in commercial markets. With an equal attention to recording item and price, the pages of middle-class diaries and journals in the period accounted for the purchase of Bibles together with fabrics to make fashionable hats. The merchandise of the moral economy moved westward along the commercial transportation routes, promoted and produced by middle-class writers like Joseph Abbot, Lydia Maria Child, and Sara Josepha Hale; clergymen like Henry Ward Beecher; and domestic advisers like Catherine Beecher.

The essays in this section discuss the connections between the products of morality and distribution in the marketplace in the spheres both of charitable women's fancy work and children's books during the Civil War. In "Charitable Calculations," Elizabeth White describes the opportunities "fancy" or nonutilitarian goods, made originally by ladies of leisure for benevolent purposes, eventually gave for women in all classes for pecuniary return and income. White argues that goods without direct use-value, and originally considered evidence of female triviality, instead served to shape the direction of market exchanges. The pleasure taken in moral principles tied to the business of profits were not incompatible. White's essay engages both the historical and current discussion on income-producing women's work in the nineteenth century, including changing meanings of pecuniary value for middle-class women in the domestic marketplace of respectability.

In "Bringing Up Yankees," James Marten examines the burgeoning marketplace for Protestant morality tales in children's books. The increasingly popular genre was promoting such middle-class assumptions and values as pious ambition, orderly and temperate conduct, and especially the commitment to a meaningful life contributing to a higher good. In the growing child nurture movement in the 1850s these character virtues helped differentiate the middle classes both from the elite and the working classes in the North in whom they were perceived as absent. Marten argues that the crucible of the Civil War added a powerful new dimension by focusing parental attention on the deeply flawed and self-destructive southern character. The narrative richness stimulated by the war contributed to the stuff of melodrama, which, within the theater of stirring combat, elaborated upon earlier Sunday School Union lessons. Fictional models of patriotic fervor, heroic discipline, and moral sacrifice inspired children's play. Boys left home and proudly put on a uniform, girls played nurse, and drummer boys marched into battle. In one very popular "true story," the drummer boy hero at Chancellorsville, Marten summarizes, "displayed every virtue that northern middle-class parents prayed for in their children: piety, humility, generosity, courage, constancy, and patriotism." Amplifying upon the culture of moral conduct and distributing it widely through the marketplace were mutually dependent processes. At the same time the middleclass tradition, which Tocqueville observed in the 1830s, was defining itself in relationship to the quality of material life and would often voice concerns about the vexing ethical consequences of capitalism.

Charitable Calculations: Fancywork, Charity, and the Culture of the Sentimental Market, 1830–1880

ELIZABETH ALICE WHITE

The refinement of society is dependent on the perfection to which needle-work is advanced, and the estimation in which it is held; and, consequently, that woman, to whom this branch of ingenious industry is almost entirely conceded, wields over the destiny of nations a weapon more powerful than the sword of the conqueror. Such a dissertation is foreign from my purpose; however, my readers will easily, without any prompting, refer the improvements of manners to different eras in the art of sewing, from that of necessity to the needle-work of convenience, of elegance, of luxury; and then comes the crowning grace, when the work of fair fingers is made subservient to the luxury of doing good.
—Sarah Josepha Hale, *Traits of American Life*, 1835

The image of a nineteenth-century parlor as a room of whatnots filled with knick-knacks remains both compelling and repulsive to the modern imagination. It conjures up sentimental nostalgia for an elegant, genteel era, or caustic musings on the psychological implications of *horror vacui*. In both visions, however, the knick-knacks are objects of fascination, through which a modern eye can read an encapsulated history of nineteenth-century middle-class culture. This essay does not address the question of the origins of middle-class culture, or try to assign a specific date to the rise of a middle class. By using the term "middle-class culture," I intend to imply a process of definition and change, an arena in which men and women engaged in the rise of a market economy and attempted to understand, define, delimit, and shape the public and private behavior of exchange. The characteristics of a nineteenth-century American middle class are a matrix of cultural, social, and economic factors, and thus an investigation of this class must by necessity be a cultural history of the economy.

Despite contemporary popular interest in fancywork, it has received little scholarly attention. The critique that proponents of the Aesthetic Movement and the Arts and Crafts Movement leveled against fancywork in the late nineteenth century remained substantially unchallenged in intellectual circles until the late twentieth century; the penchant for materials like fish scales and human hair contributed to the aesthetic condemnation of fancywork.[1] Collectors and craftspeople have lavished attention on the accouterments of sentimentalism, but only recently have historians begun to explore the material culture of the nineteenth-century middle class as more than just the *mise-en-scène* for cultural history.

"Fancywork" was a term that described not only fancy sewing, like embroidery and tatting, but also parlor crafts, from wax flowers to hair jewelry. Nostalgia for the needlework skills of previous generations shaped the nineteenth-century fashion for fancywork. As a display of genteel industry, fancywork was a social investment in the appearance of leisure. The word itself contained a dichotomy that was at the heart of middle-class culture. "Fancy" was the opposite of utilitarian; it implied leisure, aesthetic taste, and gentility, but had overtones of frivolity; "work" tempered this impression of flightiness, stressing that something was produced.[2] As a labor of leisure, fancywork embodied the unresolvable dilemma that faced middle-class women: their leisure was an important and visible marker of class, but their idleness raised anxieties associated with the dissipation of the rich. Middle-class women had to find a way to portray their labors as *fancy* work and their leisure as fancy *work*. Because fancywork was, by definition, both leisure and work, it maintained the cachet of feminine accomplishment and deflected accusations of idleness.

Fancywork provided the opportunity for both moral improvement and pecuniary gain, a dualism that appeared in the instruction manuals for fancywork as the pairing of pleasure and profit. The leisure time required to make fancywork was part of what made it valuable; it was a profitable way to spend time.[3] It allowed women to decorate their homes at a reduced cost; the new objects that filled the parlor were made as well as bought.[4] The personal production of goods distanced them from the cost of the materials, transforming them into something new with sentimental value: "A house is not to be a mere show-room, or a museum; but a home!"[5]

Despite its continuing popularity as a women's pastime, fancywork has been predominantly regarded as kitsch, evidence of the triviality of middle-class women's lives and their obsessive consumption of gew-gaws. This dismissal of fancywork as insignificant, and unimaginative, busywork ignores its importance in the definition of a middle-class culture. Although Beverly Gordon's more positive interpretation of fancywork suggests that "given a limited, constricted arena of acceptable activity and behavior, women's 'airy trifles' and 'fancies' were imaginative expressions of amusement and play, fantasy, escape and transformation," her argument is only the positive inverse of the previous condemnation; it does not change the assumptions of its negative counterpart.[6] Most discussions of fancywork examine it in the context of private, female domestic life. This essay examines the public life of fancywork production. Fancywork "experts" marketed fancywork as virtuous leisure activity. Fancywork was not a preindustrial preserve untouched by market imperatives, as the histories of its medieval origin in the manuals implied; it was implicated in contemporary market struggles. The production of fancywork fulfilled the desire to create something that was defined in sentimental terms, and its sale at charity fairs prompted a discussion of the meaning of value and the nature of exchange.

In her influential study of the relationship of sentimentalism and mass culture, Ann Douglas ultimately dismisses sentimentalism as a failed antidote to the individualism of the market.[7] This dismissal, however, misunderstands the role of sentimentalism in nineteenth-century market culture, and assumes that sentimentalism was a symptom of decline rather than an integral part of the rise of market culture.[8] The question is not why sentimentalism failed to reform the rapacious individualism of the market, but rather how it contributed to strategies developed to make sense of the market in sentimental terms, and the legacy of these strategies to modern consumer culture. In order to explore the complex formation of a middle-class market culture, the equation of sentimentalism with domesticity and "feminization" must be reassessed. The intersections of sentiment and profit that characterized the production and consumption of fancywork demonstrate that sentimentalism was not only a language of personal relations, but also a language of market relations.

There is a growing interest in the cultural history of the economy in the antebellum period. This cultural vision of economic growth has made it possible to recover the economic lives of women, African Americans, and other groups who, although they were excluded from the dominant market, developed alternative market systems. Although the middle class is usually studied as part of the dominant market, I suggest that middle-class men and women also participated in important alternative markets.[9] The antebellum middle class was characterized as much by its particular approach toward defining market interactions as it was by economic success. I engage the current scholarly debate about middle-class formation by offering insights into the negotiations of economics and culture that defined the fragility of class rather than its consolidation.[10]

The pleasure and profit of fancywork production was both personal and charitable. Charity, according to Sarah Josepha Hale, was "the luxury of doing good." The charity fair, with its donated fancywork and benevolent intentions, was organized along the lines of a gift economy; this set up an implicit difference from a business economy that was centered on individual profit.[11] In a gift economy, the reciprocity of exchange has a moral component; the unspoken obligations of reciprocity create a web of exchange in which the failure to comply has ramifications far beyond the economic transaction. Attaching moral consequences to the acts of production and consumption associated with the charity fairs was a way to shape market exchange according to the tenets of sentimentalism.[12] The exchange of goods at a charity fair was embedded in the larger social networks of community; this exchange bore the hallmarks of an older community form of market economy.[13] The charity fair was a market that modeled itself on domestic metaphors of cooperation and reciprocity rather than the metaphors of individualism. The sentimental economy of the charity fair was defined as an alternative market to the individualism of the business world; it operated according to its own system of calculations.

The organization and management of charity fairs was dominated by women. The voluntary work for the fairs was underpinned by pressing economic imperatives. The fairs were designed to raise money for the needy, but they were also intended to create a market: to secure a larger economic framework in which women's production had economic value. Fair organizers commissioned fancywork; they encouraged mothers to set production goals for their daughters. The fair was arranged by table, with each woman selling her own work, which meant that an individual's contribution was on display, just as she was. Talent, taste, and benevolence were bound together in this system and encouraged a little competition in what was otherwise a cooperative enterprise.

The fancywork was not the only thing on display. The presence of the young women at the tables selling their work lured male consumers with the prospect of the sanctioned flirtation that accompanied this kind of sentimental exchange.[14] It was the dual exchange of sentiments—the sentiments of benevolence that the voluntary labor had invested in the fancywork, and the flirtation between producer and consumer that was considered an essential marketing technique —that defined the transactions of the fair. This calculated marketing of sentiments helped make the exchange of abstract sentiments, in this case the idea of benevolence rather than its enactment, a commonplace part of market exchange.

The appeal to sentimental benevolence that functioned as the charity fair's main form of advertising contributed to an abstracted kind of sentiment that encouraged a certain kind of consumption as virtuous, creating a rationale for purchasing items that were not strictly use-oriented. To buy for the right reasons became an accepted form of market behavior. The experiences of exchange that defined the charity fair—the production, purchase, and consumption of benevolent sentiments—suggested that the worldviews of Christianity and capitalism could be reconciled. The emphasis that fair organizers placed on the "not-for-profit" aspect of the fair was itself an implicit kind of market reform. In a market filled with all the luxury goods money could buy, the charity fair offered commodities that money *should* buy.

Women donated vast quantities of fancywork to the fairs. In 1828, women in a synod in North Carolina took it upon themselves to raise money to build a new church. They raised two hundred dollars toward that goal through the sale of needlework.[15] Frances Trollope, in *Domestic Manners of the Americans*, described, in rather acid tones, the activities of members of the Dorcas Society, which had been founded in 1833 as an auxiliary of the Female Assistance Society:

> [A member of the society] enters the parlour appropriated for the meeting, and finds seven other ladies, very like herself . . . she presents her contribution, which is accepted with a gentle circular smile, her parings of broadcloth, the ends of ribbon, her gilt paper, and her minikin pins with which the table is already covered; she also produces from her basket three ready-made pincushions, four ink-wipers, seven paper matches, and a paste-board watch case; these are welcomed with acclamations, and the youngest lady present deposits them carefully on the shelves, amid a prodigious quantity of similar articles.[16]

In addition to producing the fancy items described by Trollope, the Dorcas Society devoted its time to making clothing for the poor.[17]

The calculations of the charity fair went beyond the basic objective of raising money; they touched on all aspects of women's social lives. Middle-class women devoted a considerable amount of economic energy to what Lori Ginzberg has called the "business of benevolence." Like male reformers, women performed all the duties in charitable organizations from teaching to fund-raising. Ginzberg noted: "The emphasis on benevolence as a peculiarly female impulse from the heart, removed it from crass economic considerations, tended to conceal the fact that benevolence and money went hand in hand."[18] The sentimental character of charity gave women license to pursue economic activities under its rubric; the charity fair provided an efficient way to raise funds and an economic forum that was largely controlled by women. Women not only benefited from the economic training that benevolent management offered, they seized the opportunity to use the women's economy of the charity fair as a form of alternative market economy, an education about value and exchange that they hoped would influence all market behavior.

The "voluntary" work of benevolence was, for many women, a paid occupation. Benevolent societies hired women to perform the charitable duties essential to benevolent organizations. These women solicited contributions, distributed leaflets, wrote reports, and helped organize new auxiliaries.[19] Women continued to describe their activities in voluntary terms and as the natural extension of their domestic roles, even if they received a salary for their efforts. The appearance of their work as voluntary was an essential ingredient to the success of their cause. To admit that they worked for pay would have tainted the spontaneity of benevolence that was the centerpiece of sentimental charity: no calculation could be visible. The success of the sentimental tactics that hid the work of benevolence was particularly apparent in the fairs themselves. The sale of fancywork at charity fairs was an extension of the insistence upon invisibility of the business aspects of benevolence. Like the voluntary labor of the charity agents, and the invisible labor of housework, the production of fancywork as a leisure activity was a necessary fiction to maintain.[20] Fancywork was an ideal product to sell because its production was so easily represented as leisure.

Fairs were communal gatherings, recruitment drives, and necessary fund-raisers.[21] The activities of a fair were often reported in the newspaper. On May 17, 1833, for example, the Salem *Gazette* reprinted an article from the Boston *Evening Transcript*, about a May Day fair to benefit the School for the Blind.[22] The contents of each woman's table were described in detail: Miss Catherine Putnam's table offered manuscript volumes; Mrs. Henry Smith's table had so many fascinating items that only a few were mentioned in the article:

> We have not enumerated a twentieth part of the goods and chattels constituting the merchandize on sale at this table. We have named a few only of the most costly. To catalogue them all would be to inflict punishment on the reader, so diverse in kind and so numerous in quantity were the useful and ornamental wares exhibited here.[23]

At Miss Thayer's table, the article continues, "all the articles were of *domestic* manufacture, with the exception of one palmetto basket, being made by the ladies who sold them or their friends, from materials purchased or presented to them." Thrift, as well as usefulness and ornament, was praised because it meant greater profit for the charity.

The most intriguing items for sale at the fair were "secret packages." These little packages were sold on speculation. Their contents were a mystery, and the packages were kept in a large box under lock and key until the end of the fair, when the secret was revealed to those who had purchased them. This was a practice to keep interest in the fair alive; in this particular case the ladies who organized the fair congratulated themselves on having kept the secret: "It should be mentioned to the honor of the much abused sex, that six women kept the secret six weeks not withstanding every art and cunning device used to extort it from them." Two hundred boxes were sold generating four hundred and fifty dollars of profit from these little packages, which "contained nothing more or less than a pair of *dusters* to wipe away the dust which had been thrown in the eyes of the good people for the last six weeks."[24] Gentlemen were reported to "detest" these secret packages. Another table also had secret packages, for only one dollar, that contained a *Blue Stocking* as the prize for an obliging man's generosity. Gentlemen, especially bachelors, were encouraged to patronize the fair. The Blue Stocking poked a little fun at the real reason that bachelors came to the fair: to find a wife. The links between the marriage market and the charity fair were not coincidental; both markets tried to reconcile sentimental impulses and economic necessities.

Public flirtation was one of the objections to the Fancy Fair that Sarah Josepha Hale addressed in her essay, "Ladies' Fairs" (1835).[25] Detractors of the fairs spoke against the impropriety of such a public display of affection, cautioning that "it encourage[d] vanity in young ladies, and [made] the motive of being seen and admired, the predominating one in their hearts."[26] Hale dismissed this criticism by listing the other public events considered acceptable for young women in which the danger of display would be equal. In addition to the danger of encouraging vanity, was the threat of scrutiny from unsuitable men: "the purchase of a ticket will give to any fellow the freedom of the apartment, and the privilege of gazing on the fair managers."[27] Hale agreed that such insolence would wound the feeling of a delicate lady, but that this vicious and disagreeable sort of man could also buy a ticket to the opera, and no sensible woman would refuse to go to the opera on those grounds. It was the responsibility of the organizers to ensure that the fair was managed discreetly and that young ladies would not be in any danger. In her arguments in favor of the participation of young women in Fancy Fairs, Hale omitted any discussion of real difference between the role of spectator and the role of saleswoman. Presiding over a table at a fair invited a different kind of public interaction: as a participant in a market transaction, these young women were in public in a very different way.

Hale collapsed this distinction because it was the sentimental spectacle of the pretty young woman that promised the greatest return on the charitable speculations of the fair; the exchange of sentiments between the fair manager of a fancy table and the male consumer was essential to the financial success of the fair:

> Gentlemen may, perhaps, purchase the articles more readily when presented by a fair hand; and the beaming of a bright eye may melt their hearts to unusual generosity, in the prices they pay for what is to them of no value, but as associated with the fair—yet mingling with these visions will be the thoughts of the objects to which the money they give will be devoted, and a disposition to encourage other benevolent plans will be fostered by this exercise of benevolence. The man who purchases articles at a Ladies' Fair is more likely to bestow charity on the next applicant than he who condemns all such means of obtaining money for charitable purposes is to give at any time.[28]

What Hale described was the act of sentimental consumption; the value of the object was in the experience of the exchange, in the associations with which it was invested. A gift economy is based on the exchange of intangible things like courtesy and kindness; gift exchange is by definition a transaction of emotions.[29] Flirtation was another manifestation of the reciprocity that the charity fair endorsed. It was sanctioned because it fostered benevolent actions. The importance of the act of exchange was accentuated by the sentimental potential of the exchange between the seller and the buyer; the Fancy Fair was part of the marriage market, the investment in charity was also a speculation in love.

In *Little Women*, Louisa May Alcott described a fair scene in which Amy, who has been unfairly removed from the art table, the hub of the fair, to the flower table, a decidedly unpopular one, is rescued from obscurity by the good will of Jo, who sends Laurie and his friends to buy all of Amy's flowers, and to make her table the center of social attention. In a further act of good will, Amy sends her admirers over to the art table to buy her rival's wares:

> To May's great delight, Mr. Laurence not only bought both the vases but pervaded the hall with one under each arm. The other gentlemen speculated with equal rashness in all sorts of frail trifles, and wandered helplessly about afterward, burdened with wax flowers, painted fans, filagree portfolios, and other useful and appropriate purchases.[30]

Alcott's arch characterization of the gentlemen's purchases suggests that the male impetus for buying fancywork remained unchanged thirty years later.

The second objection Hale discussed was a more serious one. The fancywork produced for the fairs was made by women who could donate their time and effort, who did not need the money, and this deprived poor women of employment. This was a central dilemma of charity: money earned by employment was preferable to alms.[31] The fairs, Hale argued, did not rob poor women of their livelihood, but instead increased the overall market for fancywork by making it fashionable:

> The articles sold at the Fairs have increased the demand for fancy works of a similar description. . . . Whatever is fashionable is soon necessary; and the circumstance, that such articles as have been sold at the Ladies' Fairs are now kept at many fancy shops, is proof that the ingenious and industrious poor are reaping the benefits of this trade in trifles.[32]

Caroline Dall, Virginia Penny, and Dinah Mulock, all writing at midcentury, contradicted Hale's prediction. Each of these women argued that for wealthy women to work without pay devalued the labor of all women.[33]

The poor to whom Hale referred were often the unfortunate counterparts of the women at the tables in the fair. She did not suggest that these worthy poor be allowed to sell their work directly at the fairs, however, because she argued that the production of fancywork promoted industry in women of leisure that was essential to their health; it also revived the teaching of needlework which had become, Hale feared, a neglected part of women's education. The industry of fancywork saved leisured women from a dangerous "excess of mental culture" as well as indolence and selfishness.[34] Although Hale was explicit about the value of the production of fancywork for women, she acknowledged that it had no value to the gentlemen who purchased it. The value lay in the context of the exchange. The charitable efforts of the woman recommended her as a wife, and the benevolent impulses of the man recommended him as a husband. The fancywork was a vehicle for the sentiments of production and purchase: the luxury of fancywork production was equated with the "luxury of doing good." The experience of buying an item from a beautiful and wealthy woman made a second experience of buying such an item from an impoverished woman more imaginable.

Confining the transactions of the charity fair itself to exchanges between members of the same class was a central component to Hale's definition of the fair as an alternate economy organized as a gift economy. The goods being sold at the fair were gifts; they had been donated to support the specified charity, so the act of production was itself a gift. The act of consumption was also a gift, particularly for a male consumer who purchased an item, often with no use-value for him, as a way of donating to the charity. The purchase of a gift created the possibility for giving the gift of charity at the moment of transaction and in future potential transactions, thus keeping the gift in circulation.[35] Both production and consumption were gifts because neither producer nor consumer engaged in the transaction based on personal need. A charity fair could be organized as a gift economy because the goods exchanged were secondary to the sentiments which governed their exchange: they never became commodities.

Although charity was the motivating factor in the organization of the fairs, it was a secondary consideration in the transactions at the fair itself. The gift economy was organized by the relationship between buyer and seller as well as by the gift of charity itself. Within the transactions of the fair, there was the possibility for reciprocity that was not assumed in the charitable act itself. Hale explicitly stated that in order for charity to work, it must "bless those who give and those who take" and the "value of the benefits conferred" had to be balanced.[36] Because no reciprocal gift could be expected, the giver of the charity had to ensure that the reciprocity of the act was built into the initial exchange; the moral value of the charitable sentiments had to offset the pragmatic value of the alms given. Therefore, although Hale did not explicitly say it, poor women could not be allowed to sell their work directly at the fairs because class barriers prevented them from participating in the gift economy of the fair which, in its links to the marriage market, depended on the possibilities for reciprocity. The act of charity was one way of defining the boundaries between the participants in that economy.[37]

Although Hale found ways to rationalize what she so aptly called the "trade in trifles," other women questioned the intellectual leap from the "valueless" commodities of the Fancy Fair and the valuable work of charity. Juliana Tappan commented in 1837:

> It does not seem to right to raise money for any benevolent society, or cause, by selling *useless* articles . . . silk bags *are* useful, and so are many things that might be, and often are sold at fairs. . . there is so much time consumed, and so much consulting of fashion, and conformity to the world that I doubt much whether fairs, *as they are now conducted*, are pleasing to God. How little of *Christ* there is in our actions.[38]

Tappan's religious concerns highlight the absence of this kind of discussion by Hale, whose primary focus was the definition of the terms of market exchange at the fair rather than the originating charitable impulse.

The criticisms of Fancy Fairs diminished as their success in fund-raising became a mainstay of charitable enterprises. With the advent of the Civil War, the charity fair became a material outlet for a sentimental patriotism. The United States Sanitary Commission was founded to alleviate the suffering of Union soldiers, and women played a large role in all aspects of the work, especially fund-raising. The Sanitary Commission, in particular its male administrators, took an antisentimental stance that was extreme, drawing criticism for callous behavior, and insisting on common sense over sympathy as the basis for its operations. The male members of the Sanitary Commission rejected sentimentalism as an obstacle to efficient benevolence rather than its impetus.[39] Female administrators, however, held a more balanced view of the relationship between efficiency and sympathy, channeling "sentimental" energy away from the grueling business of nursing and toward the business of fund-raising. Sentimentalism was mobilized as a motivational force in the organization of the vast fund-raising machine that the charity fairs became.

The regional organization of the Sanitary Commission created a national network of benevolence. When the Commission began to organize fairs to raise money, communities large and small held fairs to raise money for the soldiers: "Unity of plan, earnestness, patriotism, great humanity of purpose, and a broad and positive *nationality of sentiment and influence*, are inscribed upon all methods, counsels, suggestions, publications and labors of the Sanitary Commission."[40] Fancywork became a labor of patriotism as women began to donate useful goods like socks and shirts for the soldiers' use and fancy items to be sold at fairs to raise money to buy medical supplies and other necessities that could not be made. Even poor women did their share: at the Great Central Fair, held in Philadelphia in 1864, for example, the bookmarkers, Berlin work and bead work on sale had been made and contributed not only by the wealthy, but also by "poor needlewomen, who have found spare moments to throw in their mite to the success of our Soldier Brothers."[41]

Mary Livermore was instrumental in organizing the first large-scale Sanitary Fair in Chicago, which began on October 27, 1863. Initially, the idea of a fair had met with some skepticism on the part of the male members of the Sanitary Commission, but Livermore calculated the profit made at the fair at $80,000, which was increased to $100,000 when the remaining goods had been sold.[42] She emphasized the organizational role of women in the fair: "This first Sanitary fair, it must be remembered, was an experiment, and was pre-eminently an enterprise of women, receiving no assistance from men in its early beginnings. The city of Chicago regarded it with indifference, and the gentlemen members of the Commission barely tolerated it."[43] The networks of benevolence that developed out of these fairs changed the opinions of these original skeptics, transforming charitable fund-raising and influences other forms of business, as well.

The total amount of money raised by Sanitary Fairs during the course of the Civil War was close to $2,750,000.[44] Even children contributed to the fund-raising fever. Livermore recounted that "during the July and August vacation of 1863, the little folks of Chicago were seized with a veritable sanitary-fair mania" and held their own fairs on the lawns and in the parlors of their homes. In addition to its recommendation of fancywork patterns for ladies to make for Fairs, *Godey's Lady's Book* and *Peterson's* published fancywork patterns for children to make for Fancy Fairs.[45]

The involvement of women in the Sanitary Commission and other charitable organizations of the war changed many male opinions about women's business aptitude.[46] The language of benevolence itself took on a more businesslike cadence, emphasizing the parity between business and benevolence that reformers had carefully masked before the war. The war created a national network of charitable organizations and sewing circles. This encouraged a coordinated effort so that small sewing circles would not duplicate the efforts of others, creating a surplus of socks when shirts or scarves were needed.[47] The charity fairs of the Civil War brought about a dual revolution in fancywork production. The fairs legitimized women's sentimental business activities, but by the end of the war the enthusiasm for them had worn thin. This disenchantment with the fairs was balanced by an increase in women who had hoped to augment their incomes in this manner. In an attempt to generate a fashion for novelty, women embraced fads, like rustic work. These pine-cone creations caused a reaction against fancy-work rather than a new fashion for it.

The Decorative Arts Movement of the Gilded Age scorned these fancy-work fads. Women's exchanges refused to accept objects made out of hair, feathers, wax, cardboard, rice, and other plebeian materials.[48] This kind of production was no longer considered worthy of a woman's time; more important, there was no longer a market for it.[49] Despite their dismissal of these unfashionable forms of women's work, the organizers of the women's exchanges and craft cooperatives owed a debt to the charity fairs of their youth.[50] Just as the Sanitary Commission had pulled the disparate charity organizations together into a network of benevolence, sloughing off the language of sentiment in favor of the efficiency of business, the Gilded Age organizations insisted on a new aesthetics of production.

Embroidery was held up as a form of authentic and beautiful work that was resistant to the commercialism to which other kinds of fancywork had succumbed. Pre-Raphaelite artists like William Morris, Walter Crane, and Edward Burne-Jones designed patterns for embroidery based on natural forms that emphasized their beauty rather than their transformation into whimsy. The participation of male designers in the field changed the definitions of value; what distinguished this new kind of production was its overt market value—it was "real work," not fancy work.[51] Candace Wheeler, and the other women who organized and supported women's exchanges, expressed a dual purpose in promoting the minor arts and creating a market for the production of gentlewomen in reduced circumstances. Wheeler envisioned a way to create a reliable market for women's needlework by adopting a language of art, craft, and history that made the work of fancy-work visible again and replaced the language of fancy, whimsy, and trifles that had masked it. Although Wheeler and her contemporaries appropri-ated the discussion of fancywork, and reshaped it in aesthetic terms, the networks of production and consumption initiated by the charity fair and refined by the Sanitary Commission continued to foster the business of women's needlework: the women's market of the charity fair was easily transformed into the women's exchange, and sentimental entrepreneurship became nonprofit entrepreneurship.[52]

By the 1890s, the networks of a women's economy became a hindrance rather than an asset, in Lucy Salmon's opinion. Salmon, a historian at Vas-sar, objected to the continuing rhetoric of charity that characterized the women's exchange, and insisted that it diminished rather than augmented its ability to help needy women, because it ignored the rational imperative of competition she deemed necessary for successful business. By advocating a network of women producers and consumers and a cooperative work aes-thetic, the women's exchanges, Salmon complained, did more to arrest the success of women's enterprise than to aid it by defining women's work according to different market standards.[53] The work of the women's economy of fancywork had come full circle. The sentimental strategies that had been so important to a rising middle class attempting to define a virtuous relationship to the market had become rationalized. The logic of the alternate market of the charity fair had become part of the rationale of the dominant market. The networks of women's business that had made the charity fairs so successful also helped to define market interactions that distinguished a middle class from other economic actors. Charity fairs, like the benevolent associations they helped to support, had changed the social fabric of the economy.

Bringing Up Yankees: The Civil War and the Moral Education of Middle-Class Children

JAMES MARTEN

A children's story published just after the end of the Civil War declared the southerners' rebellion to be "a stupendous piece of folly, as well as stupendous wickedness." Yet the collapse of the Confederacy signaled the victory of the "brightest blessings of freedom" over the "dark ages." Perhaps southerners "wouldn't be so violent-tempered, and go round stabbing folks with bowie-knives," suggests a little girl from another story, "if they hadn't been used to beating and banging slaves about when they were boys." These stark images of southern violence, ignorance, and arrogance provided sharp counterpoints to the values avowed by middle-class northerners, who found their beliefs challenged and defined in the crucible of war.[1]

Although the dramatic economic expansion, unprecedented immigration, and rapid urbanization during the half-century after 1860 would further shape middle-class ideals, a number of ideas were already solidly entrenched in the middle-class belief system by the beginning of the Civil War. Acknowledging that there were, in Anne C. Rose's words, "a cluster of middle classes" in the antebellum North just "beginning to sense their kinship," it seems nevertheless clear that that kinship included a number of shared assumptions. In some ways, the war provided the opportunity to confirm and to consolidate some of these ideas, to test their applicability to the nation as a whole.[2]

Rose writes that "the Civil War, conceived as a struggle over profound issues . . . convinced" members of the northern middle classes "that human effort . . . still had value." Rose's study specifically examines religious doubts and spiritual searching, but her belief that members of the middle class insisted on "tailoring the facts of war to their own cultural ends" certainly resonates in the less mysterious but no less important arena of applying their peacetime values to war.[3] Called to action when southerners threatened to destroy the Union in which they believed those values could flourish, middle-class northerners expanded Union war aims beyond political and even humanitarian goals to include the inculcation of their particular set of values—a set of values that grew out of economic and social conditions rather peculiar to the North—whenever they could. The war gave middle-class northerners the opportunity to articulate what they believed they stood for, lent urgency to their conviction that their values represented a truly American vision of the world, and helped them focus on those characteristics that they prized above all.

Indeed, the terms of their criticism of the South bore striking similarities to the rhetoric the middle class employed in its search for a comfortable niche between the rich and the poor, which revolved around several distinctive assumptions: the centrality of pious ambition as the basis of personal and national progress; the importance of a formal, value-based education; the respectability of living calm, orderly, temperate, and purposeful lives; and the fervent belief that one's life should unfold in meaningful ways. Their antebellum commitment to voluntary associations that campaigned against the evils of drink and slavery, even as they helped to differentiate themselves from the northern elite and laboring classes, also provided points of contrast to southern society. When members of the burgeoning middle class in Providence, Rhode Island, argued that the rich and poor in their community shared such negative traits as "idleness, extravagance, and dissipation," they foreshadowed Yankees' contemptuous descriptions of southern society.[4]

In the war's second year, for example, Union soldiers advancing up the York and James Rivers described a South bereft of civilization. "The people . . . found in Virginia," wrote a reporter covering the Army of the Potomac's Peninsula campaign for the Philadelphia *Press*, "seemed to be an entirely different race from that living in the North—one which had degenerated in intellect, energy, and every thing which makes up the character of true manhood." They were, Joel Cook observed in terms that revealed much about his other Yankee biases, "as debased and degraded as the poor negroes who surrounded them." Their poverty of spirit and of material goods were equally apparent; their drawling speech was indistinguishable from their slaves', they were so gullible that they eagerly accepted poor copies of Confederate paper money sold as souvenirs in northern cities, and even the women smoked clay pipes. Although the youngsters occasionally did a few chores, they were never "usefully employed a tithe of the day."

Although he acknowledged that the war and the presence of the Union army had doubtless "changed the aspect of society and driven off the higher classes," Cook still had little good to say about this corner of Virginia. In fact, his description of southern people focused less on what they were than on what they appeared not to be: responsible, hardworking, sober, ambitious Yankees. Their lazy speech, somnolent attitude, and inexplicably contented demeanor set them in stark contrast to the hustling, bustling, and entirely more progressive northerners.[5]

Cook was hardly alone among northerners in his disdain for southern society, although many focused as much on the shortcomings of the slaves as on the weaknesses of the slaveowners. For instance, white northerners of all classes unsympathetic with the cause of antislavery found African-Americans lacking in energy, discipline, and self-reliance; they seemed lazy, literal, and slow to learn. These notions were not necessarily altered by contact with the desperately poor and understandably hesitant former slaves encountered by northern soldiers in the South. During and immediately after the war, well-meaning northern missionaries to the freedmen found serious shortcomings in their character and ambition, while, throughout the remainder of the nineteenth century, middle-class northerners traveling through the South wrote of the "picturesque," rather lazy blacks who lent authenticity to the Old South landscape, fitting in perfectly with the relaxed, rural, comfortable southland that offered vacationers relief from the fast pace of the bustling North.[6]

And yet most northerners who discussed the blighted South found these faults entrenched in the larger society and described them in terms that revealed their prescription for a successful, progressive country. Middle-class officers and men viewed the South as a backward, even foreign land. The cities were pitiful, graceless places with few schools, businesses, or other civilizing institutions. The run-down southern plantations, wasteful farming practices, and inefficiency of the slave labor system betrayed the hollowness of southern boasting about the "King Cotton" economy, and even the "better" classes in the South seemed to be all charm and no substance. Central to northerners' criticism of the South was the flawed domesticity they found there. Neither fathers nor mothers appeared to be model parents. The men were violent autocrats who raped their female slaves, while the women had obviously failed in their roles as "Republican mothers" by nurturing a generation of traitors to the Union. The looting and destruction Union soldiers committed, Reid Mitchell suggests, reflected their "belief in the South's cultural and moral inferiority."[7]

Northerners were actually trumpeting their own virtues as they catalogued southerners' failings. Southerners were shiftless, short-sighted, and domineering. Yankees put forth a number of theories to explain these evils (perhaps it was too hot!) but most placed slavery at the center of southern shortcomings. The peculiar institution degraded labor—northerners rarely admitted that any white or black southerner would willingly do a day of honest work—and encouraged cruelty and the debasement of human life.

But it also destroyed the families of both its black and white participants. As Harriet Beecher Stowe demonstrated in *Uncle Tom's Cabin*, published a decade before the war began, and as abolitionists had been arguing for decades, among the slave owners' greatest sins was their refusal to let their bondspeople marry, care for their own children, or even live together as families. Slavery also had a deep impact on white families through the well-known practice of slave owners impregnating female slaves, as well as in the arrogance spawned by their absolute power over their bondsmen and women. In short, southerners completely failed to demonstrate the self-control and discipline central to middle-class gentility. Some soldiers thought that without an infusion of Yankee common sense and values, the South would never change. "The greatest need of the South, is an army of Northern Schoolmasters," wrote a Yale-educated officer, while a Maine private believed that, "with New England taste and enterprise to develop the resources of the country," much of the South "would prove an earthly paradise." Yet another soldier declared that the South, lacking energy and enterprise, could only be reborn with "Yankee skill energy Enterprise, with the LEAVEN of free labor, free schools."[8]

Obviously, Civil War–era Americans overwhelmingly believed that the North and the South had become two distinct cultures.[9] Bertram Wyatt-Brown argues that the moral universes of northerners and southerners "had grown more, not less, distinctive" in the decades leading up to the Civil War. Even before war broke out, these differing perceptions had helped form destructive stereotypes, but as casualties mounted and Union forces encountered escalating hostility from southern civilians, it became increasingly apparent to northerners that the South would have to be swept clean of its corrupt social, political, and economic systems. Many of the invaders—privates and generals alike—insisted that the South would be inhabitable and productive only with the infusion of northern ideas, not to mention teachers and other ambitious emigrants unafraid to work. Slavery would be destroyed, poor whites uplifted, and elite planters cut down to size.[10]

These grand objectives did not become articulated in any coherent way as aims of war. But many northerners constructed their own personal agendas about what the war should mean. Rose argues that the Civil War became "a vehicle for spiritual resolution," and James H. Moorhead shows that this "American Apocalypse" of civil war focused the attention of northern Protestants on the "moral rebirth" of their nation, which they pursued by establishing a wide range of benevolent organizations for soldiers and freedmen.[11]

The crusade to reform the South was easily incorporated into northern attempts to inculcate important values in their own children. Many middle-class northerners had long before the war rejected older styles of child rearing that relied on physical punishment, shame, and extremely paternalistic patterns of discipline. Rather, aided by a complex of institutions, organizations, and publications, they sought to instill self-restraint and thoughtful obedience—virtues they believed to be absent in southern families.[12] This concern for bringing up children within a specific moral template continued during the war, as absent fathers repeatedly instructed their children in letters written on battlefields and in campgrounds, to live godly lives, work hard, mind their mothers, and take their schooling seriously—all values promoted by children's authors, educators, and child-rearing experts for decades. Some fathers realized that their own sacrifices gave them the high moral ground from which they could assail their children's shortcomings. One Union soldier scolded his daughter for attending a dance against her stepmother's wishes. "Oh, my dear daughter," wrote David Coon, "your father may be lying dead on the field of battle and you may not know it. . . . O, Emma, Emma! How can you have the heart to go to dancing parties, against your kind mother's wishes and advice and your own conscience and judgment?" To underscore his message, he regretted that he had no ink to write with—this was a lesson she must remember always—"as I perhaps may never write to you again."[13]

Even as fathers extended advice and encouragement to their sons and daughters to live good middle-class lives, other forces incorporated children into the war effort. Boys and girls of all ages made bandages and scraped lint for wounded soldiers; packed food and clothing and reminders of home into "boxes" for absent fathers and brothers; avidly followed war news in the newspapers, collected stationery with patriotic cartoons and messages; memorized stirring and patriotic poems and addresses for weekly "speaking days" at school; and eagerly played soldier and nurse.[14]

Some of the most intense efforts to make children aware of their role in the great conflict appeared in books and magazines published for children during the war and in the massive efforts to raise money to aid soldiers by the United States Sanitary Commission. Children were publicly reminded of their duty to uphold the values that shaped the country for which their fathers and uncles and brothers were fighting. Dominated by members of the northern middle class, the children's publication industry outlined those values; the fund-raising activities encouraged by the Sanitary Fairs gave children a chance to act on them.

Perhaps no Civil War–era institution was so determinedly middle-class as the children's publishing industry, whose publishers and editors shared the same goals as northern educators: preparing children for solid, if unspectacular, adult lives characterized by prudence, respectability, self-reliance, modest achievement, and good citizenship. As Marilyn Dell Brady argues in her analysis of the "model" middle-class family of this period, the "moral rearing of children was necessary for national survival." Part of the self-conscious development of middle-class values depended on a literature that would promote moral uplift, Protestant religious standards, and orderly and respectable conduct, while at the same time warning of the dangers posed by the worldly spheres of business and politics. As a result, adult and children's literature was dominated by what one historian calls "conduct-of-life books"—inspirational stories, novels, and magazines purporting to show true examples of how worthy lives were led.[15]

In fact, juvenile magazines, books, and schoolbooks, had, through much of the antebellum period, expressed middle-class values. Responding to the changes rocking American society, children's literature during the four decades before the Civil War showed the benefits of hard work, obedience, generosity, humility, and piety as well as the consequences of their absence, providing moral guidance and examples of the benefits of strong families. Authors stressed character and framed the world in moral terms, combining a faith in virtue with a confidence in the American political and economic systems. Patriotism, good deeds, hard work, and unselfishness together would guarantee individual success and national honor. As Ann Scott MacLeod has shown, pre-1860 fiction for children "was written entirely as an adjunct to . . . moral education."[16]

During the war, that education included a rather large dose of patriotism. In fact, wartime writing for children reflected no conflict between peacetime and wartime values; the term "Christian soldiers" became more than a stirring metaphor. The children's magazines and books produced in the 1860s continued to provide models of moral behavior and of youths dutifully obeying their parents, working hard, and accepting their lots in life with humility and gratitude. But these notions were amplified by the war, which made it seem patriotic as well as moral to live out the middle-class ideal. These values appeared in articles explaining the causes and history of the war, in stories spinning tales of bravery and patriotism, and in pieces showing readers how to contribute to Union victory.[17] Because the "boys and girls of today will . . . affect all future time," wrote one editor, "a knowledge of our country's history," including its troubled present, was a vital part of their moral and political education, and the connection made between loyalty and virtue was both obvious and seamless. The war induced authors to add at least two new values to their didactic repertoire. Antebellum pacifism was replaced with martial enthusiasm, as fictional boys donned homemade uniforms, built makeshift guns and swords, and practiced the art of war. And slavery finally became a target of northern writers for children. In the 1850s, publishers, reluctant to alienate potential customers in the South, had avoided the issue of slavery, and even when Jacob Abbott and other authors featured African Americans in their stories and novels, they were presented in broad stereotypes. The magazines and novels written for children during the war would continue to be condescending toward African Americans, but they would also contain scathing critiques of slavery—they would attack racism somewhat less effectively—and of the South.[18]

Indeed, descriptions of freed slaves in the South sparkled with middle-class assumptions. Letters from women working among the freedpeople of the occupied South, for instance, were designed to win sympathy for the poor "contrabands," as they were called, and to mobilize northern children to collect supplies and funds on their behalf. "I want to tell you something about these little colored children," wrote G. N. Coan to *The Little Pilgrim* in mid-1864. She described them as fast learners, enthusiastic students, and eager singers who were constantly bringing their teachers flowers and other little presents. If northern children could only "hear them answer questions from the Bible, I am sure you would be delighted, and think they were anything but stupid." Coan also related that "many of these children are as white as any of you are, with blue eyes and straight hair, or pretty auburn ringlets." Although Coan does not say so directly, these are obviously the children of white men. Yet they had nevertheless been "put up on the auction block to be sold far away from their mothers." Another of the burdens of slavery was the fact that, as slaves, "these children have not had the good teaching you have had, but have been taught to lie, and steal, and strike and throw stones at each other." With the help of their northern friends, however, they can be made into useful and good boys and girls. The letter closed with an appeal for help: "will you not send them some of your old dresses, quilts, sacks, or shoes, so that they may be able to go to school, and learn to read the word of God, and thus become good men and women?"[19]

Although the subject of race was rarely featured in the fiction, poetry, songs, short plays (called "dialogues"), declamation pieces, puzzles, and games published in the leading juvenile periodicals of the Civil War, all promoted middle-class values amid the wide-ranging information they presented about the war. Oliver Optic's editorials in *The Student and Schoolmate* often drew moral lessons from the war. Comparing disobedient boys and girls to southerners refusing to obey the Constitution, Optic declared that "Jeff. Davis, the arch rebel, is only like a bad boy who will not mind his parents or his teachers." But the most useful measure of middle-class appeals for patriotism and morality emerged from short stories. The child heroes and heroines were clearly middle-class boys and girls growing up in relatively affluent, Protestant homes in suburbs or small cities. Far removed from the actual fighting, of course, they acted like real-life children by incorporating the war into their lives. Boys drilled in their own military companies and fought their own faux battles. Girls could play at war in more gender-appropriate ways, as did Nelly, the main character in Louisa May Alcott's charming story "Nelly's Hospital." Inspired by her convalescent brother's tales of the work of the United States Sanitary Commission, Nelly resolves to create a hospital for wounded animals she finds in her yard. She builds a tiny ambulance and gathers up a fly trapped in a spider's web, a gray snake, a crippled bird, and a litter of sick mice. Her efforts cheer her brother to recovery and shame neighborhood boys into forsaking their sport of throwing rocks at innocent animals. Both boys and girls could join in the war effort, as did the children in "A Box for the Soldier," who carefully choose the presents they send to their father in the army. One son sends his favorite knife while another sends a crudely whittled gun, sword, and cannon; daughters make mittens and socks and a sleeping cap "to keep his precious head from the frosty ground."[20]

Many longer works for children, such as Oliver Optic's pair of trilogies on two young boys who join the army and navy, concerned themselves more with adventure than with political reality.[21] Yet a few novels also reflected more clearly typical middle-class assumptions about the war. *Frank's Campaign*, an early effort by Horatio Alger, showed how patriotism and sacrifice made it possible for a determined, honest boy to get ahead. Its hero, Frank, wins a school contest with his composition on what boys can do to help win the war and gets a chance to put theory into practice when his father enlists in the army. In the typical literary style of the time, with multiple subplots and surprising coincidences, Frank deals with Squire Haynes, a war profiteer who tries to foreclose the mortgage on Frank's father's farm; helps out a family of African-American refugees; and befriends a mysterious stranger looking for the man who had cheated his father in a business transaction (who, of course, turns out to be the shady army contractor). Everything turns out well in the end: Haynes is ruined, the mortgage is paid, and Frank's new friend promises to pay for Frank's education.[22]

Stories not only encouraged children to support the war directly, but also taught humility and generosity, two cherished values in prewar literature. The spoiled middle-class children in Lydia Maria Child's "The Two Christmas Evenings"—bored with their gifts within minutes of opening them—learn the true spirit of the holiday by raising money for local orphans and for African-American children in South Carolina with a year-long series of tableaux, speeches on liberty and patriotism, and sales of handicrafts. A girl in another story gives the money she had hoarded to spend at a local fair to a poor soldier's orphan, while Gertie, "the Discontented Girl," finally does her share for the soldiers after her older brother calls her a "rebel" for her lazy refusal to get to work. In stories such as these, readers learned the valuable lessons that such fictional characters had been demonstrating for years.[23]

Such charitable efforts were encouraged in children's fiction. But in keeping with their application of civic responsibility and moral correctness to wartime exigencies, authors showed that there were wrong and right ways of helping the less fortunate. In Christie Pearl's "The Contraband," the half-dozen children of a solidly upper-middle-class family pack castoff clothes in a barrel meant for freed slaves in the South. Their condescension turns the effort into a farce, as they laugh at improbable images of the contrabands wearing their "dickeys," bracelets, and old hats and rejoice that now they can buy new wardrobes. Their father interrupts the fun with "a loud 'Ahem!'" and asks sternly, "are there any things there that you want or need?" They admit that their contributions are merely clothing too ugly or unfashionable for them to wear themselves. "Then you have not given properly," he admonishes them. "Your clothes may keep the 'contrabands' warm, but they will bring no additional warmth to your own hearts. You must make sacrifices in order to reap the benefit of giving." Promptly and properly chagrined, the childen repack the aid barrel with some of their favorite clothes and toys.[24]

Although winning the war was obviously a chief concern of writers for children, in some cases family responsibilities and moral prerogatives loomed larger than the war itself. Of course, if the moral threads of the American society were not sustained during the war, the country would unravel even if the military effort was successful. The teenage title character in *Kathie's Soldiers* fulfills her duty to her country by working for the local Sanitary Fair and watching over the motherless daughter of a soldier. But she also performs her moral duty by refusing to engage in the constant gossiping and back-biting among the fashionable girls at her school and persevering against the self-absorbed daughter of yet another dishonest army contractor. Discovering that their duty lies at home, Kathie's uncle avoids conscription into the army by hiring a substitute so he can remain at home to support his widowed sister and her family, while her brother submits to going off to boarding school rather than becoming a drummer. Even Kathie's little brother Freddie does his duty by staying out of trouble and by eagerly supporting the war effort in his miniature soldier's uniform. As a young lieutenant tells the troubled hero of *Battles at Home*, "Our battles must be just where we are put to fight!"[25]

Like the wise lieutenant, many authors cast the war as a metaphor for the struggle within between good and evil. In Gail Hamilton's "Small Fighting," young Holly boisterously proclaims his patriotism and criticizes Union commanders for recent battlefield reverses, declaring that he would never allow himself to be taken prisoner by the Rebels: "I'd never surrender! I'd die a thousand times first." He later wishes "I was old enough to fight." A bemused uncle, who overhears Holly's bombastic rhetoric, intervenes. Just the previous evening, he told the children, he had watched a "skirmish" between Holly and his arithmetic lesson, from which the boy had retreated ingloriously. Later he lost a battle with a stubborn shoe lace. Beset by "Gen. Self-Indulgence" and his own temper, "Gen. Holly" had surrendered unconditionally. To the pouting Holly, the wise uncle said, "You can't go to Virginia, but you can throw out your pickets at home, and give battle manfully."[26]

For the children in this genre of wartime story—a number of examples of which were published by the American Sunday School Union and the American Tract Society—the war between the states gave them an opportunity to test their good intentions and Sunday school training in the crucible of wartime pressures. After his father is reported killed, a little boy is haunted by his last words before leaving for the army: "always obey your mother"; a teenage immigrant to "Bleeding Kansas" links her country's honor to her piety, insisting that "to rally for its defence is not less a duty of religion than of patriotism"; for Andy Hall, steadfast service in the Union army is the culmination of his reformation and redemption after a life of poverty and petty crime. Other books showed young drummer boys converting grizzled soldiers or inspiring adults with their pious deaths.[27]

That wartime writing for children reflected the application of middle-class values to the Union war effort is even more succinctly demonstrated in publications produced expressly for freedmen in the South. Tens of thousands of former slaves crowded into churches, houses, warehouses, and barns to learn from missionaries who came from the North to educate the victims of slavery. As almost stereotypical middle-class northerners, these teachers sought to instill the same discipline, self-reliance, and work ethic in the newly freed African Americans as writers for white children in the North inculcated in their readers. The American Tract Society offered the largest catalogue of reading material for freedmen, ranging from a pamphlet called *First Lessons* to *The Ten Commandments Illustrated* to short *Tracts for Beginners* all printed in outsized letters. The Society's most widely circulated publications were *The Freedman's Spelling Book*, *Primer*, *Second Reader*, and *Third Reader*, which were modeled after antebellum schoolbooks, but with the addition of stories about productive, hardworking, temperate, and patriotic African Americans like Frederick Douglass and Phillis Wheatley.[28]

The Society also published a monthly, four-page newspaper for former slaves, *The Freedman*, which, the editors suggested, could be used first by adult learners and then "given to the children as a reward for diligence and good conduct." The paper's format followed closely the contents of juvenile magazines or Sabbath school publications, with scriptural references, simple analyses of the Ten Commandments, moralistic vignettes, penmanship and grammar drills, and a few short stories and features. Each issue was infused with middle-class values like thrift, hard work, forethought, temperance, honesty, and perseverance.[29]

Readers were obviously meant to learn how to be productive citizens on the Yankee, rather than the supposed southern, model. A writing exercise reminded them that freedom only gave the former slave the chance "to be a good and noble man, and not an idle, bad, worthless fellow." "The Story of Nip" showed soldiers rewarding a young contraband woman for her long hours of work in the military hospital by teaching her how to read; she passed each day's lessons on to other former slaves. "Do you take as much pains to learn as Nip did," the author asked pointedly, "and when you have learned, are you as eager to teach those who can not go to school as you do?" Other pieces, couched in homely, if condescending language, urged

African Americans to save their money and to "lay up" such things as food and firewood for stormy days; instructed freedwomen that "If you do not know how to work—to wash and scrub and cook and sew, you will not make a good wife"; and tried to impose order on the lives of freedmen by teaching them the numbers of months in a year and days in the months. The lives that former slaves should aspire to would be decorated with middle-class values, at least according to an article entitled "Home." Describing a typical day in the life of a freedperson, it focused on cleanliness, Godliness, and order. The author admonished readers not to eat "too fast, nor with a noise like the pigs." As proper free people, their lives should be characterized by quiet fortitude, hard, honest work, and kindness.[30]

The former slaves may well have resented the patronizing tone of *The Freedman*, not to mention the clear implication that they had to be built from scratch into men and women worthy of northern philanthropy. They may have also tired of the fairly constant reminders of the great debt they owed to northern whites. Several extended articles showed the sacrifices borne by northern soldiers and their families in the fight to free the slaves. A front-page engraving late in 1864 showed a young wife rocking her baby to sleep; the accompanying article refers to the pride she feels that her husband is off fighting in the war. But the objects of this sacrifice, the recipients of the God-granted opportunity "to help yourselves," must demonstrate their gratitude by "exert[ing] yourselves to the utmost, that you may prove worthy of it all, and save and elevate yourselves and your kindred" by being "honest, sober, diligent and patriotic." Only by accepting the middle-class values to which they were being exposed—and which bore a striking similarity to the expectations authors established for middle-class northern children—would the former slaves repay the debt they owed to the North.[31]

The heavy-handed advice given by the *Freedman* meshed perfectly with two northern middle-class assumptions: the impulse to lead orderly, productive, Godly lives and the belief that such lives were virtually impossible in a South choked by the corruption of slavery. In their single-minded devotion to the middle-class ideal, *The Freedman* and other publications for former slaves resembled nothing so much as magazines produced for northern children, who also needed to be sternly nurtured onto the middle-class path.

For many wartime northerners and their children, that path led them into the enthusiastic fund-raising that was an important element of the war effort on the Union home front. Building on the prewar voluntary associations that formed one of the bases of middle-class society, the United States Sanitary Commission (USSC) became the preeminent philanthropic organization of the war. The swirl of voluntary activities that propelled them and the martial imagery central to the displays and performances held at the Sanitary Fairs further linked middle-class ideals to the war effort.[32]

All told, local branches of the USSC raised $4.3 million at fairs held in cities all over the East and Midwest between the fall of 1863 and the spring of 1865. Hundreds of thousands of Americans paid the minimal entrance fee, wandered the crowded aisles, packed into the booths sponsored by communities and organizations, attended concerts, and shelled out cash for souvenirs, home-made pastries and clothing, toys, and other goods donated by businessmen, church groups, and individuals. Among the fairs' enticements were "New England Kitchens," where young women served hot food and desserts to hungry visitors; historical artifacts and war-related relics from the American Revolution as well as the current "Rebellion"; and appearances by such political and military luminaries as Edward Everett, Abraham Lincoln, and Gen. Ulysses S. Grant and his family.[33]

Organizers obviously believed that children could become potent consumers of the patriotism the fairs promoted. Chicago public schools closed so students could attend the fairs held there in 1863 and in 1865, and newspaper descriptions show why children flocked by the thousands to the fairs. The Great Central Fair in Philadelphia offered automaton rope dancers, stereoptican views, magic shows, ventriloquists, an indoor playground, and a huge restaurant. The Children's Department of New York's Metropolitan Fair, according to *Leslie's Illustrated Newspaper*, was "a treasury of useful articles, toys and knick-knacks, almost realising the fables of fairyland." Youngsters in Albany could cluster around the "very remarkable animal called the Gorilla" at the "Gipsey tent" and the "life picture" of Indian life—complete with a canoe, baskets, and ladies dressed in Native American costumes—at the "Wigwam." Boys elbowed through crowds sometimes "so immense that locomotion was well nigh impossible" at the other exhibits to get into the 1,800-square-foot "Military Department," where they admired Cornwallis's pistol and Lafayette's camp kettle. Even more interesting were the clothes worn by the Union martyr Elmer Ellsworth when he was killed, scores of firearms, fragments from a Confederate shell that exploded in Fort Sumter, and the flags of dozens of Union regiments. The "Trophy Room" offered captured Confederate battle flags as well as metal splinters from a Confederate ironclad and an iron plate from a Union monitor. Children at the Brooklyn Fair clustered around the "Rebel war memorials" that included muskets, pistols, sabres, pikes, swords, and "Arkansas tooth picks."[34]

Like all worthy entertainments for Victorian children, Sanitary Fair displays were supposed to educate rather than merely titillate, to motivate observers to appreciate the sacrifices of the soldiers and the strength of the Union for which they were fighting. But they also encouraged children to embrace the volunteer spirit by joining in the great northern war effort. At New York's 1864 fair, a separate "Children's Department"—occupying the entire east wing of the Union Square Building—offered booths and displays by public and private schools, a toy store, and soldiers' orphans. According to the newspaper published by the fair, the items sold in the

Children's Department "represent probably a greater devotion than in almost any other department." For instance, "the little children of the Home for the Friendless" gave hundreds of pennies and made "lamp-lighters" out of colored paper. Other institutions donating hand-made items included the Deaf and Dumb Asylum, the Blind Asylum, the Wilson Industrial School, the Birch Church Mission School, the "girls of the House of Refuge," members of the Hebrew Orphan Asylum, children from the "Colored Home," unidentified "blind girls," and the "Children of the Sacred Heart" in Harlem.[35]

Some middle-class children held their own fairs in backyards, front porches, or parlors decorated with flags, patriotic pictures, and banners, where adults could buy pastries, lemonade, and craft projects made by the children themselves. A young New Englander named Willie Kingsbury earned a penny for every pin he found, which he donated to soldiers' causes, and soon, his sister recalled, "he was selling everything he could," even kisses from a "pretty little fair-haired boy" to neighborhood children and "organizing little fairs entirely of his own." Ten-year-old Emma Andrews earned a measure of fame by attending the Saturday morning work sessions of the Woman's Soldiers' Aid Society of Northern Ohio, where she sewed well over two hundred small towels. Emptying their "tin boxes, savings' banks, and stockings," Chicago children contributed several hundred dollars to the Chicago Fair, while young girls working in four-hour shifts at the Brooklyn Fair and in other cities sold dolls dressed as the Old Woman Who Lived in a Shoe. The most famous was Nellie Grant, who took on the role in St. Louis in 1864. Tad Lincoln, after attending the Philadelphia fair, organized his own in the corridors of the White House, where startled office seekers were asked to purchase pastries, candy, and fruit while waiting to see the president.[36]

In addition to these individual efforts, children also participated in more centralized activities. The public and private schools of New York raised $24,000 by holding reading lessons and entertainments for their families and friends during the Metropolitan Fair. Philadelphia's schoolchildren were even more active. Fourteen hundred teachers and 72,000 pupils worked for months sewing and soliciting, rehearsing concerts, readings, and tableaux, and holding tea parties and festivals to raise money for the Great Central Fair. Cincinnati schoolchildren put on "gymnastic exercises" and other entertainments at the Great Western Fair, while a chorus of children dressed in white and wearing wreaths of flowers opened Chicago's Great Northwestern Sanitary Fair. In St. Louis, 1,700 students from the city's many German schools sang during the ceremonial procession and recession, while a single performance of "Cinderella," featuring two hundred child dancers and Gen. John C. and Jessie Benton Fremont's son as the prince, earned $2,500 in New York City.[37]

Very late in the war, a Chicagoan named Alfred L. Sewell linked the voluntary and literary aspects of the mobilization of middle-class children by devising the "Army of the American Eagle" and founding *The Little Corporal*, a juvenile magazine. According to a short history of the movement that appeared in the first issue of his magazine, Sewell had been trying to think of a way to "marshal the children . . . and give them a chance to show how well they love their country and her brave defenders." His plan was to entice boys and girls to sell "beautiful Album pictures in oil colors" of "Old Abe," the "War Eagle" of the 8th Wisconsin Regiment, which had led his regiment into numerous battles and emerged unscathed. The Chicago attorney made children "privates" in the Army of the American Eagle simply for buying pictures for a dime each. Recruits were then supposed to organize clubs and to sell copies of the pictures to other patriotic children and adults. As children sold more pictures, they advanced through the "ranks" of Sewell's "army," starting with a corporal's rank for selling ten copies and progressing up to major general for selling four thousand copies. Other incentives included gold, silver, and bronze medals for the best selling salesmen and saleswomen, and a booklet about Old Abe for every "colonel" and "general." One picture at a time, twelve thousand children throughout the North raised well over $16,000. The "army" "recruited" by Sewell provided a ready-made subscription base for *The Little Corporal*; he reported 35,000 subscribers in December 1866 to the magazine that included dozens of articles and stories about the war.[38]

By joining Sewell's "army," taking part in school-sponsored events, and attending the mammoth USSC fairs, middle-class children experienced firsthand the increasing centralization and bureaucratization of philanthropy that characterized the massive efforts of the Sanitary Commission. The USSC was not without its critics, despite the millions of dollars of aid it poured into soldiers' welfare. Some volunteers complained that the organization favored national over local interests; others feared that its administrators' detached professionalization would undermine the moral imperative that lay behind volunteers' efforts. Yet its methods prevailed, providing a sense of unity to the home-front war effort and confirming for many northerners the efficacy and power of northern middle-class ideals and practices.[39]

Perhaps no story better illustrated the ways that cultural assumptions and patriotism could come together for middle-class children in the North than "The Boy of Chancellorsville," which appeared in the classic children's magazine *Our Young Folks* shortly after the war ended. Purported to be a true story, it was the account of a twelve-year-old drummer boy who discards his drum and picks up a musket during the vicious fighting near the Chancellor House in northern Virginia in May 1862. His captain soon sends him to the rear, where he helps care for the wounded, including a young Confederate whose life he saves by somehow convincing surly stretcher-bearers to take him to the field hospital. He is later captured and sent to Libby Prison in

Richmond, where cruel guards consign him to the dungeon. He takes ill, but is nursed back to health by a kindly Yankee officer, who also tutors him during their long hours of incarceration. Finally, the boy is released and returned to his widowed mother in Ohio, where he was now "fitting himself to act his part in this great world, in this earnest time in which we are living."

The boy hero of Chancellorsville displayed every virtue that northern middle-class parents prayed for in their children: piety, humility, generosity, courage, constancy, and patriotism. In addition, the southerners depicted in the story nearly all sound like the southerners described by Union soldiers as they encountered the South. The commander of the guards at Libby is a product of the commonnest sort of white trash, "a coarse, brutal fellow, with breath perfumed with whiskey, and face bloated with drink and smeared with tobacco-juice." He robs the helpless prisoners and shows his contempt for respectable society with his crude language and idle cruelty. At the other end of the southern socioeconomic—but not the moral—spectrum was Gen. Robert E. Lee, whom the hero also encounters on the battlefield shortly after his capture. When the boy bravely announces to the Confederate chieftain that "I came out here, sir, to help fight the wicked men who are trying to destroy their country," Lee angrily sends him to prison with the other captured Yankees. That is about all one can expect from a southerner, the author suggests. Even the great Lee, "the man who neither smokes, drinks, nor chews tobacco; who has . . . none of the smaller vices"—in short, a man who displays all of the virtues promoted by the northern middle class—undermines those values by "deliberately, basely, and under circumstances of unparalleled meanness, betray[ing] his country, and, long after all hope of success was lost, carr[ying] on a murderous war against his own race and kindred."[40]

Most authors for children did not put their fictional subjects in harm's way. But they never forgot a principle expressed by Edmund Kirke in his introduction to "The Boy of Chancellorsville": that even the most inconsequential person plays a vital part in the machinery of the universe. "If the moon," for instance, "one of the smallest lumps of matter in the universe—should fall from its orbit, the whole planetary system might go reeling and tumbling about like a drunken man." Readers must remember "the great importance of little things—and little folks are of much greater importance than little things."[41]

Those little folks would carry northern middle-class values into the future, and authors and community leaders seized the opportunity provided by the South's rebellion to hammer home those ideas. In magazines and novels, authors defined what it meant to be an American—insisting that southern morals disqualified them from true citizenship—and through Sanitary Fairs and other fund-raising efforts, organizers showed children how to put those values into practice.

THE CULTURAL USES
OF THE SPIRIT

Chautauqua. COURTESY OF STATE HISTORICAL SOCIETY OF WISCONSIN, NEG. NO. WHI B53 328.

Search the Scriptures. GODEY'S
LADY'S BOOK, VOL. 42, MARCH
1851.

The antebellum middle classes styled themselves as "go ahead"
classes. They scoffed at the elitist authority of a Federalist bureaucracy, both
in relationship to an intrusive administrative state and a tax-supported
church establishment. They ridiculed the pretensions of deference to hierarchy where it appeared to impose arbitrary restrictions and regulations on
common people. In response to a popular movement, for instance, state
governments permitted any man to serve as his own lawyer by removing all
qualifications for appearing before the bar. To critics, however, the middle
classes seemed to elevate ignorance and promote a self-serving "individualism." Middling interests appeared profane, motivated neither by spiritual
principles nor by respect for sacred values but rather by selfish gain and one
of democracy's most corrupting "isms"—materialism. In the 1850s, one
critic's anger at the spiritual irreverence and religious insincerity of the middle classes boiled over in satirical mockery. The disaffected Samuel
Goodrich observed that once upon a time,

> Professional men had good health and good digestion no clergyman
> was known to have bronchitis. I seldom heard of dyspepsia, body or
> mental. . . . The people drank hard cider, and relished sound doctrine:
> it was not till . . . afterward that—imbibing soda-water, champagne,
> and other gaseous beverages—they required pyrotechnics in the pul-
> pit. . . .
>   Thus was ushered in the Age of Talk, which soon grew into a rage.
> The mania kept pace with democracy . . . and at last, at the end of this
> national flatulence, the world grew light-headed. . . . Under the influ-
> ence of ... new notions, some took to cold water and some to mint-
> juleps, some to raw vegetables and some to hot slings. . . .
>   Everything grew intense . . . religion got mixed up with transcen-
> dentalism . . . until at last, professors took to table-turning and judges
> to spirit-rappings. . . . What I affirm is, that demogogism and democ-
> racy, dyspepsia and Transcendentalism, vegetarianism and spiritual-
> ism, have all come up . . . since old federalism went down.[1]

The rhetorical blast made a serious point about the middle classes' profa-
nation and corruption of the spirit, a charge that continues to resonate in
the historiography: R. Laurence Moore on "selling God" in the American
marketplace, Stephen Nissenbaum on the celebration of Christmas gift giving, and William Leach on the spectacle of Wanamaker's department store
Christmas season, Roland Marchand and Jackson Lears on the exploitive
uses of religious symbolism by advertisers.[2]
  A primary assumption in this section on the middle classes is that religion—respect for the holy and fear of the sacred—needs to be appreciated
beyond the secular analytic liberal tradition of the modern Western world.
Karl Marx, for instance, dismissed the Judeo-Christian heritage as an "opi-

ate," and Max Weber tightly tethered the Protestant ethic to the "spirit of capitalism." A deeper perspective, however, is being heard in recent work by historians such as Leigh Eric Schmidt and Colleen McDannell.[3] Religion, converting spiritual interests into worldly domains, was a powerful force shaping and helping to direct authority in middle-class life. Beyond formal worship, church ritual, and theology, religious feelings and sacred meanings were adapted to everyday cultural, political, and commercial exchanges.

Each of the three following essays focuses on the variety of cultural techniques skilled religionists used to create audiences for their spiritual services, and advance careers. First, Henry Ward Beecher was the most popular preacher in mid-nineteenth-century America and pastor to the largest congregation. Debby Applegate examines the specific means by which Beecher cultivated and presented his carefully honed message for a national congregation beyond the walls of his Brooklyn church. In an era of voluntary church membership, audiences needed to be made in a marketplace for congregants. Leaders needed to master a mix of organizational techniques, emotional messages, and professional skill at shaping incentives in order to build congregations. Beecher was the best, a consummate performer who grasped the importance of the new technologies, especially the network of railroad transportation and the mass distribution of print. A reassuring personality, he received thousands of letters from across the social spectrum from folks unsure of their economic and social position. They needed the support of faith to act on the belief that in this world the God of love and sympathy trumped the God of denial and fatalism. Beecher connected to people by convincing them of his friendship and his concern for their circumstances. Applegate concludes that Beecher neither was a huckster nor a con man, but one of the "first modern celebrities to make a living by turning his persona into a popular commodity."

In turn, Edward Kilsdonk emphasizes the little noticed significance musical styles had in attracting and sustaining middle-class church congregations. There were historic differences in approaches to church music, all cutting across denominal lines: "lining out," the old New England choirs, improvisational revival traditions, the formal aesthetics of musical performance, and "scientific" music. Kilsdonk concludes that increasingly "scientific" music prevailed as "part of the cultural literacy" of the middle-class church experience. Developed by Lowell Mason and Thomas Hastings, scientific music emphasized not the power of music as a force but instead its effects: harmony, restraint, and the controlled mechanics of singing. The regimentation had, as one contemporary put it, a "business air" about it. Interest in popular music was the rage in nineteenth-century America. Indeed, Mason made the sale of song books into a successful business, and he set a musical fashion for the middle classes that spread beyond the churches into the secular culture.

Finally, Andrew Chamberlin Rieser reconsiders the meanings of secularization in the history of the popular Chautauqua movement. By making room in the story for a large group of ethical humanist Christians like Jane Addams, he pushes aside the modernist polarities between sacred and secular, ministers and managers, religion and business. Chautauqua was committed to extended education as the college of life, emphasizing the connection between religious faith and the democratic process. The movement included a "polyglot" of middle-class identities. Rieser tells a layered story about people, performers, an organization, a movement, and an idea. Chautauqua, with its famous lectures, family reunion, and vacation atmosphere, was not for intellectuals like William James yearning for a strenuous religious experience at the psychological edge. Contrary to James, Rieser concludes that Chautauqua was no less real as a spiritual experience, and it was more effective and interesting than historians since have considered. Spiritual striving at Chautauqua persisted in being a vital force for the "preservation of middle-class authority."

Henry Ward Beecher and the "Great Middle Class": Mass-Marketed Intimacy and Middle-Class Identity

DEBBY APPLEGATE

"Jesus felt instantly that there were affinities and relationships far higher and wider than those constituted by the earthly necessities of family life."
—Henry Ward Beecher,
"Moral Affinity, the True Ground of Unity," December 6, 1868

Studying the middle class offers all the fascinations and frustrations of an optical illusion—what seems plain as day out of the corner of the eye can become hopelessly muddled when examined directly. Few terms are used so frequently, with such confidence, to encompass so much. When polled, the majority of contemporary Americans use the category "middle class" to describe themselves, blithely disregarding the efforts of sociologists and economists to delineate them according to income, occupation, or property ownership. Contemporary political and cultural commentators use the term so loosely that it seems to include all but the far fringes of society.

For most historians, the middle class is something they know when they see it. The concept of middle class is treated as something of a syllogism—readily identified by a catalogue of characteristics: individualistic, respectable, domestic, white-collar, teetotaling, novel reading, and so forth. Yet those who have tried to define the nature of the middle class more thoroughly are plagued by something of an optical illusion. Sociologists, cultural theorists, and historians have been unable to establish consensus on even fundamental questions about the composition, status, or structure of the middle class. "Indeed," concludes one surveyor of the field, "few problems in social science have proved more persistent and more strongly colored by both ideological commitments and political context."[1]

This confused state can be traced, in large part, to a more general sense of stagnation in the study of class over the last two decades. By contrast, the study of race and gender as categories has undergone revolutions in the same period of time, primarily through the ascent of discourse analysis. Analytical techniques associated with deconstruction (using the term in the broadest sense) have been used to undermine the conviction that race and gender are inviolable biological categories. In documenting the way modern concepts of race and gender were invented and deployed we have become increasingly aware of them as rhetorical constructs that structure our preconceptions of social experience. Yet, while definitions of race and gender have been radically destabilized and demystified, often by showing how these concepts served as screens for class interests, class itself has remained a relatively stable concept.

Class as a category is deceptively, yet significantly, different from that of race and gender. Bourgeois cultures, the United States in particular, tend to invoke race and gender as essential categories of human nature, while insisting that class is a transitory, self-created state. Unlike traditional notions of race and gender that are based on a belief in natural binaries— white/nonwhite, male/female—the concept of class as a provisional state has been used in the United States to deny the binary of conflicting interests. Class has been conceived as a matter of personified, temporal progress in which all potentially conflicting interests can be harmonized over time. Economic and social disparity is merely a matter of stages of development within an individual or group. In Abraham Lincoln's famous epigram, "The man who labored for another last year, this year labors for himself, and next year he will hire others to labor for him."[2] Because class identity is defined as an alterable cultural creation, class *per se* has been resistant to deconstructive techniques designed to excavate the way unitary identities mask social and ideological contradictions.

This fluidity has made it difficult to parse the contradictions of class. But the resistance to alternative analytical approaches is also rooted in an equally fundamental tension between the study of class and the study of class consciousness: should we examine class as a cognitive, cultural construct through which we interpret economic relations or as a statistical cohort of people with similar social and economic resources? The last major reassessment of this question occurred twenty-five years ago when E. P. Thompson revolutionized labor history by extending the understanding of class consciousness to encompass more subtle cultural factors as well as economic structures. Yet even today, when the cultural and discursive forces bearing on class are explored there remains a presumption that class identity is based on integral, shared economic interests. While the new labor history has included noneconomic forces such as leisure, mass consumption, and politics in their descriptions of class formation, the definition of social class remains economic.

In the study of the middle class, this tension is magnified by the contradiction between the fiercely individualistic ideology that seems to characterize the middle class, and the communal nature of class consciousness. While historians have had great success in depicting how the mores of individualism correlate with the spread of capitalist modes of production, they have been less successful in explaining how individualism fosters the collective bonds of class consciousness.

In the introduction to his benchmark survey, *The Emergence of the Middle Class*, Stuart Blumin declares that his mission is to resolve this "central paradox in the concept of middle-class formation, the building of a class that binds itself together as a social group in part through the common embrace of an ideology of social atomism." Yet even in this admirable attempt at synthesis, Blumin returns to the familiar ground of the economic, charting his argument directly from Thompson's maps. Blumin intends to circumvent this "central paradox" by reformulating "the hypotheses of middle-class formation in terms of the 'structuration' of certain types of social and cultural experience, to which expressions of class consciousness or awareness are related as a matter of secondary importance."[3]

Blumin sidesteps this central tension by offering the thesis that middle-class consciousness is primarily a local phenomenon based on changes in the workplace that create newly homogeneous daily associations. He synthesizes the data on occupational circumstances and social norms, examining five key areas of personal and social experience—work, consumption, residential location, formal and informal associations, and family organization and strategy.

Blumin argues that in the three decades before the Civil War the expansion of large industrial enterprises, and the proliferation of artisans-turned-entrepreneurs during the economic boom of the 1840s and early 1850s, created a convergence of structural circumstances and social experiences that served to distinguish the lives of manual workers from those employed in an expanding nonmanual sector. Drawing on Anthony Giddens's distinction between "middle-class awareness" and "middle-class consciousness," Blumin maintains that this new convergence of daily experience created a sense of middle-class *awareness*—that is, as neighborhoods and workplaces became more stratified, those who possessed a modicum of economic and educational capital began to associate primarily with each other. They then adopted new habits to protect and justify their social solidarity and relative economic security.[4]

Middle-class *consciousness* develops in the postwar era, Blumin argues. As "white-collar" workers—such as retailers, wholesalers, clerks, salesmen, accountants, and supervisors—were less bound by an artisanal skill base and traditional sources of social and economic support, increasingly they "became aligned with a national culture of business institutions and practices, such as banking and credit."[5] The events of the postwar period, "most notably, widening differences between the worlds of nonmanual and manual work, the expansion of middle class suburbanization, and the resumption and expansion of social and economic conflict that was phrased in class terms" heightened a sense of class consciousness, particularly in urban areas.[6] As the battles between capitalists and laborers became more violent and intractable, in many cases those in the middling socioeconomic strata chose to align themselves ideologically as petit bourgeois rather than part of a broader category of workers.

However, Blumin's own discussion of the nineteenth-century taxonomy of class undermines the neat distinctions. A remarkably wide range of wealth, occupation, and education falls under the heading "the great middle class." The demographic evidence of middle-class self-identification has demonstrated how difficult it is to correlate the use of the term "middle class" with economic indicators such as occupation, income, real estate, or education. An exemplary letter to the *New York Tribune* of March 10, 1855, captures just how fluid and encompassing class definitions were throughout the midcentury:

> But, our population is mostly made up of the middle class, (if there be any classes in democratic America). We have a large sprinkling of builders, master-masons, carpenters, &c.; we have merchants and brokers, who do business "down-town"; printers, bookbinders, book keepers, clerks, journeymen of every trade, whose daily work is performed "down-town," have their abodes here.[7]

Moreover, the social and economic fortunes of the average nineteenth-century family were drastically unstable. New studies reveal that bankruptcy was almost epidemic in the nineteenth century, including a high incidence of multiple failures over the course of an average lifetime. An individual might move out of the ranks of manual labor or wage work, to property ownership, or to salaried or non-manual work, only to fall back into them after misfortune. As Melanie Archer and Judith Blau conclude in their summary of existing historiography, the nineteenth-century middle class is, above all, a "middle class characterized by heterogeneity and a historically shifting social composition."[8] There is ample evidence suggesting that by the end of the nineteenth century "the great middle class" was not replaced but joined by a more narrow concept of the middle class based on occupation and economic resources.

This essay will not search for the "authentic" middle class but for the factors that could bind a diverse and mobile people together into a sense of class consciousness. What remains most puzzling about the middle class is not its criteria for exclusion, but how it maintains such a powerful ethos of inclusion in the face of great economic stratification. I will address this fundamental mystery: What conditions made it possible for such a great variety of people, engaged in such varied economic roles, to identify themselves as part of a middle class—using the term "middle class" to indicate not a set of inert qualities (domestic, property owning, etc.) but a group affiliation based on perceived similarities?

This essay argues that middle-class consciousness was shaped less by structural circumstances than by ideological and emotional incentives. It required an act of imagination for such diverse individuals to conceive themselves as a community united by shared aspirations and cultural practices.

Ideology and middle-class identity have long been linked—from the classic Marxist claim that the very notion of a "middle class" is a spurious category produced by a false consciousness among workers, to more recent argument that the middle class is fundamentally hegemonic in its power, making narrow economic interests appear universal in an effort to preserve its own relative privilege. But this pejorative concept of ideology gives only half the picture. To explain the possibility of a national class consciousness—the sensation of affirmative bonds—that can cut across economic status requires a positive dialectic that lays bare the utopian urges that bring people together.

To answer this question, we will take as an exemplar one of the most famous and influential men of the nineteenth century, the Reverend Henry Ward Beecher (1813–1887). A cross between P. T. Barnum and Ralph Waldo Emerson, Beecher was considered *the* great popular phenomenon of the era. His heyday, from the 1840s to the 1880s, coincided precisely with the emergence of the middle class and the rise of the mass-market economy. He was heralded as the spokesman for middle-class America, as well as the quintessential figure of the new national mass culture. The press simultaneously characterized his Brooklyn congregation and his broad national audience as both a "cross section" of America and as the "great middle class." Demographic evidence drawn from his church rolls and readership confirms that his appeal cut a wide swath from the urban well-to-do to the rural poor. Moreover, at a time when religion was dominated by women, he was unusually popular among young men.[9]

Henry Ward Beecher's career suggests that the consolidation of an inclusive middle-class consciousness was intimately linked to the emergence of a national "commodity consciousness," in which the ideological implications of mass production infiltrated American culture. During this period, Marx observed that the fungible nature of a commodity detaches it from its innate use value, allowing it to connote characteristics, values, and impressions that often have little to do with the product itself. Beyond the basic issue of financial access to goods, the reification of these symbolic properties—focusing consumer desire on the commodity's aura or attributes rather than the commodity itself—allows them to be used as tools of class distinction. The market's tireless quest for emotive experiences and ideas that would appeal to a heterogenous mass audience helped foster the belief that class identity could—and should—be based on personal sensibility rather than socioeconomic similarity.[10]

Henry Ward Beecher was born into one of the most prominent families of the nineteenth century, a clan long associated with the formation of the middle class. As reformers, writers, speakers, and critics, for two generations the Beechers had a hand in most of the major movements that defined middle-class culture: temperance, abolitionism, domesticity, public education, spiritualism, and popular literature, to name only a few.[11] Henry's father, the renowned Calvinist minister Lyman Beecher, was a crucial force in spreading new evangelical notions of free will and personal responsibility. The senior Reverend Beecher pioneered the voluntary association movement, regarded by historians as the foundation of horizontal class affiliations. Henry's eldest sister, Catherine Beecher, was one of the most rigorous theoreticians of domesticity as the noneconomic criterion of social status. Henry's closest sister, Harriet Beecher Stowe, was the author of *Uncle Tom's Cabin*, long considered the great masterpiece of middle-class sentimental individualism.

The national influence of the Beechers rests largely upon their close ties to the rise of mass media. But there were significant generational differences between Henry and Harriet, on one side, and Lyman and Catherine Beecher (who was a half-generation older than Henry and Harriet and more closely aligned with Lyman's ethos). Both Lyman and Catherine recognized that in the burgeoning culture of the early Republic, success would come to those who learned the arts of persuasion and exploited the power of the press. But their writings were generally doctrinaire treatises and sermons, focused on creating organizations that would nurture a superior class of Christians—in effect, a hegemonic coalition based on spiritual merit rather than economic status—who would eventually rule the nation.

Henry and Harriet began their careers in the late 1830s, when print was being transformed from a tool of citizenship into a creature of commerce, in which the goal was to sell papers and books first, and to inculcate ideas second. Driven as much by a quest for fame and financial stability as by a desire to improve society, both Henry and Harriet were deeply influenced by the new commodity consciousness. Despite their reputations as reformers, they had little interest in building formal organizations or coalitions. Instead, they used the media to create ideological and emotional effects rather than actual social bonds. In the words of *Uncle Tom's Cabin*'s famous manifesto: there is one thing "that every individual can do—they can see to it that they feel right." It was, perhaps, a less ambitious mission, but it was perfect for an increasingly diverse, far-flung population. By the 1850s,

Henry and Harriet were heralded as masters of the new mass media, reaching fantastic levels of financial success and social influence.

Both Henry and Harriet loved the spotlight. But Henry, in particular, craved the sensation of "animal magnetism" between him and his audience. He courted controversy with iconoclastic, mercurial opinions on politics, theology, and social reform. His personal life was common gossip for decades, culminating in a sex scandal that shook the soul of the country for two years. The congregation of his church in Brooklyn, New York, was the largest in the nation, numbering over 2,000, although the sanctuary held more than 3,000 spectators, at standing room only, on a typical Sunday. Tourists by the hundreds took the Sunday ferries, nicknamed "Beecher Boats," from New York City to see the flamboyant preaching of "Beecher's Theater."

Beyond Brooklyn, Beecher addressed millions of readers who would never hear him. He used stenography to reprint his sermons and lectures in a national network of newspapers, served as an editor and regular columnist for both religious and secular newspapers, and published more than thirty books, including a best-selling novel that was adapted into a hit play. As one of the most sought after lecturers in the country, he gave more than 125 lectures a year, commanding the highest speaking fees available. Near the end of his life, he lent his name to advertisements and product endorsements, but he had made himself a brand name long before.

From the late 1840s to the mid-1870s, Beecher deliberately allied himself with the "prosperity of the common people," championing causes like the 10-hour day, chastising hypocritical businessmen, and often earning the derision of the urban elite.[12] (He became more conservative on class issues after his adultery scandal of the mid-1870s.) Beecher was famous for his inconsistencies and vacillations, but he remained steadfast in his attitude toward the public. "Popular sovereignty," he liked to remark, now meant consumer sovereignty: anything of worth must be aimed at a mass market.

As one of the first modern celebrities to make a living by turning his persona into a popular commodity, Beecher offers a particularly rich opportunity to parse the relationship between mass culture and the middle class. Like many celebrities, he received thousands of letters from strangers over the course of his career. These fan letters provide a detailed picture of Beecher's audience, often describing their occupational, educational, financial, and spiritual histories. They include day laborers, carpenters, masons, ministers, farmers, mechanics, undertakers, clerks, teachers, lawyers, bakers, peddlers, manufacturers, milliners, doctors, dressmakers, and small businessmen. They come from every corner of the country, from urban areas but just as often from the West and the hinterlands of the East. Some letters convey very high levels of education and cultivation, others almost none, but they are on average literate.

The one consistent theme in the letters is sympathy—virtually all testify to an intense and intimate bond of affinity between themselves and

Beecher. The fan letter was then a new phenomenon, reflecting a crucial shift in public heroism, away from older forms of civic fame based on a record of public achievement—wars won and deeds done for their own sake. By the eve of the Civil War, renown was not a by-product, but rather a crucial component of achievement—people were famous for being famous. (As Beecher's editor once informed him, he didn't care about the length of his story, since "the eclat of a story by Henry Ward Beecher that will run for three months is just about as good for me as if it were to run four or five months."[13])

A "term used more for its resonance than its definition," sympathy dominated American vocabulary until the end of the nineteenth century as a means of conceptualizing social relations within an increasingly complex society.[14] The rhetoric of sympathy was the foundation of sentimentalism, although it often served radically different purposes. Many "genteel" speakers used the term to indicate the existence of essential cultural similarities. Alternatively, reformers conceived it as a way to create bonds across the social spectrum based on individual emotional responses. They used sympathetic identification or empathy to institutionalize the concept of individual rights and extend those rights to the disenfranchised, to those who had been discriminated against on the basis of perceived differences. Sympathy was also considered the cornerstone of powerful persuasion in writing and oratory.

Sympathy was the foundation of Beecher's career—it would be no exaggeration to say that Beecher was considered the most sympathetic man in America. Like many of his generation, Beecher grew up feeling deeply oppressed by the harsh Calvinist doctrines of original sin and divine wrath preached by Lyman Beecher and his late-Puritan peers. By the time he reached New York in 1847, Henry was eager to embrace a more cosmopolitan, compassionate ethos.

With remarkable speed, Henry shed his father's vision of God as ruler and man as miserable sinner whose only hope for salvation was self-sacrifice and fearful submission to God's laws. Instead, he preached the radical belief that love, not fear, was the basis of Christianity, or what came to be called "The Gospel of Love." Beecher shifted focus from the Old Testament to the New, recasting God from sovereign judge to loving father and placing new emphasis upon the humanizing role of Jesus Christ as a "living friend with the profoundest personal interest in me."[15] All relationships, Beecher insisted, between God and humanity and among fellow men, should be based on an individuated, personal bond of "affinity." Conversion became falling in love, instead of the total obliteration of human will, and the key motif of Christian life became fellowship rather than worship.

It would be difficult to overestimate the revolutionary impact of the Gospel of Love on American culture. It shifted the focus of Christianity from salvation in the afterworld to happiness and self-fulfillment in this world. Love and sympathy were God's tools for coping with the vicissitudes of worldly life. Unlike the reformers who counseled sympathy for the extremes of society, the poor, the ill, the enslaved—or the genteel sentimentalists who made it an implicit term of exclusion—Henry counseled sympathy for everyone, rich or poor, black or white. He offered, in the words of one newspaper editor, "a rational and affecting appeal to men to 'Put yourself in his place' and look at things from other people's point of view; to see the other side; to make allowances for differing circumstances and consequent opinions and sentiments; and so—in consonance with his theological and religious teachings—a plea for liberty of opinion with harmony of feeling."[16]

The link between liberty and sympathy was at the heart of Beecher's broad appeal. In this period of transition between an agrarian and a market economy many people were struggling to define the relationship between the prosperity of the individual and the community. Many felt the pull of the older republican ethic of yeoman independence made possible by mutualism and community solidarity. At the same time, there was strong cultural and economic pressure to adopt the new individualistic ethic of self-advancement, or what David Montgomery has called "the ideological syndrome of 'free agency,' self-improvement, and temperance."[17] It was an ideology that was belied by the difficulty of achieving independence in an increasingly integrated market economy; and that, even when successful, often increased feelings of isolation and anxiety. Speaking from his Brooklyn pulpit to a congregation in which over sixty percent were recent migrants to the city, Beecher's rhetoric of individual liberty and interpersonal sympathy maintained that it was possible to experience both personal autonomy and community feeling.

Beecher addressed an audience that felt alternately empowered and beset by the spreading influence of the market. His first big surges in popularity came during the Panics of 1837 and 1857 when he spoke extensively on the economy, captivating a population that felt acutely insecure at every level of society. Unlike many middle-class moralizers, Beecher acknowledged that fortunes were as likely to fall as rise, and that people needed a way to maintain a sense of security and self-respect in the face of these fluctuations. He spoke extensively on the pain and isolation of bankruptcy, personal hardship, and geographical dispersion. He counseled love, confidence, and sympathy as an antidote to shame and fear.

Beecher offered hope and stability to those readers, in his words, "miserably shifting from one thing to another, till the grave or the poor house gives them a fast grip."[18] At the same time, he gave a geographically and socially mobile population permission to discard ties and values that no longer suited them, insisting that personal affinity was more important than "mechanical" obligations. Jesus, he proclaimed, "comes to every man's heart to make him free—free in thinking, free in choosing; free in tastes and sentiments; free in all pleasurable associations."[19]

In dwelling on bankruptcy, economic fluctuation, and the need for interdependence as well as independence, Beecher addressed an audience shifting among proprietorship, wage labor, and salaried labor. In his fan letters, we can trace a complex relationship between the accoutrements of respectability—money, home, goods, occupations—and self-perception. Many of the letters portray a population struggling to attain modest property ownership but with limited access to cash, and thus constantly poised on the edge of wage labor. When their need for cash had grown so great that they had to give up their property, his correspondents claimed it was nearly impossible to sell their farms, houses, and shops in an economy marked by scarce credit and scarcer coin. They write of the shame of bankruptcy and the pain of losing their "pleasant" homes through unpaid mortgages. They often describe complex family relations, where kinship networks were loaned to the hilt and if one member fails the whole family is threatened. These correspondents stand as both hopeful adherents and reluctant challengers to the ethic of individualism.

William T. Craig, writing twice from Liverpool, Pennsylvania, in the summer and fall of 1875, offers a typical life history. At age 40, he has a wife and four children and is working as a clerk in a general merchandise store, "at small wages." He farmed until age 26, when he married, and then took to day labor on the canals, railroads, and local farms, often leaving his family for long periods. Eventually, he was able to buy a small tract of land and build a house and stable but was soon forced by debt to give it up. He then began "boating" lumber and coal along the rivers to Philadelphia and Baltimore ("a slavish business"), finally taking a job in a country store for four years "at extreme low wages at $200 to $240 per year, quit that business, took to cauling again like a vagabond and travelled seeking the most advantageous and profitable labor."

Now he owns a half-acre, "a sweet home," and some outbuildings, but is again away from home clerking at $275 a year, and will have to sell the house soon to pay his debts. He seeks "a BONUS of $800 or $1000" so he can pay his debts and live with his family by doing a little day labor near home for food and clothing, for "it is the utmost desire of my heart, to enjoy myself with my family and their welfare." He offers character references and declares "I use neither tobacco, nor liquor but make the best use of my earning to the welfare of my family and endeavor to lead an honest and upright life."[20]

Letters such as Craig's undermine the neat distinctions among manual and nonmanual labor, proprietorship and wage work. We can take Craig as a representative of traits traditionally ascribed to the middle class, such as small proprietorship, clerical work, and visions of domesticity and upward mobility. At the same time, he was a day laborer, a migrant manual worker with low literacy skills, near the bottom of the economic and social scale. Craig's narrative of reluctant migration, shifting fortunes, and multiple occupations is repeated throughout the letters to Beecher. In such circumstances, occupation and ownership could not be the primary term of class affiliation. Manual work, nonmanual work, and petty ownership all failed to provide Craig, and many others, with a consistent, comfortable livelihood. Moreover, given Craig's geographical instability, it is difficult to attribute his class affiliation to associations based on local culture.

What does Beecher's audience tell us about the ideological links that might unite this diverse middle class? One answer lies in Beecher's attempts to resolve, however tenuously, the fundamental tensions within the concept of "free labor." The term free labor, as the historian Eric Foner argues, "referred to two distinct economic conditions—the wage laborer seeking employment in the marketplace, and the property-owning small producer enjoying a modicum of economic independence." These contrasting conditions provoked heated debate over the freedom of free labor and its relationship to social status.

Critics of the wage system, particularly those affiliated with the growing labor movement, envisioned freedom as economic autonomy based on the equitable distribution of property. Being forced to sell one's labor treaded dangerously close to the idea of selling oneself. Champions of the wage system conceived of freedom as arising from "the noncoerced nature of the [wage] contract itself, not whether the laborer enjoyed economic autonomy." Autonomy would come from individual mastery of the marketplace rather than equitable distribution.[21]

In large part, according to Foner, it was the rise of the Republican Party that allowed these two definitions to coexist, albeit uneasily. The new Republican synthesis proposed a stark contrast between free labor and slave labor, insisting that every man had property rights in himself, rights that allowed him to sell his labor as a marketable commodity until he could acquire enough capital to become a property holder himself. Beecher was a prominent Republican orator who harbored secret presidential ambitions, and who was widely (if mistakenly) considered a founding father of the party. Although Beecher's actual political power was not great, he was one of the party's most valued propagandists. In particular, he used the Gospel of Love to give emotional resonance to the arguments of the Republican synthesis.

Beecher employed the concept of sympathy to ameliorate the tensions between the "lure of the ladder" and the longing for economic independence, community bonds, and stable identity.[22] Although he addressed himself, in his words, to "those who are struggling from the bottom to the top of society," Beecher did not counsel unwavering faith in upward mobility as the way to make sense of society. Instead, he focused on resolving the apparent contradictions between the injunction to seek both upward mobility and contentment with one's place. "We must not make the ideas of contentment and aspiration quarrel, for God made them fast friends," warned Beecher. "A man may aspire, and yet be quite content until it is time to rise."[23] The key to a happiness that transcended the vagaries of the market was not prosperity, nor was it genteel "respectability," that is, adherence to social conventions. Rather, he maintained, contentment came from the cultivation of personal character as both ends and means.

Commentators associated with the middle class commonly counseled the cultivation of character as an asset that would help one master the marketplace, and later help one get into heaven. Beecher's conception of character was simultaneously more realistic and more idealized. He maintained that, in fact, one's character is a marketable commodity, but at the same time life itself is a form of capital. As an ardent proponent of pleasure and self-fulfillment rather than self-denial, he insisted that character should be cultivated not only for trade but for personal enjoyment. Investing in the cultivation of sensibility—personal tastes, benevolent feeling, and enriching experience—provided a kind of petty proprietorship that did not repudiate the market but freed one from its tyranny. "Love is ownership," Beecher declared; "he owns a thing that understands it best, and gets the most enjoyment from it!"[24]

Beecher's concept of personal or cultural capital was meant to resolve the tension between class distinctions rather than contribute to them. "That is true cultivation which gives us sympathy with every form of human life, and enables us to work most successfully for its advancement," Beecher insisted. "Refinement that carries us away from our fellow-man is not God's refinement."[25] The accrual of cultural capital through sensibility and self-expression was specifically intended as an alternative to ruthless economic criteria or self-abnegating piety in calculating social status. Its worth was not derived only from its exchange value in the marketplace—the extent to which good character helped one make money—but also by the extent to which it allowed one to transcend economic fluctuation by providing a stable sense of identity and status. "A man is not to be known by *how much money* he has," Beecher insisted, "but by what that money is worth to *him.*"[26]

Beecher's assessment of life's worth had powerful resonance for a population constantly moving into strange new communities where their characters were unknown. It also made sense for those who found that, despite the homilies of ministers and magazines, character had little cash value in a tight economy. As one J. W. Tripp, of Marietta, Ohio, explained to Beecher after writing Beecher for a loan three weeks earlier and receiving no answer: "Perhaps you think I had better go where I am known but I do not know of but one man that has money to loan in Marrietta and he will not loan a dollar unless a man has real estate to secure him with two dollars for every one he loans." In desperation Tripp asks Beecher to lend him money, with the security of "a life insurance policy that has four hundred payed [sic] up now, in case I should stop paying on it but I do not intend to stop for every year I secure another hundred on it."[27]

Beecher's insistence that life experience was not beholden to the demands of the capitalist marketplace held appeal at midcentury for those who were themselves searching for alternatives to industrial capitalism. A remarkable letter from John W. Browning, the recording secretary of the Workingmen's Union in New York City and one of the most visible leaders in the New York labor movement at the time, makes clear that Beecher's meditations on contentment and aspiration were not dismissed as mere sentimental pap.[28]

Written on March 22, 1869, at the height of his labor activism, John Browning's letter shows that Beecher elicited strong sympathy from a man who was acutely aware that the ideology of upward mobility was more myth than reality. "I know exactly how I feel about riches and power in my present condition," Browning wrote to Beecher.

> I am a Mechanic. I am poor and I don't expect ever to be rich for the reason, as my wife says, that I am too free and cannot say no to a poor fellow who is out of work and wants to borrow a dollar or two. But I often ask are we not as happy as those who are much better off in this world's goods.

Browning speculates that he would be modest and generous if suddenly bestowed with wealth, that he would run for the state legislature and "let the people know that there are men who though not church members are at least honest enough to stand up for honest people." He continues,

> But say for arguments sake that I should be elected and finding myself worth twenty five thousand dollars, might I now say to myself, John you may never be elected to this post again. Here on the one hand is fortune and ease for winking at a little corruption when there is a great deal, and on the other hand is a return to a life of hard labor and misfortune, and chose the former. I doubt if I would do it because I have never been a lover of riches or had any desire for more than will provide for my little family and because I would rather have it said of me after I am gone: "I knew your father boy, He was an honest man. You will do well to imitate his acts and make such a record for yourself" but at the same time it is impossible to say just how I would act until tried.

Browning ends the letter on this sentiment, hoping that his musings might offer a text on "the 'consistency of human nature,'" (adding in a postscript that Beecher's "letters on labor are very satisfactory to all I have conversed with upon the subject"). Browning contemplates the lure of the ladder, and decides in the end that what determines worth is the ability to live by his own values. This is not to say that a major labor leader was "actually" middle class, but that Browning's connection to Beecher at this crucial moment in class formation reveals the depth and breadth of the utopian vision that animates middle-class identity: the faith that in an unstable economy, one could achieve stable status based on sensibility rather than income or occupation.

Even more significant than Browning's message is his urge to share his feelings with Beecher, a man he has never met and with whom he has little in common, socially or politically. Contemporary accounts agree that what made Beecher so powerful was not simply his message of compassion but the *experience* of sympathetic exchange that he created between himself and his audience. Beecher is a "cannibal," as the critic Adam Badeau observed disapprovingly: "he stirs you up in all sorts of queer intentions utterly contrary to those of your whole life; he exhorts sympathy and emotion and tears from his bitterest opponents, but 'tis all by chance."[29]

In fact, it was not at all by chance. Beecher's fan letters suggest that this idealized identification derived from his successful efforts to turn sympathy into a marketable commodity in itself. The Gospel of Love developed not only in rebellion against the oppressive theology of the past, but also in response to the new market revolution in religion.

By the late 1820s, the Calvinist denominations had been disestablished as the state-sponsored religion of the North, thrusting the clergy into an increasingly competitive spiritual marketplace. In losing their state-sponsored monopoly, Beecher and his peers were forced to compete for souls, not only with the devil but with other denominations (especially the aggressively populist sects like the Methodists and Baptists), as well as an ever widening array of secular distractions. Older preachers like Lyman Beecher lamented the loss of their traditional authority and the homogenous culture it represented. But Henry leapt at the opportunities for innovation and personal ambition offered by the new entrepreneurial atmosphere.

Henry Ward Beecher was at the forefront of a national trend in preaching that rejected dry, doctrinal analysis in favor of graphic illustrations, parables, and narrative storytelling, which would engage the imagination rather than reason. Storytelling, he explained most famously in his *Yale Lectures on Preaching*, was the only way to reach a broad, heterogeneous population. Beecher went further than most ministers, however, becoming notorious for his use of slang, jokes, mimicry, autobiographical anecdotes and confessions, and an uncanny ability to dramatize his visions through his physical presence. Beecher's stories were meant to be neither allegorical nor typological, but experiential, to spark the imagination into internalizing and experiencing these images, thus making God manifest in the individual.

Personification—or what Beecher called "the great principle of anthro-pomorphism"—was his key to the process.[30] Prior to this era, Jesus Christ played a surprisingly minor role in American Christianity. Christ was regarded primarily as a legal scapegoat within God's justice system. Beecher recast Christ as the very locus of faith. The figure of Jesus Christ, he maintained, allowed the human imagination to grasp the vast mystery of God by casting Him in human form.

The core of Beecher's preaching was that, for the average person, it was almost impossible to love God except through Jesus, and that one cannot know Jesus "until you have been intimate with him."[31] Thus the minister should, by the same token, personify Christ—"to have every part of you living and luminous with Christ"—giving Him human form to facilitate sympathetic connection between Jesus and the audience. Through mimicry, dramatic enactment, and self-revelation, Beecher used his imagination to identify with, and virtually embody, Christ, then persuaded his audience to identify with him. Beecher's efforts to be a living conduit for Christ were wildly successful. As he read from the pulpit, observed Matthew Hale Smith, "the idea that Jesus is speaking to them pervades the assembly."[32]

Beecher catapulted from popular preacher to modern celebrity by his canny use of the press. His flamboyant personal style immediately caught the attention of the New York newspaper editors, who began reprinting his weekly sermons and speeches, and reporting on his comings and goings. These reports were soon picked up by regional papers, which filled out their pages with items from the city papers. Beecher capitalized on the attention, joining the lyceum circuit, and becoming a columnist and then editor for the influential anti-slavery journal, the *Independent*. Over the course of the 1850s and 1860s, his controversial proclamations on a host of secular topics, particularly slavery and secession, brought him international notoriety.

While the *Independent* made Beecher famous, his affiliation with the serialized story paper the *New York Ledger* made him truly popular. In 1858, Beecher was approached by the publisher Robert Bonner, a pioneer in advertising and mass marketing who transformed the *Ledger* into the first form of mass media, with a national circulation of over half a million and a casual readership estimated as ten times that.[33] Like Beecher, the *Ledger* was considered *the* paper of the middle class and *the* icon of mass popularity. Already boasting a stable of famous authors, including E. D. E. N. Southworth, Fanny Fern, and Edward Everrett, Bonner offered the minister a regular column and quickly turned Beecher into a huge commercial success.

What Beecher did on stage, Bonner taught him to do on the page: to give readers who would never actually hear or see him the experience of sympathetic connection, and to get them to pay for it. Publishers in the antebellum period faced many of the same challenges as did preachers. New innovations in technology, transportation, and the organization of labor had transformed printing from an extension of local oral culture into one of the first industries capable of national mass production. Like the clergy, publishers turned to writing that engaged the private imagination and the common human condition, rather than specific, often contentious, public issues.

Robert Bonner followed this trend to its logical conclusion, founding the *New York Ledger* on the motto: "Plenty of sensation and NO PHILOSOPHY." Bonner's great insight was that, unlike oratory or local newspapers that build upon the context of a community, mass-produced reading lacked external context and thus drew its appeal from the intimate experience of reading itself. Instead of feeling connected to other readers or listeners surrounding them in the audience, mass-media readers felt connected to the authors and characters on the page. Recognizing the appeal of respectable sensationalism, Bonner built an early, extremely profitable version of brand-name recognition for his writers, pioneering the concept of the celebrity author.

Bonner's great gift was in mass-marketing. He spent enormous amounts of money to acquire exclusive contracts with well-known authors and public figures. After signing them, he then created unprecedented, lavish advertising campaigns that publicized both his new acquisition and the amount of money he paid to secure the author, offering the outrageous salary as evidence of the quality of his authors and of the *Ledger* readers' cultivated tastes. His advertisements were deliberately designed to flatter readers, often spinning humorous scenarios of elites like Queen Victoria, the Czar of Russia, and President Buchanan proclaiming their love for the *Ledger*. In a discriminating, democratic country like the United States, Bonner insisted in each issue, popularity was proof of merit.

Once under contract, Bonner directed his authors to write in a familiar, conversational tone, to develop a strong, consistent, narratorial presence by the use of direct asides and autobiographical details, and to portray themselves as in direct dialogue with an actual reader. The nonfiction columnists, in particular, were encouraged to speak on universal topics and to convey their ideas through personal stories, told in a confiding, almost gossipy tone. The columnists were advocates, above all, of "common sense" and sympathy for people's differences as well as their similarities. *Eyes and Ears*, a collection of Beecher's *Ledger* columns, was advertised in typical fashion as a volume "to form a kindly habit of judging men and events."[34] Bonner was by no means the only figure who exploited the appeal of vicarious sensation by publicizing the private, but he turned it into the driving force of successful commercial publishing. Beecher thrived on this formula of mass-marketed intimacy, riding it to international success.

Beecher's career suggests that it was the reification of social sympathy, the turning of sympathy into a commodity that could be bought for the price of a newspaper or a ferry ticket, that made it possible for ideological or "taste" affinities to *seem* more crucial to personal and group identity than structural or socioeconomic similarities. Although Beecher characterized himself as a mere conduit to Jesus and a more loving society, he laid himself open to a very real kind of commodity fetishism.

The new forms of sociability and social equality that Beecher nurtured were more ideological than actual. With a congregation of over 2,000 members, people did not join Plymouth Church to re-create the old village community that they had lost, nor did they join such a public, populist church for "fashionable" social status. It was the welcoming, sympathetic presence of the pastor that gave his audience a sense of equality and community, in direct contrast to the acutely felt social differences within and among his audience. Over and over, his fans indicate that what they craved, and paid good money for, was an illusory sensation of intimacy with Beecher himself.

It was a common cliché, borne out in his fan letters, that Beecher's audience felt they knew him as they knew their own friends and family. His correspondents wrote just for the opportunity to express their deep affinity with the minister, informing him, as did Lester Hills of Hartford, that "you are my friend in *thought* if not in personal acquaintance." They wrote with the fervor of romantic language that was Beecher's stock-in-trade. John Henry Barrows of Lawrence, Massachusetts, speaks warmly of kissing Beecher's picture, while Crammond Kennedy declares that "every time I look into my wife's face, I know that I love you."[35]

The desire for Beecher's friendship seems to have been greatest for rural readers and those isolated by illness, misfortune, or migration, whose main contact with the larger world came through newspapers. F. A. Burnam, a lonely spinster and reluctant migrant to Ohio, who claimed "respectable parentage" and had once known "home comforts," but lacks money, position, and advanced literacy, is typical. Having read a few scraps about the minister copied from the big city papers, and in need of "a *good, true friend*," she wrote to ask if Beecher would fix her up with a nice, eligible physician or minister.[36] It was this marriage of unstable economic and social position, domestic desires, and a strong response to mass media that characterizes Henry Ward Beecher's middle class.

This emphasis on ideological affinity over social circumstance is the foundation of the heterogenous American middle class. Unlike other models of class affiliation, which are horizontal and based on the recognition of shared economic interests, this vision of the middle class is structured more like a hub. Members of the "great middle class" are not joined directly through their tastes and ideologies, but obliquely through a set of central mediating icons or ideals—they measure their status through their personal identification with images propagated by popular media, rather than through direct comparison with each other.

Modern celebrities like Beecher are significant because they personify, and thus foster vicarious identification with, the flattering ethos of elevated classlessness that is the basis of most mass marketing. As a writer, speaker, pundit, and celebrity persona Beecher became the ideal middle-class self-proprietor, who made his living neither as a capitalist nor a laborer, but as a magnificent but flawed man who was justly compensated for cultivating his true self.

Scientific Church Music
and the Making of the American Middle Class

EDWARD JAMES KILSDONK

Andrew Fletcher famously commented that he would not care who wrote the laws of a nation so long as he could control the songs.[1] The early nineteenth century was marked by a dramatic change in the style of church music, particularly in the moderate evangelical churches. These churches formed the heart of the reform institutions that composed the benevolent empire, and their members formed the vanguard of the transportation and industrial revolutions while simultaneously struggling to make sense of the social and economic transformations that they were creating. Historians of nineteenth-century America have long noted the relationship between the members of the reform organizations that burgeoned after 1820 and the rhetoric of self-control and self-restraint. And recent students of manners, of the interiors of houses and churches, and of the process of personal presentation, have shown that these people defined themselves not by income or wealth, but rather by their habits and activities.[2]

Yet musicologists have only recently begun to place music into its context in the changing daily lives of ordinary Americans.[3] This paper will use changes in styles of church music and in the discourse about those styles to explore the connections between the rhetoric of self-control and self-restraint and the public performances chosen by the churchgoing individuals who formed the core of the emerging American middle class in the 1820s, 1830s, and 1840s. By comparing the new mainstream with the forms of popular church music that fell by the wayside, we can see the people who would go on to make up the American middle class selectively choosing styles of deportment and public conduct while attaching moral values to their actions.

In the eighteenth and early nineteenth centuries there were many styles of church music. Most religious groups did what they liked, and although there were occasional arguments within groups, as for example the *note versus rote* controversy in which urban Congregationalists tried to persuade rural and conservative congregations to give up improvisatory singing for tunebooks, most people did not care what their neighbors were singing, much less what people in other regions were singing. Starting in the 1820s this changed, as proponents of "scientific" music tried to convince the members of the emerging Protestant mainstream that there was one single proper musical style that should be used in churches of every denomination in every region of the country. This debate grew heated in the 1830s and 1840s, and there was an extended discourse about the nature and purpose of church music. The issue died down again during the 1850s as scientific musicians gained a partial victory. By this point, there was a mainline Protestantism that espoused widely shared notions of respectability and propriety. In this the reformers had won.

The common pattern for psalm and hymn singing in nineteenth-century America was for the words and the tune to come from different sources. Tunebooks and hymnbooks proliferated, with the contents arranged by meter and subject matter so that it was a simple matter to combine words with a tune, and then to use a different tune the next week. Although publishers aimed their hymnbooks at fairly wide markets, doctrinal and catechismal hymns were popular and necessarily limited any particular hymnbook to congregations that took a particular view of the extent of the redemption, the relationship between free will and salvation, the possibility of human perfection, and any of the other doctrinal issues that antebellum denominations used to distinguish themselves. As a result hymnbooks were, if not strictly denominational, generally limited to Calvinists, to Arminians, or to Unitarians. Tunebooks were more open: a Methodist and a Presbyterian congregation could use the same tune even though the texts they sung had been altered to express Arminian or Calvinist views of salvation. If hymnbooks were distinguished by doctrine and aimed at denominations, tunebooks distinguished themselves by the nature of their music: one might have an extensive selection of tunes for family worship and social meetings; another would be long on strophic psalm tunes for use in church services; and a third might feature a complicated composed piece at the end of the book or perhaps a wide collection of "revival songs." The combination of text and tune meant that any congregation could easily find musical selections that matched their conception of religion and their preferred form of religious worship. The music in the various churches in a locality was well known, and often affected individual decisions about which church to attend.[4]

By the second decade of the nineteenth century, there were several distinct approaches to church music in America, and they all cut across denominational lines. Prominent among these were: lining out; the old New England choirs; shape note singing; the revival songs and spiritual ballads of the Second Great Awakening; the scientific music promoted by Lowell Mason and Thomas Hastings; and the aesthetic tradition of musical performance.

"Lining out" simply refers to the practice of having the clerk or precentor read each line of the psalm or hymn aloud, following which the congregation sings it. Then the next line is read and sung, and so on through the piece. Unlike the call-and-response pattern of much African music, the precentor does not generally engage in a sustained duet with the congregation but rather states the words in a speaking voice or a rapid chant. Lining out is an efficient way to give a congregation the words to a number of hymns without requiring all to have and to read hymnbooks, and it works best when the tune is known to the congregation or is easy to pick up.

The old New England choirs, most of which grew out of the singing schools that formed the "note" side of the *note versus rote* controversy, commonly sang tunes by William Billings and the other New England tunesmiths, as well as some secular tunes rewritten to accompany sacred lyrics. They started as an attempt by Boston elites such as Cotton Mather to reform the musical practices of the countryside. These choirs were popular in the late eighteenth and early nineteenth centuries, going out of favor during the 1810s before being revived in the Old Songs movement of the 1850s.

Shape note singing also grew out of the New England choirs. The first books of patent notes were created by New England tunesmiths seeking an easier way to instruct their pupils. Unlike improvisational styles of lining out, shape notes were a printed form of music, with tunes transmitted by books and enforced by the text and not by the collective ear of the congregation. They remained an important part of the antebellum music market, and the innovation and creativity of the various schemes has made them a favorite subject for musicologists. Shape notes were, however, a printed form that was used most extensively in the West and the South, and not in the seaport cities or the scattered cultural centers of the old Northwest. By the late 1830s, urban musicians treated shape notes as a rustic makeshift that impeded proper music. Shape notes were, however, closely related to the revival music and popular traditions of sacred song.[5]

Also common in the South and West were the musical practices that had grown out of the revivals and spiritual meetings that we now refer to as the Second Great Awakening, practices that often showed strong African influences. These included the spiritual ballad, a narrative song telling of doubt and salvation, often following the narrative structure of the folk ballad it was based on. Another popular musical form took scraps of lyric or portions of the Methodist Hymnbook and combined verses to make new songs. Choruses, simple verses that contained one or two words that could easily be altered—come brothers let us meet them . . . come sisters let us meet them . . . come preachers let us meet them—were often sung for hours at a time, and were one of the many places where African influences shaped American hymnody.

In turn, the scientific music movement was originally a product of Boston culture and New Haven theology, but its ideals and practices soon spread more widely. Scientific music focused on regular harmonies, stately melodies, and on tunes and arrangements that members of the congregation could sing well if they were given a little bit of choir practice. The music tended toward cheerful tunes in the major key, and choir masters were reminded to emphasize precise enunciation, especially beginnings and endings, and proper harmonies. The name for this music, "scientific," refers to its obsessive pursuit of harmony and order, and the science or rules of musical practice that were followed to these ends. Some of the better-known compositions of the scientific musicians are Mason's "Missionary Hymn" (From Greenland's Icy Mountains) and "Nearer My God to Thee" and Thomas Hastings's "Toplady" (Rock of Ages). In some cases—Mason's "Missionary Hymn" for example—the melodic line was weakened in order to make the harmonies more regular. By writing, arranging, and performing their music, and by engaging in the larger discourse about church music and public behavior, scientific musicians were engaged in the difficult search for a regular and systematic way of displaying religious emotion.[6]

Drawing more on the oratorio tradition, and with the forms of musical performance associated with European models of professional performance, were a group of aesthetes or "amateurs of music"—people who loved music, who cared for it, and who had studied the rules and methods of European classical music. These were the proponents of high culture, and the most vigorous exponents of Romantic notions of art and beauty. They tended to discuss church music as a particular form of music, one that remained subject to the customs and rules of all other performances. The aesthetes claimed "that certain progressions of musical sounds are adapted to express and excite certain emotions of mind," and that music is an external effect that acts on the worshiper and not a particular action performed by the worshiper.[7] To them, the science of music was a means of raising emotion, and a sense of love or reverence that had been raised by church music was the same as the secular emotions of love or reverence that might have been raised in a concert hall. Aesthetes generally conflated religious and aesthetic emotions. As Lawrence Levine points out in his provocative *Highbrow/Lowbrow*, similar individuals worked hard to sacralize Shakespeare and to improve concert life in the early Republic. Unlike Levine's narrative of a top-down imposition of sacralized culture that dampened vibrant popular traditions, however, the aesthetes lost the battle over church music. [8]

There was an active discourse among Jacksonian Americans about the nature and purpose of church music. This discourse focused on matters of taste, which was inextricably linked to social class. As a result, musical decisions were driven not just by the internal qualities of the music but also by the manners and customs that became associated with the various musical styles. Church music was part of a larger aggregate of taste, and people associated particular personal qualities with congregations that preferred the various forms of music. The conflicts over church music, then, were part of a national conversation about social roles and personal identity in the era of canals, steam, great personal mobility, rapidly changing business cycles, and struggles over the meaning of being middle class.

Most prominent scientific musicians were from New England, and like many New Englanders, they moved west during the first half of the nineteenth century, bringing their culture with them. The musical form the scientific musicians created, however, was not limited to the New England diaspora. It was adopted by people in all regions of the country and it altered singing styles and popular attitudes, although it seems always to have been more of an urban than a rural phenomenon.[9] Most individuals who bought music books preferred scientific music, and this is true of the South and West where Mason made his largest sales, not just of the North and the old Northwest.[10] During the 1830s, first in Boston, then in the Ohio Valley, and then in most cities, scientific musicians decided to improve church music by teaching everyone to sing, and they convinced the public school system to add vocal music to the regular curriculum.[11]

The discourse of scientific music entered the common language. Anna Campbell of Petersburg, Virginia, wrote in her diary in 1851 about life as a newlywed when she and her husband, Charles, climbed into the rocking chair at twilight:

> *it* holding C.C. & he holding me, sometimes we amuse ourselves, & edify all within hearing, by singing duets in the most scientific manner of course, little `bo peep,' being a great favorite second only to "Cats in the cream pot" . . . [12]

"Cats in the Cream Pot" was not what Mason and Hastings had thought was proper scientific music in the late 1820s and early 1830s. Campbell's wry use of the word "scientific" indicates that she very clearly knew the difference between "Cats in the Cream Pot" and "Rock of Ages." That wry, ironic distance, however, is the most intriguing part of the family duet. It is not just that Campbell knew the notion of scientific music, not just that she parodied its call for serious and significant display of emotion and propriety. It is that, knowing this, she and her husband sang "bo peep" and "Cats in the Cream Pot" regardless, because they were fun, and because they suited the couple.

The language of scientific music was part of the cultural literacy of the middle class, like a few words of Latin or a line or two of poetry: it confirmed the speaker's class credentials. While it had been created in the 1830s in an attempt to define proper behavior amid cultured Bostonians and religious conservatives of the Middle Atlantic States, scientific music debate had, by the 1850s, come to inform the varieties of middle-class culture.

The career of Charles Grandison Finney illustrates the link between scientific music, the mellowing of revivalism, and the popularization of the tastes associated with the emerging middle class. While in his twenties, before his dramatic conversion, Finney was active in the local Presbyterian church. He led the choir and played the bass viol, an instrument commonly used in churches in the late eighteenth and early nineteenth centuries. He also regularly had been attending Methodist meetings since he was an adolescent, and had experienced their loud, uninhibited, and spirit-driven community. When he began his later career as an evangelist, he brought these experiences with him, and they were experiences that many in his audiences had also shared.

Finney's first revivals were much looser and less restrained than his later work in Boston and New York. Finney and his fellows amalgamated low-church Methodist fervor with Presbyterian organization, the plain speech of the law and new businessmen of the canal district. These revivals used new forms of music. The most popular tunebook in upstate New York during the middle part of Finney's revivals was Charles Leavitt's *The Christian Lyre*, released in 1830. Leavitt took melodies from popular tunes and attached them to new lyrics, as Luther had done during the early days of the Reformation. Leavitt's *Christian Lyre* went through more than eight editions in the first six months, and was praised by New Haven's prickly *Christian Spectator* for the musical options it offered in the new revival meetings.[13] He presented his tunes simply, often using only the tenor and bass, and because of this simplicity and because so many of the tunes were familiar from other contexts, his book was a readily accessible source of music.

Leavitt's popularity quickly brought forth imitations. Of these, the most popular was *Spiritual Songs for Social Worship,* the 1831 collaboration between Lowell Mason and Thomas Hastings, aimed at the same revival market as Leavitt's work. It also featured more restrained tunes, more complicated harmonies (using three- and four-part arrangements fairly regularly), and Mason's talent for putting together attractive little melodies that had a modest range and could be sung by most people. As early as 1834, the *Christian Spectator* was condemning Leavitt for using tunes whose secular associations destroyed the religious effect of the hymns, and calling for a more chaste and serious music such as that in *Spiritual Songs*. Mason and Hastings used "better" tunes and harmonies, but in practice the musical effect was not always what they had imagined. The more complicated harmonies and less frothy tunes in *Spiritual Songs* were not always easier to manage, and the "imperfections" in the harmony that resulted from partially skilled singers attempting works above their skill level were surely quite painful to many listeners, but the book still appealed widely.

Both Hastings and Leavitt tried to convince Finney to accept their books and use them in his services. He refused, arguing that music was a distraction to a revival. For Finney, as for many other Americans in the early 1830s, music was not an essential part of the religious experience. It was important and it had its place, but the shared experience and concentrated focus of the revival meeting was the proper center for religion. This was one way in which Finney's revivals were distinguished from the Methodist, Baptist, and Cumberland Presbyterian revivals of the South and West. There, music was a central part of the excitement of the great social meetings, while the hymn lyrics often served as a catechism for the new converts.

During his long attempt to break into the ranks of Eastern ministerial respectability, Finney calmed down his revivals and disavowed some of the rhetoric of his more radical upstate New York colleagues; he also grew more sympathetic to scientific music. When he established his Brooklyn Tabernacle, he invited Thomas Hastings to become its musical director. Hastings played the organ, led the choir, edited New York's *Musical Magazine*, and used his prominent position to help him sell more tunebooks. Based on the statements in his tunebooks, it appears that Finney's congregations in the mid-1830s were singing compositions that did not remind the congregation of secular lyrics, that were arranged to move at a moderate pace and with a solid and singable harmony, and that were instructive rather than exciting.

While young Finney was regarding music as a diversion and a distraction from the real purposes of a revival, Lyman Beecher was working with Lowell Mason in Boston, and Mason's choir grew into something of a Greek chorus. Mason would lead bursts of song or brief interludes that—sometimes in the middle of a sermon—would invite the congregation to reflect on the point just made, and would try to bring the point home to the listeners by phrasing the same moral or religious lesson in musical terms.[14] Mason and Hastings agreed that the musical director was more of a subordinate minister than a professional musician, and should be chosen for his piety and religious effectiveness and not for the mere quality of the music he was able to lead. Scientific musicians like Hastings and Mason were public moralists, using the press to urge their peculiar combination of strong piety and regularized music. They were not alone; the upwardly mobile Methodists who wrote for the *Methodist Quarterly Review* made similar arguments, as did young men from most other denominations.

By the 1840s, the language of scientific music, which called for proper harmonies (according to the musical rules laid out by Handel and Haydn), for melodies without easy secular associations, and for arrangements that emphasized the words of the hymn and not the surrounding musical embellishments, became the dominant language in discussion of music. This music was directly linked to the notions of deportment and control pushed by the reform associations. As one scientific musician put it while creating a usable past for himself, "At first sacred music was simple *melody*, but as the intellectual began to predominate over the sensual, and as men began to act more from reflection than impulse, the need of *harmony* began to be felt, and the art became more severely scientific."[15] Scientific music appealed to those who stressed reflection over impulse, who were in search of consistency and regularity in their actions and their self-images, and the acts of writing and singing harmony were taken as proof that the musician was able to restrain his or her "sensual" nature.

Scientific musicians did not have the rhetorical field to themselves. Much of their energy was devoted to improving congregational singing by improving the choir, so that it might both serve as an example and also guide the congregation in their singing. Primitivists distrusted choirs in general, and low-church Baptists could accuse choristers as well as ministers of being hireling priests and impersonators of devotion.[16] Aesthetes made a more complicated critique of the work of the scientific musicians, based on the low quality of much of the actual music. Lowell Mason urged the use of a choir because it was a more efficient way to get the congregation to sing. A large choir, consisting of everyone who wanted to belong, was guaranteed to have people in it with ugly or discordant voices. These people were sure to ruin the music, and thus prevent the congregation from being edified. If they could not have a truly good choir, such as the quartets and small ensembles found in Philadelphia and Boston, then the aesthetes would rather the entire congregation bellow in unison. Either would be better than hearing a half-trained choir singing a new tune each week, especially when "all is perpetually new, cold, and purely scientific."[17] These criticisms arose because the scientific musicians had been too successful at wedding their notions of proper music to a particular form of performance. The word "scientific" quickly came to mean not only the practice of harmony and the rules of music, but also the use of a choir in church. It did not matter what music the choir was singing or how it was singing it; it was a choir and so it must be "scientific."

The fairly modest musical demands that the scientific musicians placed on their singers were subject to ridicule, as were their claims to consistency and order. The discourse cut both ways. One classic example occurred in Cincinnati in 1836 when James Freeman Clarke, Boston intellectual and Transcendentalist leader, commented on the choir led by Timothy Batelle Mason:

> Let us enter yon handsome church. It is vaulted, gilded, carpeted, and cushioned. It is filled with gentlemen and ladies, fashionably attired, and extremely punctilious in their behavior. The Minister announces

the hymn. There is a general rustling of leaves and dresses. The flock are finding the place. The performer, with a business air, has taken his seat at the organ. Orchestral fingers are hastily running up and down the index, of the Handel and Hayden [sic] collection. Their hearts are on bars and rests, tones and semitones. They are amateurs; great at solos, catches and rounds. They are resolved to make an impression. It is wonderful what responsibility can rest on the shoulders of a few. Scientifically doth the symphony die away. Involuntarily do the faces of the amateurs lengthen, for great is the importance of Time. Expression, too, is essential. Not a *forte* or a *piano* must be neglected—not an interval miscalculated. What a concentration of mind doth the science of music demand! What reputation is at stake! What a moment for an amateur! Down goeth the wand of the leader. The assembly rises. The rustling of silks goeth up, and the first line of the hymn is lost in the noise. A hundred fans are in motion; a hundred eyes are curiously raised to the choir, and then employed in wandering about the room. Their books are open in their hands, but where is the voice?—Where is the mighty chorus of praise, that should burst from that large assembly? Are they all silent? Are they indeed permitting a band of musicians to sing alone, while they amuse themselves with the sounds, as if it were made but to tickle the ear, and relieve the tedium of a worship, which to them is a mere form?[18]

For Clarke, scientific music was a false reform that emphasized the mechanics of singing while destroying the natural language of the heart. It led to formalism of the most pretentious sort, with both the choir and the congregation interested in display—in fashion—rather than in meaningful worship.

Scientific musicians worked hard to teach their choirs the mechanics of good singing, and with some concentration many of the choirs learned to sing well. But there was a cost, and that cost is at the center of Clarke's critique. The music may have been more precise, but it was not spiritual. Scientific musicians talked a great deal about the need for truly religious sentiments in the choir and in the choirmaster. For Clarke, however, these sentiments were constrained by the lamentable nature of a choir singing for itself, a congregation listening for enjoyment. In neither case were religious sentiments being expressed. The concert hall had come to church, and crowded out the worship.

The charge that worship was devolving into mere formalism was not new. More significant was the style of formalism that Clarke identified: the "business air" of Timothy Batelle Mason as he sat down at the organ. Music was a business for Mason; it let him live comfortably while pursuing something he enjoyed. The "business air" combined with the concentration that the choir applied to the scientific mechanics of the music suggested that the emphasis that scientific musicians placed on process and order sometimes appeared to be a regimented, narrow-minded, paint-by-numbers sort of music. This regimented music, joined with the "fashionable dress" and "punctilious manner" of the inhabitants of this urban church, suggested that these individuals were desperately trying to act properly. To Clarke's eye they failed miserably.

Clarke was a product of the New England intellectual aristocracy, a Harvard classmate of Oliver Wendell Holmes, Sr., and like Daniel Drake and the other members of Cincinnati's elite, disconcerted by representations of the new middle-class people as they struggled with their deportment.[19] For Clarke, deportment was not about dress; internal and personal refinement did not come automatically with a vaulted church and cushioned seats. Despite the claims of the musicians, in the end, scientific music also was captivated by the allure of fashion.

Most of the people participating in the public debate over church music were men. Most church members and attendees were women. This gender ratio extended into the choir loft, where a large female contingent had a chance to publicly participate in worship services. When men complained in print about the idle and superficial tunes sung by the choir, and about the way that the choir was more interested in personal display than in religious worship, or even when they recognized that singing in the choir was the attraction that brought many young people into the church on a Sunday, their complaints suggested that they were not happy at the style and manner of the young women in the choir. Part of the subtext in all discussions of church music, and especially in discussions that invoked fashion, was whether the collective voice of the church should speak with a male or a female timbre.

Many Americans were apprehensive about being thought fashionable. Display for its own sake, or to impress others, was the emblem of the secular world. This sentiment was most pronounced among Methodists and Baptists, where popular tales circulated in which fashionable observers at religious meetings were overcome by the spirit but were unable to experience conversion until they divested themselves of their finery. Told and retold in Methodist class meetings and love feasts, in Baptist gatherings, in Finney's revival sermons, in preacher tales and autobiographies, and most likely around the kitchen table as well, these stories all emphasized the spiritual danger of a concentration on outward finery at the expense of the inner adornments.[20]

Fashion was display. Fashion was vanity. Fashion was purely superficial. And, most important, fashion was counterpoised to sincerity. Understanding the discourse of fashion and sincerity lets us understand what exactly was at stake in discussions of church music and in the decisions that church members were making as they decided who should sing and what should be sung during worship. On the one hand, people were engaged in self-display during worship services. Getting dressed up in "Sunday go to meetin' clothes" implies a level of self-conscious self-presentation, which in the end blurred the line between using dress to show respect for the presence of the divine and using dress to show respect for the social occasion. If western ministers struggled to keep their gentlemen from stretching out on the benches to sleep, from talking during the prayers, and from chewing tobacco in church and spitting on the floor, it was from an awareness that some manners and decorum generally were appropriate for religious assemblies. Fashion, display, and decorum were constant concerns.

The 1830s and 1840s were full of worries about the nature of performance, the moral dangers of having secular or theatrical performers leading prayers from the choir loft, and the need to find a hymnody that was appropriate for sacred time. By the 1850s, two traits emerged. Many of the louder or tawdry musical styles had slipped away. Here the scientific musicians had won. On the other hand, secular tunes were back in the churches just as they had been in the 1820s. By the 1850s, people knew who they were and how they were expected to act in church, and they were then able to relax their musical guard: popular tunes with religious lyrics were making their comeback in churches and religious meetings across the country. Some churches took Stephen Foster or waltz melodies and adopted them for the service. This also was not what Mason and Hastings had had in mind, and they were exasperated when waltzing churches described their music as "scientific," and their choirs as respectable. Scientific musicans were more successful at defining how a song should be sung than declaring which tunes were appropriate to church services, and although popular tunes kept coming back, lining out and disharmonious singing were far rarer in the 1850s than they had been in the 1810s.

Clearly people were aware that their actions in church had larger social significance. Fashionable clothing, rustling fans, and the like were aimed at one's neighbors as much as or more than they were aimed at the divine. Similarly, musical choices were made in a climate that gave moral, aesthetic, and social dimensions to tunes and harmonies. Lowell Mason, Thomas Hastings, and the other scientific musicians argued that a music of controlled harmonies and easy melodies was the best way to show both sincerity and good taste. They articulated a personal style that promised to resolve some of the tensions of the market economy, and then attached that style to a particular set of musical performances. In doing so, they gave the emerging American middle class a reason to choose a distinctive performance style. And, by establishing scientific music in the schools, they taught this style to subsequent generations of urbanites. As a result, scientific music not only became the dominant style of, and discourse about, church music for the rest of the nineteenth century, but it also led new generations of the middle class to internalize the values that the scientific musicians had extolled.

Secularization Reconsidered: Chautauqua and the De-Christianization of Middle-Class Authority, 1880–1920

ANDREW CHAMBERLIN RIESER

Ministers," wrote journalist Walter Lippmann in 1914, "are as bewildered as the rest of us, perhaps a little more so." Given the historical context, it was a startling observation with terrifying implications: that as Americans faced industrial strife and the specter of European war, they would find their religious leaders paralyzed and confused. Lippmann linked society's future to a regime of disinterested technocrats whose authority rested on the cognitive superiority of science. Only the rigorous application of scientific management principles, Lippmann suggested, could save society from disintegration.

Historians have often gravitated to Lippmann's *Drift and Mastery* for its insights into the spiritual crises of modernity. My intent, however, is to place the Lippmann-esque connection historians have drawn between modernity and secularization in a critical light. By focusing on the cultural experience of participants in the Chautauqua movement between 1880 and 1920—mostly native-born, Protestant Americans who rarely identified themselves as working class or wealthy—we can highlight the importance of religion in shaping middle-class identity at the cusp of modernity. Chautauqua and other quasi-religious movements survived the rise of a secularized, managerial elite; indeed, far from casting about in bewilderment, they seemed to flourish during the height of the organizational revolution of the turn of the century. This riddle points us to a vital but long-ignored field of exploration: how have religious beliefs and institutions helped to shape the organizational revolution? While many have identified *secularization* as the leitmotif of early twentieth-century public culture, I argue that historian David Hollinger's term *de-Christianization* more accurately describes the shifting terrain of moral authority during this era.[1]

The Uses of Secularization

We turn first to the theory of secularization and its echoes in the scholarship treating of the American middle class. Mid-twentieth-century historical scholarship considered health fads and the rise of consumerism—harbingers of secularization in subsequent revisionist interpretations—as colorful but unintended consequences of religious freedom and prosperity.[2] Americans in the Progressive Era, the argument went, were too preoccupied with immigration, labor strife, and corporate trusts to worry about a few mind-cure zealots, theosophists, and advertising hucksters. With little to contribute to the ever more violent conflict between participatory democracy and the coercive impulses of middle-class "status anxiety," these *dramatis personae* rarely appeared on the stage.[3]

Since the 1960s, as consumerism and legal precedent have sharpened the boundaries separating religion and public space, the uncritical reliance upon secularization as a tool of interpretation—or an assumption underlying other arguments—has grown increasingly common. Robert H. Wiebe's masterful *The Search for Order* paved the way for a deeper understanding of the middle-class cultural experience by linking the collapse of nineteenth-century agrarian values to the rise of "an aggressive, optimistic, new middle class" of technocratic managers.[4] His portrait of a society coping with the transition from a traditional to a modern economy contained a hidden narrative of secularization. Wiebe's dichotomies—traditional versus modern, rural versus urban, personal versus impersonal—mirrored the shift from *Gemeinschaft* (natural will, oriented to the collectivity) to *Gesellschaft* (rational will and individualism) theorized by late nineteenth-century sociologists Max Weber and Emile Durkheim.[5]

American disciples of Weber had long since applied modernization theory to explain changing middle-class social customs, moral norms, and religious practices. For Lippmann, the twilight of traditional society and its "simple rules of a village civilization" ushered in a frightening age of spiritual uncertainty. "Our souls have become disorganized," he wrote, "for they have lost the ties which bind them." And American sociologist Thorstein Veblen was so convinced that "economic causes work towards a secularization of men's habits of thought" that he confidently (and wrongly) predicted the collapse of organized religion among the classes exposed to modern industrial processes.[6] "It is among those who constitute the pecuniary middle class and the body of law-abiding citizens," he wrote, "that a relative exemption from the devotional attitude is to be looked for." In addition, the theme of secularization remained very much alive through the 1960s in the work of sociologists Talcott Parsons, Thomas Luckmann, and Peter Berger. When one considers that *The Search for Order* appeared during something of a renaissance of Weber studies in the American academy, Wiebe's decision to exclude religion and culture from his analysis is all the more striking.[7]

Other historians stepped in to make these connections explicit. In an impersonal, mass society, argued Warren Susman in 1979, nineteenth-century virtues of sacrifice, duty, and integrity no longer made sense. A new ideal of self, popularized by the growing legions of self-help authors, advertisers, and public relations experts, exalted the value of outward charisma, the cultivation of a magnetic personality, and self-realization. "The vision of self-sacrifice began to yield to that of self-realization," Susman concluded.[8]

In 1981, T. J. Jackson Lears's *No Place of Grace* provided important insights into how the new culture helped to preserve class hierarchy.[9] He attributed the frenzied search for natural or premodern sources of authentic experience at the turn of the century to the need to win the "'spontaneous' loyalty of subordinate groups to a common set of values and attitudes." "Modernization was not a neutral or impersonal process," Lears wrote "it was primarily furthered by the dominant social groups who stood to benefit, however indirectly, from corporate expansion." In later publications, Lears stressed the role of advertising and mass culture in creating "a new and secular basis for capitalist cultural hegemony."[10] As with Wiebe, secularization was crucial to Lears's analysis. He defined it, in Lippmann-esque terms, as a "cultural strain" expressing "a loss of the gravity imparted to human experience by a supernatural framework of meaning."[11] And because of the persuasiveness of *The Search for Order* and *No Place of Grace*, an unexamined narrative of secularization was deeply implanted into the cultural history of the middle class.[12]

The myth of the secularizing middle class is nowhere more evident than in William Leach's *Land of Desire*. To "a considerable degree," argued Leach in 1993, "no religious tradition" had the power to resist seductive neon advertisements and retail window displays. The resulting "new culture" was "unconnected to traditional family or community values, to religion in any conventional sense, or to political democracy." Yet this sweeping assertion appears to be called into question when the reader learns that Leach's main protagonist, Philadelphia retail magnate John Wanamaker, was a teetotaling Presbyterian who read the Bible constantly, founded and taught at the Bethany Mission Sunday School, decorated his stores with crèches during the holidays, and financed several urban revivals staged by his friend Rev. Dwight L. Moody. Undaunted, Leach maintains that Wanamaker's religious beliefs served a psychological role as a crutch to justify his worldly success, providing him with the "moral authority" to "sanctify what he was doing." This way of coping with the new commercial order, Leach concludes dubiously, is "the way most other middle-class Americans dealt with that order and still deal with it today."[13]

The struggle to reconcile sacred and worldly obligations is a truism of

American religious and social history. Wanamaker's quandaries were not dissimilar to those faced by colonial-era merchants and antebellum industrialists. In our effort to expose the inner workings of class formation—to "denaturalize" the middle class, in current scholarly parlance—we must not fall prey to the temptation of simply dismissing those aspects of a subject's life that seem incompatible with our preconceptions of modernity. If we treat religion as the psychological by-product of a presupposed drive for material acquisition, we render a distorted critique of the cultural experience of the middling sorts.

Granted, there is much to critique. Despite four decades of scholarship on the rise of managerial hegemony, religion never lost its salience in the mythos of the American middle class. As late as 1976, the foremost encyclopedia of United States history defined *middle class* as "the embodiment of the 'American Way,' with its dedication to business, emphasis on ambition, faith in progress, and devotion to the pervasive influence of the Protestant ethic."[14] The seeming permanence of such deductive logic, the continuing mythology of the God-fearing, middle-class American, and his stubborn unwillingness to secularize, as predicted by modernization theorists, provides a rich field for the examination of the process by which capitalism reproduces itself in a liberal state.

Students of the *fin-de-siècle* middle class have much to learn in this regard from historians of religion. Reports of the death of religious conviction, they remind us, have been greatly exaggerated. "Out in America's heartland," Lawrence Moore observes, "religion seemed healthy by all external signs." During the early twentieth century, Protestant denominations attracted the newly assimilated and upwardly mobile, while in the cities, Catholic churches swelled with new immigrants from eastern and southern Europe. In addition, the effects of technology were ambiguous, as radio church services competed with parishes but the automobile placed more churches within commuting distance. The fundamentalist schism attracted legions of urban working-class and rural conservatives, many of them deeply dissatisfied with the watering down of Christianity by modernist theologians and politicized preachers of the "Social Gospel."[15] As Jon Butler has observed, the failure of the Social Gospel to make good on its promises of social renewal—or worse, according to Susan Curtis, its eventual degeneration into a provider of goods and services barely distinguishable from for-profit commerce—does not necessarily correlate to the decline of religion. In the largest cities, where middle-class exposure to liberalized creeds and consumer aesthetics was most direct, Christian denominations either held steady or flourished. In a rejoinder to Lears, Butler suggests that the late nineteenth-century spiritual crisis "transfixed only effete and unimportant intellectuals and that the age of the new American city should be best known for a remarkable advance in institutional religious commitment."[16]

If so, the question around which studies of the middle-class experience have traditionally revolved—"What happened when the cultural authority of the nineteenth-century Protestant elite declined?"—ignores important aspects of the experience of ordinary, non-elite middle-class Americans. The question more likely to elicit new knowledge of the culture of the middle class is "Why did the American middle class remain so religious?"

Traditional religion and the organizational revolution converged most directly in the proliferating numbers of middle-class voluntary associations and reform societies. Adorned with churchly titles such as the Salvation Army, Woman's Christian Temperance Union (WCTU), and Young Men's Christian Association (YMCA), these institutions adopted the latest business techniques to achieve their respective missions. Thoroughly modern in many ways, they formed the vanguard of the church's renewed competitiveness in the face of multiplying secular diversions. The YMCA and YWCA, for example, stubbornly refused to shed their divine missions while reshaping Christian brotherhood and sisterhood to meet the needs of modern bureaucracies.[17] Of course, there is no disputing that the liberalization of Protestant theology and the rise of advanced marketing techniques, made necessary by overproduction, created an atmosphere conducive to what Leach called a "culture of desire." Nevertheless, how widely this new ethos was accepted, how much it enlarged the cultural authority of its makers, and whether it reveals evidence of secularization (as opposed to de-Christianization or religious pluralism) are matters of potentially fruitful investigation. As the example of Chautauqua suggests, the erasure and redrawing of the boundaries separating the sacred and secular realms—and not simply absorption of the one into the other—helped shape what it meant to be middle class between 1880 and 1920.

The Chautauqua Movement: Useful Knowledge and Its Critics

As one of the foremost institutional embodiments of the Social Gospel, the Chautauqua Movement—a complex matrix of overlapping institutions that provided a platform for education, reform, and piety—is a useful point of departure. Although rarely mentioned by contemporary academic historians, Chautauqua's centrality to middle-class culture was conventional wisdom among discerning witnesses. "No one can understand the history of this country and the forces which have been shaping it for the last half century," insisted sociologist Richard T. Ely in his autobiography, "without some comprehension of the important work of that splendid institution that was, and is, Chautauqua." Declared the *New York Times Magazine*, "He who does not know Chautauqua does not know America." Though not everyone approved of its solutions, few questioned Chautauqua's importance in sacralizing middle-class responses to the dilemmas of modernity.[18] "In these days of growing secularization and materialism," wrote historian Herbert B. Adams in 1897, "Chautauqua is a good object lesson in what might be called a religious survival or revival in concrete, wholesome, visible ways."[19]

For Chautauqua's co-founder, Methodist Bishop John Heyl Vincent (1832–1920), Chautauqua was fueled by the conviction "that life is one, and that religion belongs everywhere." "All things secular are under God's governance," he insisted, "and are full of divine meanings." Even science could be "brought to the support of Christianity." Unconcerned about the objections such views might raise in a post-Darwinian age of technology and theological liberalism, Vincent pressed forward. As early as the 1850s, Bishop Vincent predicted that the great evangelical awakening would mature into an educational movement. An ex-circuit rider himself, he valued the camp meeting as a proselytizing tool; but he was convinced that the "malicious clamor" and untidy outbursts accompanying the penitent's entrance into the Kingdom would be gradually replaced with a more orderly "cultivation and strengthening of the moral and religious principle. . . ."[20]

In partnership with Ohio industrialist Lewis Miller (1829–1899), Vincent realized this prediction in 1874. In search of a summer retreat for Methodist Sunday school teachers, Vincent and Miller discovered Fair Point, a Methodist camp meeting site on the shores of Lake Chautauqua in far western New York. At its core, Chautauqua, as it came to be called, was an "outdoor university" taught by professors from the University of Chicago and Johns Hopkins University (among others), combining Bible study with courses in science, history, literature, and the arts. For the more casual vacationers, gate fees funded an eight-week summer calendar of sacred music, calisthenics, domestic science classes, and a lecture program of Social Gospel–minded missionaries, politicians, preachers, prohibitionists, and reformers.[21]

Vincent's fusion of the sacred and secular included a political element. Chautauqua's intellectual atmosphere produced a flowering of proto-Progressive sentiment before the turn of the century. At Chautauqua, reformers constructed a cultural consensus that might meet the challenges of rapid industrialization, urbanization, and immigration. Most Progressive causes, including compulsory education, child labor legislation, food and drug inspection, conservation, and public hygiene found their way—somewhat haphazardly—into Chautauqua's lectures, sermons, and publications. Jane Addams's appeal for sympathy and understanding might share the stage with Willard F. Mallalieu's "March of the Anglo-Saxon," a speech by Josiah Strong on responsibilities to "the heathen world," or a John R. Commons diatribe on the "inroads of alien stock." On economic issues, presentations by William Jennings Bryan, Terance V. Powderly, Richard T. Ely, and Edward Bemis outnumbered those by proponents of strict laissez-faire principles. But when renowned Social Darwinist William Graham Sumner served up his usual quip at Lake Chautauqua—"if you ever come to live in a socialist society, make sure you get on the committee"—the audience laughed.[22]

Those who completed a four-year home reading course called the Chautauqua Literary and Scientific Circle (CLSC) received their symbolic

Entrance to Shelbyville Chautauqua Assembly, Shelbyville, Illinois, circa 1909. COURTESY OF THE SHELBY COUNTY HISTORICAL AND GENEALOGICAL SOCIETY.

diploma at an elaborate commencement ceremony. One CLSC member in Georgetown, Texas, a doctor, led the argument for the socialization of transportation during a debate in 1890, concluding that "he was inclined to the opinion that state ownership was the best solution of the vexing problems connected with the operation of the [railroads]." Later that evening, a woman quoted approvingly from Edward Bellamy's best-selling book *Looking Backwards*: "The author compared their conditions to a coach which some had to pull, while others sat on cushioned seats enjoying the ride, while occasionally giving vent to the expressions of their sympathy for those who toiled in their traces."[23] Ideas about the need for proactive governance spread in "a moderating way," reflected the New Dealer Rexford Tugwell, whose mother was an avid Chautauquan. "Even a mild sort of socialism was given a hearing in the literature going out to the Reading Circles."[24]

Consistent with the egalitarian undertones of evangelical Christianity, Vincent's Chautauqua Idea linked religious faith and democratic progress. "The right of the ballot brings with it the need of general intelligence," he wrote; and Chautauqua would provide the tools for a growing populace to better exercise their rights.[25] But we should be careful to define democratization in context. For Vincent and his supporters, democracy did not mean freedom from religious duty, moral order, or respect for property. Rather, it rested on allegiance to fixed moral and ethical laws. "There are two freedoms," insisted a fellow Chautauquan, anticipating Isaiah Berlin: "the false, where a man is free to do what he likes; the true, where a man is free to do what he ought."[26]

As the founders of Chautauqua, Vincent and Miller claimed membership in a strata of educated, white, mostly Northeastern elites known variously in the scholarship as the "Genteel Tradition," "Best Men," "moral guardians," or "Victorian connection."[27] Troubled by the spiritual implications of science and the problem of maintaining social order in a growing capitalist society, they shared an optimistic faith in the ability of men and women to arrive voluntarily at fixed moral truths and act accordingly. Cognizant of the revolutionary potential of shifting moral authority from the church to the individual, Victorians insisted that social order should be maintained by the enlightened governance of society's "best" people capable of selecting the "best" culture for mass consumption. As Vincent put it, "Let them read the same books" and "observe the same sacred days—days consecrated to the delights of a lofty intellectual and spiritual life." This cocksure didacticism occasionally manifested itself in a refusal to accept the increasingly pluralistic nature of American democracy. Vincent, for example, raised the specter of popish domination in a virulent anti-woman's suffrage diatribe in 1884: "Too many people vote at present . . . Romish authority which now dictates Patrick's vote, would control Bridget's."[28]

Ironically, Chautauqua's inchoate liberalism, embodiment of participatory democracy, and respect for alternative views within its limited moral boundaries resonated with those whom Vincent hoped to keep on the margins. In the 1890s, Catholic and Jewish groups created their own Chautauqua assemblies, unaffiliated with the "mother Chautauqua," in Plattsburg, New York, and Philadelphia, respectively.[29] By appropriating Chautauqua's patriotic discourse for themselves, these groups rejected Vincent's exclusive definition of good citizenship and declared their intent to converge with the mainstream on their own terms.

Chautauqua flourished in ways its founders and critics could never have imagined. Consistent with his self-image as an evangelist of education, John Heyl Vincent inaugurated the first Chautauqua Literary and Scientific Circle (CLSC) in 1878. More structured and ambitious than previous reading clubs and literary societies, the CLSC offered a four-year course of reading, structured discussion sessions, and correspondence exams. Chautauqua reading circles popped up wherever middling folk yearned for self-improvement. Over the next four decades, 275,000 enrolled students and hundreds of thousands of *ex officio* readers were exposed to the "college outlook." Nearly 50,000 passed exams and graduated. The CLSC mimicked the formal education process, right down to its elaborate graduation ceremonies and symbolic diploma. The lack of vocational training was, of course, the whole point. Vincent's early opposition to women speakers, his celebration of women's maternal qualities, and his frequent clashes with Susan B. Anthony, Carrie Chapman Catt, and Anna Howard Shaw earned him a national reputation as an opponent of women's suffrage.[30] The CLSC, Vincent hoped, would educate the housewife while strengthening the home as a refuge from the ills of industrial society. As Chautauqua made "one's own house the centre of the whole world of science, literature, art, and society," society would reap the benefits of enlightened motherhood without exposing the mistress of the domestic realm to the dangers of college. Moreover, Vincent insisted, education should not facilitate material acquisition, but should reveal insights into the "Word and Works of God."

Yet Vincent never fully controlled Chautauqua's political culture. Despite his hard-line stand, Chautauquans generally favored woman suffrage. And despite his exertions on behalf of the Victorian conception of home, the collective experience of the CLSC widened horizons, gave rise to new perspectives, and suggested priorities undreamed of by its conservative founder. The CLSC membership, well represented in all regions except for the South, was 85 percent female, 99 percent Protestant, and so thoroughly white that the administrators of the program did not see the need to include race as a response in their application questionnaire. Between 1882 and 1891, only 22 percent of the male members of the CLSC could be classified as working-class and agricultural (i.e., farmers, firemen, conductors, millers, and mechanics), with the remainder of the occupations generally considered to be the preserve of the middling sorts (in order from highest representation to lowest: clerks, ministers, teachers, merchants, students, bookkeepers, lawyers, doctors, and manufacturers). The figures for female CLSC members show a disproportionate number of teachers.[31] At the height of the movement, nearly as many women received CLSC diplomas as graduated from U.S. colleges. To the women of Katytown, wrote novelist Zona Gale, "the C.L.S.C. came not as a process, but as a power."[32]

The few women's historians to examine Chautauqua have noted this irony. Observing the overwhelming majority of women in the CLSC roll books, they stress the CLSC's role as a "conduit for feminist ideas," imparting to women the "ideological and intellectual tools to claim new authority in the Progressive Era." In Chautauqua, as in the WCTU and YWCA, middle-class women extended the obligations of motherhood and homemaking into the social sphere, thereby transforming domesticity into a powerful argument for heightened political influence.[33] Religious belief remained a vital source of meaning for the architects of the emerging feminist consciousness.[34] We should not forget that the CLSC's appeal was to an exclusive strata of white, Protestant, middle-class women—a group poised to leverage its class and racial status against the inequalities of gender. More, this was a group with access to the credit, law, and advanced business techniques of industrial capitalism. Women rarely spoke openly of how Chautauqua's administrative hierarchy, financial workings, and adherence to *Roberts Rules of Order* trained them for entrance into competitive labor markets in education and business. Still, a nexus of religion, class, and race positioned white clubwomen to assume the advantages, at least in a limited fashion, of the organizational revolution.

Among intellectuals, Chautauqua did not fare so well. While millions of middling sorts flocked to what Theodore Roosevelt acclaimed "the most American thing in America," avant-garde authors and cultural rebels recoiled in horror. Chautauqua popularized everything they opposed: Victorian prudery, feminized religion, and a cultish allegiance to all ideas European. "One never gets to believe in the proper destiny of woman," complained Rudyard Kipling while visiting Chautauqua in 1890, "until one sees a thousand of 'em doing something different." A different masculine objection came from another outsider to the Chautauqua scene, Boston intellectual William James. "I long to escape from tepidity," James wrote to his wife from the assembly. Utopia, he discovered, was boring. In an effort to create a place free from the trials of industrial life, Vincent had created a "middle-class paradise" bereft of the conditions of competition and struggle ("human nature *in extremis*") which, in James's view, gave rise to the best in creative accomplishment and made life significant. James found himself wishing for "something primordial and savage," for "heroism and the spectacle of human nature on the rack."[35]

As long as the national movement grew, Chautauquans could abide the occasional barb from male members of the new intelligentsia. Chautauqua focused its recruiting efforts on scholars still operating in the Whig paradigm, older academics whose dual faiths in religion and progress had not been distracted by the new biblical scholarship or the turmoil over Darwin. The "living teacher" who could guide students through "the labyrinths and the steeps of knowledge" was a critical figure in Vincent's vision.[36] And for advocates of university extension like Herbert Baxter Adams of Johns Hopkins University, Chautauqua presented an opportunity for summer employment, jobs for their graduate students, professional networking, and the broader dissemination of their work.

But if Chautauqua embraced academia, not all scholars embraced Chautauqua. In order to sharpen the boundaries of the scholarly canon, some academics in the 1880s and 1890s distanced themselves from Chautauqua's priggishness, flowery rituals, crowd-tested conventions, and—as some male academics saw it—feminine superficiality. In some cases, Chautauqua emerged as the *vox popula* against which academics defined their professional identity as objective social scientists.

Merging with Modernity:
Religion, Commerce, and the Independent Assemblies

To be sure, Chautauqua's social profile shrank as the knowledge professions (academics, teachers, librarians, and archivists) developed rigorous new standards, streamlined practica, and rationalized categories of knowledge. Chautauquans cleaved to the Renaissance ideal of a broad-minded mastery of arts and sciences, even as that ideal lost salience in the wave of specialization and professionalization. But if a Chautauqua education brokered little respect among intellectuals and technical specialists, Chautauqua's institutional innovations secured its place in the organizational revolution. For Chautauquans were remarkably successful at forging alliances with the sources of local bureaucratic authority.

Chautauqua's successful (if temporary) adaptation to the new institutional fabric of turn-of-the-century America rested upon the so-called "independent Chautauqua assemblies." In addition to its powerful annunciation of a relatively inclusive ethos of moral uplift, the great strength of Chautauqua lay in its decentralized organizational structure, made possible (or necessary) by the rising demand for respectable vacation resorts. In keeping with the larger trend in Protestant thought, Vincent and Miller embraced the summer vacation as a fact of modern life and made it an integral part of their broader mission of spiritual and social renewal. Leisure was encouraged, so long as it was self-improving and productive.[37] The idea of a lucrative (yet moral) tourist attraction spread quickly. By 1900, more than one hundred towns across the country held assemblies on grounds resembling Vincent's original Chautauqua. Like the original, many took over preexisting Methodist campgrounds.

The independent Chautauqua assemblies took root and flourished on narrow tracts of land where the class interests of ministers, boosters, streetcar owners, and railroad executives overlapped. Chautauqua brochures described these spaces as a blend of pastoral purity and urban sophistication. Installing a Chautauqua assembly was in many ways the perfect compromise between another church (provident but unprofitable) and a secular resort or industrial factory (lucrative but morally objectionable). Seeing Chautauqua as a means to both moral and economic ends, boosters issued bonds to raise funds, bought land, incorporated themselves as nonprofit institutions, built hotels and auditoriums, and hired speakers and personalities to attract vacationers from nearby towns and cities. Spending sprees enriched local construction companies and distributors. Railroad companies, seeing an opportunity to spur passenger traffic, offered land, cash, advertising, revenue kickbacks, specially built train stations, and excursion fares as incentive for communities to relocate their assembly close to the rails. In exchange, some railroads secured free admittance passes for their employees.

There was, of course, nothing new in the sight of sacred organizations jockeying for advantage in the commercial economy. In the sacred space of the Methodist camp meetings, "the culture industry and religion learned from and adjusted to each other."[38] Theirs is a story not of alienation, marginalization, and defeat, but of new strategies to preserve the delicate equilibrium between sacred and secular space. Methodist camp meetings flourished during the so-called "Holiness movement," a midcentury revival of John Wesley's concept of "entire sanctification" in which a penitent who surrenders to God's grace is cleansed of corruption and is henceforth "so far perfect as not to commit sin." In the late nineteenth century, as the townships adjacent to the camp meetings prospered, the Methodist elders encountered new challenges to their authority over the religious landscape. Many of these religious enclaves were annexed by their municipal neighbors, gaining basic services but losing their nonprofit (and hence nontaxable) status. With larger crowds came more concessionaires; retailers, ever more numerous, allied themselves with the interests of the railroad; and before long, this coalition of shopkeepers and railroad executives would challenge the elders' prohibition against the running of trains on Sunday, which the Methodists felt disturbed the peace and calm of Sabbath observances. Increasingly, the elders found themselves in the role of carping reactionaries to the "progressive" relaxation of strict sabbatarianism.

Chautauqua offered a workable solution, and many of the elders jumped at the chance. The reasoning went something like this: convert the camp meeting into a Chautauqua and let the trains bring crowds all weekend; immerse them in the best that the culture industry can offer, the most ennobling thoughts, the most praiseful entertainment; remain vigilant against immorality. In this context, Chautauqua's growing appetite for dramatic impersonators, musical revues, and popular plays reflected the softening of the Methodist hierarchy's opposition to the stage.

The independent Chautauqua assembly, seemingly schizophrenic in its ability to house ideals of Protestant uplift and coarse real estate motives under the same roof, reveals much about the changing cultural experience of the middle class. It shows us how, in Christopher Evans's terms, "social Christian principles moved beyond churches to interpenetrate larger social-political institutional structures."[39] In our effort to assess some progressives' skepticism about the individual's capacity for self-rule and the mania for efficiency and expert control, we should not overlook their equally powerful faith in popular education, participatory democracy, and Christian citizenship—as Jane Addams put it, "Paul's formula of seeking for the Christ which lieth in each man."[40] Chautauqua's popularity, despite the upturned noses of William James and some academics, suggests as much. Far from simply rendering religion vulnerable to the expanding consumer culture, the Chautauqua's version of the Social Gospel reassured Americans that they could import many of their religious beliefs into realms often viewed as secular, such as municipal governance and popular entertainment; further, that the summer vacation, a child of industrial growth and a sign of the expanding middle class, would mature within the boundaries of religion.

In addition to its impact on political and social discourse, religion's influence on the use and aesthetics of commercial and residential space must not be minimized. According to Emily Raymond in 1885, Chautauqua was a "Mecca" where "many thousand pilgrims" went for "truth and inspiration." As if to clear up any doubts of God's immanence in the assembly's sacred enclosure, the makers of the original Chautauqua in New York carved a three-dimensional scale model of the Holy Land into the lakefront, just yards from the bathers. An even more startling inscription of a biblical myth system into the middle-class landscape could be viewed at the railroad-owned Chautauqua in Rome City, Indiana. Its featured attraction was the "model car," a scale model of Palestine in plaster of paris, complete with

*Park of Palestine, circa 1900.
In this remarkable mix of religious, leisure, and industrial
space, the scale model of the
Holy Land, built in the early
1870s, is visible in the foreground. The beach is immediately to the left. Beyond the
ditch in the foreground, representing the Red Sea, the institution's power plant is running
at full steam. In 1903, this
castlelike structure would be
converted into the Men's Club.*
FROM THE COLLECTION OF THE
CHAUTAUQUA INSTITUTION
ARCHIVES, CHAUTAUQUA, NEW
YORK.

mountains, cities, and rivers, and exhibited permanently on a bright yellow
flatbed with the words G.R. & I. RAILROAD COMPANY emblazoned in
black letters across the side. If the Holy Land could fit on a railcar, then anything was possible—even a drive-in church.[41]

It was one thing to reconcile biblical iconography with the railroad. Rec-
onciling religion with the newest technology of corporate production—
advertising and public relations—would require more effort. When this reli-
giously oriented movement of popular education took on the characteristics
of a modern corporation, it rendered itself vulnerable to both sacred and secular forces. Chautauqua's success as a player in the culture industry meant
that its influence would forever be limited by its market share. And in the
first two decades of the twentieth century, its market share fell precipitously.
There are many reasons for the decline of the Chautauqua assemblies. Just as
it stepped in to assume the churches' welfare burdens, the semiwelfare state
socialized Chautauqua's civic function as a clearinghouse for useful knowledge. The rise of public health programs, university extension and summer
schools, and state teachers' licensing boards reflected both Chautauqua's
success as an advocate for the Social Gospel and its increasing ineffectiveness
as a medium of mass education. Furthermore, Chautauqua's daughters
rarely followed in their mothers' footsteps. Seeking direct avenues to political influence, younger feminists left the CLSC for groups aligned with the
General Federation of Women's Clubs. In the early years of the century,
many CLSCs were annexed as the educational arm of women's clubs.[42]

Finally, Chautauqua's reputation for respectability diminished in the early years of the century when for-profit lyceum organizers appropriated the Chautauqua name for their network of mobile "circuits." Using aggressive sales tactics, one-sided contracts, and a carefully orchestrated "tight booking" system, circuit Chautauquas hastened the decline of the independent assemblies and elicited a new backlash among educated elites. To modernists like Sinclair Lewis, the circuit Chautauqua, with its "animal and bird educators" (i.e., pet tricks), William Jennings Bryan lectures, inspirational speeches, sentimental plays, and crude wartime patriotism, symbolized the shallowness of middle-class culture. Despite ridicule from the urban avant-garde, the circuits launched the careers of numerous performers and served as vital links to the outside world for some 6,000 small towns. After a precipitous fall in attendance in the late 1920s, the last tent show folded in 1933.[43]

Even in decline, Chautauqua's formula of Christian citizenship stamped its imprint deeply up on the emerging corporate aesthetic. As the circuits forced independent assemblies into receivership in the 1910s, municipalities and cottage associations took over. The assembly's middle-landscape charms made it valuable real estate. Land developers saw profits in its winding streets, attractive landscaping, and proximity of railroad and streetcar lines; even more, Chautauqua's reputation for respectability seemed consistent with the emerging suburban ideal. Chautauquas did not endure their conversion to suburban (or ex-urban) residential neighborhoods without conflict. Legal covenants still prohibited drinking, card playing, and music, prompting one cottager to insist in 1904 that "the hide-bound laws must be loosened a little." To preserve their tax-exempt status and low rent and gate fees, owners' associations often resisted internal improvements to the assembly infrastructure. This prompted complaints from trustees and casual visitors alike. One correspondent to the original Chautauqua assembly in 1900 described the Cottage Holders' Organization as "a class of people who have banded themselves together like a pack of pirates to make every dollar they can by taking boarders."[44]

By that point, the dialogue was largely between factions within a white, middle-class consensus, spoken in the language of individual property rights and increasingly shaped by a managerial stratum of real estate professionals.[45] But even as Chautauquans organized in ever more demanding professional regimes, they would not be forced to relinquish their fundamentally religious worldview. The loyalty demanded of them by the professional-managerial strata and the larger system of class relations it represented channeled spiritual stirrings into de-Christianized—but still spiritually and often theologically driven—institutional structures. The Rev. Shailer Mathews, a professor of religion and a dean of the divinity school at the University of Chicago, spent twenty-two summers at Chautauqua devising, in essence, a de-Christianized mode of moral authority suitable for the suburban middle class. In the "modern social order," he argued in 1914, as if reacting to Walter Lippmann's dire warnings about the acids of modernity, "God uses human agencies to bring men and himself together."[46] Historians have too often mistaken such examples of religious adaptation as evidence of the rise of a secular, managerial order. But the reality is much messier. Although Shailer Mathews and the Chautauquas faced an increasingly de-Christianized public culture, religious competition and spiritual striving continued to play vital roles in the preservation of middle-class authority.

Conclusion: De-Christianization and the Middle Classes

Chautauqua's vitality until 1920 suggests that we must be more cautious in our reliance on such concepts as "modernity," "rationalization," or "professionalization" to explain broad changes in the politics of culture between 1880 and 1920. It is not only a matter of modernity acting, religion reacting. Rather, religious organizations and motives were deeply ensconced in the organizational revolution. The decline of the Chautauqua assemblies did not necessarily mean the collapse of Victorian moral order in the face of professionalization, or the replacement of a decrepit, evangelical middle class with a new, managerial one. Arguments posing a model of class hegemony must come to grips with the rich tradition of resistance and pluralism within the middle-class oeuvre. Modern class relations were shaped not from the ashes of an imagined Protestant moral consensus, but carved into an ambiguous environment of demographic change and religious pluralism. Subsumed under the contested civic ethos of Americanism and consumer prosperity, religious ideals would manifest their influence on a pluralistic public culture stealthily, through interest-group advocacy and through the individual choices of conscience.

Chautauqua's example, therefore, reminds us of the polyglot nature of middle-class identities, the possibility of multiple middle classes vying for supremacy, the emerging (but rarely monolithic) power of the managerial ethos, and the dense intertwining of class with religious, national, ethnic, and gender affiliations.[47] The continuing diversity of America's ethnoreligious and spiritual movements today suggests that despite efforts to manufacture moral consensus on a religious basis—or, alternatively, to impose a secular social order based on the alleged "decline" of religious consensus—the pluralistic effort to derive transcendent meaning from the modern world would not be so easily controlled or predicted. The crisis of modernity led to manifold avenues of inspiration. In a century in which the corporate stewardship of the individualized pursuit of private desires increasingly defined the cultural experience, Chautauqua, social Christianity, and religious faith more generally lost many of their claims as symbols of social progress while gaining new appeal as an alternative discourse of personal liberation, communal life, and public virtue.

THE MIDDLE IS MATERIAL

Mark Twain Carte de Visite.
COURTESY OF THE MARK TWAIN
PROJECT, THE BANCROFT LIBRARY.

Cover. THE LADIES' HOME JOURNAL,
FEBRUARY 1912.

Tocqueville observed in the 1830s that the middle classes declared
their faith in democracy in America by means of personal dramas. The act of
buying goods, for instance, more than utilitarian, assumed the significance
of a symbolic performance. Acquiring clothing or furnishing a parlor
aroused in the user an awareness of status and the power of self. Eighteenth-century historians have identified a burgeoning "consumer society"
among middle classes in the Anglo world. The appearance of refinement,
scrupulous attention to body manners, and patterns of spending within the
context of rising standards of living have received the recent attention of
historians such as C. Dallett Hemphill, Richard L. Bushman, Carole Shammas, and Robert E. Gallman.[1] Karl Marx's conclusion that a bourgeois
"commodity fetish" spurred greater material consumption does not begin
to explain the material as well as psychological needs and desires motivating
the middle classes to expand the nineteenth-century marketplace for everyday goods.

By the 1840s, observers were surprised and impressed by the speed with
which the material economy was democratizing. George Fisher for one
commented in his diary:

> At any little village in New York . . . are well-stored shops and artisans
> in abundance who can minister to the wants not merely of comfort,
> but of elegant refinement. The canal brings everything from New
> York. They can build you a house with every modern convenience
> and improvement, make every sort of carriage and harness, paint,
> paper, and furnish in excellent style. . . . The astonishing thing is the
> rapidity with which it has been done.[2]

Ordinary middling folk confirmed Fisher's point. Consistently they listed
each domestic purchase with an exact accounting of cost in their diaries and
journals, while documenting the spreading abundance of small domestic
articles including foodstuffs, kitchen utensils, appliances, furnishings, and
reading matter. Catherine Beecher's *Treatise on Domestic Economy* (1841)
cautioned that every housekeeper needed applied knowledge of current
technologies in order to succeed in the modern household. Beecher
included information about stoves as well as businesslike skills for managing schedules and budgets.

According to the census, national wealth in consumer durables jumped
from $800 million in 1850 to $6.5 billion in 1880, and assets in nonfarm
residential structures from $2.1 billion in 1850 to $11.6 billion in 1880.
Walt Whitman, returning to Brooklyn from Washington during the Civil
War, observed that "the great cities and towns through which I passed look
wondrously prosperous—it looks anything else, but war—every body well
drest, plenty of money, markets boundless and of the best, factories all
busy." By 1880 the wordsmith in Whitman rose to the occasion:

In modern times the new word *Business* has been brought to the front, and now dominates individuals and nations. . . . Business, not a mere sordid, prodding, muck-and-money-making mania but an immense and noble attribute of man. . . . Business shall be, nay is, the word of the modern hero.[3]

The following two essays highlight the historical importance of small-scale technologies and their representation in visual culture among the middling classes. Picturing people and things increased apace with the marketplace. Photography, first in the form of daguerreotype and soon as the cheap and mass-produced carte de visite and stereograph, was an immediate success. Seeing was believing; in its realism, the picture appeared to tell no lies. Following the California gold rush, young people throughout the nation in pursuit of a better life, wealth, and opportunities were leaving home in unprecedented numbers. The demand for album-size collections of a "likeness" for keepsake, display, and family legacy was insatiable. Sam Clemens's daguerreotype as a printer's apprentice on his fifteenth birthday in 1850 was only the first in a library of self-images. By the later 1860s, when Mark Twain was securing his success as a writer, he was slipping his most recent cartes de visite into all his outgoing correspondence.

In "Cartes De Visite Portrait Photographs and the Culture of Class Formation," Andrea Volpe moves inside the photographer's studio. She describes in detail the mechanics of the posing stand as well as studio techniques used by professional photographers to create the effect of a controlled body displaying respectability. Moreover, she interprets the changing meanings of the pictured card for personal identity as well as the making of a middle-class culture awareness. The multiplying consumers of the cartes de visite were witnessing an innovative representation of themselves as a collective type. Accompanying the new sciences of phrenology and physiognomy in the nineteenth century, a visual culture of standardized body forms was making claims for social authority. The image of the chemically produced middle-class portrait was immediately discernable as different from the corresponding photographer's mug shot of the primitive, insane, and criminal. "Cartes de visite," Volpe summarizes in conclusion, "were made possible by the perfecting accuracy of photography, the corrective embrace of the posing stand, and the desire for self-discipline and increased visibility among the emerging middle classes."

Pictured trade cards and trade catalogs traveled widely through the domestic landscape: packaged with every product sold in the marketplace, distributed by manufacturers and businesses at exhibitions, sent to individuals through mail order. Incorporating high production values by the later nineteenth century, the trade pamphlets and broadsides were designed to highlight the quality of a product by means of images set in relationship to information. In "Public Exposure: Middle-Class Material Culture at the

Turn of the Twentieth Century," Marina Moskowitz probes the complexity of emerging marketing processes through the making of a familiar, intimate, and homelike atmosphere in the furnishings of public space. The private home had traditionally been the site for an education in the middle-class way of life. As part of a middle-class marketing initiative to raise the quality of life of the many, sites now expanded to include the new public settings in which daily life was occurring, "railroad cars, hotels, restaurants, clubs, apartment buildings, schools and other spaces." Moskowitz focuses on the personal services provided by the distribution in public places of silverplate flatware and bathroom fixtures. Expectations for the relationship between the private and the public were shifting into reverse. "It was more," she argues in conclusion, "than specific technological innovations or styles of decorations that provided the parallels between domestic and public spaces." Middle-class demeanor, values, and principles for organizing place were now visible in office buildings and hotels, and marketers advertising in popular domestic journals like *The Ladies' Home Journal* were betting that ordinary people would gradually introduce the innovative conveniences into their homes. Middle-class standards of consumption had completely come out of the closet, for everyone to witness and experience.

Cartes de Visite Portrait Photographs and the Culture of Class Formation

ANDREA VOLPE

In his 1852 novel, *Pierre, or the Ambiguities*, Herman Melville's Pierre offered this commentary on daguerreotype portraits and the standardization of identity and image production suggested by photography at midcentury:

> Whereas in former times a faithful portrait was only within the power of the moneyed, or mental aristocrats of the earth. How natural then, the inference, that instead of, as in old times, immortalizing a genius, a portrait now only dayalizes a dunce. Beside, when everyone has his portrait published, true distinction lies in not having yours published at all. For if you are published along with Tom, Dick and Harry, and wear a coat of their cut, how then are you distinct from Tom, Dick or Harry?[1]

By contrasting the ability of the painted portrait to memorialize a subject with the daguerreotype's ability to momentarily represent the ordinary, Pierre sees that photography could multiply the visual marks of distinction to the point of formula, and in the process visually transform distinction into its opposite. His observation can also be read as marking the emergence of a standardized, conventional social and visual identity that came to distinguish the respectable, middle-class body in the middle decades of the nineteenth century.

Pierre's insight foreshadowed the rise of a new form of photographic

Anonymous Carte de Visite. COURTESY OF
HISTORICAL COLLECTIONS AND LABOR
ARCHIVES, PENN STATE.

portraiture, cartes de visite, that by 1860 would replace the daguerreotypes of which he spoke. Just two and a half by four inches in size, cartes de visite were the first form of commercial portrait photographs made as multiple paper prints. Cartes were invented in Paris in 1854 by A. A. E. Disdéri, and capitalized on the bourgeoisie's interest in self-representation. They first gained notice in the United States in 1859 and had become the preeminent form of portrait photography by 1861. "Cartes de visite" translates as "visiting card," although there is little evidence that the little portraits were used literally as visiting cards. They were, however, incorporated into rituals of social exchange, display, and collecting, all of which locate them in the culture of a coalescing American middle class. The genre, as one account in the photograph trade papers described it, formed a "deluge," and the sheer volume of images prompted the first photograph albums.[2] Cartes sold for a dollar a dozen, or for as little as a dime each, and their economy, both for photographers and sitters, sustained their popularity through the end of the 1860s.[3] Detractors criticized urban, high-volume portrait studios as "picture factories," implying that the mass production of conventional portrait photographs yielded correspondingly indistinct social identities.[4]

Cartes are viewed traditionally as a conventional and derivative genre unworthy of scholarly consideration because they were made in such great number, by far too many now-nameless, or minimally skilled, photographers to be of significance. But conventionality, rather than serving as evidence of aesthetic shortcoming, provides historians with evidence of collective forms of expression with wide appeal. The ubiquity of cartes points to what Jane Tompkins calls "cultural work": popular and conventional texts should be read "as attempts to redefine the social order" and for the ways they "[tap] into a storehouse of commonly held assumptions, reproducing what is already there in typical and familiar form."[5] Cartes are conventional, in other words, not because they are the product of ill-trained photographers, but because the genre's visual formula offered a template for individual and collective identity that resonated with the social and economic lives of nineteenth-century Americans.

The rising demand for photographic portraits was grounded by the portrait's place in American cultural history and galvanized by the expanding market economy of antebellum America. Portraiture had appealed to Americans as a representation of economic and cultural status since the early Republic, when finely painted portraits were embraced by the urban gentry to visualize their position in the social order. In the antebellum Northeast, self-trained itinerant limners traveled through the countryside, "creating countless images from stark black-and-white silhouettes to colorful full length-oils" for a growing circle of farmers and craftsmen seeking visual representations "to consolidate their position in a new bourgeoisie," explains David Jaffee.[6] By the 1840s, traveling portraitists were trafficking in the new technology of photography, offering first daguerreotypes and then ambrotypes (both techniques yielded single, unique images) as cheaper and more accurate portraits for the growing ranks of the middling sort. Historians often view this effect as evidence of photography's "democratization" of visual culture from the 1840s onward, as if the dispersion of photographic portraits merely expanded, but did not change, the essential cultural work of portrait images. The ability of cartes de visite to be printed even more cheaply and as multiple copies could be read as further evidence of such a democratizing impulse. But in the 1860s, the mass production of cartes did more than simply make the portrait more accessible: the expanded availability of portrait photographs quickly reduced a portrait sitter to conventional pose and formulaic form, and by so doing helped produce a collective middle-class body. So rather than consider visual culture as simply a progressive mirror onto social formation in this period, this essay considers the constitutive role of cartes de visite portrait photography in the culture of class formation.

"There is little question," Michel Foucault writes in volume one of the *History of Sexuality*, "that one of the primordial forms of class consciousness is the body."[7] Foucault identifies the body as a form and product of class consciousness because of its central position in modern forms of power. Social, political, or economic power is not exercised through prohibition, but through discipline, and its component techniques of observation, administration, correction, improvement, normalization, examination, and surveillance. Bodies, in this account, become both the subject and object of knowledge and are themselves deployed actively as agents of power in social formation. Foucault's conceptions of power and the body are, as Patricia O'Brien writes, "an alternative model for writing the history of culture," because rather than reducing "culture to the product of social and economic transformations" or reading cultural forms that transparently convey the events of the past, his method proposes that the visual and textual rhetorics, deployments and strategies of culture must themselves be the central subject of historical inquiry.[8]

This emphasis on the agency of cultural formation is crucial to my reading of cartes de visite in the cultural work of nineteenth-century American class formation. As the literary historians Wai Chee Dimock and Michael Gilmore formulate:

> Our sense [is] that the boundaries of class are unstable, that the experience of it is uneven, that it is necessary but not sufficient for the constitution of human identities. . . . Our desire [is] to build on these limitations, to use the analytical inadequacy of "class" as a rallying point, a significant juncture from which to rethink the concepts such as "identity," "explanation" and "determination." We are interested . . . in the category of class less as an instance of "reality" than as an instance of the "made-real," less as an empirical description of social groups than as a theoretical enterprise, an attempt to attach a cause and give a name to "something which in fact happens (and can be shown to have happened) in human relationships."[9]

In this conceptualization, class is a fundamentally unstable category that is "fixed" and stabilized by representational practices, such as literature or visual culture. It is through representations, in other words, that social formation is visible. Because photographs employ what Foucault calls "the view point of the objective," they are particularly powerful in making class seem an unquestionable fact.[10] Against this framework, cartes de visite photographs can show us how middle-class identity was made more visible and, as a result, "made real" in the 1860s. The carte de visite photograph combined the traditional associations of portraiture with the visual authority of mechanical realism, which allowed the portrait photograph to be read as "proof" of social position, when in actuality the carte is evidence of the cultural production of such claims.

In the United States at midcentury, the American middle class embraced a wide range of cultural forms—education, religion, moral reform, and child rearing among them—that created a distinct physical body associated with economic and social position. Bodily pedagogies, directed by school books, hygiene, and self-culture manuals as well as phrenological magazines, instructed readers on how to manage the individual body and read the social body. Social and cultural historians argue that these preoccupations with appearance, manners, and bodily discipline offered ways to cope with the rapidly changing political economy of nineteenth-century America and ultimately came to be seen as the signature forms of middle-class culture. Control over the body was not only the focus of lessons in self-improvement, it was also a crucial element for establishing social and cultural authority: the shape and behavior of the physical body itself enacted class formation. Contemporary concern with bodies as expressions—indeed embodiments of class—suggests that cartes de visite can and should be read for the ways in which the popular photographic genre helped to visually invent a respectable body. This approach suggests the contribution of cultural history to the study of social formation.

The primary mechanism for producing the body as it appeared in cartes de visite were the posing stands used by photographers to hold the body in place during long exposure times. Stands shared a common design, in which a waist-high metal rod was anchored to a broad wooden or metal base. Two adjustable clamps extended from the spine of the stand, one to rest against the small of the back, and one to hold the neck. Ideally, the posing stand was hidden from sight, behind a woman's billowing skirts or a man's carefully crossed legs, but was often left visible. The limited-light sensitivity of glass plate negatives and cameras put real constraints on photographic practices, but these mechanisms did not single-handedly determine the poses in which sitters were put before the camera. To notice the legs of the stand peeping out from behind a sitters' legs is to be reminded that posing stands were an exoskeleton for the aspiring middle class: an exterior, visible mechanism by which bodies were held and molded. These stands were both brace and caliper. As instruments, they suggest the correcting of individual bodies and the comparison and measurement among them championed by comparative anatomy. If we consider the posing stand not as a simple technical tool, but as an instrument of culture—the most palpable mechanism for imposing ideas of respectability onto the body—then it becomes possible to trace the visual construction of a respectable *type*. The repeated application of the stand imposed a standardized bodily form on the individual body, and by doing so, visualized a generalized form associated with upstanding social position.

Together posing stands and cartes de visite exemplify what Foucault called a "positive mechanics" for producing a sort of body and type of social identity through visual and textual representations that naturalized and empowered the respectable body by subjecting it to heightened visibility.[11] This positive means of disciplining, and thus producing, the middle-class body is evident in directions from the photographic trade press on how to best pose sitters, as well as in commentaries on and evaluations of the visual formulas that emerged among commercial photographers as cartes de visite

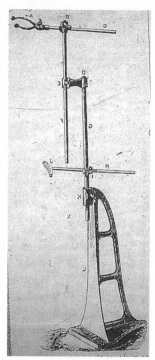

LEFT: *Anonymous Carte de Visite.* COURTESY OF HISTORICAL COLLECTIONS AND LABOR ARCHIVES, PENN STATE. RIGHT: *Posing Stand.* PHILADELPHIA PHOTOGRAPHER, MARCH 1868.

portraiture took shape as a genre. The posing advice of trade journals published in New York and Philadelphia worked as a "literature of correction," in which posing advice instructed photographers to use the posing stand as an instrument of correcting and controlling improvement.

The trade press depicted operators as eager to control and eager to please, caught between their desires for an efficient pose and a satisfied sitter. The problem of posing was most immediately a practical one for photographers: how to get a sitter to sit still?[12] Photographers came to rely on the stand to enforce their hold over the body, all the while working to distract sitters from the control implied by its cold embrace. To let a sitter take a pose without the stand threatened disaster for the photographer and subject alike. The photographer would fail to obtain a satisfying pose and would lose time and money to an unhappy customer. At the same time, overuse of the stand would immobilize sitters so completely that they could not move, drawing too much attention to the instrumental authority of the procedure. Posing often began with the photographer arranging the sitter "in an attitude entirely devoid of ease," only to "delude him, or her, into sickly contortions of countenance they facetiously denominate 'looking pleasant.'" Editors and advisers pointed to stiff poses as evidence of the "tyrannical officiousness" of the photographer and pleaded with them to emphasize comfort over control.[13] *Tyrannical officiousness* shows contemporary awareness of the power dynamics and the particular form of bodily discipline embedded in the production of cartes de visite, as photographers were instructed to walk the fine line between flattering and restraining their sitters.

In the hands of a capable operator, the cold arms of the posing stand were felt not as instrumental coercion but as comforting control during a procedure that was compared to the anticipation of sitting in the dentist's chair.[14] Photographers were instructed to use the stand to secure "complete rigidity so as to afford complete immobility" of the sitter so that their efforts yielded a "natural, graceful and harmonious pose."[15] The tension between control and comfort evident in directions to photographers reveals how management of the body depended on authoritative use of the stand that would also conceal its interventions.[16] Photographers coerced their sitters into the embrace of the posing stand by complimenting and composing them. Photographers were advised to use the posing stand to find a position "perfectly free from all constraint," even as instructions for using head rests and posing stands emphasized a tight hold on the sitter's body: "First, raise the main rod the proper height and tighten the screw; let it remain; then put your back-rest to the sitter, crowding him forward as much as you please, and tighten the screw. This holds him firm," advised one manual.[17]

The literature of correction, intended to aid photographers and ease the problems of posing, helped produce a respectable body by standardizing poses. "The majority of photographers have two or three different positions in which they submit all their models, whether tall or short, long or small," concluded *Humphrey's* in 1863.[18] Standardized compositions prevailed to

Photography Studio Interior. HARPER'S NEW MONTHLY MAGAZINE, SEPTEMBER 1869.

such an extent that, by 1865, the journal complained that "the conventional pillar and curtain" used in so many cartes de visite had become "untolerable."[19] Standard posing was bemoaned as a shortcoming of the profession; "Is it absolutely necessary that every member of the family should lean on the same pedestal or stand staring over the same balustrade?" asked one critic, noting hopefully that diversity of pose would not be a bad thing.[20] If a photographer relied too heavily on the posing stand, John Towler feared that portraits would reveal the sameness produced by the "silly clinging to uniformity in the position of the sitter."[21] Edward Wilson, editor of *The Philadelphia Photographer,* chastened his readers: "None of you are so ignorant as to be told that it is not well to choose a stereotype set of positions, and make all your sitters assume one or the other."[22] But photographers did not resort to predictable poses out of ignorance. Just the opposite—formulaic poses were the product of careful study and the literature of correction offered in the trade press.

When photographers used the stand to fit their customers' bodies into prescribed poses, they were imposing on each body common ideas of what a particular type of body should look like. The practical concerns of commercial photography joined with the positive motivations of photographers to naturalize the way posing stands were used to enforce bodily attitudes. Directions for shaping the body that informed the iconography of cartes had thus become indispensible and seemed the only possible and productive way to pose a sitter. Ultimately both the rhetorical formula of photographic advice and the visual composition of cartes de visite became so familiar as to be accepted as fact. The posing stand standardized and multiplied the respectable body through an aesthetic defined by comforting control; the resulting portrait photograph was an enactment of, and representation of, what Foucault refers to as "membership in a homogeneous social body" and what historians call the middle class.

Cartes de visite visualized the respectable body in a social climate in which the signification of the body and assumptions of its transparency weighed heavily on the national consciousness. The popular sciences of phrenology and physiognomy, alongside the new sciences of comparative anatomy and physical anthropology, provided the visual and intellectual framework for reading a sitter's body and for deploying the posing stand. Posing stands were the most explicit instrument used to gauge a sitter; they enacted a visual and intellectual vocabulary for reading and producing the body based upon ideas of physical essentialism, visual transparency, and social classification. Scientists from Samuel Morton to Louis Agassiz based their work on visual inspection and the self-evident authority of physical bodies, where "a glance might suffice to read an individual's character and destiny," explains Cynthia Eagle Russett.[23] The result was a social and physiological determinism that used the shape of head and the proportions of limbs to chart the progress of human society from the primitive to the civilized, from the slouched to the upright. Together sight and body were the basis for an essentialism that found meaning in typologies and comparisons, rooted in the assumption that the respectable body could be distinguished on sight from the primitive or criminal body.

The trade press endorsed the terms of comparison, hierarchical social organization, and visual evaluation of the human figure articulated by these popular and scientific theories of the body.[24] Photographers agreed that physical and visual generalization was the key to evaluating and posing their sitters.[25] The doctors, scientists, and physiologists who dispensed directions for managing the body inhabited the same intellectual universe as the journal editors and manuals authors who directed photographers on questions of pose.[26] Photographers shared with physicians the belief that the entire human frame represented a more accurate index of inner qualities than the head and face alone. "The whole body manifests the character, or comparative strength of a man's intellectual faculties," wrote reformer Dr. John Ellis. Photographers expressed similar views. The directive from *Humphrey's* was that "the entire figure, from head to toe," was "the most suitable of any to express the complete resemblance of the individual, from expression of the physiognomy down to fine attitude and proportion."[27] Belief in the natural transparency of the body, and photography's visual realism, figured heavily in the poses that photographic writers recommended to their readers. Titles from the trade press such as "Anatomy, Phrenology, and Physiognomy and Their Relation to Photography," "A Hint for Posing Your Sitter," and "Defects in Our Sitters," suggested that the visual vocabulary of physiognomy was the key to reading the body.[28] "Attitudes, dresses, features, hands, feet, betray the social grade of candidates for portraiture. The picture tells no lie about them," penned Oliver Wendell Holmes in his 1863 discussion of the card photograph in *Atlantic Monthly*.[29] Praised as "photographic aids to physiognomy," the visual authority of cartes were at once shaped by these assumptions about bodily transparency and used to verify the accuracy of the theories they represented.

The Philadelphia photographer M. A. Root advised that bodily position should conform to the sitter's social position.[30] The traffic in sitters made quick study of the human form a necessity, so that the transparency of the body was naturalized as a visual truth that would be self-evident to a photographer. A visual reading of physical form started with running "your eye over the subject, regarding the dress, its color, style and trimmings . . . all the time studying the face and expression."[31] Once the photographer had sized up the face and dress of a sitter, he should then turn his eye to the body, turning it this way and that, in order to find the best view, just as a sculptor modeled clay or a painter rendered a figure.[32] This practice was one of constant measuring and comparison, with the result that the photographer's judgment reflected "just how we would have the world estimate and rank us, and how we rank ourselves," as one sitter put it.[33] The repetition of this comparing, gauging, and ranking process, combined with ideas of bodily form institutionalized by the posing stand, visually produced the respectable body. Notably, social position determined bodily position, even as bodily carriage was read as evidence of social position.

Bodily difference was considered self-evident, so that Root, for example, recommended poses and settings that mirrored natural gender difference: "the whole and every part of the male form, taken generally, indicates an aptness and propensity to action, vigorous exertion and power," he wrote in *The Camera and the Pencil*. The female form, in contrast, "gives the idea of something rather passive than active . . . created not so much for the purpose of laborious utility as for the exercise of all the softer, milder qualities."[34] Yet, by using photographs to reflect well-established white, middle-class gender roles, the photograph helped to produce them as social reality. The *American Journal of Photography* suggested that cartes de visite were best suited for portraits of sitters engaged in appropriately gendered activities. A woman, for example, might be positioned "examining a bouquet, arranging a vase of flowers, buttoning a glove, examining a picture, reading a letter."[35] *Humphrey's Journal* explicitly directed that a "mother be represented playing with her children," and cartes de visite albums are filled with images of maternal tenderness.[36] All these labors emphasized a woman's natural capacity for moral influence, tenderness, and gentleness, captured by moments of thoughtful reflection or delicate tasks, such as turning the pages of a photograph album. The sentimental emotions attached to cartes emphasized feminine feeling, deference, and dependence as natural qualities that could be depicted in portraiture.

Posing conventions for men, in contrast, reinforced the cultural authority of patriarchal individualism. Photographers were coached to pose male subjects as upstanding and self-controlled figures. Photographer H. J. Rodgers instructed his readers that temperance, self-control, and constraint were the most worthy qualities a man could display in a portrait.[37] Self-control was the preeminent value of middle-class masculinity, which in part may explain men's willingness to endure the posing stand: amidst directions for physical and pecuniary restraint, the arms of the posing stand assured that they would display the physical marks of their social position. Poses such as the "contra posto" standing pose were reproduced on such a wide scale that the viewer sees an individual portrait that is also, simultaneously, a social role and identity into which the portrait sitter has been fitted.

Both popular and scientific understandings of bodies in the nineteenth century turned around the concept of *type*, in which differentiations from standard forms were understood as distinctions of varying degrees from norms of physique, behavior, and biology. Typological photographs rely on

Two Anonymous Cartes de Visite. COURTESY OF HISTORICAL COLLECTIONS AND LABOR ARCHIVES, PENN STATE.

comparative categories, finding meaning not in an individual image, but in the organization of a group of images in relationship to each other. Stylistically these images emphasize generalization, clinical observation, and classification of generic examples. The typological photograph both generalizes about and visually constructs a category of identity and a region of the social body, such as "the criminal."[38] The appearance of any one body in typological photographs is besides the point, because one photograph of a thief stands for the appearance of all thieves: the viewer does not see an individual but a type. The most instrumental of nineteenth-century photographs, those in which the circumstances of production deny agency to the point of coercion (such as the daguerreotypes Louis Agassiz commissioned to prove his theory of the separate creation of the white and black races), visualizes the taxonomic qualities of typological images. Yet nineteenth-century preoccupations with classification, physiognomy, and the reading of exterior physicality as the mirror onto interior substance were not limited to the visual construction of "the insane" or "the criminal " but also extended to the "respectable" bodies visualized in cartes de visite. Cartes de visite were representations of "the normal," in opposition to which other images, such as those produced under the eye of science or reform, were understood. Standardized representations of visibly respectable bodies staked out the upper ranks of a social hierarchy that was as dependent on representations of respectability as it was on visual depiction of otherness.

But like the asylum inmate or the criminal, the respectable body became recognizable not by marks of individual distinction, but for its reference to a particular segment of American society.

Cartes made visible the defining physical features of the individual middle-class body and positioned the middle class as part of a larger social body. The carte was both proof and artifact of status and position, naturalized by the cultural authority of photographic realism that located status in the body itself. The respectable body became recognizable and powerful, not by marks of individuality, but for its reference to a particular segment of American society, identified by posture and props. Through repeated representation of the upright and the upstanding, cartes de visite linked a particular *kind* of visual body with essential physical distinctions, so that the appearance of restrained bodies in these images both reinforced and constructed the importance of bodily control as an element of respectability.

Not only did the cartes de visite help produce the physical form of the middle-class body, the purchase and exchange of such images further enacted and verified class position. Cartes visually constituted the changing meaning of culture and its implications for representations of the body. In these decades the concept of culture was "becoming a form of consumption necessary to the maintenance of one's class standing," as Mary Kupiec Cayton observes.[39] Culture, as Cayton defines it, was a familiarity with a particular body of knowledge as a measure of status and position, not the embrace of transcendent values. The commercial photographer's studio and the legions of cartes de visite produced in the 1860s helped negotiate this redefinition of culture as an object of consumption. Cartes de visite photographs made it possible to mass produce and mass market a bodily form increasingly associated with middle-class position. In the process, they helped consolidate middle-class social authority and solidify the changing meaning of culture.

From the late 1850s to the early 1870s, the posing stand mobilized a social body in the culture of class formation by immobilizing individual bodies before the camera. Cartes de visite were made possible by the perfecting accuracy of photography, the corrective embrace of the posing stand, and the desire for self-discipline and increased visibility among the emerging middle class. Together, these elements constitute what Foucault called "the gentle way in punishment."[40] Posing for a photograph was not an explicit punishment of the body; it was, ideally and often in practice, a partial and indirect form of control, veiled by the attentive impatience of the photographer. The dynamics of obliging regulation voiced in the trade press echo what Richard Brodhead has called "disciplinary intimacy, or simply, discipline through love." This tender control, visible in cultural institutions and practices such as schools, child rearing, and sentimental fiction, was distinct to the "thinking of the American middle class as it "redefine[d] itself in the antebellum decades."[41] Directions for posing the sitter were not simply a matter of technical instruction, nor were the images produced in the photographer's studio mirrors onto nineteenth-century social formation. The literature of correction used to direct posing should be viewed as a commercial variation on the sentimentalized discourses of corporeal control, that, like the circulation and reproduction of cartes de visite photographs themselves, helped to produce a particular kind of body and identity associated with the consolidation of middle-class social authority.

Cartes de visite did not cause middle-class consolidation, nor do they simply reflect its composition. But causation, in this instance, is productively explored and probed by considering the role of visual images in representing middle-class identity and social formation for its nineteenth-century participants. Just as important, cartes de visite complicate and enrich historians' accounts of the mid-nineteenth century by suggesting that middle-class formation ought to be as much a question of representation as of narration. For it is only by exploring the interior workings of cultural forms and bodies of thought that we will begin to see how a middle-class identity was "made real."

Public Exposure: Middle-Class Material Culture at the Turn of the Twentieth Century

MARINA MOSKOWITZ

> When the history of the architecture and the history of the trend of taste in interior decoration of the present time comes [*sic*] to be written, the historian will make very poor work of his task if he fails to intelligently recognize the influence of the great hotels of this country.
> —Matlack Price, 1924[1]

In February of 1875, Joseph H. Rines of the Reed & Barton Company traveled from the company home in Taunton, Massachusetts, to San Francisco. Rines established himself at the Grand Hotel with an important mission: to secure a commission for outfitting the Palace Hotel, then under construction, with silverplate.[2] The Palace Hotel was the joint venture of William Ralston and Warren Leland. Ralston was president of the Bank of California and one of San Francisco's biggest boosters; he wanted the city to host one of the world's grandest hotels and set out to build the 755-room hotel on an entire city block. Leland was one of five brothers who were rapidly making a name for themselves in the American hotel business.[3] The salesman Rines realized that this commission represented a major new market for his company, and that with clients as well-known as Ralston and Leland, the hotel trade, and perhaps more individual purchasers, would come to trust Reed & Barton's wares. Rines's lengthy stay in San Francisco shows the importance of a new sector of public spaces to manufacturers of furnishings that might at first be considered "domestic" goods.

As the resting place for myriad manufactured goods, the home was not the isolated haven from the world of commerce that advocates of domesticity painted it. The family stood simultaneously as the basic unit of middle-class communities and the basic unit of the consumer market, around whom the world of commerce revolved. Still, goods associated with the home were increasingly marketed to a variety of institutional customers, including corporations, hotels, schools, and whole municipalities. Companies like Reed & Barton, and other producers of furnishings, had not only to image their products for advertisements and catalogues, but to imagine them—their settings, their uses—for the public, particularly individual purchasers. One way of doing this was to place their wares in public settings where they might attract notice. While the design exhibitions and competitions of industrial and world's fairs were one type of setting, another important category consisted of public spaces where the goods were actually in use. Railroads, hotels, clubs, restaurants, hospitals, and schools all had the need for large quantities of goods: for example, silverware for dining rooms or furniture for lounges. These spaces might serve as the sites of exposure to furnishings and spatial organization for new members of the expanding middle class, who might later incorporate these designs into their households. Though the tenets of Victorian domesticity and business culture were often posed as rivals for the attention of the American family, the two were bridged by the ways in which the home and public institutions such as hotels, department stores, clubs, and railroad cars echoed one another in organization and decor.[4]

As public and domestic spaces reflected one another, they were also increasingly alike from place to place across the country. Mechanisms of transportation and communication, from the train on which Rines brought samples to California to the telegraph he used when information from the home office was critical, made a national distribution network possible. The rise of the railroad made possible the transport not only of goods but also of people. Traveling salesmen established routes across the country for the distribution of goods, and a slowly burgeoning tourist trade emerged. Temporary lodgings for these travelers provided a new market for the producers of furnishings, as did the railroad cars themselves. At the same time, in larger metropolitan areas, apartment dwellings opened their doors. The increasing split between work and leisure time in the industrial era contributed to a rise in public spaces such as clubhouses and restaurants. Hotels were not just for transient visitors but provided gathering spaces, particularly in smaller cities and towns, for families, friends, civic groups, and social clubs in their lobbies, restaurants, and lounges.[5] All of these developments together provided the new settings in which daily life occurred; railroad cars, hotels, restaurants, clubs, apartment buildings, schools, and other spaces provided institutional buyers for goods and design services.[6]

The rise in public venues for American material culture occurred in the era that Mark Twain and Charles Dudley Warner labeled "the Gilded Age" in 1873, the years of the late nineteenth century in which the effects of American industrialization became entrenched. The era announced itself in part at the

Centennial Exposition, a display of not only postbellum national unity, but also the country's productive capacity and diversity. While the great Corliss Engine stood as a reminder of the technological power driving production, surely as overwhelming to many visitors was the sheer abundance of manufactured consumer goods, displayed according to materials and production modes as they had been at industrial exhibitions common to the second half of the nineteenth century, but on an even larger scale.[7] While perhaps only the wealthiest industrialists could afford the glittering goods and palaces that lent the era its name, their companies mass-produced more affordable versions of goods and their riches underwrote the large institutions in which a broader public might mix. These goods and spaces, both necessities and luxuries, were accessible to a growing middle class, who for their part increasingly took what had been considered the latter and recast it as the former.[8]

The increasing disparity between the power—consumer, economic, and political—of the richest and poorest strata of the country, as expressed in their material environments, became a cause for concern as the nineteenth century gave way to the twentieth, and the Gilded Age ceded to what is now known as the Progressive Era. Characterized broadly as an "age of reform," the first generation of the twentieth century saw a rise in the civic concern of the managerial classes. They sought not to exist passively between the wealthy industrialists and the poor who labored for them, but to actively mediate between the groups in everyday life, as they did in the industrial settings they managed. Centered primarily on urban concerns, progressives adopted a wide variety of tools to try to effect change, ranging from neighborhood settlement houses to large-scale urban planning projects. While their do-gooder instincts ran strong, embodied in such noted persons as Jane Addams and Jacob Riis, the progressives often stood to gain in economic and political terms from their efforts. They could be as patronizing in domestic matters as they painted the captains of industry of being in the workplace; in fact, they relied on these captains for philanthropic funding of their causes. Rather than erase stratification, reformers sought to improve all tiers, and encourage upward mobility, but largely maintain the status quo in terms of the organization of industrial life. The push for betterment and progress did not stay the tide of material goods and the creation of new environments, but rather encouraged them, as long as production and distribution of goods were well managed and regulated. While the progressives might have questioned the gilded luxuries of the previous generations' elite, they also sought to raise the quality of life for many Americans, including their material circumstances.[9]

At the root of both the Gilded Age abundance and Progressive Era reforms was a belief in environmental determinism, that the material world not only reflected the status of those who lived in it, but could in fact help shape that status. Aspirations for material goods and physical environment would result in behavior and shared values appropriate to middle-class life, according to much of the public sentiment of the day. While the home was often presented as the site of inculcation of these values, public settings could serve just as well. Architecture critic Matlack Price wrote in the 1920s, "People of every land and every walk of life are susceptible to the kind of building in which they find themselves, be it a cathedral or one of our great modern hotels . . . if people come to understand and appreciate architecture as a part of the life of our times, their appreciation will come through the modern hotel."[10] Material goods and the organization of the physical environment were a means of expressing an increasingly shared national experience; with the social mixing in public spaces, they were also a means of introducing the tenets of that experience to those not yet sharing it. Spaces and the objects within them were freighted with, and thus carried, significant values of middle-class life, such as the importance of etiquette and social codes, privacy, and careful investment and management.

That some of these values were borrowed from business parlance is not accidental. The growth of the middle class, in both quantitative and geographical terms, with its ranks of clerks, managers, merchants, as well as professionals, was linked to the rise of American business at the turn of the century. For manufacturers, wooing institutional customers was good business sense. In the first place, outfitting public buildings simply made for large sales. In some instances, however, because the commissions were highly competitive, their true value was marketing potential rather than direct financial gain. Manufacturers used public settings both to highlight their design sensibilities and prove the durability of their wares under heavy use. If a large concern such as a hotel chain or a university trusted and valued a manufacturer's wares and business dealings, so, too, should a family purchaser.

Thus, there were two ways in which a company promoted its wares in public spaces: a potential buyer might on the one hand respond to the actual artifact upon seeing it in a public space, and on the other hand might trust the imprimatur of an institutional customer. There were infinite steps in this process; for example, in Rines' long view, while few people in the country would actually visit the elite Palace Hotel, its reputation might encourage commissions from more modest sites in smaller towns. Furthermore, the booming press of the day could carry news and images of such commissions to an even broader audience.

As manufacturers drew attention to their specific brands by placing them on public view, they also helped more generally to familiarize consumers with the goods they made. Public institutions were more likely to incorporate luxury versions of everyday objects, such as flatware made of silverplate, and large-scale durable goods, such as bathroom fixtures, while these goods represented a major investment to a domestic consumer. Thus, public settings might be a venue for learning about not only interior furnishings, but also the behavior and values associated with those furnishings. Again, representations of public spaces, both verbal and graphic, could disseminate these lessons as well as the spaces themselves did, and to a wider segment of the national population.

Dining in Public

The continuing story of Joseph Rines shows many of the factors involved in placing goods in public spaces, from the balance between design quality and price in winning a competition to the lasting promotional effects of a commission. Though Rines apparently expected to be able to offer a bid for the contract in February of 1875, his visit to San Francisco became a longer one. Construction on the Palace proceeded more slowly than had been anticipated, and silverware appeared to be far from Leland's first priority among all the decisions he had to make about his new hotel. As Leland stalled, more silverware manufacturers learned of the opportunity and gravitated toward San Francisco. In a letter to the home office on February 17, Rines mentioned that both the Tiffany Company and "an english house" had arrived to furnish samples for Leland, as he had earlier been asked to do; later he mentioned both the Gorham Company and Meriden Brittania as main competitors. Leland further frustrated Rines by not explicitly stating what he was looking for in the way of furnishings for the hotel. In the meantime, Rines made it his business to examine Leland's choices in other appointments for the hotel; Rines predicted that a variety of patterns would be acceptable, as long as they "seem best and prettiest." It was not until over a month later, on March 22, that Rines first had the opportunity to show the Reed & Barton samples to Leland. Rines believed that the Reed & Barton silverplate fared well in Leland's estimation, but still without a list of goods needed, he had a hard time gauging the proprietor's interest. This meeting was also his first opportunity to see what his competitors were offering for the Palace. On the grounds of design, Rines dismissed the competition: "After seeing the samples of all parties I think you have a fair chance with the rest. Tiffany has no show at all and the Meriden offer nothing stylish unless they are keeping back other patterns." But he also realized that the commission would be won largely on price, and began to strategize about the bid he would soon have to submit. Rines expressed doubts about Leland's business practice, saying, "They have acted about ordering other goods in a manner that I don't call 'square' so that if they like your samples and others will promise to furnish them less than you offer you will lose the order."

Rines was an excellent sales agent. As he looked to earn this commission, he took a broad view of what it could mean for the company. The mounting anxiety that is expressed in his letters to the home office in Taunton stemmed from his belief that this one commission could, if won, substantially further the company's business. In Rines's estimation, the financial cost of placing a low bid would pay off in the end; he wrote, "They say today that they expect to give the entire order to one party. I would rather lose a trifle now than not get it and if they divide it up there will be no honor about taking nor will the advertisement be of any account." Thus, Rines was already viewing his potential sale as fodder for more, perhaps both within the hotel trade and without. He wrote later that same day, with the order numbers in hand, "Adding both lots together for Dining room and private rooms and it makes quite a large order. Gorham is very anxious to get it. The dealers here all enquire every day if it is decided yet and I would prefer you should not lose the other as your sales would probably be affected by it."[11]

Joseph Rines's experience in San Francisco in 1875 reveals many of the issues involved in the manufacturing, selling, and purchasing of silverplate wares, and durable goods in general, in the last quarter of the nineteenth century. The forms of silverplate were functional, used in the daily experience of eating, but this version of them also connoted a quality of luxury suitable for the finest hotel. Still, the pieces were also not sterling silver, too great an investment for many a consumer, whether domestic or institutional. Related to the combination of function and luxury inherent in the pieces was the combination of cost and design as factors affecting purchasing decisions. While a low bid was an important element in the "competition," with Leland's ability to manipulate prices, the aesthetic qualities—what was deemed "best and prettiest"—emerged as the actual grounds for the decision. In special instances such as this one, customers might even influence the design of goods and would certainly determine quantities produced.

The rising importance of early forms of publicity, marketing, and company identity also figured in this story; while Leland would not trust "the honor of . . . any company," Rines presumed that other potential purchasers might trust Leland's judgment of the wares, and perhaps by extension, Reed & Barton. This type of information could be carried to a significantly larger audience than the actual clientele of the hotel, through publications in both trade and popular periodicals. Or Leland's choice might affect owners of smaller hotels in smaller cities; while Leland might purchase goods to maintain his reputation as a proprietor of luxurious spaces, other purchasers might use similar goods, in smaller quantities, to introduce this element of luxury. For many families seeking such a symbolic investment, the pieces chosen were flatware—forks, spoons, knives, and occasional serving pieces—used to lend an air of luxury to the daily task of eating.[12] The public setting of a railroad car or school cafeteria was one place where potential purchasers might become accustomed to the ideal of a matching set of flatware defining the community that dines together. Further, in these settings, those dining might learn to trust the quality of a particular company's wares or even grow to favor a familiar pattern.[13]

The importance of association with well-known public sites could even outweigh the financial value of the specific commission. Indeed, in some instances companies went so far as to take a loss on sales to their institutional customers, estimating more highly the long-term promotional benefits. For example, in the 1870s, the branch manager of Reed & Barton's New York office was instructed to make a very low bid for some pieces needed by Delmonico's restaurant: "There would be no money in them at this price but we would like to have them in Delmonico's as an advertisement. . . ."[14] As such tactics show, even as early as the 1870s, long-range marketing strategies were employed by American manufacturers.

The actual settings of the businessman's hotel, Masonic lodge, or department store tearoom of small cities were one level of influence, while written accounts of the grander spaces of large cities provided another level. Other cultural productions also contributed to the ideas about product, building, and urban design that Americans held at the turn of the century. New magazines, appealing primarily to women and promoting ideals of domestic design, proliferated in the late nineteenth century. New printing technologies allowed magazine editors, as well as mail-order catalogue purveyors, to picture the objects and plans they were discussing.[15] Even when consumers might not actually go to well-known restaurants or hotels, popular periodicals' coverage of them as significant public places could still plant ideas in the minds of the public far away. For example, while certainly few members of the burgeoning middle class had the opportunity to eat at Delmonico's in New York City, a broad public could learn "How Delmonico Sets a Table" by reading the November 1891 issue of *Ladies' Home Journal*. The article not only explained the "correct" manner for table service, suggesting what pieces were requisites, and also that they should certainly match, but also lent popularity and exposure to the New York restaurateur Delmonico as an arbiter of these rules of etiquette.[16] Readers of *Ladies' Home Journal* in Taylorville, Illinois, who might never venture to New York themselves, would still know what pieces to buy from their local jeweler, who advertised with electrotyped images of Reed & Barton wares.[17]

In addition to being a form of advertising, institutional commissions also served as a testing ground for new forms. For example, Reed & Barton introduced its patent cutting-fork to the hotel trade before it was included in the general merchandise catalogues. The fork was included in an 1882 general catalogue with the explanation, "In our line of Flat Ware especially adapted for Hotels, Steamboats, etc., etc., we have introduced the Improved Forks, and their superior strength and durability have already been fully tested, with perfect satisfaction in all cases."[18] Public customers were also a good test because they had more at stake in providing high-quality furnishings. An 1885 series of letters to the *Jeweler's Circular*, the trade periodical for the industry, explained developments in steel knife blades set into decorative silverplate handles as a corrective to earlier complaints that when knife blades were dulled, customers attributed their difficulty in cutting to the quality of the food rather than the furnishings.[19]

Having started in the hotel trade early on, Reed & Barton maintained its interest in this sector of the market, furnishing not only hotels, but all manner of public spaces, including railroad dining cars, clubs, schools, steamships, and the new apartment houses being built across the country. In 1883 the company began actually producing the hotel line in a separate division of the company. Marketing and sales of all goods were unified; sales agents appear to have incorporated the hotel trade into their regional routes, rather than divide lines of wares between them. Jewelers might act as middlemen for these large orders, just as they did with individual purchasers. For example, Reed & Barton's southern agent H. W. Graves worked with a local jeweler to win the commission for the Piney Woods Hotel. The home office in Taunton certainly helped manage the process, keeping track of hotels furnished and new hotels under construction.[20] Since there were concentrations of these public venues in metropolitan areas, the Reed & Barton branch offices also coordinated this marketing effort. George M. Howard, running a branch office for Reed & Barton in the opening years of the twentieth century, made it his business to keep abreast of construction of new public spaces and solicit commissions for silverware. Howard's solicitation letters were tailored to give examples of Reed & Barton's work in a particular line of public space; a letter to Col. W. G. Price, developer of a new apartment house in Pittsburgh, Pennsylvania, detailed: "Among some of the Hotels and Apartment Houses we have supplied we may mention The Plaza, Manhattan, The Ansonia, Majestic and various others in New York, The Rittenhouse, Gladstone, Colonnade, Bartram and Greens in Philadelphia, The Raleigh, New Willards, and the Dewey of Washington, and several others through out the country." Beyond this commercial trade, Howard also noted the Pennsylvania Hospital and local schools. He wrote, for example, to the president of Bryn Mawr College, "We desire to call your attention to the fact that we are now represented in Philadelphia with a full line of samples of goods suitable for the table service of Schools and colleges. . . ."[21]

Whether or not the institutions were specifically schools, they were nonetheless sites of education in middle-class ways of life. Silverplate flatware indicated "dining," or a refined approach to eating, even for a seemingly simple meal. In the sanctity of the home, or in more public settings, these meals were breaks from the daily routine. The rise of silverplate flatware also went along with the rise of separate spaces designated for dining; they provided a furnishing for these new spaces, whether domestic dining rooms or larger banquet areas of clubs, hotels, and restaurants.[22] Flatware also symbolized the space in which dining took place. Special patterns created for specific public places or monogrammed pieces designating a family home were means of unifying the experience of dining in a specific place. The luxury quality of the items spoke of the attention given to mealtimes as a break from the work day in places distinguished from work settings. The concept of luxury was itself often defined or described in the era in terms of dining, the act in which economic consumption of accouterments and bodily consumption of food were combined into one.[23]

Dining could be a ritual, in specialized places with specialized tools. Participating in these rituals meant not only being present—having a place at the table—but also knowing the codes of the rituals, etiquette. The settings for dining, whether public or private, might also be sites where exposure to etiquette rules were stressed. Dining was bound into a set of rules, not the least of which was what piece of flatware to use for what course or food item, and the correct way to hold it. In his 1911 work *Jennie Gerhardt,* novelist Theodore Dreiser used the occasion of a meal in a hotel restaurant to capture the title character's lack of familiarity with these codes, even while she was aware of their existence. Describing Jennie's dinner with Lester Kane, the son of a wealthy industrialist, Dreiser wrote, "Another time in the Southern hotel in St. Louis he watched her pretending a loss of appetite because she thought her lack of table manners was being observed by nearby diners. He could not always be sure of the right forks and knives, and the strange-looking dishes bothered her; how did one eat asparagus and artichokes?" When Lester assures her that her "table manners are all right," Jennie admits to feeling "a little nervous at times." Still, in Dreiser's depiction, through these occasions, "Jennie grew into an understanding of the usages and customs of comfortable existence."[24] The tools for eating were bound to rules of social conduct, and knowing those rules was one way in which a community recognized itself; etiquette went beyond just knowing the proper uses of flatware to a way of ordering middle-class life.

A matching set of flatware might be a way of defining a circle—whether a family circle, or the addition of close friends, or a professional sector eating together at a club—but would also indicate the refining element of etiquette, the rules and regulations to which that circle tacitly agreed to adhere.[25] Social standards were played out with standardized goods. The notion of owning a matching set of flatware did become a standard of home furnishing for the middle class. And within a community, a family, or school or club setting, the "standard" of eating with the same utensils was a manner of defining that community. As silverplate flatware increasingly became a standard possession of the American town dweller, this act of ownership was a way to consider oneself part of a larger group, and became an identifier of a group sharing such rules of etiquette, such styles of dining, across geographic boundaries.

Bathing in Private

While dining in public contexts was increasingly accepted at the turn of the century, other personal activities, particularly those connected to bodily hygiene, were withdrawn from public view. Bathing, for example, was increasingly granted a designated space of its own within the middle-class American home, and large investments were made in the fixtures that furnished these rooms. Still, the inspiration for creating such a private chamber might have been initiated via their elaborate inclusion in public locations, such as hotels, department stores, and apartment buildings. Fixture manufacturers recognized these large-scale clients for both their large orders and their associated value, just as silverware manufacturers had.

In general, fixture companies at the turn of the century needed to market not just their products, but the idea of establishing a space for them, and making a significant investment in furnishing that space. In 1914, the Kohler Company of Riverside, Wisconsin, published a large catalogue of enamel cast-iron plumbing fixtures. The first few pages of the catalogue depicted modern bathrooms with a wide range of appointments, shown in photographs of actual rooms. In contrast, these pages also had line drawings of various scenes of bathing, washing, drinking, and other activities that suggested a need for running water. The drawings were paired so that the images of facing pages loosely corresponded to one another, but suggested different eras in the settings and implements for bathing. The eras were not necessarily fixed in historical time, but clearly showed the "before and after" stages of a certain development: the incorporation of interior plumbing received into modern bathroom fixtures. The convenience of running water and the rising standards of privacy together contributed to the acceptance of the bathroom as a necessary use of interior space, its furnishings worthy of attention. The elaborate décor of bathrooms in public buildings were one model that legitimated such attention on a domestic level.[26]

By the turn of the century, the leading American hotels had a reputation for providing private access to the means of cleanliness. The trend could be traced as early as the provision of a bowl, pitcher, and free soap at Boston's Tremont House in the 1830s and continued with the modernization of the Astor Hotel in New York in 1875, installing private bathrooms in order to keep up with the city's newer hotels. As one early history of the American hotel trade recounted in 1930:

> One of the first and important innovations of modern hotel-keeping was modern plumbing and its bright particular jewel the modern bathroom. Our hotels were the chief beneficiaries of modern plumbing throughout most of the nineteenth century. They gave two generations of American an opportunity to scrape their first acquaintance with bathtubs, hot and cold running water, water-closets, and steam-heat. It has been said that today the American public worships the bathroom. If that be so, the birth of that worship was in America's hotels in the 1840s and 1850s. Of all the many ways in which American domestic life has been influenced by hotels, the influence of the hotel bathroom stands pre-eminent.[27]

Maintaining a private bath for every room gained importance as an advertising claim as competition for transient hotel traffic rose, particularly in larger cities. By the 1920s, accounts of "modern" hotels in architectural and domestic periodicals routinely specified the number of bathrooms and the quality of their furnishings, as in this description of the Benjamin Franklin Hotel in Philadelphia: "On the upper floors are the 1210 bedrooms of the house, each with a private bath with the highest type of plumbing—sunken tubs, tiled floors. . . ."[28] Thus, the publicity for new hotels or other public spaces might also provide publicity for its outfitters.

While public settings might introduce the concept of privacy, they were also a place to show the consistently high quality of goods produced in large quantities. As with flatware, hotels, schools, hospitals, and other institutions provided not only large-scale sales for companies such as Kohler but good advertising as well. By the time the company started publishing the house organ *Kohler of Kohler News* in 1916, it could run a monthly column devoted to these commissions in public "buildings that are modern in every respect." In describing renovations to the Windsor Hotel in Jacksonville, Florida, an article stated, "As the dominant idea in remodeling was to introduce modern conveniences and unusual features, 51 'Viceroy' baths were added to the hotel's bathroom equipment." The Viceroy bathtub model was adopted in hotels across the country, most notably in New York City's vast Commodore and Pennsylvania Hotels, which served as tourist attractions in their own right. [29] American novelist Sinclair Lewis commented on this new form of tourism and its benefits to manufacturers in *Babbitt* (1922). On his way to Maine from his hometown in the midsize, midwestern city of Zenith, the title character, George F. Babbitt, makes a stop in New York. Lewis explains his primary destination: "They had four hours in New York between trains. The one thing Babbitt wished to see was the Pennsylvania Hotel, which had been built since his last visit. He stared up at it, muttering, 'Twenty-two hundred rooms and twenty-two hundred baths! That's got everything in the world beat. . . .'"[30]

The Viceroy bathtub used at the Pennsylvania Hotel was also the focus of the Kohler Company's first national advertising campaign, beginning in 1915. As the focus of this campaign, the Viceroy was also prominently featured in promotions within the trade.[31] The company featured its large hotel commissions in advertising run in architectural and other trade journals, using that forum to build confidence with the professionals who might promote their products. Most fixture companies did not sell directly to consumers, but rather relied on architects and plumbers to specify and install their wares. Architects in particular were seen as an important entrée into the nonresidential market, requiring large numbers of fixtures. The emphasis on reaching architects directly resulted in commissions for public buildings that might inspire confidence in other purchasers.

World War I offered another opportunity to inspire confidence, on a number of levels. Kohler sold large quantities of its wares to companies building emergency war housing for increased ranks of workers and thus linked its name to the need for "efficient" settings for production. This trade promoted not only the company as taking part in the war effort, but also the importance of sanitary plumbing as a necessary part of the American home. In the early 1920s, Kohler would make the association between its products and the standard of living even more explicit, using the phrase in its advertising. A 1922 advertisement depicted a bathroom with a built-in Viceroy tub, a wall-mounted lavatory, and low-tank toilet, headed by the phrase "The Index to Your Standards of Living." This headline, an obvious reference to contemporary attempts to enumerate a standard of living for American families, took the "bundle of goods" that normally constituted the "index" and reduced it to one item—the household bathroom, described in the copy as the "one room in every home which is the key to the real standards of living of that household." In contrast to early national advertisements of the mid-1910s, this one featured an image of the room itself, with no people in it. The message here was not about introducing good habits of hygiene to one's family, but that the objects themselves, when placed in a proper setting, brought a certain status to the family that owned them. With its picture of the "index to your standards of living," Kohler assumed that the "standard" was one to which the middle class aspired and promoted its products as the necessary first step toward achieving that goal. Because of the connection to a family's health and well-being implied by the rhetoric of hygiene in the home, such a purchase could be justified as a necessity rather than a luxury. As "the index" to a family's standard of living, Kohler implied that this one purchase could establish a family's place within the middle class that shared that standard.[32]

At Home in Public

If new ideas regarding domestic furnishing or organization were gleaned in a public setting, the measure of their acceptance occurred in the home. Norman Hayner, a professor of sociology at the University of Washington, looking back on the influence of hotels over the previous generation, wrote in the 1930s: "'Homes are becoming more hotel-like,' the hotel men say, and they are thinking of the way in which hotels have pioneered in such things as bathtubs, modern heating arrangements, and comfortable beds. Travelers have become acquainted with these 'new fangled notions' in hotels and have gradually introduced them in their own domiciles."[33] Still, it was more than specific technological innovations or styles of decoration that provided the parallels between domestic and public spaces. The very principles around which members of the middle class organized their domestic spaces were seen in institutions ranging from hotels to office buildings.

Though there was a wide variety of housing stock in the United States at the turn of the century, certain forms gained prominence, popularized by large-scale producers of housing. Large industrial firms used economies of scale to efficiently produce houses, or rather the pieces that together made up a house and distributed them via railroad across the country. This mail-order architecture, or kit-house, business constituted a significant part of the market in new houses in the 1910s and 1920s. Because of the lower costs, primarily of materials but also of simplified labor, the option of home ownership was extended to those who might not otherwise be able to afford it, thus broadening the potential market for certain house forms. The earliest firm, the Aladdin Company, was founded in 1906 in Bay City, Michigan, and was rapidly joined in the trade by large-scale competitors, such as Sears, Roebuck and Montgomery Ward.[34]

One of the popular styles distributed by the mail-order architecture firms was the square-type house or box house, now commonly called a foursquare. The name referred to the geometric shape of the floorplan and volume of the house, particularly in contrast to the irregular plans and massing of Queen Anne and revival style houses that preceded it in popularity among American house dwellers. The foursquare did often rise from a perfectly square footprint, or at least a rectangle with perpendicular sides close in measurement to one another. Two stories topped by a hipped roof, the side walls of the foursquare were also roughly square, with no gable ends to break the cube-like volume. The fenestration, at least in the front of the house, was usually symmetrical, though there might be one projecting bay window, and the front entry was often preceded by a porch. Three or four bedrooms and a bathroom occupied the second floor, while the living room, dining room, kitchen, and sometimes an extra bedroom or den made up the first-floor rooms. True to its later name, the foursquare often had four roughly square rooms on each floor. Box houses often maintained some sort of entry or central hall space separating and mediating between the rooms.

Regardless of the interior floorplan, the room arrangement was not apparent from the outside of the house. Unlike some earlier styles with jutting bays and turrets, the box house was designed "from the outside in"—the overall form determined the arrangement of space within it. While there were certainly precedents in domestic architecture for this type of design, such as Georgian or Federal architecture, the foursquare may also have shown the influence of public buildings of the day. From factory buildings to downtown business blocks to banks and hotels, rectilinear plans and massing were common in cities and towns across the country. As the description for one of Aladdin's foursquare models explained:

> In design the Rochester is truly American—simple, strong, and substantial; conservative lines bespeak dignity and personality of which this design is a shining example. Its features are not composed of novelties that come and go, but are made up of the more careful touches that have stood the test with home builders for many years. The Rochester has the added advantage in point of design of being square in shape, which always expresses massiveness and strength.[35]

Aladdin staked its claim for helping to create a national architecture, both by labeling the qualities so often found in public buildings "American," and by promoting nationwide distribution of its products.

If the exterior connoted strength, the resulting interior projected efficiency, a watchword of the day. From the floor plan to the roof line, the interior space of such geometric buildings could be divided into regular units, seen to provide the most efficient use of space; each resulting space could be assigned its own task or user. On the domestic scale, these units also lent more privacy than might have been had in the more open-plan bungalow, another popular form of the era. The box houses were large enough to provide bedrooms for members of the slowly shrinking American family and almost always included a separate bathroom. This second-floor design seems similar in particular to the upper floors of hotels or office buildings, with similarly sized individual rooms around a central core to maximize light to the rooms. Sinclair Lewis in fact depicted George and Myra Babbitt's bedroom by writing, "It had the air of being a very good room in a very good hotel."[36] The foursquare matched one description offered by the Aladdin Company of modern dwellings. Commenting on the wastefulness of overly large houses with unused spaces, the company declared, ". . . the modern home is like a good business. It has resources enough for the unexpected emergency but carries no dead surplus investment."[37] While the passage was certainly meant metaphorically, it could read as a literal description of the spatial qualities of the building, and what they shared with "a good business," such as a factory or office building.

The hallmarks of the modern home, as presented by numerous articles in shelter magazines and other popular periodicals, as well as the kit-house catalogues, were "comfort" and "convenience." Interestingly, these were the same words often used to describe the interior arrangement of new hotels and other public spaces. For example, one account of a new hotel in Los Angeles praised its architects, the firm Schultze and Weaver, and commented on the relation of both the structure and its décor to contemporary houses. The article in *Arts and Decoration* explained:

> Architecturally, too, they have made provision for comfort and convenience, and have made it (as is the way of the modern hotel) so inconspicuously and effectively that it is taken for granted without conscious thought. Nonarchitecturally, they have created an environment the enjoyment of which is not privately restricted to a small group. They have provided a permanent and compelling general suggestion for standards of home decoration; the modern hotel has influenced and affected the trend of taste in interior decoration more than is commonly recognized.[38]

As Schultze and Weaver were praised, so, too, did Aladdin tout the abilities of its designers in similar terms; the designer of their popular Marsden model was described as a "'home man,' a man who loves his family, one who takes his greatest pleasure in a home of comfort and convenience."[39]

Providing for "comfort and convenience," Aladdin and other mail-order architecture firms worked primarily on the domestic scale. Still, the companies did find ways to garner more public attention for their products. Much like the separate hotel trade catalogues of the silverware companies, Aladdin began producing "special interest" catalogues, most notably its 1920 publication, "Low Cost Homes Designed Especially for Industrial Purposes."[40] With large orders of homes, Aladdin offered to supply, free of charge, a town plan for the new town and public buildings such as a town hall. In these ways, even companies in the business of making houses, and for the most part single-family houses, gained a broader recognition for their product.

What all of these manufacturers of varied products acknowledged with their marketing efforts was the fact that as much as the industrial era brought divisions of spaces devoted to work, leisure, commerce, and the home, there were nonetheless strong parallels in the ways in which these spaces were organized and decorated. For previous generations, the extent to which lives were lived in public or sheltered within the bounds of the home had been considered a mark of social and economic status, but at the turn of the twentieth century, the pattern of interaction between the two realms became more fluid.[41] This fluidity was particularly a hallmark of the expanding middle class, which had both greater ability to maintain its own domestic spheres than in earlier eras and access to a wider variety of clubs, stores, hotels, and offices, as well as to transportation mechanisms between these sites, to augment the settings of their daily lives.

In the new attempts of social scientists to study, and quantify, the quality of life shared by the burgeoning middle class, these forays into public arenas became part of the "standard of living." While the new community studies by sociologists such as Jessica Peixotto and Robert and Helen Merrell Lynd shared with earlier studies of the working classes a focus on the family household as the basic unit of community, they looked beyond the issues of subsistence that these works had charted. For example, Peixotto, in her 1927 work, *Getting and Spending at the Professional Standard of Living,* completed a detailed analysis of household budgets of professors at the University of California. In addition to traditional categories of costs for shelter, food, and clothing, Peixotto included the expenses of vacations, meals away from home, dues for both professional societies and local clubs, and other cultural entertainment as items in the standard professional budget. She noted that many of her subjects spent beyond their base salaries in order to meet a standard of living that was defined by aspiration rather than income.[42] If being a member of the middle class increasingly meant sharing a set of aspirations with others, then both manufacturers and consumers looked to public spaces as sites where those aspirations could be created and disseminated.

BUSINESS CAREERS IN MODERN TIMES

Chain Belt Co., 1913. COURTESY OF STATE HISTORICAL SOCIETY OF WISCONSIN, CLASSIFIED FILE NO. 585.

Stenographers of the Firm, 1884. COURTESY OF STATE HISTORICAL SOCIETY OF WISCONSIN, NEG. NO. WHI(X3)41932.

The most influential scholarly book ever written about the Ameri-
can middle class is C. Wright Mills's brilliant 1951 volume entitled *White Collar*. If you ever come across a copy in a used bookstore, look carefully at the cover. You will see a small man with a thin tie and bland gray jacket, tucked away nearly out of sight in the bottom left-hand corner. The man's head is tilted downward so that his hat is more prominent than his face. It is impossible to make eye contact with Mr. White Collar, but we can tell that his mouth is drawn tight in a determined, even grim, manner. He is lonely but without even a crowd; the black urban canyon dwarfs him.

This iconic image of the lilliputian middle-class worker speaks power-fully about hopelessness and helplessness in the face of larger social forces. Indeed, the mysterious man on the cover of *White Collar* is one of the stock characters of twentieth-century literature as well as social science. The pop-ularity of the recent Broadway revival of Arthur Miller's *Death of a Salesman* demonstrates the continuing power of this cultural symbol. And the tradi-tion of condescending to white-collar workers goes back well into the early twentieth century, with Sinclair Lewis's *Babbitt* serving as the supreme achievement of those intent on establishing that most members of the mod-ern American middle class were ridiculous—if not downright dangerous.

The essays in this section, however, force us to revise, if not overturn, our inherited wisdom about those who seem to have made it only to the margins of genuine middle-class respectability. Andrew Cohen, Clark Davis, and Jeffrey Hornstein instead discuss these entirely human people in terms of creativity, power, and imagination, as well as in terms of the much more familiar status seeking, anxiety, and political weakness.

Cohen first asks us to expand our vision of whom we might consider as fully middle class. He argues that we need to use the concept of a "lower middle class" in order to capture the grittiness, as well as the fluidity, of life at the edge of the collar line. In the decades preceding World War II in Chicago, workers—especially immigrants—went back and forth between being unionized proletarians and small entrepreneurs. Theirs was a com-mon world that demonstrates the survival of Bruce Laurie's "popular bloc" well into the twentieth century. Moreover, this middling class remained economically and politically powerful; Cohen provides compelling evi-dence about how these skilled workers and petty enterprisers placed signifi-cant roadblocks in the way of elite attempts to establish a modern, corpo-rate economy.

Clark Davis, in turn, takes us into the heart of the "new" middle class of salaried corporate employees that Mills identified and so relentlessly carica-tured. Davis's exploration of the corporate frontier in Los Angeles reveals how wrenching a cultural change white-collar work was for men who had exchanged the promise of self-employment for a mere salary. Yet despite the representation in contemporary cinema of these workers as mindless drones, they actively shaped their work environments, and companies had to labor hard to convince salaried men of the masculine virtues of the system of career ladders and managerial hierarchies. Davis's workers might, in the end, be as economically dependent as those that Mills portrays, but they are much more reflective and, in the end, much more active in forging their own destiny.

Jeffrey Hornstein takes the consideration of gender and agency even further as he reveals the intricacies of how first men, and then women, shaped the would-be profession of realty to fit prevailing conceptions of manhood and womanhood. Male Realtors realized that, in order to create a realm of occupational autonomy, they would need somehow to place themselves within long-term American discourses relating to property and merit. Just as they succeeded in doing this, however, women increasingly became able to wrest much of their business away—and thus empower themselves—by borrowing from an even more traditional ideology of domesticity and the home.

Professors would rarely be caught thinking that they might actually learn something from the lives of people as prosaic as Realtors. Perhaps, however, it is time for academics to discern that we, too, have always been a species of white-collar worker and that we are enmeshed in webs of careers, ambitions, and organizational imperatives that are not necessarily qualitatively different from those that supposedly trap the more lowly and mundane. In that sense, we might also recognize that it is time to include in our vision not only the romantic proletarian struggles for workers' control favored by labor historians. As we come to move middling white-collar workers from a belittled speck at the left-hand bottom corner to the center of our vision, we might well find not only a complex history but also an inspiring humanity.

Obstacles to History? Modernization and the Lower Middle Class in Chicago, 1900-1940

ANDREW WENDER COHEN

At the turn of the century, thousands of urban craft workers and small businessmen lived in Chicago, dominating local politics and affecting the terms for economic development until the Great Depression. This lower middle class proposed a combination of association, unionism, partisanship, and collective bargaining that proved a successful alternative to both the hierarchical class relations desired by corporate capitalists and the outright class warfare envisioned by radical social critics. Though their vision was neither egalitarian nor revolutionary, it did fundamentally alter the development of Chicago's economy and significantly shift the trajectory of social policy.

In the past, historians of the twentieth-century United States have shown these tradespeople little consideration, a profound irony given the stature of the independent businessman and artisan in American national mythology. Central to this neglect is an implicit modernization narrative that portrays the lower middle class as a roadblock to progress. Many labor historians have condemned craft workers and their unions for emphasizing the improvement of material conditions for themselves rather than a broad revolutionary program dedicated to helping all workers. Historians of business and law have described small proprietors as backward-looking individualists, hostile to technology, unions, and government. Political historians see the "old middle classes" as blind to any public interest beyond the accumulated private desires of individuals, even viewing them as susceptible to fascism.[1]

Theoreticians, Marxist and anti-Marxist alike, have also ignored the lower middle class, either predicting its disappearance or decrying its continuing existence. Anthony Giddens notes that neither Max Weber nor Karl Marx left a "detailed analytical account of the notion of class and its relationship to other bases of stratification in society." Though Weber named the petite bourgeoisie one of four distinct classes (with manual laborers, white-collar workers, and the business elite), it was the least significant group in his historical framework, which portrayed experts, bureaucrats, and professionals as the agents of social change. Similarly, Marx predicted the lower middle class would dissolve as capitalism eroded its economic power. Marx optimistically believed shopkeepers and craft workers would have a vital role in the coming revolution, but only after they became proletarians.[2]

Theoretical successors to Weber and Marx have roamed little from these formulations. C. Wright Mills and Daniel Bell, for example, speculated that the lower middle class would lose its distinct identity and join the expanding middle class. Marxist critics like Lenin and Gramsci, and more recently Ernest Mandel, have viewed craft workers and small businessmen as vestigial obstacles in the path of a socialist future.[3]

In recent years, some scholars have tried to restore the lower middle class to history. Labor historians have reclaimed craft workers' most progressive and egalitarian tendencies. Business historians like Philip Scranton study smaller manufacturers. Scholars of social mobility like Olivier Zunz trace the decline of the petite bourgeoisie. And political historians like Alan Brinkley describe lower-middle-class anxiety with some compassion. But such works still express a tacit modernization narrative that effectively diminishes the significance of lower-middle-class life. For labor historians, selected craft workers become significant when they realize their destiny as members of a working class. Other scholars consider small businessmen interesting because they represent an alternative lost, or a community in decline. Still others acknowledge the plight of the tradesman in a changing society, but emphasize his fascist flirtations. Though these approaches help reestablish the historical significance of the lower middle class, they nevertheless present it as radical, doomed, or reactionary, rather than as a vital mainstream force shaping the economy or polity.[4]

By questioning modernization teleologies, scholars can restore the lower middle class to history. Some recent scholars have moved away from standard narratives to give greater attention to previously slighted communities and cultures. In *Rethinking Working Class History*, a study of workers in Bengal from 1890 to 1940, Dipesh Chakrabarty rejects the assumption that "premodern" cultures must wither as part of an inevitable liberation struggle. Likewise, scholars such as Alice Kessler-Harris and Christopher Tomlins have demanded historians deemphasize traditional narratives like industrialization in order to study the millions of farmers, women, and people of color who have toiled outside of factories. At the very least, as Kessler-Harris concludes, scholars must emphasize how economic transformation affected different groups and institutions, including (and perhaps especially) those who managed to survive its direct effects.[5]

The lower middle class was one such group: significantly affected but not entirely subordinated by capitalism. This essay seeks to examine the reaction of the petite bourgeoisie to economic transformation in Chicago. It contends that skilled workers, contractors, and shopkeepers actively participated in the struggle to determine the shape of the urban economy, confronting corporate power, technological change, and the reorganization of work. Though hardly radical, these tradespeople antagonized Chicago's economic elite and successfully defended a distinctive moral economy into the Great Depression.

Though turn-of-the-century Chicago contained hundreds of corporate manufacturers and thousands of factory workers, the city was not entirely industrial, and a lower middle class had developed among the craft workers and small employers who built the city's homes, cut its hair, and delivered its coal. Between 1890 and 1904, the city gained more than 830,000 new residents, as well as thousands of new businesses. Immigrants to the city required food and shelter, services and government. Businesses required transportation and infrastructure. If steel and oil were the sinews of the new national economy, bread and meat, coal delivery and garbage removal, housing and plant construction underpinned Chicago's commercial life. Restaurants, bars, and barbershops did not provide essential goods, but they were the important neighborhood institutions and spaces that defined public life in the city.[6]

A significant percentage of the city's residents worked in these trades. In 1900, more than 55,000 men, or 10 percent of all working males over ten years old in the city, found their occupation in just eleven construction trades. An additional 34,864 men (6.3 percent) and 45,747 women (30.5 percent of working women) engaged in selected service fields including barbering, laundering, and building maintenance. Many men engaged in local transportation; teamsters, draymen, and hackmen alone accounting for 23,203 men, or 4.2 percent of all male workers.[7]

A surprising number of men and women were shopkeepers and semi-independent producers. In 1905, the city sustained 852 bakeries, most of them small retail shops owned by individuals. In 1900, more than 23,000 men, or one out of every twenty-four, were "retail dealers," the third most common occupation among the 555,515 employed males in the city. Significant numbers of women also operated small businesses. At the turn of the century, more than 1,500 women, or a little over 1 percent, were retailers, with an additional 3,432 (2.3 percent) working as milliners and millinery dealers. In 1910, more than 15,000 women worked outside factories as dressmakers and nearly 5,000 more as tailors. Combined, these two jobs constituted 8.5 percent of the female workforce.[8]

These tradespeople had immigrated to the United States not only from Germany, Ireland, and Scandinavia, but also from southern and eastern Europe. Neither "old" nor "new" immigrants dominated the city's lower middle class. Rather, specific ethnic groups dominated tightly defined niches. German-Americans were building tradesmen and shopkeepers in disproportionate numbers. Irish-Americans were slightly overrepresented in construction and transportation, but greatly underrepresented in retail and service sectors. Polish-Americans often worked in industrial manufacturing, but many Poles became masons, carpenters, and bakers. Few Russians worked in construction, but nearly 12 percent of all Russian men were retail dealers, and significant numbers were bakers, barbers, and other tradesmen.[9]

Technology had touched these trades, but it had not radically remade their day-to-day operation. Factory production was uncommon. For barbers and retail dealers, machines were of little use. In retail baking and butchering, mixing, kneading, chopping, and wrapping were done by hand. Into the 1920s, local commercial transportation continued to rely upon the horse-drawn wagons, loaded by powerfully built teamsters, rather than by forklifts or pallet trucks. In the building trades, manufacturers had begun producing materials in factories, but skilled journeymen still did most work with hand tools devised centuries before, while thousands of laborers lifted, carried, and hauled materials with little mechanical assistance at all.[10]

However prominent corporations had become in manufacturing, they had made few inroads in the construction, retail, and service sectors. Of the 284 teaming firms listed in the 1902 Chicago city directory, 256 (90 percent) were individuals, partnerships, and family firms. Only twenty-eight (10 percent) were large enough to call themselves "companies." Small firms dominated the teaming trade because of its minimal capital requirements. Statistics from 1905 reveal that contractors owned only $200 in capital for every employee; the average Chicago manufacturing company invested thirteen times as much. Such firms were small and hired few employees. Despite the emergence of bread, cookie, and cracker factories, baking remained diffused among a large number of small establishments with few workers. Between 1904 and 1914, the number of bakeries in Chicago grew from 852 to 1305 firms, while the number of workers per establishment actually declined, from 6.80 to 5.89.[11]

Nor were such employers wealthy or well educated. Thomas Kidd, the president of the Amalgamated Wood Workers Union, admitted that, "I was a small employer once, and after every pay day I discovered that my men had more than I. So I went back to work." Labor economist Royal Montgomery noted that "the rugged, 'self-made' businessman . . . for some reason, seems to be more common in the construction industry than in other lines of business." In 1899, F. B. Robinson, the assistant secretary of the

Chicago Masons and Builders Association, described his constituents as "ordinary common laboring men," not "college bred men." Some prominent contractors and material manufacturers had attended technical schools such as Bryant & Stratton Business College to learn bookkeeping, but few had university degrees.[12]

Employers and employees frequently shared remarkably similar backgrounds. Of the large pool of immigrants who entered trade apprenticeships in youth, some remained journeymen, while others became foremen and then contractors. One example was Joseph Downey. After his father's premature death, Downey and his family migrated from Ireland to the United States. A Chicago man named James McGraw took Downey on as an apprentice mason, eventually making him a partner. One biographer called Downey "a self-made man in the truest and best sense of the phrase, and yet [he] is absolutely devoid of the egotism which is so often apparent in those who have been the architects of their fortunes." The contracting class contained sufficient numbers of former journeymen both to justify American myths of upward mobility and to rebuke those who had inherited their station.[13]

Chicago's lower middle class coalesced in such trades, which provided comparatively high-paid work for some residents and entrepreneurial opportunities for others. Modest businessmen and prosperous craft workers enjoyed relative equality and familiarity. If social relations within the class were fluid, this fluidity merely provoked a broader community of interest committed to preserving skill and independence against those who planned to modernize the urban economy.

A Common Problem and Response

In May 1903, more than one hundred master and journeymen barbers picketed outside a Chicago barbershop whose owner, John Kluck, had refused to close at 8 P.M. The police arrived at the corner of Madison and Wells Streets and arrested two sheet-metal workers for "trying to incite the crowd to violence." The crowd dispersed but re-formed around five other renegade shops. Stephen McCauley, the vice president of the barbers' union, told the newspapers, "Kluck is the man we are after. All the others have told us they would close if he shuts his doors." To this, Kluck defiantly responded, "I will never close my shop so long as I can get a barber to stand by me."[14]

As this anecdote indicates, intense rivalries existed among Chicago's tradespeople, but they expressed a set of preoccupations rather different from what previous historians have assumed. Though Kluck's story features angry workers, coercive picketing, and a staunch union, it is not a straightforward tale of Marxian class conflict. Instead, protest enforced the standards of a broader economic community that included both workers and small employers. The story shows how the mutual desire to limit competition and enforce wages, hours, and conditions could unify segments of the lower middle class. It also shows how craftsmen effectively responded to their hotly competitive environment and suggests how they would confront the development of new corporate enterprise.

Competition threatened these producers from below, undercutting their prosperity without fundamentally transforming their trade. Every day, men and women came to Chicago from Europe and from the American countryside, eager to work as craftsmen in the city's expanding construction and transportation markets. Ambitious small businessmen like John Kluck built clienteles by undermining trade standards. Thousands of small businesses scrambled for trade, many of them earning meager profits. A magazine for teaming contractors complained in 1910:

> The larger teaming contractors when consulted as to the future of the teaming business in Chicago usually say "Future? There is no future; look at it right now, a man can't figure on a thing; it's cut, cut, cut, the competition is so keen in the teaming business that there is not a cent in it . . ." Says another: "What's the use of looking to the future? Everything is so expensive all the possible profits go into show bills, doctor bills, harness bills, feed bills, etc. If we have a good contract there are three or four other fellows after it. They will install new equipment, wagons, harness, to be new and painted, lettered to suit and at a price so low that it's folly to try to meet it."[15]

The pool of able workers, some only a small investment away from independence, continually threatened to undercut existing firms.

More fearsome were the large corporations, ambitious local entrepreneurs, and out-of-town investors that generated new competition and threatened the character of many trades. Chain stores, for example, threatened to replace the city's scrambling shopkeepers and restaurateurs with elite corporations and salaried managers. Herman Kohlsaat, an emigrant from western Illinois, turned a single lunch counter into a wholesale bakery and a chain of eateries. Kohlsaat became one of the city's elite merchants, investing in real estate and newspaper publishing, and developing close political ties to Republicans like Theodore Roosevelt and Governor Frank O. Lowden. His daughter Pauline married Potter Palmer, Jr., the scion of a prominent Chicago family.[16]

Corporate manufacturers attempted to undermine traditional building techniques, shifting production from construction sites to factories, and replacing skilled craftsmen with a mass of semiskilled machine operatives. In the nineteenth century, skilled carpenters customized doors and window sashes. Journeymen masons sawed stone in pieces at the building site. After the Civil War, a new group of manufacturers began mass-producing wood trim and cut stone using motorized lathes and planers. Corporate manufacturers thus moved certain trades from the urban public economy to the private sphere of the factory and rural quarry.[17]

Such corporations threatened to eradicate the fluid, labor-intensive, proprietary character of these trades. In 1904, the Illinois Tunnel Company accumulated thirty million dollars in capital stock and bought the telephone conduits beneath Chicago's downtown. Running small electric freight trains from the rail yard to the basements of the largest Loop concerns, the company promised to replace public streets, teaming contractors, and teamsters with a private, corporate, and "modern" form of transport.[18]

Most drastic was the transformation of Chicago's heating industry. At the turn of the century, gas lit Chicago's streets and homes, but coal warmed its residences and businesses. Looking for new markets, People's Gas, Light and Coke, or "the Gas Trust," began persuading businesses to use gas for heat as well as light. The rivalry between coal and gas was representative of the struggles initiated by economic modernization. Coal epitomized an older mode of production and distribution. Sold by small neighborhood dealers, delivered by teamsters, burned in cast iron stoves by residents, and shoveled into steam furnaces by stationary firemen and engineers, its distribution required thousands of small businessmen and craft workers. Although the "Gas Trust" also used coal, burning it in a factory to produce methane, its distribution was the very definition of "modernity": corporate, centralized, and mechanized.[19]

These corporations and their new technology startled older producers. Reflecting upon his career in the teaming business, Howard Levansellaer Willett noted the market's deadly power:

> Here in America, just one weapon . . . cut-throat competition. Respectable old businesses who clung to old ways . . . old methods . . . quietly passed away. Hundreds of thousands of them . . . millions of workers displaced. Most found new skills and a few forty-five year-old men threw in the sponge . . . refused to work. They puttered around the house . . . one suspender unbuttoned. . . . "Everybody works at our house but my old man." Dead is dead! Firing squad or competition. . . . But competition is an American word. It is a friendly everyday, "on our side" word, so we shrug it off, forget its deadly implications.[20]

The lower middle class responded to these pressures by intervening in the economy and actually attempting to govern the market. Chicago's craft workers and proprietors established a wide range of unions, associations, and agreements that regulated prices, wages, and production though self-styled laws, enforced by fines, strikes, boycotts, and, if necessary, violence. These orders, although privately controlled, claimed to be legitimate, authoritative, and exclusive governments, challenging both property rights and the sovereignty of the state. As such, their ordering schemes were a militant response to the transformation of the American economy that, at the time, seemed a genuine threat to corporate capitalism in cities like Chicago.

This governance depended above all upon organization. Craft workers were feverish organizers. The first Chicagoans to unionize were construction workers, but employees in transportation, retail, and service followed closely behind, obtaining charters from the American Federation of Labor. Though commentators today sometimes contend that retail and service workers are unorganizable, history suggests otherwise. By 1904, the Retail Clerk's Protective Association had seventeen local unions in Chicago. Transportation workers were even more successful. Between 1902 and 1905, teamsters formed forty-eight new locals with more than 20,000 members. Until manufacturing workers unionized during the Great Depression, such craft workers formed the backbone of the Chicago Federation of Labor. As late as 1929, 72 percent of the city's unionists worked in construction, teaming, service, trade, government, and amusements.[21]

Small businessmen also fervently associated, filling Chicago with local business organizations. In 1897, the Lakeside Directory of Chicago listed groups of plumbers, bottle dealers, carpenters, cooks, drapers, jewelers, liquor dealers, masons, plumbers, tailors, retail druggists, theatrical mechanics, and undertakers. In the coming years, more emerged, including the Chicago Grocers and Butchers Association, the Chicago Master Steam Fitters, the Master Horseshoers Protective Association, and the West Chicago Liverymen and Undertakers Association, among many, many others.

The men who administered these organizations were typical, if extreme, examples of their class. Labor leaders were socially mobile, leaving unions to become employers and even to administer trade associations. As a young man in 1905, James B. Barry led the railway express drivers in a strike against the powerful express delivery companies. By 1917, Barry was the secretary of the Chicago Contracting Team Owners Association.[22] William D. O'Brien, a powerful mason contractor and president of local and national trade associations, had been president of the local bricklayers union in the 1870s. In 1900, the current president of the bricklayers' union, George P. Gubbins, referred to "Billy O'Brien" as:

> a man who stands around with a fat roll of money in his pocket, and
> he calls men everything under the sun. It is fortunate for O'Brien that
> I never worked for him, or else there would be a case for the coroner.

By 1912, however, Gubbins himself no longer held union office. Like O'Brien, he had become a mason contractor.[23]

The lower middle class dominated Chicago politics in the Progressive Era, and partisanship drew unionists and employers still closer together.

Labor leaders like George Gubbins, William C. Pomeroy, and Martin "Skinny" Madden stood behind Democratic mayor Carter Harrison II. In return, Harrison gave these men city jobs. An 1899 investigation showed that between thirteen and twenty-two union officials held public offices such as brick inspector, examiner of engineers, and others. Meanwhile, as the writer Hoyt King notes, local government was the province of "business men, with politics for a specialty."[24] King referred not to wealthy merchants like Marshall Field, but to men like U.S. Senator William Lorimer (a brick dealer), as well as to lesser lights like Sheriff James Pease (a painter) and Appellate Court Clerk Thomas N. "Doc" Jamieson (a druggist). Among the thirty-five victors in the 1905 aldermanic elections were a city cement tester, a contracting plumber, a paint dealer, a general contractor, and a mason contractor.[25]

Leaders in politics, labor, and small business often sprang from the same families. Over the course of his career, William H. "Red" Curran worked as a bailiff, a deputy sheriff, a brewery agent, a Republican aldermanic candidate, a plumbing contractor, an officer of the plumber's union, the president of the Chicago Building Trades Council, and as Illinois state factory inspector. Curran's "long tailed tribe" included Thomas Curran, a Republican state representative and former saloonkeeper, as well as a county employee, a city bridge tender, a municipal court judge, a bailiff, and the superintendent of the Bridewell jail. Jimmy Carroll, brother of Plasterer's Union president Edward Carroll, was a saloonkeeper and alderman in Evanston. Siblings Anthony and Joseph D'Andrea controlled unions of hod carriers, sewer diggers, tunnel workers, water pipe extension laborers, and macaroni manufacturers. In addition, Anthony was at different times a priest, linguist, pimp, alderman, and committeeman in Chicago's Nineteenth Ward.[26]

Labor leaders and their bosses were rivals, yet the civility and even affection that often followed violent strikes and lockouts were notable. Organizations fought when agreements lapsed, as both sides sought new rules favorable to their interests, but unionists still praised their employers for their "fairness," while employers cast their workers as members of a business family. This rhetoric enabled the concrete relationships developing in this period. Workers and employers overcame their differences by directing their energies toward mastering the marketplace and asserting exclusive "legal" powers over wages, prices, and work rules. Sometimes governance was internal to unions, which claimed both workers and employers as members. The Chicago Federation of Musicians (CFM), for example, established a court to enforce its wage and price rules. In September 1904, the CFM suspended Henry Doehne, the musical director of the Garrick Theatre and a member in good standing for thirty years, and fined him $260 for thirteen violations of the union price list. Without his union card, Doehne could neither continue as an employer nor obtain employment as a musician in Chicago.[27]

In other cases, organizations of workers and small employers signed exclusive agreements, promising mutual assistance in controlling economic conditions. The most potent agreements existed in the teaming industry. For example, on May 21, 1902, the Coal Teamsters' Union #4 and the Coal Team Owners' Association signed an agreement stating:

> Party of the first part (the Coal Team Owners' Association) agrees to employ none but members of the Coal Teamsters' Union, Local #4, in good standing and carrying the regular working card of the organization.
>
> We (the Coal Teamsters' Union) further agree that we will not work for any firm that does not belong to the Coal Team Owners Association.

In December, fearing an indictment for conspiracy to restrain trade, they changed the language of second clause to read:

> We agree that we will use our best endeavors to have all employers of coal teamsters become members of the Coal Team Owners' Association.

The new language did not alter the effect of the agreement. In 1903, journalist Ray Stannard Baker asked Milton Booth, the secretary of the union, whether any nonunion teamsters worked in the city. Booth answered: "No, unless they are in the hospital." When Baker asked the equivalent question of John C. Driscoll, the representative of the team owners, Driscoll responded "You'll have to look for them [independent contractors] with a spy glass."[28]

Similar agreements closed the market to new entrepreneurs and laborers, some of them African-American and some female. Many historians have noted the racism and sexism of craft unions, but often without describing the broad context for this discrimination in the period before World War One. First, not all craft organizations were equally biased; some local unions of janitors, hod carriers, and teamsters admitted African Americans on an equal basis. Second, though some organizations explicitly barred blacks and women, the demographics of Chicago's labor force before 1914 dictated that closed shop arrangements actually most frequently hindered white male nonunionists seeking employment in the city's shops, yards, and building sites. Blacks and women challenged the exclusivity of skilled trades in Chicago primarily during major lockouts, when the largest firms hired them as replacement workers. Such clashes created a vicious circle that perpetuated animosity between these groups; exclusion prompted excluded individuals to "scab," which only encouraged more restrictive policies among unions and associations.[29]

Racial and sexual restrictions were aspects of a broader preoccupation with governance. Craft workers defended the notion of exclusivity itself, claiming that a diverse membership threatened "the validity, tenacity and family of the trade union, and the unity and discipline therein." Perhaps this was a rationalization, but it suggests the functional and ideological justifications for exclusivity. A racially and sexually homogeneous membership strengthened solidarity within each local, reducing the threat of factionalism. Moreover, exclusivity was central to a moral economy that prized organization and control above equal opportunity and freedom of contract. The continuing squabbles between different craft unions over jurisdictional lines further exemplified their near-obsessive dedication to governing their trades.[30]

This broad governmental mentality clashed directly with the ambitions of Chicago's corporate elite. Labor historians have correctly argued that exclusivity impeded the organization of mass-production workers in the city's steel mills and slaughterhouses. Yet the teamsters' agreement directly restricted the access of corporations to markets controlled by the lower middle class, engendering the fevered resentment of Chicago's commercial elite. In 1902, the Coal Teamsters Local #704 and the Chicago Coal Team Owners demanded that downtown buildings including Marshall Field & Co., downtown hotels, and other businesses stop using gas for heat and power during the summer. Fearing that People's Gas, Light and Coke would eventually put them out of business, the drivers and dealers demanded these buildings remove their gas appliances and threatened to stop all coal delivery to defiant firms during the colder months. The department stores initially refused to capitulate, but they finally acceded when they ran short of coal the next winter. The "Gas Trust," Marshall Field, and the downtown corporations had bowed before the lower-middle-class alliance.[31]

Rules governing workers, technology, wages, and hours angered elite businessmen and represented a real threat to their power in the city. Many scholars have suggested that small businessmen were more hostile to unions and trade agreements than corporations. In fact, while many small businessmen in Chicago actively engaged in collective bargaining, the city's corporate elite rejected any and all unions during this period. In 1903, frustrated by the cooperation between unions and associations in trade like construction and teaming, wealthy businessmen including Charles Thorne, the general manager of Montgomery Ward and Company, founded the Employers' Association of Chicago, the city's foremost open-shop group. These men viewed craft unions and allied associations as a more immediate threat to their interests than emerging radical unions like the Industrial Workers of the World. Indeed, the bloodiest labor dispute in Chicago's history—the teamsters' strike of 1905—pitted the Employers' Association and its corporate constituents against a petit bourgeois alliance of drivers and contractors, not against insurgent industrial workers.[32]

Later, the lower middle class and its organizations influenced New Deal policy, perhaps more so than better-known "corporate liberals." The trade agreements favored by New Deal architects like Raymond Moley were present in Chicago as early as the 1880s. National policies like the National Industrial Recovery Act (NIRA) ratified the long-standing arrangements that governed urban craftsmen and their bosses. Not coincidentally, contractors and shopkeepers were strong supporters of Chicago's Kelly-Nash Democratic political machine, which helped sweep Roosevelt into power during the 1930s.[33]

In the end, the lower middle class was an active participant in history, establishing its own communities and refusing to accept the boundaries imposed by the wage relation. Craft workers dabbled in business and politics, while businessmen allied themselves with militant workers. Together they used unions, associations, and trade agreements to govern competition and resist economic transformation. In this sense, they were conservative, for they opposed both radically egalitarian social change and the modernization of their crafts. But their conservatism placed them in direct opposition to a corporate elite who envisioned a technologically sophisticated, hierarchically organized, and nationally integrated economy.

The Corporate Reconstruction of Middle-Class Manhood

CLARK DAVIS

In the summer of 1925, *Sunset Magazine* published an article entitled "Making $5 Grow to Millions," which chronicled the story of retail magnate George Pepperdine. The author effusively described how Pepperdine, with "little formal education and in poor health," initially worked as a bookkeeper but had "no intention of working for someone else all his life." In 1909 Pepperdine started a mail-order accessory catalog for auto parts that grew by the mid-1920s into a lucrative chain of 125 stores.

The tale of Pepperdine's dramatic rise to independent wealth resonated in middle-class culture. Though faced with challenging circumstances, he steadfastly pursued independent business success, and in doing so, epitomized the masculine ideal for ambitious white men. Yet ironically, in the midst of praising this "self-made" entrepreneur, the author of this article discussed the benefits of working as an employee in Pepperdine's company. He reported that "it is not easy to get into the Pepperdine organization, but if he passes the test and is accepted as one of the family, the salaries and bonuses are attractive and the opportunities for promotion extraordinary."[1] In celebrating both Pepperdine's business achievements and the rewards of employment in his company, the author straddled a growing chasm between lingering nineteenth-century expectations of middle-class manhood, which emphasized individual accomplishment, and the twentieth-century reality that increasing numbers of American men worked as salaried employees in bureaucratic hierarchies.

The *Sunset* article's conflicting themes illuminate a clash between a long-held middle-class ideal and capitalism's new realities. The dominant middle-class construction of occupational success had long glorified economic independence as a means of providing security and perhaps opportunities for capital accumulation. Andrew Carnegie expressed the traditional (and notably anticorporate) American success ethic in a speech to students at Cornell University: "Is any would-be businessman before me content in forecasting his future, to figure himself as laboring all his life for a fixed salary? Not one, I am sure."[2] The increasing presence of large corporations around the turn of the century, however, made lifelong salaried employment in a large bureaucracy a distinct possibility. While historians speak of this as an era of bureaucratization, career ideals did not transform in perfect sync with changes in economic and social organization. Instead, business structures evolved more quickly than attitudes regarding work, success, and careers. The prospect of corporate employment subsequently raised troubling concerns for ambitious white men. What kind of status would a corporate position offer? What were the advantages and disadvantages of corporate employment in comparison to other potential occupational choices? Ultimately, what meaning would a corporate career have for its holders?[3]

The rise of American big business required a new generation of Americans to reconsider meanings of success, community, and security in a rapidly urbanizing and bureaucratizing society. In this process, the corporate workplace became the shopfloor of the nation's modern middle class. This article explores a critical part of this history by probing the challenges emergent corporate capitalism posed to traditional notions of middle-class masculinity and then by examining the subsequent struggle between business leaders and broader categories of Americans to redefine "manhood" in the new organizational order.[4]

Because we know that large corporations became the dominant force in the American economy, it is easy to assume that American men simply came to accept an occupational culture that posed disturbing challenges to their ideals. Indeed, we know that conceptions of manhood during the Progressive Era increasingly centered on activities outside the workplace. This reality, however, obscures the intense early twentieth-century struggle over corporate careers' social meaning. Leaders sought the services of a privileged group of Americans—young, educated white men—and needed to win them over from viewing bureaucratic employment with disdain; business officials thus endeavored to present corporate employment as a reasonable trade-off between desires for security, autonomy, and status. Young white American men, in turn, could not simply dismiss or accept the new corporate order but instead tried to negotiate the best possible opportunities. The business office itself became contested terrain as leaders and employees struggled to understand and shape the new occupational order and new manly identities.[5] By the end of the 1920s, advancement up the corporate ladder had become a legitimate route to the attainment of virtuous manhood, even as entrepreneurial ideals continued to reverberate strongly in middle-class culture.[6]

Southern California, where business development progressed at a frantic pace between 1900 and 1930, serves as a natural setting for this story. Los Angeles emerged in the 1920s as the nation's "corporate frontier," a setting where economic accumulation occurred more rapidly than any other place in the country during this period, and where new business enterprises did not have to displace an earlier industrial economy. From 1880 to 1930, Los Angeles grew from a small agricultural town of barely 10,000 inhabitants to a metropolitan center with more than 2,000,000 residents. Its economic infrastructure correspondingly transformed from small farms and businesses to massive, heavily capitalized corporate bureaucracies.[7] By the 1920s, Los Angeles was home not only to some of the largest companies in the region, but to national leaders in oil, banking, insurance, utilities, and transportation.

Southern California's social, political, and economic landscape was distinguished in important ways from other urban centers. First, because turn-of-the-century Los Angeles businesses emerged in a small-scale, largely nonindustrialized economy, they were able to influence the local culture more profoundly than their counterparts in well-established eastern urban centers. Second, Los Angeles's economy had a comparatively large service sector and, thus, a larger proportion of nonmanual employees than eastern industrial centers.[8]

Despite these differences in the nature and process of southern California's economic development, the evidence suggests that while emerging western corporations had greater opportunities than eastern firms to innovate policies and shape the local milieu, and greater opportunities to negotiate corporate cultures, business experience differed there by degree, not kind. Distinctive features of western life affected the way southern California companies operated and dealt with employees, but *process* took precedence over *place* in molding corporate cultures. Large businesses, be they in Los Angeles, Chicago, or Atlanta, ultimately faced similar difficulties when it came to recruiting, securing, and motivating talented young men. More often than not, they adopted common strategies. While southern California's distinctive environment shaped the interaction between companies and employees, a truly national corporate culture had developed by the 1920s.

In their efforts to recruit long-term, dedicated employees, business officers in Los Angeles and throughout the nation drew from a society that had for generations held economic independence as the cultural ideal for white males, and even the very essence of what it meant to "be a man." This anti-bureaucratic tradition in the construction of Anglo-American masculinity had flourished since the colonial era. For the nation's privileged, native-born white males, responsible manhood entailed working toward and ultimately achieving this status, whether through farming, a craft, or business proprietorship.[9] Opportunities for such independent employment, however, waned in the late nineteenth century as the development of a capitalist market economy created a middling sector of white-collar workers employed in bookkeeping, clerical work, and sales. In an environment of increasing occupational stratification, these nonmanual positions became associated with improved social relationships, including an annual salary rather than daily wages, higher overall pay, the ability to specialize in certain trades or professional activities, and a removal from factory work's more grueling and dangerous environment. Yet because of its dependent context, white-collar work seemed in many ways distinctly unappealing to ambitious white men—not unlike factory toil.[10] Many thus viewed these jobs primarily as stepping-stones to independent business proprietorship. The idea of a business life-cycle culminating in occupational independence became a tenuous compromise in middle-class Americans' career aspirations.[11]

But if middle-class men had thus grown accustomed to the idea of white-collar work as an acceptable career starting point, the widespread appearance of the corporate enterprise in the early twentieth century threatened this settlement. By World War I, expanding oligopolies dominated key economic sectors. Corporate rosters in every major national city included supervisory and managerial positions in sales, operations, accounting, and numerous related departments, as well as scattered general office personnel.[12] The number of white-collar employees surged. By 1930, more than fourteen million Americans, greater than 30 percent of the civilian labor force, claimed employee status in office, sales, or professional jobs.[13]

Whereas many Americans had traditionally believed that nonmanual positions in smaller firms offered modest opportunities for individual initiative and some control over the working environment, the size and systematization of the new bureaucracies seemed to limit prospects for independence. Employees, even those in fairly high managerial positions, found themselves entangled in complex operational hierarchies, subordinated to a chain of command, and with no realistic opportunity to direct the enterprise.[14] Corporate employment thus often required troubling degrees of subservience. In 1913, Pacific Mutual Life Insurance Company's vice president informed employees that "when a certain agent once told me that he was going to take a week off, I wondered how or why. He had not really been on the job and therefore could not, logically, get off. His week would be a dismal one because he had not earned it." By the mid-1920s, Pacific Mutual required its employees to keep elaborate productivity reports charting the number of clients interviewed and policies sold per hour, and thereby the value of their time. [15]

The broad nature of corporate operations also meant that personnel were vulnerable, like small businesspersons and farmers, to larger market forces but had less control over the firm's response to such difficulties. Many serving "successfully" found their jobs abruptly terminated when their employer suffered financial setbacks. Pacific Mail Steamship personnel received pink slips in 1925 and 1926, for instance, when despite solid profits, the company's failure to regain its rights to government-contracted shipping routes resulted in its dissolution. Employees such as Eugene C. Walsh, who served with the company for seven years and garnered two promotions, received a letter reading: "we very much regret the necessity of severing your connection with the company . . . during the long period that you have worked for the company your service has been most satisfactory and it is with the utmost regret that it must be terminated." Less senior employees received more terse notices.[16]

Women's increasing presence in corporate offices made the likelihood of dependent employment still more problematic. During the Progressive Era, women came to dominate the lower clerical rungs. The percentage of stenographers nationally who were female, for instance, grew from 5 percent in 1870 to 96 percent in 1930. The prominence of women within the white-collar workforce imperiled the acceptable manly identity that office work had earlier offered. American men increasingly viewed the corporate workplace as a "feminized" institution.[17]

While the presence of women challenged male identities, corporate executives responded to young white men's reservations about white-collar careers with multi-layered strategies to define big business employment as the new standard of middle-class male success. Leaders implemented strict hierarchies of gender that underscored male privilege and sought to essentialize the masculinity of white-collar work. By 1925, women held one-third of all white-collar jobs nationwide, but, with only rare exceptions (notably in the insurance industry), employers relegated women to the lower-rung clerical positions. From 1910 to 1930, the number of Americans working as proprietors, managers, and officials, and as agents in real estate and insurance, more than doubled; women, however, never constituted more than 6 percent of this group.[18]

Female office-worker demographics in part reflect many young women's decisions to assume entry-level posts and subsequently quit within a few years to get married. Evidence suggests, however, that employers themselves often imposed this "marriage bar." Executives sought to discredit female clerical workers' grievances by claiming women left for marital reasons, rather than out of frustration over poor pay, tedious work, and no opportunities for advancement. Both subtle and overt discriminatory hiring and promotion practices assured that men retained control of the corporate workplace, even as women outnumbered them in many offices.[19]

Los Angeles executives further limited salaried "career" positions largely to white men, accentuating a correlation between "whiteness" and middle-class masculinity that flourished throughout the Progressive Era.[20] In Los

Angeles, a city where business elites openly described the region as the new "cradle of Anglo-Saxon civilization," race and occupational status became intimately tied. By 1930, Los Angeles ranked second only to Baltimore among large cities in the proportion of people of color, including Mexican Americans, Asian Americans, and African Americans. The city's Anglo-American ruling class made this racial and ethnic fragmentation, compounded by communities of southern and eastern Europeans, a central issue in labor strategies. It ultimately racialized the region's workforce and carved out not only a "White" but also a near "Anglo-Saxon" monopoly on white-collar jobs.[21] Southern California's significant communities of Asian, African, and Mexican Americans worked largely in manual labor and domestic service. Los Angelenos of southern and eastern European descent served primarily in working-class jobs or pushed for upward mobility through small business initiatives. Male office jobs in the region's largest companies, on the other hand, became the domain of white men, particularly native-born persons of British descent. "Company" men were distinctive among other major occupational groups in this regard. In samples taken from the 1910 and 1920 censuses, native-born men constituted a higher proportion of white-collar employees than any other occupational category. Eighty-six percent of the 1910 sample was native born; in 1920, 80 percent was native born. In both census years, more than two-thirds of the parents of white-collar men had also been born in the United States, a figure matched only by professional and technical workers.[22]

By largely excluding women and people of color from salaried "career posts," business executives defined many rungs on the white-collar ladder as "masculine," that is, acceptable for white men. Such boundaries furthermore assured that nonmanual positions would continue to hold an element of middle-class status, even as the tasks of many white-collar jobs and the structure of much white-collar work became increasingly clerical and monotonous. Simple racial and gender segregation, however, did not necessarily give these jobs "manly" status. In other words, an occupation might be acceptable for white, male, middle-class aspirants, but not all "male jobs" conferred the peculiar status and identity this ambitious group ultimately sought. Only those professions that combined nonmanual status and a decent income with opportunities for individual achievement matched prevailing middle-class notions of male virility.[23]

Business officials responded to young men's sensitivities about the long-term prospects and manliness of white-collar jobs by constructing within their company cultures a distinct new vision of white-collar manhood. They did this by arguing that white-collar tasks called for the very best attributes of manhood, and that their business would provide opportunities to fulfill this noble destiny. To be a corporate employee, most executives argued, meant that one had gained access to a system that allowed "manly" advancement over the course of a lifetime. Accepting an office job, even a lowly clerkship, meant not that one had agreed to a low-paying routinized assignment. Rather, signing up with a large enterprise meant that one had tied his future to a major corporation whose grand successes would become his.[24] Historians who have studied the practical structure of white-collar work are well aware of the gulf of experience, power, and authority between lower-level white-collar male workers and senior managers. Yet business leaders usually ignored this chasm, at least rhetorically, in their efforts to construct corporate cultures.

The metaphor of the "ladder" emerged as the nearly universal response among business leaders in Los Angeles and throughout the nation to the widespread reservations about white-collar positions. If companies provided occupational ladders, then any position in the firm could in the long run prove a good one since it provided a basis from which to advance.[25] There were high rungs and low rungs, but the corporate ladder offered all men the same opportunity to ascend. Southern California Edison leaders, for instance, argued that "any Edison Company employee can hope to become its head since the differentiation of tasks is not permanent. There is a constant promotion of those who show ability and who have a capacity for initiative and for making decisions."[26]

The concept of the company ladder rested on the practice of promotions, which sought to fill all vacancies from within and to allow present employees to advance. For many reasons, promotion systems seemed to make good business sense and received much discussion in management circles. Numerous early twentieth-century managerial institutes published detailed treatises on the importance of internal promotions. One 1919 study spoke bluntly about the need to utilize promotion systems if a company wanted to retain its best employees: "Concerns who do not adopt the policy of making promotions from the inside cannot hope to maintain a force of ambitious capable workers." The report cited that "the lack of opportunity for advancement is a frequent cause for men leaving their jobs just at the time when their experience is becoming a real asset to the firm."[27]

Los Angeles executives listened carefully to such advice, and most major corporations implemented well-defined promotion systems. These policies allowed local firms to promote honestly the possibilities for advancement since their rapid growth created a relatively fluid labor market. Such systems flourished, for instance, in large industrial firms like Union Oil. Between 1893 and 1926, employee ranks there swelled from fifteen to more than 9,000. In the midst of this expansion, the company established promotion policies, termed "civil service policies," which mandated that vacancies be filled from within in all possible cases.[28]

Los Angeles banks also instituted policies designed to promote lifelong corporate careers. In turn-of-the-century Los Angeles, most banks were small enterprises with compact managerial hierarchies and few opportunities for advancement. During the 1910s and 1920s, however, as small banks merged with larger enterprises administered by complex chains of command, the prospect of rising through the ranks became an important enticement. Promotions soon became an institutionalized aspect of banking operations. The Farmers and Merchants National Bank, for instance, noted in 1927 that four of its top officers had risen through the ranks; three started in the entry-level position of messenger in the years 1894, 1901, and 1904.[29]

Pacific Electric, a public-regulated utility, also institutionalized promotion policies. At least by the 1920s, company materials indicate that for agents and other white-collar employees, such strategies became the rule. In 1927, Pacific Electric formalized a five-part promotion policy: 1) Station subordinates will be notified of all openings; 2) Employees must request the position in writing; 3) If qualified people exist, men from the company will fill the position; 4) Assuming all else is equal, seniority will be the basis of preference; 5) When restructuring results in staff reductions, senior employees will take the posts of juniors if their own job is cut.[30]

Yet large firms needed not merely to institute promotion policies; they had to sell the concept to employees. This required marketing the very notion of a corporate career. Los Angeles companies took up this challenge with reckless abandon and touted a new vocational path appropriate to modern urban society. Discussions of advancement opportunities and the virtual canonization of those who had risen up the company's ranks pervaded corporate cultures. When a major bank merger created the Security-First National Bank in 1929, for instance, its employee magazine heralded that promotion from within would be the new firm's organizational rule. That fall, the company magazine printed an article entitled "Making Good a Promise" that listed the names of employees receiving promotions. Los Angeles' Pacific Southwest Savings Bank went so far as to publish a detailed list of advancements its employees could expect should their service be exemplary.[31]

Union Oil enthusiastically heralded its "civil service system" in a steady stream of "mobility editorials" that emphasized the promotions possible with long and dedicated service, as well as corporate odes:

> Promotion comes to him who sticks
> unto his work and never kicks
> Who watches neither clock nor sun
> to tell him when his task his done
> who toils not by a stated chart
> defining to a jot his part
> But gladly does a little more
> than he's remunerated for
> The man, in factory or shop,
> who rises quickly to the top.[32]

The Los Angeles First National Bank repeatedly published articles promising promotions for meritorious service, including an adaptation of a Shakespeare line that began, "All The Bank's A Ladder."

Through such propaganda, Los Angeles business leaders articulated a vision of "white-collar manhood." In a particularly blatant example, Pacific Electric's "New Year's pledge" on the cover of its company magazine in 1922 literally accented its employees' manhood: "[I pledge] to be a *Man*, filling a *Man's Place* in a man's game, and prove ours the best manned industry in southern California."[33] Corporations continually linked discussions of white-collar occupational norms and ideals with images of powerful, successful men. Every local firm vividly recounted the biographies of employees receiving promotions as illustrative models of manly success. At Union Oil, those who advanced into middle- and upper-level management positions might have found their picture, short biography, and praise for their personal qualities featured prominently in the company magazine. In Pacific Electric ranks, no story was more important to company leadership than that of D. W. Pontius, who had truly worked his way up from an entry-level clerical position. In 1929, he was named president, and the firm spared no effort in promoting his career history, regularly reminding employees of his lowly beginnings. In 1928, for instance, the company magazine printed his baby picture and declared: "Know the determined-looking little fellow? Sure you do! Up the ladder to rank and fame he has lost neither the determination nor the see-all piercing eyes that are evidenced in his young childhood." The following year the magazine heralded his appointment as president by noting that Pontius "really ought to be written up for the success magazines, for no man's career more strikingly proves what an average man may accomplish. Thirty-eight years ago he started in about the humblest job a railroad could give him."[34]

The practice of masculinizing corporate careers with targeted mobility editorials and real-life accounts of corporate success occurred in most large firms. Companies also employed other more subtle strategies. Numerous issues of the *Pacific Electric Magazine*, for instance, featured articles or texts that in some way singled out, diminished, or made fun of women. In July 1924, for example, a lengthy poem entitled "A Wail 'bout the Frail," lamented the difficulty of understanding women. It opened: "A Woman is queer; there's no doubt about that, she hates to be thin and she hates to be fat; one minute it's laughter—the next it's a cry. You can't understand her however you try. But there's one thing about her that everyone knows. A woman's not dressed till she powders her nose." In another case, an article that highlighted how three women had proven themselves extremely capable in the company's engineering drafting department was followed by the joke: "It is almost as difficult for a man to live up to his ideals as for a woman to live up to her photographs."[35] Perhaps by continually singling out the difference between male employees and their female counterparts, leaders assured men of masculine status.

Amidst their frenzied efforts to cultivate a cadre of dedicated agents, Pacific Mutual leaders faced a particularly difficult challenge in affirming male identities since they also hired large numbers of female agents. Throughout the 1910s and 1920s, American insurance companies had turned to saleswomen, believing them more effective in securing women customers. By 1930, Pacific Mutual's Los Angeles agency employed sixty women who, in 1929, wrote nearly $5 million in new business. While this sales record thrilled company leaders, it put them on the defensive against some male employees who struggled with the challenge successful women posed to their occupational identity. Pacific Mutual executives responded to concerns raised by the presence of female agents in several ways. Executives occasionally wrote articles defending the practice of hiring women. The March 1930 issue, for instance, of the company magazine reprinted a newspaper column that argued: "Most working women are working because they have to, not because they want to. The modern world is giving them, not a new freedom, but a new duty." In most offices the company also established separate "women's departments" so that men and women were not technically under the same command. Finally, the company magazine discussed the activities of its female agents in a separate section called "Women and their Activities." [36]

Corporate strategies to transform career ideals raise important questions about the intersection of business structures with social practices and mores. Would ambitious young men buy into the corporate career ideal? Would success in white-collar bureaucracies become the new standard of manly achievement? Changing occupational realities clearly aided corporate efforts. The increasing dominance of big business resulted in declining opportunities for independent entrepreneurs in some sectors of the economy as small businessmen struggled to compete in the corporate world.[37] Large firms readily advertised the struggles of small businesses by way of contrast to the stability of big-business employment. Southern California Edison warned its employees in 1916 that notions of quick riches were unrealistic in comparison to "starting at the bottom of the ladder in some substantial industry and progressing rung by rung to the great things which are at the top."[38]

Measured against the promises of company rhetoric, however, opportunities for dramatic success often fell short. The simple arithmetic of corporate hierarchies dictated that not all could advance to the upper rungs of business ladders. Many employees served for long periods in stable companies yet received few if any promotions. Born in England in 1870, Edward J. Adams moved in 1891 to the United States, where he found a job as bookkeeper at Standard Oil Company. He worked at Standard Oil for twenty years before becoming clerk in Union Oil's Seattle office, a position he held until 1934 when the company promoted him to assistant agent at the Tacoma office. Despite twenty years of service in a semiprofessional position with another oil company, Union Oil's adherence to promotions from within forced Adams to enter at one of the lowest white-collar positions. He worked another twenty years before being promoted. For every story of a rapid corporate advancement, there are others of men like Adams who spent years with a company yet advanced little or not at all.[39]

Between the fading ideal of business entrepreneurship and the equally idealized picture of new corporate mobility, young men tried to carve out a delicate compromise amongst competing desires for independence, security, and status. As critics of social mobility studies have pointed out, occupational success is often subsumed by other factors as individual career aspirations are played out within a complex array of desires and needs.[40] Lloyd McCampbell, for instance, obtained a job as lease clerk for a Texas oil company in 1920, but the cold winter that followed led his girlfriend to persuade him to move to Southern California. McCampbell quit the position and moved with her, obtaining employment at Union Oil in 1922. Several years later, when the company tried to transfer him to a different city, McCampbell quit, preferring to remain at his present residence.[41]

Many employees moved from job to job for reasons not so obvious. Oliver Palmer worked as a clerk at six different companies between 1913 and 1920. The Pacific Mail Steamship Company hired the thirty-five-year-old Palmer in 1920 as a freight clerk, noting that his letters of recommendation from previous employees were all very positive. Pacific Mail began grooming Palmer for a position in their Hong Kong office. After several months, however, he resigned, obtaining an additional positive recommendation from this most recent firm. For unknown reasons, Palmer moved from city to city around the United States, generally staying less than a year at each location.[42]

Evaluating men's reaction to white-collar life is difficult because it requires one to analyze conflicting data. We can find significant numbers of American men who embraced the corporate career ideal and experienced significant advancement, just as we can find significant numbers who either rejected corporate dictates or were unsuccessful by its standards. Recognizing that salaried white-collar employment did not offer a uniform experience, young Americans became keenly sensitive to what kinds of conditions and rewards various positions would offer. A 1926 survey of office workers revealed that only slightly over half expected promotions. These already held the higher positions. Those on the lower rungs expressed the greatest pessimism.[43]

Yet as men moved up the corporate ladder, they recognized that large companies offered reasonable opportunities for social mobility, steady income, and good salaries, especially when compared to other career options. This was because most large firms experienced high turnover at the lowest rungs, but their middle- and upper-level positions were considerably more stable and comprised significant numbers of men who had risen steadily up the corporate ladder. Personnel statistics reveal that most firms encountered widespread turnover at entry-level positions. From 1904 to 1909, for example, the Pacific Mail Steamship Company hired 252 salaried male clerks. Seventy-seven of them quit shortly after being hired, never receiving a raise or promotion; eight who received a raise or promotion quit; and thirty-two were fired shortly after joining the firm. Barely half of the company's new hires during this period remained for more than several weeks.[44]

The high turnover most firms faced at entry-level positions likely reflected two factors: first, many companies did not screen terribly closely at the time of hiring but did do so after a quick evaluation of on-the-job performance. Firms soon eliminated men who seemed ill-suited to serve the company well.[45] Second, most men in these positions were young, single, and thus in a position to change locations if personal situations altered or better opportunities arose, and as these lower-level white-collar positions lost status and advancement opportunities, better opportunities likely seemed easier to find. Meanwhile, the rapid feminization of clerical positions stripped these posts of status and authority. As opportunities for promotions from these positions decreased, fewer men sought them, and those who did often remained only a short time.

In sharp contrast to the high turnover in entry-level positions, employee rosters at many companies showed greater stability in midlevel positions. At Pacific Mail, loyalists staffed managerial positions. Among the ten general officers at its San Francisco office in 1922, only two had served fewer than ten years with the company; five had served more than twenty years, one thirty-eight years, and another forty-six years. At Pacific Mutual, the twenty-nine leading agents in 1928 had held their positions for an average of 11.5 years, and most probably served the company even longer in junior positions. At Sothern California Edison, most departments reported little turnover by the 1920s. The Dispatching Department, for instance, employed, on average, between thirteen and nineteen people from 1923 to 1927, but it lost no more than two employees per year and generally experienced the departure of only one employee per year.[46]

Whereas lower-level workers could be rather easily persuaded to transfer to another firm, midlevel and senior managers felt they had much to lose. The prospect of corporate employment thus posed a perplexing picture for the ambitious young men large firms hoped to recruit and retain. On one hand, they recognized that many white-collar positions offered little hope for advancement and thus abandoned the low-status and low-paying positions as soon as other opportunities arose. And yet with each rung on the corporate ladder, men found heightened status, pay, and opportunities to advance. At some point, most employees came to believe that a career with one firm offered adequate status, security, and money, as is evidenced by the increasing personnel stability as one progressed up corporate hierarchies.

J. E. Brick started his own drilling company in the early 1920s, but quickly discovered that it was difficult to lure men from other large companies to help manage his operation. He finally found a superintendent, but only at the price of $750 a month, a salary much higher than most peers would have made.[47] Brick's difficulty in recruiting managers from established companies reflects the extent to which they enjoyed secure positions with good salaries, benefits, and promotion opportunities.

As corporations sought to shape workforces appropriate to their needs, and ambitious young men juggled competing desires for security, wealth, and status, the popular construction of masculine identity became a central test of corporate cultural power. In the late nineteenth century, white middle-class culture celebrated the rugged individual who struggled for athletic, economic, or other personal achievement as the epitome of true manhood. The white-collar employee of the twentieth century stood in sharp contrast to this construction. If the nation truly became a "corporate society" during the Progressive Era, then certainly manly ideals would have had to change.

Yet, through the 1920s, white-collar men were the object of sharply conflicting representations in popular culture. Just as the "collar line" itself evolved to distinguish between working- and middle-class status, an equally powerful pecking order developed among the various steps on the corporate ladder to define acceptable variants of white male identity. In films and literature, senior figures in corporate hierarchies increasingly appeared as strong-willed individuals with considerable power. Such characterizations hinted that corporate ladders, as promised by leadership, did in fact offer ambitious and talented men opportunities for agency and achievement. Cultural depictions of employees farther down the ladder, however, yielded less flattering portrayals. Books, magazines, and films more often showed middle- and lower-level workers as faceless pawns with no initiative or control. The antibureaucratic tradition in earlier constructions of American masculinity lingered as those working in subservient positions appeared pitiful and effeminate.

Safety Last, a popular 1923 Harold Lloyd film, captured the varying degrees of status and respect on the white-collar ladder. The movie opens with Lloyd at a small-town train station leaving for the big city. His fiancée tells him at the depot, "It would break my heart if you failed." Once in the city, the best position Lloyd can find is as a lowly sales clerk in a fabric store. Embarrassed by the job, he seeks to make his fiancée believe he is "making it big." He sends her jewelry and writes false notes about his prosperity. Ironically, all the talk of Harold's success leads his fiancée's mother to worry about him being all alone with so much money, so the fiancée decides to visit. When she arrives, she first spots him working behind the sales desk, and gasps in horror, but seeing her panic-stricken face, Lloyd pretends to be a manager helping to train clerks. Harold then receives a note to see the real general manager about a complaint, and coyly excuses himself, but minutes later, his fiancée observes him coming out of the general manager's office and again assumes *he* is the manager. This makes her deliriously proud. Lloyd ultimately escapes the predicament by gaining his fiancée's love and approval through scaling a twelve-story building in a heroic act.

Safety Last offers a powerful commentary on the precarious status of bureaucratic employment. Although nonmanual work gained middle-class status during the nineteenth century, by the period of corporate emergence it alone did not convey masculine identity. Senior management became esteemed figures, yet according to both the employee and his fiancée, the lowest clerks within the company occupied positions of near-shame. Notably, Lloyd wins his fiancée's approval only through an act of physical prowess, a clear reversion to blue-collar notions of physical masculinity.[48]

Yet if growing corporate interests could not entirely rewrite constructions of masculinity, the emergence of corporate capitalism did begin to influence representations of employment in popular culture. Surveys suggested that the common nineteenth-century derision of "hirelings" and dependent employees in American literature faded somewhat. During the Progressive Era, American authors and playwrights sometimes, though not always, gave corporate employment greater recognition and status.[49] The mere fact of changing occupational realities no doubt led to shifting cultural understandings. As corporations came to dominate American business, executives became key players in the nation's economy and public life, and writers increasingly drew on business themes in their work. The increasing representation of corporate life in American literature had the reciprocal effect of granting it heightened cultural legitimacy.[50]

As the corporate model took hold, many middle-class publications celebrated the white-collar career ideal. Los Angelenos read of the merits of corporate advancement not only in company publications, but in various local magazines. Since its beginning in the late nineteenth century, *The Graphic*, a Los Angeles progressive journal, had highlighted business leaders in a column entitled "prominent personalities." By the 1910s, these personalities frequently included men who had climbed company ladders. In the 1920s, *Sunset* began to feature essays by corporate personnel directors and career counselors that not only affirmed corporate careers, but also offered tips on how to get promoted.[51] *Saturday Night*, which catered to affluent southern Californians, reported regularly on significant promotions within local companies. With descriptions similar to those found in company magazines, it highlighted recent promotions as symbols of regional pride and heralded corporate executives as role models for young men.[52]

While advancement up bureaucratic ranks became a promising route to a successful masculine identity, powerful critiques of bureaucratic employment continued to offer steady challenges to the voice of corporate interests in middle-class culture. For every representation celebrating one who had advanced to a leadership position, critical indictments of corporate employment focused on the plight of men who had not. In 1912, the *Atlantic Monthly* ran an article titled "The Man Who Failed," which chronicled the story of a washed-up thirty-five-year-old former manager. Fired after failing to gain a big promotion, the man could not obtain a new position because no one trusted him.[53] A 1923 *Sunset* article depicted the plight of a man whose wife left him after twenty-three years of marriage. Among her reasons, she felt "ashamed" of her husband's position as a clerk. The man noted that "he had no intention of remaining a clerk always," and he went on to start a successful business of his own.[54]

Perhaps no stronger critique of white-collar employment ever appeared in American popular culture than King Vidor's 1928 film *The Crowd*, seen by hundreds of thousands of American moviegoers. Released at a time when big business seemed to reign supreme, the two-hour silent movie presented evidence of the continued challenge facing corporate leaders in their efforts to lure young men into white-collar employment. The story begins on July 4, 1900, with the birth of Johnny Sims in an idyllic small town. Upon seeing his new son, Johnny's father triumphantly announces, "There's a little man the world is going to hear from all right. . . . I'm going to give him every opportunity." Twenty-one years later, however, Johnny Sims is working as #137 in a New York City insurance company, toiling away in what can only be described as white-collar hell. His desk is placed in a vast room where hundreds of identically dressed young men sit in evenly spaced rows turning page after page of documents in perfect unison. Johnny's home life proves equally stifling as his wife and in-laws grow bitter over his inability to climb in the firm. When he finally gets a break and wins $100 in an advertising jingle contest, an automobile strikes and kills his youngest child during the celebration. Despondent with grief, Johnny then quits before being fired for poor performance. The film closes with Johnny and his wife escaping to the movies. He sits in the theater having a great time, but as the camera fades, viewers see him watching amidst a crowd of thousands whose appearance and actions are exactly the same as his. Even in this brief moment of pleasure, he remains immersed in the crowd.[55]

The Crowd offered Americans a bleak appraisal of modern life in the 1920s. Small-town kids moved to cities only to find themselves enveloped in urban jungles where opportunities for personal autonomy and individual achievement were, at best, rare. If a young man already leery of white-collar work saw the film, it likely reinforced his fear of "working for someone else" any longer than necessary. Executives, as well, no doubt winced at its depiction of company life, recognizing the message it sent to young men searching for promising ways to start their careers.

The United States may have become an urban, corporate society in statistical terms by the 1920s, but the cultural corporate transformation of middle-class career expectations and ideals was far from complete. The dominance of corporate business structures in the nation's economy during the early twentieth century did not fully overturn the long-standing anti-bureaucratic tradition in the construction of American masculinity. Indeed, even a century after the period of corporate emergence, the nation's major employers continue to confront a society in which many ambitious men disdain the thought of bureaucratic employment.

Yet despite the persistence of a powerful individualistic strain in the social construction of masculinity, corporate leadership could claim substantial success by the 1920s in their efforts to rewrite the standards of success. Through internal promotion systems and widespread publicity of promotions, they sought to create a new social ideal of middle-class corporate mobility that would attract talented young Americans to their firms, and large numbers of Americans did indeed cast their lots with corporate interests. This shift was reflected in the popular culture that increasingly featured and often celebrated corporate management as a social ideal. Corporate career ideals did not replace entrepreneurial and individualistic desires, but they did become an accepted alternative. By the 1920s, constructions of middle-class manhood had expanded to encompass both entrepreneurial or professional independence and ascendance up the corporate ladder as legitimate avenues to success.

The Rise of the Realtor®: Professionalism, Gender, and Middle-Class Identity, 1908–1950

JEFFREY M. HORNSTEIN

In 1917, the word "Realtor" appeared for the first time in *Webster's International Dictionary*. Seeking a way to differentiate in the public mind the professional from the unethical practitioner, Minnesota real estate dealer Charles N. Chadbourn came up with the term after a "street urchin . . . thrust a newspaper headline under my nose" decrying the fraudulent practices of unspecified "real estate men." The generic "real estate man" in question was not a member of Chadbourn's local real estate board, but "only an obscure speculator with desk room in some back office." Nevertheless, he had, Chadbourn claimed, "besmirched every 'real estate man' in Minneapolis." The 1916 Convention of the National Association of Real Estate Boards (NAREB) approved the adoption of the term as the official designation of an active member of the Association. In 1920 the District Court of Hennepin County, Minnesota, decided in favor of the Realtors in a case against a telephone directory publisher that had indiscriminately used the word in listings.[1] The court asserted that the word "had never been used in any way whatsoever until so invented" and could thus be used only by those duly licensed by the National Association of Real Estate Boards. Until the Lanham Acts of 1948 changed federal patent regulations to allow protection for registered collective marks, the National Association fought and won sixteen cases on the local and state levels to protect its symbolic property.[2]

"Realtor" quickly gained popular currency. In 1920 writer Frank Ward O'Malley misused the word in a *Saturday Evening Post* story satirizing the travails of a young, home-seeking couple.[3] He was swiftly informed of his error by William H. Wilson, district vice-president of the National Association and president of the Philadelphia Real Estate Board, who dispatched a letter to *Post* editor George Horace Lorimer informing him of the dictionary definition of the term. Wilson noted pointedly the Minnesota court decision. Lorimer apologized publicly to the Realtors, affirming the word's remarkable circulation in just four years. "Probably nine men out of ten" would be willing to place a wager upon their "ability to give a correct definition of the word . . . yet eight of them would lose their bets." The proper definition was not obvious—"for though all Realtors are real estate brokers, not all real estate brokers are Realtors by a long shot." The editor praised the real estate men for having "hit upon an exceedingly clever and ingenious device to assist them in the achievement of their aims" to become recognized as professionals.[4]

Critic H. L. Mencken was less impressed by the symbolic innovation. Commenting upon the lofty rhetoric of the Realtor's Code of Ethics, Mencken wrote, "In the conduct of business a *Realtor* is bound by much stricter rules than incommode an ordinary business man; in fact, he is cribbed, cabined and confined in a way that almost suggests the harsh working conditions of a justice of the Supreme Court or an archbishop." He proposed an etymology for the term, suggesting that Realtor was "derived from two Spanish words, *real* meaning royal, and *toro*, a bull," and that it thus connoted "*royal bull*." Chadbourn replied, apparently without irony, that, "*Real estate* originally meant royal grant. It is so connected with land in the public mind that *Realtor* is easily understood, even at a first hearing. -*Or* is a suffix meaning a doer, one who performs an act, as *grantor*, *executor*, *sponsor*, *administrator*. *Realtor*, a doer in real estate."[5]

My purpose in this essay is twofold. On one level, it is to tell a story about the consolidation and rationalization of real estate brokerage, a fascinating case study in the history of the professionalization of business.[6] On another level, though, the essay explores what this particular professionalization project, the rise of the Realtors, tells us about the making of the American middle class in the twentieth century.[7] I propose that a complex tension between "professional" and "entrepreneur," themselves historically variable categories, defined the twentieth-century American middle class. Simultaneously and constitutively a believer in the authority of expertise and occupational autonomy, the corporation and free enterprise, public service and private profit, the Realtor exemplifies the twentieth-century American middle class. The Realtor embodies a variety of early-twentieth-century cultural, social, and economic trends, including the drive to professionalize business, the rapid expansion of white-collar labor and its heterosocialization, and the enormous expansion of the homebuilding and home-selling industries. An analysis of the rise of the Realtor can shed new light on a central problem in the history of American culture: How did the vast majority of Americans come to think of themselves as "middle class" by 1940?[8]

The story of the rise of the Realtors can be told in two parts. During the first period, roughly 1908–1929, leaders in the field institutionalized the occupation. The real estate men attempted to create and deploy cultural capital by inventing a masculine professional mystique. They gathered prominent local boards together into the National Association of Real Estate Boards, fashioned NAREB into a formidable political influence, constructed a Code of Ethics to govern professional behavior, and established a regime of standard real estate practices. They invented and adopted the word "Realtor" in an attempt to create exclusivity and prestige by symbolically associating a particular set of professional claims with a brand name. The Realtors rose to national prominence during World War I with their generally lauded work as "Dollar-a-Year Men" in the Real Estate Division of the United States Housing Corporation. In the immediate postwar years through the late 1920s, the Realtors reached the apogee of their pre–World World II influence and prestige. NAREB's postwar "Own Your Own Home" campaign coincided with the unprecedented housing boom of 1922–1928.[9] The leaders of the National Association became advisors to federal officials on housing and other real estate matters, particularly during the Hoover years. This wartime and postwar collaboration set the pattern and agenda for national housing policy for much of the subsequent forty years.[10] Finally, during this period the National Association commenced its educational and research programs, forging links with prominent academicians in its quest to create a scientific basis for claims to professional status.

Two trends emerging in the mid-1920s posed serious challenges to the masculine-scientific professional model, and this challenge defines the second part of the narrative. First, a housing bust in the late 1920s delegitimized the Realtors' claims to science-based professionalism. Second, while there had long been women dealing in real estate, their numbers increased dramatically in the late 1920s, and many applied for brokers' licenses in those states with license laws. Many of the older and larger boards in the East and Midwest refused to admit women as members prior to the 1940s, but women Realtors from the West Coast began to make appearances at national conventions in the late 1920s. This influx of women posed a serious challenge to the early masculine model of the profession. The rhetoric of the profession clashed with women's culturally resonant claims for admittance to the masculine world of brokerage and sales. In the context of first the Depression and then the demographic, social, and economic pressures of World War II, the profession was re-gendered. Women captured the largest segment of the profession, residential sales. Venerable old boards, such as those of Philadelphia, Pittsburgh, and Chicago, finally admitted women into their ranks in the postwar decade. Women Realtors broke the gender barrier by strategically deploying the ideology of domesticity to create a female dominion in real estate, in the process participating in the creation of a new flexible, heterosocial model of professionalism.[11]

While ideal notions of "home sweet home" may be traced to the 1820s, it is with the emergence of "domestic science" in the postbellum years that the American home truly became an object of expert knowledge and professional intervention. By the first decades of the twentieth century, social workers, home economists, architects, urban planners, housing reformers, housing officials, and real estate agents planned, regulated, inspected, designed, and sold houses, wrote and spoke prolifically on the subject of the American home. Never before had "home" become such a sustained focus of scientific, technical, reformist, and business discourse, shaping the occupational identity of several emerging professions. A particular, narrow conception of the home became a symbol for ideal family relationships and notions of citizenship.[12] The conception of a real estate brokerage as a profession depended upon the existence of this intellectual-cultural object and the discourse of professionalism surrounding it. As putative home experts, Realtors reserved central roles for themselves in the promotion of homeownership and the creation of housing policy from the early 1920s onward.[13]

The Rise of the Broker and the Local Board

Conditions in the United States in the late nineteenth century were ripe for the emergence of a specialized class of persons dealing in real property. While partly a myth, the closing of the frontier, announced by Frederick Jackson Turner in 1893, meant that the vast land resources of the continent were now in either private or public hands; there was little uncharted territory remaining.[14] As the forces of industrialization drew rural people and immigrants into the rapidly growing cities, informational asymmetry, particularly with regard to finding a domicile or a place to establish a business, became a considerable problem. And since most Americans purchased their houses, their most precious and expensive durable goods, from amateur vendors—other homeowners—this created a niche for expert negotiators. Real estate brokerage rose also, in part, to fill and profit by this social need.[15]

As in many other spheres of American life, the organizational impulse struck real estate brokers after the Civil War. While a few boards, such as Baltimore (1856) and St. Louis (1877) were established earlier, the first major organizational wave took place in the 1880s. A second wave of board formation followed on the heels of the founding of the National Association of Real Estate Boards in 1908. Modeled after stock exchanges, early real estate boards brought owners and purchasers of real property together to negotiate. Real estate boards aimed to facilitate transactions, to standardize commission schedules and leases, and more generally to stabilize values by centralizing information about real estate.

After a dazzling rise in property values from the 1860s through the early 1890s, real estate markets suffered a depression from 1893 through about

1907. Stories of real estate fraud proliferated. Brokers in established boards suggested that large numbers of "irresponsible" men were being drawn to the business, due largely to a lack of entry requirements. William Douglas, president of the Milwaukee Real Estate Board, founded in 1901, asserted that it was easier in Wisconsin "to become a real estate man and handle thousands of dollars worth of property and money" than to become a "barber charging ten cents for a shave." A barber, Douglas pointed out, must "go before the investigating board and if he is not a good barber they don't give him a license." A real estate man, however, was not required to pass a preliminary examination, nor was he questioned as to his "mental training, education, honor or anything of that kind."[16]

Professionalizers in real estate were faced with the problem of defining what constituted a "good" real estate broker. Local boards relied on character screening. The board desired men of character and standing, "gentlemen," at least in deportment, who had been in the business long enough to acquire a solid reputation, and who were likely to enhance the board as both a business organization and a social institution. Its boardrooms functioned as a clubhouse, an alternative to the haven of the home, a refuge for the weary businessman where he could engage in sociability with other men. Social functions created a sense of belonging to an occupation that transcended day-to-day concerns of financial success.[17]

NAREB and the Professional Real Estate Men

[H]ere and now I wish to impress upon every man in this convention and all those who deal in real estate along ethical lines that ours is a profession, for if years of training, study, knowledge of values and principles and up-building of character does not warrant to us the title of profession, then medicine, law and other kindred professions are trading on but what is a title and OURS by right.[18]

It was through his local board that the broker established himself as a fraternal member of the "high-class" real estate order, but he found his identity as a "professional" through the National Association of Real Estate Boards. The most active local boards conjoined in Chicago in 1908 to spread the gospel of professionalism, standardize real estate practice, and try to raise public consciousness about the positive and progressive role of real estate brokerage in American history. On balance, at least judging by press accounts, NAREB raised the prestige of real estate brokerage. It also had a marked influence on housing policy and local land-use regulations.[19]

An immediate objective of the 120 men representing nineteen boards from thirteen states who met in Chicago on May 12–15, 1908, was to convince the public that the depression of 1893 was finally over and that real estate could be trusted as an investment, at least if handled by a "high-class" broker. Their goals included standardization of transaction procedures, enhancement of the public image of the occupation, and lobbying for laws, such as easier access to mortgages, that would facilitate investment in real estate and restore confidence in real property as a commodity.[20]

NAREB established its headquarters in Minneapolis, and began to publish the *National Real Estate Journal* in 1910. From its inception the *NREJ* contained a mix of technical advice, real estate news, and profiles of various member boards and real estate men and their achievements. From the beginning, the editors of the *NREJ* and the leadership of NAREB made a concerted effort to associate "real estate man" and the established professions of law, medicine, the ministry, and engineering. The real estate man was a confidential advisor like a lawyer or minister, a diagnostician and healer of society's ills like a physician, and a planner and builder like an engineer.

The primary function of the *NREJ* was the creation of a common language and the rudiments of an occupational culture with which men scattered in local boards across the continent could imagine themselves as a community of interest. The journal published legal news and disseminated "how-to" information about organizing local boards, establishing multiple listing systems, drawing leases, and selling various types of property. Its advice paralleled national trends, publishing timely articles on topics like the "psychology of selling," the scientific management of a real estate office, and dealing with women as consumers. The *NREJ* regularly published stories in which real estate men could see themselves as part of the national "fraternity." Readers of the *NREJ* were regularly told that they were "live real estate men," and there were frequent profiles of other such men.

The first and most interesting of these narratives was published in the *NREJ* in 1912 as a reprint of a story by Edward Mott Woolley from *The Saturday Evening Post*. "The Inner Secrets of a Real Estate Broker's Rise" is a retrospective narrative—done in a *Silas Lapham*-style interview format—of a young man's search for a meaningful career, which he ultimately finds in real estate brokerage. The protagonist confides that he had been a twenty-four-year-old "young chap in love," dissatisfied with his job as a cashier. Currently a "man who has passed the forty mark," with a smattering of gray hair marking a "right royal battle" to be his "own master," he has evidently agreed to tell his story in order to enlighten other young men, "whether they sell real estate or not."[21]

After an unsuccessful year of attempting to make money in the standard, not-quite-honest ways of the "overcrowded" and "ordinary real estate ranks," the protagonist had an epiphany that set him on the path to professionalism. Presented with an easy opportunity to cheat an old woman contemplating investing what little was left of her late husband's estate in the purchase of a business property, he was struck by the "innocence" of her "old soul." Because she knew so little about real estate "and the factors that influence it," the "sharks" had already made off with a large part of the bequest. Rising to the occasion, he provided her with an appraisal report that "fairly sizzled with honesty," pointing out that the "land was badly situated from the standpoint of business development," that "merchants of the better class were migrating from the neighborhood," and that "undesirable elements were invading the district." Having saved her from a "sham," he perceived the "dawning of a real opportunity" to "educate" and "guide" customers toward "goods that had real value."[22]

On one level, the moral of Woolley's story is clear: part and parcel of being a "professional" real estate man is the protection of the vulnerable and weak. Exertion of his masculine duty is not only honorable, but profitable. Heroism is possible even in the white-collar world. On another level, though, the story reveals something even deeper about middle-class identity. For Woolley's anonymous protagonist, the rewards for making the transition from "shark" to "professional" go beyond feelings of moral superiority or the attainment of public confidence that leads to profit. The *personal*, subjective benefit of achieving professionalism was *stability*: "I was happy when I got down to this point," he asserts, "for I was doing something definite. . . . I was through with aimless wandering. There is a magic country that hangs over the heads of most men; they see it, though it is above and beyond them; but usually there is a road that leads to it." The territorial metaphor is no accident. With the frontier only recently declared officially closed, with no *actual* real estate left to "conquer," the ambitious young man was supposed to "find his place" in the "magic country" of a stable, honorable, and, perhaps, remunerative white-collar career. Real estate deals in land, in space, in providing places for those on the move; it brings together the migrant and the hearthstone. Ostensibly antagonistic tendencies at the heart of American culture—mobility and stability—meet in the figure of the real estate man.[23]

Overall, the *NREJ* depicted real estate brokerage as a model vocation that a young man would find satisfying because it would both test his mettle and allow him to express the full range of his talents. In it, he could find the excitement, occupational autonomy, and potential pecuniary rewards of entrepreneurship, as well as the progressive prestige of white-collar "head work" and "public service." Real estate brokerage held itself out as an ideal pursuit in a world in which occupational categories and the realities they attempted to represent were in flux, as was the masculine idiom in which they were crafted. In the pages of the *NREJ* and in the meeting rooms and banquet halls of the annual conventions, by giving men in the remotest corners of the country common models and images, NAREB drew the parochial local high-class real estate man into the national profession.

The *National Real Estate Journal* could provide models, but could not, however, ensure a high standard for membership in NAREB-affiliated boards. Many in the leadership of the National Association did not think that mere character screening at the local level would a profession make. Men like Frank Craven of Philadelphia and John Kenney of Madison, Wisconsin, argued that there had to be national standards for admission. They proposed two further instruments of professionalization, a code of ethics and a state-administered real estate brokers license. They joined the Progressive Era campaign to professionalize business more generally, an effort that included the promotion of college education for businessmen, the establishment of postgraduate business and management schools, and the formation of professional managerial associations.[24]

The leaders of the National Association hoped to "eliminate the undesirable and irresponsible curb-stone broker," whom they hoped would "come to be regarded by the public . . . just as the 'Quack' in medicine is regarded, and just as the 'Shyster' in law, and the licentious 'libertine' in the ministry are regarded." The "curbstoner" was a "low-class" real estate dealer, a man without an office who conducted his business in the street. Unethical by definition, he could be seen lurking in train depots waiting for unwitting victims newly arrived to the city. He employed nefarious tactics to undercut honest brokers, such as employing "society ladies" as informants to gain leads on potential clients and customers. From 1910 through the mid-1920s, the *NREJ* was filled with articles decrying the curbstoner.[25]

Posing the image of the curbstoner as their primary obstacle to positive public recognition, NAREB's leaders proposed a code of ethics to root him out. "The real estate broker is probably depended upon by his client more than any other profession or trade," argued Ethics Committee member Frank Craven at the 1911 Convention in Denver. "The broker who would take advantage of him or her deserves everlasting censure."[26]

The initial version of the Code of Ethics was ratified by the 1915 Annual Convention. It revealed a number of general concerns about the real estate men's self-image. The language of the code is forceful and exhortative, rather than suggestive. It asserted that a "broker worthy of respect and confidence *will never* make unfair criticisms or untruthful statements" regarding a fellow broker. On the contrary, a worthy broker "*will* cultivate a friendly relationship and respect for all worthy competitors." The code warned professional real estate men to maintain a dispassionate stance, and to keep their anxieties in check rather than "knock" another broker's deal. Should a prospective buyer express interest in a property offered by a competitor, the broker should "treat the proposition as well as the absent broker with fairness, however anxious he may be to sell the property which [*sic*] he represents." Disinterestedness, a central theme of Progressive Era professionalism, clashed with the imperative of profit, an uneasy tension at the heart of business professionalism in general.[27]

Prescriptions about intraprofessional relations are important only at a historical moment and in a social context in which it can no longer be assumed that "professional" and "gentleman" are commensurate.[28] By positing norms of professional intercourse, NAREB's Code of Ethics imagined a particular type of real estate man, with a particular relationship to himself and his work. But NAREB's Code was framed almost entirely in negative terms, invoking antagonistic sets of discourses. It may be interpreted, then, as an attempt to instill gentlemanly, old middle-class modes of behavior in men presumed to be other than gentlemen. Lurking beneath the surface of the code was nagging uncertainty about the definition of middle-class masculinity in the new age of corporate capitalism. Above all, where did real estate brokers fit in a world in which high status in business was increasingly associated with large corporations?

In contrast to the relative consensus regarding the need for a code of ethics, the issue of laws to license real estate brokers created sharp divisions within the young association. On the one hand, there were those opposed to licensing *tout court*, finding the notion antithetical to old middle-class notions of occupational autonomy and voluntarism. On the other hand, those in favor of licensing were split between those who favored licensing criteria emphasizing character—essentially standardizing and generalizing prevailing board membership policies—and those who argued for licensing based on an objective test of competency. Though by the 1950s the "competency" argument won the day, the first wave of licensing laws passed in the 1920s established character as the primary basis for obtaining a license.

The majority of NAREB's leadership in the 1910s and 1920s held the view that licensing ought to combine character screening and competency testing. There was, however, articulate rank-and-file opposition to the very idea of licensing. To J. J. Kenna, president of the exclusive St. Paul, Minnesota, Board, it was immaterial what the brokers called themselves. Kenna strenuously objected to the idea that any outside agency should decide upon his qualifications to do business. There was only one measure for brokers: success, as defined in cash—"if the balance is on the right side of the ledger on the first of January." The most successful brokers "excelled in the art of influencing men" and "developed the greatest of all crafts, salescraft." Kenna was most vexed by the implications of the pro-licensing argument— that real estate men, "members of the great National Association," were asking the state to "please enact laws restraining us from doing a dishonest act," themselves raising the point "that we need watching and naturally are dishonest." This was a serious affront to his old middle-class sense of manliness.[29] To suggest that self-reliant businessmen pay a tithe to the state in order to pursue their calling was both "personally obnoxious" and an insult to "the gentle public."[30] Licensing was tantamount to occupational treason for Kenna.

The cleavage within the NAREB membership over licensing ostensibly centered on differing notions of the essential character of real estate men— were they "businessmen" or "professionals"? However, by the mid-1910s this dichotomy was eroding, as business itself was succumbing to the rhetoric of professionalism. As Louis Brandeis asserted in 1912, "business should be, and to some extent already is, one of the professions," as its accepted measure of success was no longer mere monetary reward, but recognition for public service rendered. This view, shared by NAREB's leadership, held that large incomes were a just reward for service, a result of a "demand for efficiency" far greater than its supply: "the able man" naturally earned a larger income than "one less able."[31] Pecuniary reward was transmuted from a sign of grace to a mark of competence.

The Realtor as Civilized Pioneer

In 1923 *The Saturday Evening Post* published an eight-part series by Philadelphia Realtor Felix Isman entitled "The Accountings of a Real Estate Man." The lengthy articles covered a wide range of activities engaging the new profession—in the wake of the publication of Sinclair Lewis's *Babbitt*, they introduced an authentic Realtor to a popular audience. They depicted the "shocks and thrills of the business," juxtaposing anecdotes of success and failure, of ethical and fraudulent dealing, making a case for licensing and other typical professional reforms.

The overriding theme of Isman's series was an entreaty to readers to seek guidance from competent, ethical real estate men. Isman wrote from the point of view of seasoned expertise, asserting that, "nine persons in ten have only the vaguest ideas about what a house ought to be, and that they are still more vague about buying a home." Only the Realtor was capable of looking behind "superficial things" to assess the "real value" of a property.[32]

Despite contemporary conventional wisdom about women as the "natural" "managers of the home," one of Isman's expert recommendations was to keep women out of the home-buying process.[33] Women were genetically unable to make judgments according to the proper criteria, prone to such perverse behavior as rejecting the "best value[s]" because of the shade of the wallpaper. Though men formally controlled the family finances, women were the real power behind the bankbook. Isman mused that women were "especially poor judges of the intangibles in real estate," were "skeptical, easily deceived, wanting too much for their money" and judged property "by the things in sight," overlooking "factors in location that are far more important." The professional real estate man considered objective criteria like "the trend of values" in a given section, the "kind of neighbors," possible nuisances, safety for children. "Yes, madam, it is a lovely bathroom—but could anybody build a public garage or rendering works next door? How about that objectionable quarter a dozen blocks down the street—which way is it growing? How about that parasitic development just over the boundary line of this subdivision?"[34]

Worst of all, Isman maintained, women were "the greatest suckers" in real estate, "critical and ill-informed in small operations and afraid to undertake big ones." Women lacked experience in the subject matter, had no means of acquiring it, refused to acknowledge their incompetence, and were "swayed by impulses."[35] Women represented irrationality and "sentiment," a "very expensive luxury" in business. There was little room in this conceptualization of the professional Realtor for women. This perspective, or at least the gender assumptions that informed it, was shared by many of NAREB's leaders. However, it was precisely "sentiment" that women trying to enter the field and the men supportive of their entry employed as an opening wedge. The tension between those who denied the value of sentiment and those who recognized it ran through the first phase of the professionalization project.

Complementary to Isman's attack on (womanly) sentiment and irrationality was the appropriation of the (manly) pioneer metaphor. The men of NAREB had long thought of themselves in an engineering idiom as "city builders" and "men who moved the earth," and by the mid-1920s this had crystallized into an image of the Realtor as modern "pioneer." However, the keynote speaker at the 1928 Convention, University of Wisconsin president Glenn Frank, deployed the pioneer metaphor as critique. Yes, the Realtor ought to think of himself as the "apostolic successor" to the pioneer; as the pioneer had "cleared the forests to create farms," the Realtor was "clearing the farms to make cities." Unfortunately, the Realtor sometimes did his job, like the pioneer, through exploitation, "getting while the getting was good" then moving on to "fresh fields of exploitation." Worse, the pioneer left "denuded and disorderly landscapes." The Realtor could only rise "to the dignity of a professional man" if his methods ceased to be dominated by "the mind of the pioneer"; that is, until he became more than "an exploiter of site values." Only the introduction of "beauty and permanence into a civilization" could lift the occupation "to a level of dignity out of the reach of the shafts of satire" being hurled by Mencken and Lewis. In other words, the Realtor had to become more civilized—and thus more professional.[36]

The timing of Frank's speech was not accidental. By the late 1920s, real estate men were particularly sensitive to their image, which had been tarnished first by stories of rent profiteering during the war, then by the publication of *Babbitt*, and finally by the burst real estate bubbles of the late 1920s.[37] The pioneer metaphor belied deep ambivalence about how the Realtors perceived themselves.

As if in tacit response to this incongruity, the rhetoric of male Realtors of the 1920s was saturated with metaphors of heroism, nobility, and fraternity. Seen in part as a strategic attempt to masculinize their work by associating it with perceived manly pursuits, this rhetoric was symptomatic of white-collar men's anxieties about their class position generally at the turn of the century.[38] The Realtor's articulation of his place in the social order teetered precariously between two conceptions of manhood: an old middle-class tradition of the entrepreneur, yeoman farmer, and free professional; and a newer rational, scientific, white-collar technocratic professionalism. The older rhetoric of rugged, pioneering manliness was grafted onto an occupational ideology that borrowed still older, theologically derived notions of "selfless service," as well as newer scientific notions of rationality and efficiency. Medieval notions of honor and chivalry, republican images of the free professional and autonomous property owner, and modernist social scientific impulses to standardize practice and knowledge mixed uneasily.

The early Realtors had attempted to create a masculine professional mystique. In inventing their own "mystery of profession," imagining themselves to be quasibrotherhoods, employing heroic language, creating the title "Realtor" and rites and rituals, they tried, consciously or not, to create a sense of manly belonging tied to a sense of historical continuity and purpose. The attempt to create a heroic past and a professional present was a consummate work of *bricolage*, incorporating a spectacular array of images. Yet the mixing of metaphors suggested a fundamental misrecognition or confusion, a cacophonous multiplicity of attempts to answer the question, "who are we?"[39]

Women's Ways of Selling: Separate Business Spheres

The entry of large numbers of women into the field in the mid-1920s forced many of these latent tensions to the surface. While real estate men imagined themselves as engaged in a manly calling, the commodity that they sold, the family home, was clearly of a different order. The home was still resolutely woman's sphere in the early twentieth century, and the professions that had emerged around the home, like home economics and social work, were definitively "feminine."[40] Real estate men's campaign to become professional purveyors of domestic spaces was a project latently loaded with gender troubles.

By the early 1920s, real estate men could not ignore the fact that women, too, were staking claims for professional status. Gladys Hiestand claimed in 1913 that "the most efficient real estate men are willing to acknowledge that women have the brains and ability to cope with them in this branch of business," yet women appeared in the early issues of *NREJ* only in the capacity of reformers advocating homeownership. A short series of articles on women in the profession appeared in 1921, purporting to give "the Woman's Angle" on real estate. Women possessed "certain qualities" that made them "peculiarly fit" for the profession. "Women's intuition" helped the woman Realtor "to enter into the prospect's psychology, to grasp the situation quickly and thoroughly," and once grasped, to use her "sharp wit" and "readiness to grasp detail" to "make the best of a given situation." Louise Slocomb, "Realtoress" of Portland, Oregon, contended that men had "courage, strength and foresight" and women possessed the "ability to handle details" and to understand "fellow women," a complementary relationship. Homemakers by "nature," it was equally "natural" that women should be successful home brokers. "A woman has a definite idea of what a home should be; she appreciates its comforts and conveniences as no man can." To the woman, selling a house was "more than a mere business deal." The woman Realtor took "a personal interest in every home" that she sold, and her enthusiasm was "contagious" and this was "transferred to the prospect."[41]

Gentlemen readers of the *NREJ* need not fear, as women declared that they were "not seeking to deprive men of their laurels" nor were they "trying to take unto themselves masculine prerogatives." Given that women possessed "alertness, sympathy, vision, and that elusive intuitiveness," all invaluable aids in selling homes, and since it was assumed that homes must appeal first of all to women, women should no doubt be successful in selling them. In the 1920s women's claims for incursion into the masculine world of real estate invariably were framed in terms of women's inherent qualities that distinguished them from men. Women, it almost went without saying, were "extremely well fitted to sell homes."[42]

In the 1920s women began to enter real estate in great numbers. Between 1910 and 1930, there was a tenfold increase in the number of female real estate agents, as the proportion of women in the field increased from 2 percent to over 13 percent.[43] San Francisco Realtor Grace Perego was the first woman Realtor to address the annual convention, in 1927. "Woman's place is not in the home when she wishes to embrace real estate as a career, not even in the home selling business," Perego proclaimed. She had begun her career as a builder of apartments, then sold country real estate before establishing a large brokerage firm, and she made a forceful case for gender equality, implicitly rejecting the essentialist logic of separate spheres. "Which branch of real estate would women best be fitted for?" she asked rhetorically. Though many women made their "start in the real estate business selling homes because they *seem* naturally adapted to this line on account of their familiarity with home requirements," there was no necessary connection between gender and home sales. Women would sell homes only until they "found" themselves, and developed a broader knowledge of real estate; then they would "invade any branch" they chose.[44]

As greater numbers of women obtained real estate licenses, they sought to join local boards, many of which, especially among large founding members of the National Association like Chicago, Pittsburgh, and Kansas City, Missouri, refused to admit them. The NAREB constitution contained no proscriptions against women becoming members, but membership standards were the exclusive province of local boards. At the 1925 convention the defenders of male exclusivity made a weak case, arguing that to admit women would compromise the clubhouse atmosphere of the local board. Their male opponents rejected these arguments, with a mixture of essentialist and equity arguments. Nevertheless, very few women became members of local boards, with the exception of a few West Coast boards like Long Beach, California, despite the increasing number of licensed female brokers. In recognition of this fact, beginning in the mid-1930s the leadership of NAREB encouraged women to form their own organizations.[45]

While the business press gushed about women's "conquest" of the office, it referred almost exclusively to clerical and secretarial work.[46] What explains the influx of women into the real estate field? Age and marital status played a determining role for many. Generally, women entered real estate later in life: the median age of women real estate agents in 1930 was 48, versus 30 for the general female work force. Women real estate agents in 1930 were two and a half times more likely to be married and more than twice as likely to be divorced as the average female worker. Women often began real estate to supplement family income, but if they made good tended to remain in it for life—it was, in many cases, a career, and not a mere digression between adolescence and marriage. The narrative representations that exist of women real estate agents reflect these demographic facts.[47]

It was widely acknowledged that women were the true consumers of the Realtors' main commodity, the family home, and much of the sales pitch was directed at them. Grace Perego's assertion of gender equality notwithstanding, male Realtors had long employed a species of Victorian separate-spheres ideology to promote homeownership. The "Own Your Own Home" campaign, conducted as a collaborative effort between the real estate industry, the federal government, and housing reformers in the years following the World War I, exemplified this trend. The advertisement on the next page is typical in its blatant appeal to gender anxieties, presenting home ownership as the natural solution.

What, then, was to prevent aspiring woman Realtors from appropriating this ideology as justification for their entry into the home-selling field? If "she" truly "thought of its interior plan and sketched its room arrangements" and "pictured to herself just how the exterior of her home will look," then who better than a woman to sell a home to a woman? The logic of separate spheres virtually dictated that women peddle the woman's sphere. The world of sales—a realm of business that had been cast in masculine terms since well before the turn of the century—was indeed vulnerable to female invasion, at least in residential real estate.[48]

"I'd Rather Deal with a Woman"

The Women's Council of the National Association was established in 1938. By 1944 the Women's Council had increased its membership by almost 60 percent, to 1,146 women Realtors, foreshadowing massive postwar growth.[49] As residential real estate sales began to soar in 1943, the doors of opportunity were opening for Rosie the *Realtor* as well. World War II thus left a permanent legacy of female participation in real estate.

Cut No. 106.   Price, 70c

Her Greatest Desire

She will never be happy until she has a home of her very own. Hardly a day passes that she does not think of *her* home, as she would have it. It is to be a place of comfort, contentment and harmony; it is to be practical, convenient, beautiful.

She has thought of its interior plan and sketched its room arrangement; she has pictured to herself just how the exterior of her home will look—how pleasant and inviting—and the grounds will be in keeping with her plan of her home, a place to really *live*.

Build a Home First

Nothing takes the place of this home of her own planning, nothing will be nearer or dearer to her heart, next to her own loved ones.

Build her that Home of her Dreams. Build it Now. Come in and let us show you our plans of attractive homes. Our service is free.

Her Greatest Desire. FROM SOUTHERN PINE ASSOCIATION BROCHURE, CUT NO. 106, UNDATED, RECORDS OF THE REAL ESTATE DIVISION, THE U.S. HOUSING CORPORATION, 1917–1952, RECORD GROUP 3, NATIONAL ARCHIVES, WASHINGTON, D.C.

The founders of the Women's Council were divided as to their overall objectives—self-liquidation and assimilation into the "malestream," or creating a "women's world" within the profession.[50] Were women Realtors supposed to conform to the professional culture established by the real estate men or was there to be a woman's way of doing business?

A syncretic answer to the women's dilemma emerged during the war, coming particularly from a faction within the Women's Council, led by West Coast Realtors.[51] A leader of this group, the young and dynamic Mary A. Warren of Glendale, California, delivered a rousing speech entitled "Home Selling for Women" during the 1941 Women's Council meeting. Women should aim to dominate residential sales, she said, but her justification was not the usual "women-know-homes-better" line that was coming from the leadership. The new slogan for women Realtors was "I'd rather deal with a woman"; the new strategy, to capitalize, in a highly instrumental fashion, on society's gender *assumptions*.

> Throughout history womankind has been credited with the virtues of gentleness, honesty, sincerity, and unselfishness. Whether we actually possess these attributes in undue measure would be a subject of academic interest. But tradition has endowed us, and being human, we've striven to merit the reputation . . .
>
> The man customer likes to deal with a woman in real estate for several reasons. If he has a wife, or female relatives, he assumes that a woman will know better what *they* would like. Then, once he's made your acquaintance, he's amazed and delighted to find someone who can *handle* business like a man, and *still* make him feel like a superior being. And,

on the average, he endows you unquestionably with a noble character (seeing that you're in such a difficult and competitive field) and likes to feel HE'S helping you carry your burden by dealing with you.[52]

If this new breed of women Realtors claimed the territory of home sales as their own sphere, that claim was no longer a declaration of innate moral prerogative, but only an attenuated domesticity tagged onto a self-interestedly gendered "expertise" in manipulating home buyers. The new slogan was a perfect collapse of the business motives and gendered morality that separate spheres was, indeed, intended to avoid. Women were not supposed to "deal," at least not so obviously, or in those terms. Women Realtors, at least some of them, appropriated the vestiges of Victorian mores for their own purposes, playing with the language to cash in on stereotypes.[53]

At the same time, male Realtors, perhaps unable to compete with women's powerful sales logic, beat a retreat into the masculine hustle of commercial realty and reassurances of their self-styled professional imperatives as "city builders." Women came to specialize overwhelmingly in residential sales as real estate developed its own internal separate spheres. The Society of Industrial Realtors, founded in 1941 and nominally open to all members of the profession, has tended to remain a "boys' club," in the words of a local board official.[54] By 1950, every local board except Columbus, Ohio, accepted women as full members.[55]

Professionalization, at least in real estate in the 1920s–1950s, was therefore not simply about preserving and defending masculinity. Certainly men attempted to arrogate to their sex whatever privileges accrued to being "professional," and vice versa. But women also claimed, by right of sex, a privileged access to certain career lines. In the process, they opened new areas of business, and helped to further blur lines between "professions" and "trades." It is no accident that women entered real estate at about four times the rate of men during the four decades after World War II.[56] Writing in 1977, Mary Shern, Realtor and author of *Real Estate, A Woman's World*, perfectly captured the new professional spirit:

Real estate can indeed be called a woman's world, not only because women are the backbone of the sales force, but also because their traditional role in society is an asset. Our profession might truly be the last bastion of free enterprise. Typically, salespeople manage their own careers, and profit to the extent of their own achievements. Even before the advent of the feminine mystique, women participated on the same payscale as men . . .

I fail to become upset over the shifting sands of sexual roles in society. I choose my role and let others do the same. In real estate we can pursue our course because we're women, not in spite of it, and do our task without losing an ounce of femininity. Therefore, I more or less oppose equal rights. Why should women give up the edge we've so richly deserved and so long enjoyed?[57]

While Shern's words represented in some respects a conservative, mid-1970s reaction to a particular image of feminism, they were made possible by the flexible, heterosocial culture of business professionalism, which undeniably provided broader opportunities for women as it subtly reconfigured gender and class distinctions.

The professional *bricoleurs* who attempted to transform themselves from "real estate men" into Realtors® appropriated rhetoric and strategies from many disparate discourses and created a new field of professional activity—real estate agency—that helped to crystallize a particular notion of the American home. They attempted to fashion themselves as professionals at a historical moment in which notions of professionalism were in particularly intense flux. They framed their initial professionalization project in the idiom of masculinity, but this, too, was a concept in flux, and ultimately, the attempt to accrue cultural capital as professionals via masculinity failed. The culturally predominant association of the home with the feminine predisposed real estate brokerage to become a heterosocial occupation. Yet this weakness was also its strength: unlike other emergent professions, such as home economics, which arose only to fall in a few decades, real estate became a self-reproducing, politically potent, and culturally salient occupation due in part to its gender flexibility.

Realtors—dealers in both domestic and metropolitan spaces as well as in the ideology of homeownership—attempted to fashion themselves as professional entrepreneurs. In the process, they helped to transform and reconfigure received notions of profession. This, in turn, was part of the general process whereby "middle class" became a meaningfully meaningless category of identity. Meaningful—by 1940, almost nine-tenths of Americans considered themselves members of the middle class and to this day continue to respond to its invocation by politicians, pundits, and scholars as if it were a self-evident entity.[58] Yet also meaningless—the parameters of this class are virtually impossible for the same politicians, pundits, and scholars to demarcate with any precision. The middle class continues to elude, and elide, precise definition, despite its centrality to twentieth-century American political culture. In this imprecision and amorphousness, I suggest, inheres the political and cultural power of the category.[59]

THE POLITICS
OF RACE AND COMMUNITY

Rainbow Glee Club. FREDERIC H. ROBB, ED., 1927 INTERCOLLEGIATE WONDER BOOK OR THE NEGRO IN CHICAGO, CHICAGO: WASHINGTON INTERCOLLEGIATE CLUB OF CHICAGO, 1927, 153.

When it comes to looking at issues of race, the standard narrative
of the middle class becomes decidedly ugly. Even the most committed multicultural scholars tend to view the American middle class as inherently
white. The picture that most historians paint of the middle class is not
pretty to begin with, and middling folks' almost visceral, nearly transhistor-
ical racism puts the icing on the toxic middling sludge. In one far-reaching
but not-so-extreme example, the avant-garde public intellectual Mike Davis
argues in his *Prisoners of the American Dream* that as part of "the mass ruling
class of the American world system," the middle class maintains its "bou-
tique lifestyles" within "sumptuary suburbs." Inside "the *laager* of Yuppie
comfort," those in the American middle are poised to undertake military
offensives against Third World liberation forces as well as, eventually,
inhabitants of the ghettos within their own borders. Or, when a scholar
does acknowledge that not all members of the middle class have a pale hue
to their skins, these middling folks are usually presented as renegades to the
greater cause of racial or economic egalitarianism. One telling example
comes in Robin Kelley's *Race Rebels,* where he casually mentions the "moralizing of the black middle class," implying that what is always absent from
the black bourgeoisie are wonderful working-class "collectivist values,
mutuality, and fellowship."[1]

In this volume's concluding essay, Robert Johnston discusses some of
the intellectual roots, especially in the work of sociologist E. Franklin Frazier, of the view that middle-class people of color are, at best, sellouts. Yet if
we are to attempt a genuine multicultural renovation of American history
and social thought appropriate for the new century, it is time to recast, if
not completely rethink, the received view when it comes to the relationship
between race and the middle class. The middle class is simply not the same
thing as that bane of scholarly existence: "the white middle class." Rather,
throughout modern American history people of all races have held great
dreams related to being and becoming middle class. And as Adam Green
shows in his essay, members of the black middle class—despite their supposed individualism, status seeking, and, yes, moralizing—could be effective and powerful democratic egalitarians. Green shows, through a remarkably insightful analysis of Intercollegian Wonder Books from the 1920s,
that African-American middling folks from Chicago were at the forefront of
advanced thought on issues of gender, sexuality, and labor. Green asks us to
finally confront, and perhaps banish, the ghost of E. Franklin Frazier.

Theresa Mah, in turns, provides important evidence for why we need to
continue to take seriously the standard narrative of race and the middle class
even as we work to revise it. Mah points to the importance of racial privilege in the maintenance of white middle-class identity during the early Cold
War period. Focusing on one dramatic case of residential exclusion in suburban San Francisco, Mah asks us to consider how democratic rhetoric and
the political construction of a suburban majority could work to exclude,

rather than include, those outside the charmed circle of whiteness. In contrast, Sylvie Murray shows in her essay on domestic populism in Queens, New York, that racism by no means served as the sole defining force of middle-class politics during the postwar period. Rather, community protest over such issues as public housing and the provision of schooling did not automatically lead to a meanspirited politics of exclusion but could instead inspire a kind of populism congruent with racial egalitarianism as well as New Deal liberalism.

In an academic landscape where "whiteness" has become a monolithic scourge that tends to create only victims and/or hegemonic structures of power, Green, Mah, and Murray help restore the political struggles that are the tales on which we should be focusing. Such an emphasis on politics produces a certain messiness that practitioners of cultural studies often prefer to sweep under the rug. Ultimately, though, the untidiness that historians uncover as we further explore the connection between race and the middle class will likely help us reconnect our stories with the democratic public realm, as well as with a democratic sense of hope.

The Rising Tide of Youth: Chicago's Wonder Books and the "New" Black Middle Class

ADAM GREEN

In October 1927, reviewer Dewey Jones of the Chicago *Defender* took note of a publishing venture that, despite occasional lapses, merited recognition as a "masterpiece." The 1927 Intercollegian Wonder Book, a 232-page almanac selling for $2 in paper and $4 in cloth, was a work of "gigantic proportions," constituting "the most definite achievement in its particular field ever attempted in Chicago." Produced without sponsors, the book was lauded for its capture of local life, to a degree thought unattainable: "everything and everyone," Jones proclaimed, "is represented in one phase or another." Jones stated that "10,000 copies should not begin to supply for those who really want this book—and who should have it!" The review's conclusion—"the directory will prove of invaluable aid to any person in Chicago"—agreed with the editors' own hopes that it would prove a resource to which "student, teacher, professional and business man may turn with assurance for exact information about the Negro in this city."[1]

Over time, this role has been the one for which the 1927 and, later, the 1929 Wonder Books are best known. Legendary among local residents as guides to achievement, institutions, and community life in black Chicago, the Wonder Books have also been consulted by scholars on a range of topics.[2] Yet, to date, no one has examined these works more fully as indices of their times, catalogues of black life and the ways in which African Americans—or at least some of them—understood their condition. In part, this is due to the scope of the Wonder Books. Together totaling more than five hundred pages and ranging in topic from "Who's Who" listings to organizational sketches, from history and antiquity to theater and athletics, appraising these texts is a daunting task. Still, this seems small cause for the failure to closely examine the books, which, as we shall shortly see, are unique summations of black life during the 1920s. A better explanation addresses their presumed link to elite experience and agenda.

The Wonder Books, focused on "celebrated characters" and "facts and figures about the Negroes for thousands of years...intended as a setting for the progress of the Chicago Negro," seem at first classic examples of uplift philosophy. This orientation, perfected by Booker T. Washington and his Tuskegee Machine but present in other programs advanced by privileged blacks at this time, is significant as much for its claim to authority within communal life as for its vindication of that community. According to Kevin Gaines, its most thorough critic, uplift constituted "a moral economy of class privilege, distinction, and even domination within the race." Characterizing blacks without proper ancestry or means as benighted and in need of guidance, uplift thought advocated fundamentally "bourgeois values of racial progress." Given that these poor and working-class African Americans made up the majority of the community through the years of the Great Migration, when the Wonder Books appeared, uplift appeared counterintuitive as well as class-biased: working, as Gaines trenchantly concludes, "to replicate the racist and sexist codes of the oppressive society" while "sundering African Americans from a history of group oppression and struggle."[3] In many ways, then, when historians today see works like the Wonder Books, they see reminders of the unenlightened self-interest that joined with Jim Crow law, economic and political disenfranchisement, and violent repression to perpetuate the underdevelopment of black life early in the twentieth century.

But was this in fact the legacy of the Wonder Books? As collaborative documents—each listed more than fifty editors and contributors—the two books documented uplift culture in composite form, with popular as well as elite understandings of collective advance engaged and argued in historical context. As inventories of institutions and enterprise in black Chicago— arguably the most developed of the enclaves emerging out of the Great Migration—they illuminate processes of class formation among African-Americans, in particular the rise of a "new" black middle class more distinct from elite convention than historians have credited. And as elaborate statements on the part of black students, the Wonder Books trace the animating spirit of the age—that of the "New Negro"—away from the artists and propagandists seen to be its core adherents, and back to one of its original audiences: young African Americans. Read along these lines, the Wonder Books appear vital, suggesting new application of not only class, but also generation, as useful categories of African-American historical analysis.

The Wonder Books were written and edited by members of the Washington Intercollegiate Club, an organization for black students and graduates initiated through the local Wabash branch of the YMCA in 1909. Frederic Robb, editor-in-chief and guiding spirit for the two books, served as the president of the club in 1926–27, during his last year of law school at Northwestern University. Editors Emma Nix (a Wendell Phillips High School graduate who had attended the University of Chicago) and Regina Falls (a student at Englewood High and later Chicago Normal College), along with a number of other writers and contributors, were officers. Although membership rules for Washington Intercollegiate were liberal—anyone with college credits could join—they applied to a limited cohort within the black community. Nevertheless, this group was a growing factor in community life by the late 1920s. The decade had seen expansion in black secondary and higher education, much of it tied to the massive relocations resulting from the Great Migration. Black college graduates went from 2,132 in 1917 to 13,580 in 1927, a sixfold increase. Black students of high school age (14–17) saw a less dramatic, yet still appreciable, increase, from 486,115 in 1920 to 618,150 in 1930, an increase from 54 percent to 62 percent of that age group. In Chicago in 1930, the number enrolled from this age group was 8,066, or 74 percent. To be sure, access to educational resources for African Americans was still limited. Yet it is important to note how this increase spurred the ambitions of local black students, in particular their desire to translate their intellectual capital into social and civic influence.[4]

Overviews of Washington Intercollegiate offered in the first Wonder Book reveal the extent to which members embraced this role. Forty-one percent of the club members identified themselves as officers in other organizations, 37 percent placed themselves in business or the professions, and 68 of 217 active members belonged to fraternities or sororities. At the same time, organizational histories presented in the Wonder Books portrayed a group interested in self-critique and outreach. Under the section heading "Problems," editors noted the emergence of "a very strong materialistic attitude" among their peers and lamented that "twenty eight percent of the group know little or nothing about the Negro's past in America, West Indies, South America, and Africa." Thirty-nine percent attended local lectures at such venues as the Sinai Temple, Chicago Forum, and Grace Lyceum. Sixty-four percent regularly attended group meetings in 1926–27, and when they participated in programs put on by Washington Intercollegiate, they joined 9,400 other community members.[5]

Listings of club activities in the 1927 Wonder Book further clarify the sense of mission at work within the group. In addition to recitals, dances, and outings, Washington Intercollegiate sponsored a number of speakers, including future Council on African Affairs founder Max Yergan, briefly returned from his sojourn in South Africa under YMCA sponsorship, and Max Shachtman, then working locally as a youth organizer for the Communist Party. The topics of these presentations were eclectic: M. Mason

Higgins, supervisor of the Mason School for children, discussed "The Place of Modern Women in Society," while Herbert Greenwood, a local attorney, gave a talk on "John Brown and Radicalism," and Bernard Roloff, executive secretary of the Illinois Social Hygiene League, lectured on "Sex and Happiness."[6] In 1929, the group sponsored speakers from India, Mexico, and China, as well as a forum on the question, "Does Orthodox Christianity Hinder the Progress of the Negro?" with Carey Temple pastor Reverend Frederick Jordan challenging *Modern Quarterly* editor V. F. Calverton. Editors termed the event "the largest [debate] ever held on the South Side," with "hundreds" filling Pilgrim Baptist Church on "the coldest night of the year." Also noteworthy were debates club teams led by Frederic Robb, a distinguished debater since his days in high school, took part in. Arguing affirmative positions on such questions as legalizing birth control, enacting uniform divorce laws, and recognizing Philippine independence, Robb and his partners were lauded in the 1927 Wonder Book for their near-perfect year. Indeed, the only blemish on Robb's record came in July 1927 during a clash with activist and longtime club supporter Ida B. Wells-Barnett, in a debate on whether "the leadership for the past thirty years has done more for the advancement of the Race than the leadership thirty years previous." Arguing the affirmative, Robb was no doubt lucky to escape with the draw.[7]

If Washington Intercollegiate demonstrated how, quoting E. Franklin Frazier, "Negro higher education [was] devoted chiefly to the task of educating the black bourgeoisie," then both that education's substance and the class interests it served were more complex than either Frazier or later critics have allowed. Other scholars have documented the progressive positions held by members of the black middle class on questions such as colonialism or reproductive rights. Few, though, have noted how these views served as necessary—and normative—aspects of the program of self- and community development undertaken by younger members of that class. To be sure, club leaders felt their efforts entitled them to an exemplary role in black life, as the 1927 foreword indicated:

> Students have determined the contents of this book and with much sacrifice have presented a book to the public which should be a strong incentive to the capable youth of the city and America to make the most of their lives, to begin in youth to cultivate habits of thrift and thoroughness, to lay, even before attaining their majority, the sound basis of character, practical sense, energy, integrity, without which a lasting success in affairs is practically impossible.[8]

Clearly, several disconcerting aspects of uplift philosophy were operative here—presumed distinctions of merit ("capable youth"), meant to account for the poor conditions most African Americans lived under; embrace of programs of personal achievement and improvement ("make the most of their lives"), rather than more collective strategies; faith that moral personality and reputation derived from individual effort (". . . habits of thrift and thoroughness, to lay...the sound basis of character . . . "), rather than the structuring effect of a racist environment. Yet uplift's rhetorical excesses here might obscure what was innovative rather than conservative or accommodating about the outlook of Washington Club members.[9]

A crucial theme within the Wonder Books, as indicated above, was the identification of African-American youth as its ideal audience. While the books sought to assist "student, teacher, professional, and businessmen" in providing "exact information about the Negro," young blacks were its preferred constituency. Emphasizing achievements in culture (the work of painters Henry O. Tanner and Archibald Motley, Jr., for instance), bibliographies on the race question (including curious entries such as Lothrop Stoddard's *The Rising Tide of Color* and Carl Van Vechten's *Nigger Heaven*), and local architectural landmarks, Wonder Book editors sought to mark a path toward "a sound basis for character" for young readers. Extensive sections detailed area schools—especially high schools—serving Chicago's black community. Portraits documented full-year classes at Wendell Phillips High School, the legendary South Side campus serving as an institutional beacon for southern migrants to Chicago during the previous decade. Other pictures identified Phillips teachers, staff, and participants in school organizations, such as theater groups or the school's R.O.T.C. band under the direction of Major N. Clark Smith. Graduating seniors at other high schools, including Englewood, Hyde Park, Lindbloom, McKinley, and Parker, were noted under the heading "Potential Intercollegians," making clear the expectations editors had of their junior peers.[10]

Formal education was one of several areas where the Wonder Books catalogued civic resources for young blacks: other sections appraised park facilities and "playground teachers," private scholarship programs, libraries, and recreation clubs. Taken together, these items demonstrate how pivotal youth training, broadly defined, was to collective advance as understood by the editors of the Wonder Books. Few blacks—poor along with elite—would have argued with this, particularly if they were familiar with school conditions in the Jim Crow South. By one survey, only 18 percent of all eligible black children were enrolled in high schools in the South as late as 1933–34. Although larger southern cities were opening high schools for African Americans by the 1920s, black students regionally were still severely underserved—in 1924, there were only three public high schools for African Americans in all of Mississippi, for instance. Conditions were significantly better in Chicago and other northern cities. Still, those concerned with African-American youth surely noted the deficit resulting from poor southern secondary education, given the numbers of recent migrants. Thus, the Wonder Books' didactic emphasis on scholastic ambition and discipline was not out of line with public concerns in black Chicago.[11]

Throughout the Wonder Books, young blacks were presented as a vanguard of sorts, an assessment exemplified by the phrase "The Rising Tide of Youth" used to title the education portion of the second book. Indeed, such moves indicated a "generational consciousness" organizing the books as a whole. To be sure, conditions for young black Chicagoans during the 1920s were different from those for youth generally following World War II, when terms such as "generation gap," "student activism," and "youth culture" became ubiquitous. While developed compared to the agrarian South, black urban life in Chicago was no "affluent society" of the kind later found across Europe and North America, producing adolescent and young adult subcultures "generalis[ing] internal contradiction[s] for the society as a whole," and thus constituting the subject for classic research on youth in the United States and elsewhere. Yet incrementally expanded educational access for African Americans at this moment—along with anxiety that this access might prove fleeting—suggests a broader desire on the part of Wonder Book editors and young blacks in general to comprehend community interests in age-specific fashion. This feeling, in turn, resonated with a striking shift in black thought at the time.[12]

Of the currents reshaping black life during 1920s, none were more explicitly endorsed within the Wonder Books than the Negro Renaissance. An extended passage from the 1927 book titled "The New Negro" makes this connection clear. Relating the term to "a Negro whose habits and ideas are entirely different from the Negro of fifty years ago," the editors characterized the New Negro as one who "ignored the unfounded flatteries heaped upon the Negro," yet "glories in the colored man's contribution to civilization." Thinking "in terms of the future welfare of his children," the New Negro favored "better schools, more teachers with higher salaries, numerous parks and playgrounds, sanitary alleys [and] paved streets." Pointedly recalling those blacks who had served in the military during World War I, and the repression they met following upon the war's end, the New Negro was described as someone "opposed to that loyalty and patriotism which supports a government with its all in war, to be satisfied to be Jim Crowed, segregated, lynched, [and] mobbed." In a veiled warning to established leaders, Wonder Book editors warned that "the New Negro has no respect for age for age's sake, but has respect because of their storehouse of wisdom and accomplishments." Seeking not "philanthropy, but an opportunity," relying not on "boast . . . " but "achieve[ment]," and living as "a lover of world brotherhood," the New Negro heralded the promise of the new century as "a fusion of all the races of the world."[13]

To be sure, reference to the Negro Renaissance in the Wonder Books relied also on an array of verse reprints, including Claude McKay's "If We Must Die" and "I Too" by Langston Hughes, along with poems by Georgia

Douglass Johnson, Paul Laurence Dunbar, and Jean Toomer. Yet alongside these tributes, as well as others to celebrities outside literature, like Aaron Douglas, Florence Mills, Bill "Bojangles" Robinson, and Josephine Baker, the passage above shows that editors viewed the Renaissance not only as an arts movement, but as a broader social phenomenon. Indeed, here the cultural suggestion gleaned from the age was more anthropologic than aesthetic: a millennial consciousness reworking structures of African-American existence. This, of course, was not far from the conception of the Renaissance's muse, Alain Locke, whose redefinition of collective racial condition as a "life in common" rather than a "problem in common" offered the most hopeful epitaph for the era. What Wonder Books editors sensed, perhaps better than their elders at the time and certainly better than historians since, was how this shift agreed with the age cohort they represented. After all, Locke and others (including, of course, the young artists famously clustered in Harlem) saw the younger generation as the "first fruits of the Renaissance," enjoying the capacity to realize "the voice of the New Negro" thanks to their unique experience as a self-conscious age group. Reinforcing this link was the wave of student strikes deposing presidents and reworking curriculums at historically black colleges such as Hampton, Fisk, and Howard—schools with more than their share of alumni among the creators and audience of the Wonder Books. Still, while scholars of the Negro Renaissance have noted these dynamics, they have rarely pursued them past the salons and nightclubs of Harlem, thus downplaying their impact on blacks beyond the inner circle.[14]

Indeed, the consensus among historians has been that the concepts and spirit of the Negro Renaissance were scarcely engaged within the African-American public at large. For some, this failure was understandable, given the poverty, deprivation, and other everyday concerns many blacks struggled with at this time. What, then, of educated blacks like those represented in the Wonder Books? E. Franklin Frazier, writing on the black middle class, offered an answer setting the direction for later scholarship:

> The Negro Renaissance of the twenties represented a reevaluation of the Negro's past and of the Negro himself by Negro intellectuals and artists. It failed because at that time the new middle class . . . in the Negro community rejected it. The short stories, novels, and poems which expressed this new evaluation of the Negro and his history in America by his artists and intellectuals were unread and ignored by the new middle class that was eager to gain a few dollars. Instead of being interested in gaining a new conception of themselves, the new middle class was hoping to escape from themselves.

Extending Frazier's thinking, Harold Cruse would later declare that the black bourgeoisie failed to support the Renaissance "morally, aesthetically, and financially," dooming it to social and cultural insolvency. These conclusions, it is clear, are challenged by the Wonder Books, which show that the period's greatest cultural sea-change was duly noted by members of the black middle class and integrated into their worldview and communal program. As well, the books reinforce the argument of observers in Chicago and other cities beyond Harlem that the Negro Renaissance period looked different across the Hudson River—different in ways illuminating fundamental processes of social, rather than solely cultural, transformation impacting black life at the time.[15]

New Negro thought and orientation within the Wonder Books, in fact, highlights the distinction emerging at this time between the black middle class and traditional elites within the African-American community. Despite the efforts of some historians, notably Willard Gatewood, to clarify this difference, the tendency to collapse blacks beyond the working class into the same self-interested and exclusionist category continues to confuse discussions of class within African-American life. This is unfortunate in the case of documents like the Wonder Books, for it not only obscures their articulation of class identity and politics generally, but also their capture of the historically specific meanings of class in effect during the 1920s for African Americans. The small yet self-aware petite bourgeoisie emerging during and after the Great Migration has been a recurrent point of interest for researchers: Frazier himself acknowledged its importance in a 1925 essay on black entrepreneurs in Durham, one of his few favorable commentaries on the black middle class. What the Wonder Books permit us to do is view this class as much more than simply an economic factor in African-American life.[16]

Writing some years after the appearance of the Wonder Books, sociologists St. Claire Drake and Horace Cayton noted how within black Chicago, "middle class individuals are great 'joiners' or 'belongers.'" Certainly this tendency was already apparent in the Wonder Books. College-related groups, not surprisingly, featured prominently—one article placed the total membership of the twenty-two alumni associations locally at more than 2,350 members, including 350 in the Tuskegee Club and 470 combined in the Howard and Fisk organizations. Other social and civic associations were also detailed, ranging from the Phyllis Wheatley Women's Club to lesser- known groups like the Vagabond Queens or the Plasterers' Protective and Benevolent Club. Churches received special emphasis: articles in the 1927 book detailed the Pilgrim and Olivet Baptist Churches, while, in 1929, denominational coverage was headlined by an overview of the Church of the Good Shepard and its pastor, the Reverend Harold Kingsley, whose various missions servicing "1000 people a week" exemplified its program of "democratic evangelization." While celebration of middle-class association could be seen as a claim to narrow group status and distinction, the emphasis on civic activism within these groups as recounted in the

Wonder Books challenges this assertion. The Beta chapter of the Alpha Kappa Alpha Sorority was extolled for its efforts for local scholarships as much as for its enhancement of the social calender. An overview in the 1927 Book of the Wabash YMCA noted "approximately 30,000 persons" using health and clinic programs, along with "hundreds of boys" trained through physical education, and concluded that the service "touch[ed] more people daily than any other institution among the group." Efforts to extend the foothold in professional and clerical sectors undergirding the new black middle class were indicated among occupational societies like the Social Workers Round Table, the Chicago Graduate Nurses Association groups, and the Phalanx Club, an organization of federal employees. In contrast, more traditional elite groups, such as the "Old Settlers," were cited briefly, if at all: Sigma Phi Pi, or Boule, the most exclusive association in black life at this time, received no mention in either Wonder Book.[17]

Recognition in the Wonder Books of prominent individuals sharpened the distinction of middle-class social mores from elite tradition. Biographies of Robert Abbott and Phyllis Wheatley Club founder Elizabeth Lindsey Davis, among many others, emphasized struggles to transcend humble beginnings. Such homilies to the self-made individual would not be lost on readers, aware that traditional criteria for status among black elites were largely those of ancestry. Many of the sketches portrayed local success stories, particularly those like druggist Robert Giles, finance and real estate baron Jesse Binga, and Parker House Sausage Company founder J. H. Parker, all of whom made their mark in commerce and business. Yet broader notions of service were offered in tributes to Marcus Garvey, called "Negro's greatest organizer and propagandist" in the 1929 book, and Ida B. Wells-Barnett, lauded not only for her antilynching campaign, but also her agitation against race violence in the North, pursuit of women's suffrage, and support of the Intercollegiate Club and other youth organizations.[18] Biographies of generational peers—attorneys Oscar Brown, Sr., Edith Sampson, and Earl Dickerson, Pilgrim Baptist minister Junius Austin, and organizer Irene McCoy Gaines, among others—appeared frequently, reiterating the New Negro tone of the books, and marrying celebration of ambition with ideas of common interest in what Stephanie Shaw calls "socially responsible individualism."[19]

Together with the organizational summaries described earlier, such biographies support Allan Spear's characterization of the structure of black Chicago during the 1920s as an "institutional ghetto." Yet in so doing, they make one final—and crucial—point about the break with traditional understandings of status and social roles in black life. Celebrating local institutions and their animating civic spirit, the Wonder Books offered a declaration of independence from racial clientage. Replacement of historic bonds of sponsorship and charity with a mixture of autonomy and interracial cooperation was an integral feature of reform and revitalization programs among early twentieth-century African Americans, from the NAACP to the Garvey movement, and even within New Negro philosophy itself. Historically, black elites resisted this impulse, emphasizing their alliances with the white world, often to grotesque extremes. In contrast, the Wonder Books embraced the new and more egalitarian strategy, through their portrayal of a more organic communal infrastructure and culture. Although areas where old rules of clientage still operated, such as local political parties, were noted in the Wonder Books, the desire to relegate the white world to the background was consistent and striking. Besides brief tributes to patrons like Sears, Roebuck founder and racial philanthropist Julius Rosenwald, interaction between whites and blacks was portrayed as having little direct effect on black life. Certainly the most peculiar example of this was the near-silence on the 1919 Race Riot, noted briefly in a footnote on the advertising pages of the 1927 edition.[20]

All this is in line with Spear's now-classic model of class succession in local leadership, as an "integrationist" elite yielded in the first decades of the twentieth century to the more "separatist" middle class. Yet his conclusion that, partisan rhetoric aside, race-specific strategies and institutions in black Chicago represented a narrowing of collective imagination and politics seems less accurate upon reading the Wonder Books. Far from constituting "the best of a bad situation,"[21] the break with traditions of racial obligation and fealty opened space for expanded social, cultural, and political outlooks. Among the frameworks transformed in this way was uplift itself, becoming a composite orientation melding the interests of diverse communal constituencies, rather than consolidating the authority of one. Fuller discussion of several key themes in the second Wonder Book documents this, indicating expanded—not circumscribed—notions of local community.

While the 1927 Wonder Book offered a rarefied view of expressive culture, emphasizing classical recitals by members of the National Association of Negro Musicians, the 1929 edition was fully up to date with the revolution in urban vernacular forms occurring at this time. *Defender* theater critic Jack L. Cooper's essay, "The Negro Runs Riot With The Stage," described dancer Bill "Bojangles" Robinson's record run at the Palace theater, as well as those of local performers such as the Byron brothers and Little Esther Jones. Photos joining Cooper's text depicted popular artists of the day, including jazz composers Noble Sissle and Eubie Blake, screen actor Clarence Muse, comedians Butterbeans and Susie, and blues women Ida Cox and Ethel Waters. Novelty acts featured in the piece—Coy Herndon, "the Race's leading hoop manipulator," female boxers Aurelia Wheedlin and Emma Maitland, and Jack Wiggins, "the world's greatest buck and wing dancer"—doubtless raised the eyebrows of those readers seeking more respectable examples of black creative endeavor. Other items showcased jazz innovators, including bandleader Walter Barnes and Louis Armstrong, whose exploits along the South Side "Strip" of nightclubs and entertainment palaces earned him a "Who's Who" entry in the Wonder Book. While it is impossible to wholly recast middle-class tastes on the strength of Cooper's survey, certainly it testified to the choice of speakeasy and variety stage over more highbrow offerings among the Wonder Book staff and, in turn, suggests similar interest in such new forms among its readers. [22]

If cultural commentary broadened ideas of black creativity, coverage of transnational issues further widened the horizons of collective imagination well beyond the parochial. International topics had defined the Wonder Books from their start in 1927. Washington Intercollegiate member Charles Thompson's circumnavigation of the globe was recounted there, with the stated purpose of encouraging among readers "a truer measure of realities," and "a deeper sympathy for the hopes and aspirations of humanity." A piece titled "8000 Years of Negro Achievement" vindicated blacks' place in human civilization, recounting Egyptian dynasties, Africans' contributions to the early Christian church, and the great liberators of the eighteenth and nineteenth centuries, ranging from Toussaint L'Ouverture to King Menelik of Abyssinia. Graphically, both books employed Egyptological motifs at page headings and in the advertising section in order to link black antiquity with the race's enterprising future—a signature technique of local designer Charles Dawson, a contributor both in 1927 and 1929. By 1929, the book editors had focused their interest in transnational themes toward more contemporary concerns. Captain Harry Dean, mariner and descendant of antebellum shipbuilder Paul Cuffee, sought to excite local *wanderlust* in a piece titled "The Negro Must Go To Sea," in which he improbably encouraged readers to follow river banks and lake shores out to open ocean, since like "a plant . . . not watered . . . [a] race that has no contact with the sea atrophies." An article on colonial Nigeria titled "West Africa Makes Strides" inventoried native professionals and businesses operating there, although it failed to specify what impact colonial rule was having on indigenous development. Captions scattered about the Book, such as the one reading "Africa, West Indies, and South Offer Many Themes for Artists," sought to encourage readers to define their own projects along global lines.[23]

The most intriguing discussions of transnationalism within the Wonder Books concerned their editor-in-chief, Frederic Robb. A postgraduate student in London between publication of the two books, Robb's impressions while overseas featured prominently in the 1929 Wonder Book. In "Meeting Negroes Who Achieve In Europe," Robb noted interest in various expatriates, both well known (Paul Robeson and bandleader Jim Europe, among others) and barely discovered (young Marian Anderson, whose 1928 London recital was "long to be remembered," and J. A. Rogers, future scholar and journalist known around Paris at that time for having written "many articles for the French press" and guiding "many a visitor to most interesting parts of France"). A bemused review of British classroom and campus rituals was joined by a reprinted letter from Minerveno de Oliveira, a Brazilian studying in London at the same time. Titled "The Editor as I See Him," the letter waxed eloquent over Robb, recounted his speeches, organizational efforts, and interests as "characteristics of a great leader peculiarly made for this age." Already established as a nexus for Pan-African and anti-colonialist thought and activism, London in the 1920s constituted a crossroads for Anglophone Africans and Caribbeans. This condition was captured in photo-journals of Robb's acquaintances while abroad, from throughout Africa, the Carribean, and Asia. [24]

Concern over gender and the role of women marked another progressive aspect of the social politics of the Wonder Books. In addition to Intercollegiate Club events promoting first-wave feminist concerns such as suffrage, divorce law, and birth control, biographies of local club women, social workers, and activists like Elizabeth Lindsey Davis and Ida B. Wells-Barnett offered an antidote to patriarchal sentiment within both Wonder Books. Particularly noteworthy were essays by Intercollegiate Club members Irene McCoy Gaines and Edith Sampson on the role of black women in local politics and the professions. Gaines outlined the history of local black women's involvement in electoral politics since the 1913 passage of the Illinois Women's Suffrage Bill, acknowledging those active in the National League of Republican Colored Women (Nannie H. Burroughs), the Illinois League of Women Voters (Irene Goins, Ada McKinley, Margaret Gainer), as well as those, like Gaines herself, working to deepen black women's involvement in the local Democratic Party.[25] Sampson's essay, titled "Are Our Women Holding Their Own?", depicted black women's social position through an analysis of their integration locally in the professions. Touching fields such as teaching, social work, dentistry, and medicine, Sampson reserved most of her commentary for her own occupation, the law. Noting black women practicing locally as attorneys in 1929, as well as her own efforts in organizing that group as the Portia Club in 1927, Sampson went on to commend legal studies generally as one route to personal improvement:

> The study of law is one of the greatest benefits a woman can possibly attain. There is no walk in life which she cannot the better fill for her legal knowledge and for the enlargement of mind which it brings. If all the women do not practice after studying, it is no proof that women are a failure at law, but on the other hand, the world is the richer and the power for good greatly increased.[26]

Clearly, the bare handful of women active in the professions and local politics—so small, in fact, that both articles comfortably cited all by name—could not serve as a reliable sample of local black women and their general concerns. As well, biographies of Pullman porter J. William Botts and his wife, Martha Botts, a teacher, or social worker Annie Fitts and her late husband, Bernard, publisher and advocate of youth literary societies, pre-dictably delimited women's social role in the constraining language of traditional domesticity. Yet the Wonder Books' treatment of black women also emphasized the mutualism and civic obligation Elsa Barkeley Brown locates at the center of the social and political consciousness she terms "womanism." Biographical entries on Ida B. Wells-Barnett or Irene McCoy Gaines, while noting family and marital history, presented their accomplishments primarily to celebrate their own autonomous social example.[27] Given scholarly consensus that associational activity among African-American women—what Darlene Clark Hine calls the commitment to "making community"—was the defining figuration of black women's historical agency over time, Wonder Book accounts of groups and organizations described earlier, viewed through a gendered lens, take on deeper significance and meaning.[28] The essays from both Gaines and Edith Sampson suggest that perhaps the best evidence of a progressive gender politics in the Wonder Books was the actual involvement of women within the books themselves. Six out of the twelve editors and twenty-six out of fifty-one total staff members for the 1927 Wonder Book were women. While these numbers declined in 1929, the prominence of the work of women staff, if anything, increased.[29]

A final—and surprising—evidence of the revised politics of black community advocated within the Wonder Books was their view toward black labor. Scholars have seen labor questions as litmus tests for the black middle class, forcing their elitism, archaic interpretation of political economy, and deference to white oversight above the surface and into view.[30] Locally, the record has seemed little different—stories of equivocation or indifference on the part of the Urban League and the *Defender* when asked to support unionization for black workers are well known.[31] The Wabash YMCA, midwife to the Intercollegiate Club, was an especially egregious offender, promoting company unions within the local stockyards and propagandizing notoriously for management during the 1919 Riot, in order to quell blacks' support for the mass organizing drive then taking place in the yards. Such examples support Earl Lewis's distinction between middle-class attention to the "home sphere"—the discrete terrain of household and segregated community—and mass concern with the workplace, as an ongoing tension structuring African-American politics during the twentieth century, and exacerbating class antagonisms as well.[32]

Treatment of black workers was mixed in the 1927 Wonder Book. An essay titled "Labor Must Organize" asserted that "Negro laborers as other laborers must raise their standards of living through effective organization," and recommended American Federation of Labor locals, the communist-supported American Negro Labor Congress, and the Brotherhood of Sleeping Car Porters as worthy vehicles toward this end. Entries elsewhere extolled the virtues of area unions, such as Local 208 of the American Federation of Musicians. Yet featured just as prominently were accounts of company-sponsored employee associations—like the Pullman Porter Benevolent Association of America, bitter rival of the Brotherhood—meant to preclude the rise of autonomous black collective representation. As well, little consideration was given to the role of other constituencies within black community—youth, the churches, the press, and the middle class—in the struggle for labor rights and workplace justice.[33]

By 1929, however, Wonder Book editors were portraying labor issues as central concerns of New Negro youth and conscientious leadership. Moving beyond spot surveys of employment and commercial conditions locally, the second Book featured Frankie Adams's lengthy and comprehensive essay on "The Negro Women in Industry," Vivian Garth's "Labor Thinks For Itself," an account of Brookwood Labor College in upstate New York, and Brotherhood of Sleeping Car Porters organizer Milton P. Webster's "Organized Labor Among Negroes in Chicago." An article titled "Take It or Leave It" linked workers' rights to broader use of collective economic leverage, indicating the influence of the Chicago *Whip*—the militant local paper advocating boycotts as a means to increasing clerical and sales jobs for blacks on the South Side—and its editor Joseph Bibb, a contributor to the 1929 Wonder Book. These and other pieces, in addition to documenting employment conditions and assessing progress in securing workplace reform, called on readers to recognize their role in supporting these struggles. In his piece, for example, Webster noted "the praiseworthy effort of the young men and women in the Intercollegiate Club and the International Negro Student Alliance" in providing him space to make the case for black worker organization.[34]

The centerpiece of the 1929 Wonder Book's advocacy of black labor was its digest of the National Negro Labor Conference annual meeting that year, sponsored by the Brotherhood of Sleeping Car Porters branch in Chicago. As with other activities, the book listed speakers and panelists involved in the conference. While some, including National Negro Business League official Albion Hosley and Cook County Juvenile Court Judge Mary Bartelme, focused on shortcomings of race businesses, and even black families, in creating unstable conditions, most focused on economic discrimination exacerbated by racism. Edith Sampson pointed out the difficulties working mothers experienced in supporting their families given low wages, while Frankie Adams spoke of poor health and safety conditions in industry, notably lampshade manufacturing, where 2,000 black women worked locally at that time. The Reverend Harold Kingsley, of the Church of the Good Shepard, asserted that since "the Negro worker is the basis of the church," religious bodies needed to be more pro-active in championing their constituents' interests. Frederic Robb emphasized the relationship between African-American students and labor, calling on black workers to "help educate the students up to their responsibilities," and for students to "quit criticizing the worker and get in harmony with him." Among Robb's recommendations were courses in "labor and industrial movements" at black colleges, labor scholarships for black students, and fostering of a "labor psychology" within the black church. Following speeches by Randolph and other ANLC leaders, the meeting offered twenty-two resolutions, including rejection of company unions, commitment to organizing the South, support of Haitian and Philippine autonomy, workplace, wage, and benefits reforms, and a "united front" of labor, clergy, professionals, and students within the African-American community.[35]

To be sure, this program on behalf of black labor was the product of ANLC efforts—the Wonder Book's recounting of it made Robb, Sampson, Adams, and other writers supporters, rather than sustainers, of labor's cause. Still, their solidarity begs the question as to how class-limited their outlook was at this time. In championing independent worker organizations—and, in particular, the Brotherhood of Sleeping Car Porters—Wonder Book editors were choosing sides in a heated and controversial local struggle. As William Harris has documented, local institutions, notably the Associated Negro Press, the *Defender*, and even the *Whip*, had been early opponents of the Brotherhood's efforts. While by 1928 the *Defender* had come out in support, others, such as Associated Negro Press founder and head Claude Barnett, remained opposed, fueling suspicions as to the capacity for interclass alliance on the part of the black middle class.[36] Wonder Book staff, by contrast, were unequivocal in their support: committed to solidarity since they saw that the workplace was linked to—rather than separate from—the home terrain of communal concerns.

Given its capacity to accommodate diverse approaches between its covers, one might have expected the Wonder Book to continue indefinitely as an institution. Editors predicted as much in 1929 with the promise, "Next Edition: World's Fair," emblazoned on their title page: a reference to the "Century of Progress" Exposition scheduled to take place in Chicago in 1933. Yet the Wonder Book was never published again. While no clear explanation exists, the later careers of many contributors suggest that the striving ethos within the books may have registered all too well, leading ultimately to the publication's demise. Edith Sampson pursued a celebrated career in legal work before being appointed as a special delegate to the United Nations by President Truman in 1950. Irene McCoy Gaines expanded her work as an organizer, holding posts in the NAACP, the Parkway Community House, and the March on Washington Movement through the 1940s. Jack Cooper, who already had begun a pioneering career as a black radio programmer, deepened his involvement in the new medium over the next two decades, offering popular music, dramatic, and religious shows through a time-share empire of local programming that many see as the beginning of black-appeal radio.[37]

The most intriguing personal history to emerge out of the Wonder

Books was that of its lead editor, Frederic Robb. Predictions of future success as a politician or jurist proved incorrect—by 1931, he had abandoned the law, concluding that it mostly concerned "fixing," and that he did not want "to become a part of that." Changing his name to Fidepe H. Hammurabi, he extended earlier transnational interests, organizing a Royal Ashanti Singers and Dancers program for the 1933 World's Fair and the "International or Pan-African, Asiatic, European, and North and South Americas Day" at the 1940 American Negro Exposition, also held in Chicago. Along the way he maintained his reputation as an orator, regularly holding forth at the outdoor forum held at the north end of Washington Park through the 1930s and 1940s. Explicit about his Pan-African allegiances, Hammurabi was arrested, along with Elijah Muhammad and other Chicagoans, for his objections to World War II. In 1950, he founded the House of Knowledge and the Ethiopian Research Library, a bookstore and learning center crucial to black Chicago's eventual emergence as a center for what has come to be called Afrocentric thought. In many ways Hammurabi embodied the eclecticism and innovation of the young African Americans associated with the Wonder Books—as well as offering a caution to those presuming that his life, as well as the lives of those in his generation, proceeded according to a standard script.[38]

What the Wonder Books offer, in the end, is one means through which to change—if not discard—that script. While the black middle class has, of late, regained the attention of scholars, the resulting studies have often followed classic works like Frazier's *Black Bourgeoisie* and Cruse's *The Crisis of the Negro Intellectual* in taking the black middle class to task for its conservatism and sycophancy toward the wider white world. Examination of the Wonder Books, however, argues that this sort of blanket dismissal should be reconsidered. Indeed, such sources suggest lines of revision for the study of the black middle class specifically, and offer an effective means toward sophisticating analysis of American middle-class history generally.

Within the field of African-American history specifically, the Wonder Books suggest that presuming the black middle class a homogenous and predictable entity is a flawed premise on which to base future study. Age and educational experience, it is clear, complicated outlooks within this group, as did the environment in which individuals and groups found themselves situated. Although twentieth-century Chicago produced one of the more notorious examples of modern clientage—the Democratic submachine effectively containing black political ambition for a half-century—in areas such as labor, business, media, culture, and religion, activities locally on the part of the black middle class were strikingly autonomous and self-determined. Indeed, these efforts constitute a rich and eclectic record of engagement with questions of communal development on many levels: the Wonder Books are among the first of many chapters in this story. Seen in this light, members of Chicago's black middle class appear more interested in collective cooperation and solidarity, more committed to confronting traditions of patriarchy and class elitism, more *activist*, in a word, than "imitative and unimaginative," as Harold Cruse bitterly concluded. Perhaps this was the result of the unique environment of black Chicago, flush with energy and expectation in the wake of the Great Migration. Perhaps this was symptomatic of the early and plastic phase of African-American class formation, when the Wonder Books emerged: as members of the "new" middle class, editors and contributors could indulge a future of possibilities unburdened by later trials constraining both initiative and ambition. Only scholarship based on rich sources like the Wonder Books, and engaged with the story of the black middle class on its own terms, rather than as a straw man offering easy answers regarding the enduring plight of black communities, can provide effective answers to these questions.[39]

In relation to middle-class studies generally, the Wonder Books point out the difficulty in making easy comparison across lines of race. Benefits accruing to the middle class generally through the course of national history—unfettered entrepreneurial growth and civic custodianship beginning in the nineteenth century, bureaucratic investiture and, later, reward through a "culture of affluence" during the twentieth—have been largely unavailable to African Americans until recently. Nor has this discrepancy been merely a historical coincidence. As with white workers, reproduction of middle-class identity in this country has relied upon an unapologetic stake in race privilege and an ongoing commitment to fortifying the color line, as issues shaping the social history of the past century, such as neighborhood autonomy and, later, crime and punishment, make clear. At the same time, critiques emphasizing the deactivation and social malaise that American middle-class life is understood to embody also require modification to fit African-American lives and histories, if indeed they retain validity at all. Concern over the special conditions of studying the black middle class becomes more pressing when one notes the derivation of classic studies of the African-American middle class, like those of Frazier and Cruse, from the work of such pioneer critics as C. Wright Mills. If anything, then, the tradition of studying the black middle class has often been seen as a simple problem of applying existing class theory to the conditions of African-American lives, rather than discerning whether the specificity of those lives demands revision of that theory.[40]

These suggestions, clearly, deserve deeper consideration than I have been able to offer here. As recent and robust interest in the history of the black working class has sharpened historical inquiry well beyond that topic, so, too, does future improvement in the study of the black middle class promise richer and more sophisticated scholarship in general. Few better resources exist with which to initiate such inquiries than sources like Chicago's Wonder Books. Their capacity to excite and inform continues to the present day, fulfilling the hopes of its creators many years ago.

The Limits of Democracy in the Suburbs: Constructing the Middle Class through Residential Exclusion

THERESA MAH

In 1951, a group calling itself "America Plus, Inc." proposed an amendment to the California state constitution to be decided upon by voter initiative at the following year's general election. Dubbed the "Freedom of Choice Initiative" by its sponsors, the amendment would have guaranteed homeowners and businessmen the "right" to choose their employees, guests, patrons, tenants, and neighbors. While one effect of the amendment would have been to nullify any fair employment legislation passed in California, its better-known provision was to allow homeowners to enter into contractual arrangements concerning the occupancy of private housing in their neighborhoods. This latter provision—specifically guaranteeing the "right" to choose one's neighbors—was one of many such attempts to emerge in response to the 1948 U.S. Supreme Court decision declaring restrictive covenants legally unenforceable.[1]

Though America Plus insisted that its amendment "neither segregates nor discriminates" and that, theoretically, "the contracting parties may admit all of one race into their neighborhoods or all of another race, or as many of each as the majority prefers," it was clear that the main thrust of the amendment was to enable whites to exclude racially undesirable groups from privately owned accommodations. While the organization's initiative ultimately did not pass, its two incarnations in two years—along with the popular support it enjoyed—point to significant anxiety in this period about the encroachment of "racial" groups into suburban, white neighborhoods and the erosion of "majority rights" through civil rights legislation.[2]

Arnold Hirsch has noted that between 1948 and 1968, the federal government gradually moved toward a "color-blind" housing policy, beginning with the Supreme Court's ruling on *Shelley v. Kramer* and culminating in the passage of the Fair Housing Act in 1968. This period marked a shift away from nearly three decades of federal involvement in racial segregation. Yet, as Hirsch and others have argued, these policies at the federal level did little to reverse the high levels of housing segregation and ghettoization established during the first half of the twentieth century. Instead, this period might be seen more accurately as one that saw an increased urgency on the part of those committed to reinforcing racial boundaries.[3]

The urgency reflected, for example, in the "Freedom of Choice" campaign indicated the important position that control over neighborhood composition had come to occupy by midcentury. This ability to choose one's neighbors was predicated upon what the neighborhood had come to symbolize. The expansion of the housing market, the availability of long-term, self-amortizing loans, and the general rise in wages made homeownership accessible to a broad segment of the population for the first time in history. At this time as in no other, it became possible to buy one's way into the middle class. Yet, primarily because of the widespread application of racially restrictive covenants barring "nonwhite" ownership, these privileges were limited to whites. Campaigns like "Freedom of Choice" reflected the efforts of a newly emerging, as yet insecure "majority" of Americans—a middle class built on the ability to mark its mobility through the possession of a house.

In a 1950 novel written by the national chairman of America Plus, a fictional character gives a sense of what was felt to be at stake in the struggle to control neighborhood composition:

> What gives property value? Restrictions! . . . we need more, not less of them, if the neighborhood, the basis of American democracy, is to be preserved. . . . What else is the gentleman's neighborhood agreement except the majority's demand that it have a right to choose, to determine its own standards of friendly nearness, its own familiar, intimate intercourse, its own way of life?[4]

The passage suggests the fundamental role that racially restrictive covenants had played in the creation of racially homogeneous neighborhoods. The absence of restrictions would lead to the racial intrusion that threatened not just property values, but the very security of the middle-class position.

While the failure of America Plus to win approval for "Freedom of Choice" might indicate that its goals were not, in fact, well supported by the majority, the discourses at its heart, revolving around homeownership, majority rights, neighborhood self-determination, and American democracy, were consistent with the dominant concerns of the day. The efforts of average Americans in the twentieth century to define themselves as middle class by buying into racially exclusive suburban neighborhoods also represented, on a fundamental level, attempts to realize the American Dream—at the direct expense of others. Our failure to explain the persistence of racial segregation and ghettoization well beyond the institution of legislative prohibitions may lie in our blindness to this cultural process.

An extraordinary residential segregation case in the spring of 1952 offers an excellent opportunity to explore this process. In January of 1952, Sing Sheng, a young Chinese immigrant, answered an ad in the *San Francisco Chronicle* for a house at 726 West Orange Avenue in South San Francisco. Sheng then placed a down payment of $2,950 on the three-bedroom house, where he intended to live with his Chinese-American wife, Grace, their son, and another child whom they were expecting. When news of the sale spread through the Southwood neighborhood, the owners of the house received letters and telephone calls registering their neighbors' objection. The owners were accused of breaking the restrictive covenant that covered homes in the subdivision, and they received menacing threats that they would be barred from purchasing a house elsewhere. When a group of angry neighbors later met with Sheng to try to intimidate him from purchasing the house, Sheng made the unusual suggestion of putting the matter up to a vote by the entire neighborhood. He agreed to abide by whatever decision came out of the vote and felt sure that the outcome would be in his favor.[5]

When the ballots were counted on February 16, 1952, the result was 174 "objections," 28 "no objections," and 14 "no opinions." The news of the incident made headlines all over the San Francisco Bay Area and was reported throughout the country, as well as abroad. The bitter irony of a case in which a former Chinese national, who was well-educated and trained in an American university, who had abandoned his home country after the communist takeover, and who had placed his hopes in America and in the democratic process only to see it fail him in practice was not only exceedingly dramatic, but also struck a nerve deep in the national consciousness. In a period when the idea of democracy was paramount, many wondered how an exercise that seemed to embody the high principles of the democratic process could result in such injustice and inequity. On the other hand, the participants in the neighborhood vote were baffled and angry that they were being judged for what they believed was fully fair.[6]

The way in which discussion of the issue was framed in the media in terms of either the triumph or failure of democracy highlighted the significance of "democracy" as an overarching discourse during the Cold War period. In a letter to Southwood residents before the vote, Sheng himself set up the issue in terms of a basic opposition: "The present world conflict," he began, referring to the Korean War, "is not between individual nations, but between Communism and Democracy." He then continued, "We think so highly of Democracy because it offers freedom and equality. America's forefathers fought for these principles and won the Independence of 1776. We have forsaken all our beloved in China and have come to this country seeking the same basic rights. Do not make us the victims of false democracy. Please vote in favor of us."[7]

In the end, of course, the majority did not vote in favor of the Shengs. But rather than becoming "victims of false democracy," as Sheng himself put it, it seems that the Shengs rather became victims of an intensified discourse of democracy deeply implicated in the racial and class formation of the postwar era. After the disappointing outcome, Sheng revealed, "I didn't know about any race prejudice at all until I came to Southwood. I was sure everybody really believed in democracy, I thought up this vote as a test." While Sheng and those who decried the outcome of the Southwood vote believed democracy clearly represented freedom and equality and saw the vote's outcome as a failure or betrayal of its principles, to the residents of Southwood who rejected the Shengs their victory signaled the triumph of democracy and, by extension, the legitimization of their position that exclusion was justifiable. In the words of one resident: "After all, democracy means that the majority rules."[8]

The idea that the majority rules is significant in this context because it was in the suburbs, in communities like Southwood, that "the American majority" was most fundamentally being constructed at this time. Southwood was a recently built development of modest, single-family homes in the price range of $9,000 to $12,000. The tract of 253 frame houses was built by the American Homes Development Company, which referred to itself as "developers of this representative American, residential area." Suburban homes in this era were speedily built and affordably priced, with low down payments, particularly for veterans. Like countless other communities that sprang up around metropolitan centers after World War II, Southwood was populated by a new class of homeowners whose purchases were made possible by federal housing subsidies under the Home Owners' Loan Corporation (HOLC), Federal Housing Administration (FHA), and the Veterans Administration (VA), as well as financial gains through wartime employment. As Kenneth Jackson has noted, regarding the construction of similar "Levittown-type developments" on the East Coast, the availability of these modestly priced homes meant that "even the working classes could aspire to home ownership."[9]

If the United States in the postwar period became a nation of homeowners living in the suburbs, it was in those very same suburbs that residents constituted themselves as "the majority," as well as "white," " American," and "middle class" through processes that they themselves believed to be wholly democratic. This process of racialization was accomplished in a practical sense at this (crab)grass-roots level—using Thomas Sugrue's coinage—in what he has also termed "the politics of defensive localism."[10] Whether in the form of neighborhood improvement associations, "homes associations," "protective associations," or less organized groups of home-owners, neighborhoods like Southwood became sites for a new emphasis on the democratic process, but one that ironically fostered a chilling climate of exclusion.

In practice, neighborhood associations, or even less formalized gather-ings of neighbors, exercised a great deal of power regarding the composi-tion of their communities, particularly through the use of restrictive covenants. Subdivisions like San Lorenzo Village, across the San Francisco Bay from Southwood, specified under original covenants drawn up by the developer that occupancy would only be by those "wholly of the white or Caucasian race." In the case of San Lorenzo Village, the covenant was main-tained by the governing body composed of the community's property own-ers, each of whom had a vote in electing the Homes Association's Board of Directors. The board of directors met monthly at meetings open to the gen-eral membership, who showed widespread interest and enthusiastic partici-pation in such matters of community government. In cases of communities without such governing bodies, residents would, as described by one con-temporary study of exclusionary practices, "band together" and agree not to sell their properties to "nonwhite" buyers.[11]

The Sheng case only further illustrates, if more symbolically, the perva-sive way in which acts of local participation, often couched in terms of dem-ocratic action, served to constitute and maintain a racial majority. The Southwood residents were only too happy to participate in the vote pro-posed by Sheng precisely because it was not inconsistent with their every-day actions. Though this particular incident culminated in actual balloting by the residents, the activities in the neighborhood before and after Sheng's proposition demonstrate the ordinary events of "defensive localism" that occurred with such frequency in the postwar suburb/neighborhood. For example, beginning the very day after the Sheng's deposit was made on the Southwood home, neighbors began harassing the owners with telephone calls and letters condemning them for their decision to sell to Sheng. Imme-diately following, meetings were scheduled and tactics ranging from friendly persuasion to threats of violent reprisals were used. After Sheng's suggestion of the vote, campaigning began immediately, involving, among other things, door-to-door visits instructing neighbors on how to vote. The Shengs' own letter quoted above was an insignificant gesture compared to the level of campaigning by the opposition. In addition to the residents' canvassing, even the subdivision's developers got involved, sending each household a letter warning them that property values would drop if "non-Caucasians" were allowed into Southwood.[12]

The views of Southwood's residents had wide circulation by the early 1950s. In a survey of candidates for state office in California, a questionnaire on housing asked whether licensed real estate brokers and sales representatives should be required by law to serve all clients equally without discrimination. One candidate wrote: "Every community is like a home and its citizens by popular vote must decide that question and no one else." In the aftermath of Sheng's exclusion from Southwood, state Senator Jack Tenney, one of the proponents of the "Freedom of Choice" amendment, called the incident a "true example of democracy in action. . . . If people don't have a right to vote on their neighbors, they don't have a right to vote on their President."[13]

According to a city planner in the July 1948 *Journal of Housing*, the concept of the "neighborhood unit" was one that was almost thirty years old and had been the subject of much difference in interpretation among planners and housers. Nonetheless, it was an idea that had gained increasing acceptance, largely because in a period of rapid urban development it had the ability to embody "rural nostalgia" and the idyllic image of "the kind of intimate social relationships and the stability [found] lacking in the chaotic life of the city." With the additional aid of the FHA, which believed that the neighborhood units were "more profitable to developers, offer better security to investors, are more desirable to home owners, and create enduring and stable communities," the vision of neighborhood units, and unity, became established in fact. By the postwar period, this concept had gained such importance as to be incorporated into the rhetoric of the Cold War; one subdivider who favored restrictive covenants and neighborhood associations stated, "when you rear children in a good neighborhood, they will go out and fight Communism."[14]

The vehemence with which so many newer middle-income neighborhoods sought to exclude "nonwhites" might be explained in part by the importance of homeownership in the postwar era as the primary means of securing middle-class status. Whereas previously housing had generally acted as a marker of status only for the upper classes, the dramatic growth of middle-income housing in postwar America made it possible to distinguish oneself as middle class or upwardly mobile rather than poor and immobile simply by virtue of homeownership. Since the spread of suburban/middle-income development in the postwar era promised the fulfillment of postwar affluence and upward mobility for many Americans, the purchase of even a modest frame house in a middle-income neighborhood represented more than a financial investment in a piece of property where one's family could live. The purchase of a home represented perhaps even more a serious investment in an idea: that higher social status could be acquired through ownership of a home in the right neighborhood.

As such, it was crucial that the house remain free of "value-deflating" influences. In explaining this phenomenon, one civil rights organization observed in its newsletter, "The location of one's house has become the last clear symbol of social status. Furs, a large car, jewels, art, all of the things which bear evidence that 'I have arrived' are available on the mass market; but not so with homes."[15] Thus at the same time that housing was being "democratized" and therefore made common through increased accessibility, a simultaneous act of exclusivity became necessary in order to elevate and maintain its value. The neighborhood thus may have been considered the basic unit of democracy for white Americans, but for "nonwhites," it became the site of disenfranchisement in a deeply profound way.

The history of Southwood and its development mirror the national desire to eschew working-class trappings for the ideal of upward mobility. Southwood was one of four tracts that made up part of the City of South San Francisco, on "The Peninsula" between the Pacific Ocean and the San Francisco Bay. Unlike the more pastoral suburbs nearby, South San Francisco was known as the "Industrial City," its moniker proudly festooned— even to this day—like the famous "Hollywood" sign on a hillside above the homes. It was the home of approximately 140 industries, including nationally known companies such as Swift, Armour, Fuller Paints, Bethlehem Steel, and Dupont Paint, that attracted a large blue-collar population.[16]

In the period after World War II, South San Francisco underwent a transition "from an industrial center to a residential suburban area," a transformation well reflected in the social aspirations of its residents. Thus, while there was a diversity of occupations and educational levels present in Southwood, survey data taken at the time of the Sheng case indicated a preponderance of a skilled and semiskilled laboring population even in the new suburban tract. Twenty-four percent of Southwood residents were semiskilled workers or housewives; 17 percent were professional or managerial; 15 percent skilled craftsmen; 14 percent were white-collar workers, such as accountants, secretaries, sales representatives, and clerks; and 3 percent were in the military. Remarkably, there were no doctors, lawyers, engineers, dentists, or ministers—professions generally considered upper middle class. As for educational attainment, only 19 percent of the respondents had two or more years of college. The sociologist who obtained this data remarked that the data suggest "a significant index of upward mobility, with a preponderant non-college population choosing to reside in an 'exclusive' area."[17]

In an era in which average Americans sought to redefine themselves as middle class and to hail the success of their upward mobility by claiming "classlessness," the presence of almost any class diversity threatened to sabotage their efforts. If any ruptures existed in the consensus, it became imperative to suture the breeches with a patch created from an equally patchy fabric of "whiteness." Indeed, as one observer noted in 1947, "many residential areas find their only bond is the fear of Negro infiltration."[18]

In the explanations given by the residents to justify their objection to Sheng, anxieties about status and class markers predominated. Of the 92 respondents surveyed by researcher Robert Lee, 35 percent believed that property values would drop because of Sheng's entry. An additional 21 per-cent believed that property values would drop not simply due to Sheng's presence alone, but from further "nonwhite" entry that would surely follow if he were allowed to move in. One man insisted, "If it's over in [another part of] South San Francisco [which remained industrial], it would be all right, but here in this tract, no! We bought these homes in a restricted tract." Another resident explained, "We moved here from a housing project in order to get away from Orientals and Negroes because our children are growing up. We've got to look out for our kids, ya know [*sic*]."[19]

The conflation of various "racial" groups—in this case "Orientals and Negroes"—as "nonwhite" points to the primacy of "white" as the main way in which the middle class sought to define itself at this time. As older hous-ing, overcrowded neighborhoods, and eventually public housing became associated with minority groups, a process that was intensified by wartime migration to California, these new members of the middle class imagined nonwhites as the specter of their own poor or working-class, non-upwardly mobile past.[20] The visible marker of racial difference came to stand in for class differences, and the process of exclusion from middle-class areas solid-ified the association of "nonwhites" with inferior surroundings, poverty, and crime.

The effort to sustain racial purity often involved the invocation of the taboo of miscegenation. One common sentiment that was expressed to interviewers and used to justify the residents' refusal to accept nonwhite neighbors was the conversation-stopping question, "Would you want your daughter to marry one?" The assumption that the only response could be a resounding "no" was always already assumed in the question. And the fact that the answer "why not?" was never entertained publicly suggests that the taboo of racial mixture, restrictions on women's sexuality, and faith in the need to protect wives and daughters operated in conjunction with the idea of the homogeneous neighborhood to maintain the social order of the postwar suburb.[21]

In a 1943 article on practices of racial restriction in residential areas, one commentator asserted that miscegenation was "the 'end-all' argument behind which non-thinking people retire."[22] Yet ignorance alone cannot explain the nearly culturewide adherence to the idea of segregated residen-tial space. The emphasis on racial purity was bound up with an imagined threat to an American way of life that included a deeply held belief in family, conformity, and a stable balance between the individual and the commu-nity—values which, not uncoincidentally, could be easily mapped onto the postwar conflict between democracy and communism.

Comments made by the Southwood residents and by others regarding the case made it clear how strongly the anticommunist overtones of the Cold War permeated everyday life in postwar America. There was wide-spread suspicion that Sheng was either a communist or "a tool of the Communist [*sic*]." Mrs. Warren Mooney, a resident of Southwood, revealed the extent to which the communist threat was used to frighten neighbors: "They told us so many terrible things . . . that he was a Communist, that he (Sheng) himself was racially prejudiced against Negroes, things that I know now are not true." Others voiced the suspicion that the entire incident was staged as communist propaganda to "stir up trouble" on Brotherhood Week, implying that the negative outcome of the case would prove rich fodder for critics to highlight American hypocrisy on an occasion purportedly celebrating brotherhood. Senator Joseph Knowland of California also acknowledged such a possibility, but steered clear of suggesting that the incident had been staged; nonetheless, he seemed compelled to defend American democracy by asserting that the Southwood case was an isolated incident that "undoubtedly will be put to the worst possible use by Communist Propaganda in Asia."[23]

Just as the neighborhood was the purported "unit of American democracy," the family was its private counterpart. Engels long ago pointed out the connection between the convergent establishment of the modern family unit and the system of private property in capitalist society, and in postwar America, the conflation of these two systems was quite evident.[24] Residents in the Sheng case frequently voiced concern about their children, racial mixture, and sexual threat. One man bluntly stated, "My wife was raped by a Nigger once and I don't want that to happen again."

Another said, "I don't want my kids playing with all kinds of people. I paid a very high price to live out here in the suburb [*sic*]. I moved here mainly for the sake of my daughter. She's growing up and we have to think of the kids. . . . We came from a housing project just to get away from having to live with Negroes because our kids are growing up . . . " While the threat of rape loomed in the imagination with regard to women and girls, the threat of racial mixture was a threat to the entire family: "Our children don't know the difference and might marry one of them someday."[25]

In an attempt to emphasize the value of the "Freedom of Choice" legislation, America Plus chairman Aldrich Blake explained that he owned an apartment house in which he and five other tenants lived and shared a common patio. "The relationships are close. We are a big family," he wrote. One of the units became vacant, and his wife declared that if he rented it to a "Negro," she would move. Yet he was in a dilemma because if he refused to rent to a Negro who applied, he would be liable for damages under the civil rights code. Blake claimed:

> Now, neither Mrs. Blake nor I have the slightest ill-feeling toward Negroes. We admire the progress the Negro is making. We are not haters. In short, we simply prefer to live under the same roof with people of our own kind, people whom we understand, whose culture

is the same as ours, and among whom we have been raised. We would indeed be very unhappy in any other environment.[26]

Elaborating further on the complexity of the issue, Blake described the dilemma he would be confronted with if he were to rent to a "Negro." In essence, his other tenants would move out; he would be forced to rent only to blacks lest he go bankrupt; yet doing so would alienate his friends and neighbors and ultimately destroy his and his family's happiness. These problems, Blake asserted, were "practical problems which confront others who are not bigots or racists, but just average Americans trying to live happy lives."[27]

The insistence on individual choice and property owners' rights was consistent with the ideology of liberal democracy that was prominent in Cold War discourse, as opposed to the totalitarian authority thought to be characteristic of communism. At the same time that claims were made about the primacy of the individual and his/her "rights," there was an equally forceful emphasis on the importance of "community." Statements asserting, "We are community minded," and "We live in a close knit community, with lots of community spirit" were frequently reiterated. Along with insistent claims about community there was a corollary notion that the community consisted of "average" or "ordinary" American people.[28]

To the Southwood residents, the fact that the decision to exclude Sheng was agreed upon by the majority made it justifiable, especially given that other groups or other communities could ostensibly make their own decisions about whom they want in their neighborhoods. One common refrain heard in the interviews about the case was, "Why doesn't Sheng live with his own people?" One resident stated specifically that Sheng should "stick within his own territory. . . . He should live with his own people in a Chinese tract." Another person went so far as to criticize Sheng's emigration from China—his own racially homogenous community—and conclude: "Anyone that will desert his own people like that shouldn't be allowed to live in our community." After the vote, residents argued in their own defense: "You can't blame us for wanting to live with our own kind of people, can you? We don't want to live with them. Why should they want to live with us?" In other words, the prevailing belief was that a "separate but equal" set of communities was the norm.[29]

While the above statements imply that segregation is a voluntary act, that people band together because of natural and acceptable desires to be with one's own kind, the delineation of racially segregated residential space in the shape that it took in midcentury America was a relatively recent phenomenon. In San Francisco, a racially segregated Chinatown area dated from the nineteenth century, but it was contiguous with, and often bled into, both the wealthy Nob Hill neighborhood and the poor and dilapidated, largely Italian North Beach area. The Fillmore district, which later came to be known as San Francisco's "Negro district," was still quite diverse through the 1940s and 1950s. Other studies, such as James Borchert's work on Washington, D.C., Arnold Hirsch's work on Chicago, and Kenneth Kusmer's work on Cleveland, clearly demonstrate the specifically twentieth-century formation of distinctly racialized urban space. Indeed, as Douglas Massey and Nancy Denton note, "There was a time, before 1900, when blacks and whites lived side by side in American cities." [30]

The case of *Sheng v. Southwood* was a lightning rod for cultural meanings in postwar America. At the most transparent level, it could be concluded that the case was simply about racial exclusion, that Sheng was not wanted because he was "Oriental"; that he was primarily constituted as racially different and therefore unwelcome into a racially homogeneous, white community. Yet at another level, the specter of invasion loomed in the minds of Southwood homeowners, and they acted to fortify the boundaries of their homogeneous, middle-class neighborhood. Arguments about property values and neighborhood composition dominated this discussion, repeatedly raising the issue of homeowners' rights. The opposition of communism and democracy in the rhetoric of the Cold War figured prominently in the meaning behind these discourses.

To conclude: we must remember that the effort to constitute the nation as democratic, classless, and materially comfortable operated not only in the political rhetoric of the day, but also permeated the culture at a very local level. In turn, the neighborhood in this period became one of the main sites for the formation of "whiteness," "Americanness," and the middle-class "majority" in a purportedly democratic society. In the case of postwar housing, the democracy that ultimately prevailed was severely limited. As America held up the image of itself as the shining example of democracy to the world, the country was simultaneously denying the franchise to an entire segment of its population through racial exclusion from the suburban housing market.

Rethinking Middle-Class Populism and Politics in the Postwar Era: Community Activism in Queens

SYLVIE MURRAY

Despite the unitary connotations implied by the phrase "the middle class," no single (or simple) definition of the term exists. One's access to property, one's position on the occupational ladder, even one's political sensibility (or lack thereof) are all criteria that have been used in reference to this quite elusive social category. Of these, the latter has attracted much attention in recent scholarship. Derided in the sociological literature of the 1950s for its political apathy, the middle class has been associated since the 1970s with an insurgent popular and populist conservatism. It is this image of reactionary middle-class populism that this essay seeks to challenge.

In his classic 1951 study of the American middle classes, *White Collar*, C. Wright Mills traced a profound transformation from the "old" middle class of the nineteenth century, defined by its access to a small business or a farm, to the "new" middle class of the twentieth century, identified by its white-collar occupational patterns and, most significant for our purposes, its political insignificance. Having lost the independence that property owner-ship conferred, and being subjected to the whims of the modern corporate bureaucracy, the white-collar man, or the "Little Man" as Mills put it, was completely devoid of political awareness and interest. "Estranged from community and society in a context of distrust and manipulation; alienated from work and, on the personality market, from self; expropriated of indi-vidual rationality, and politically apathetic—these are the new little people, the unwilling vanguard of modern society." In his conclusion, Mills insisted even further on the political indifference of the middle-class masses. "They are strangers to politics. They are not radical, not liberal, not conservative, not reactionary; they are inactionary; they are out of it. If we accept the Greek's definition of the idiot as a privatized man, then we must conclude that the U.S. citizenry is now largely composed of idiots."[1]

Twenty years later, the academic wisdom about the middle class had changed considerably. Occupational distinctions were becoming less relevant and politics more prominent. The "lower middle class," as the term was coined in the early 1970s, included both blue-collar and low-echelon white-collar workers—in fact, the former came to replace the latter as the quintessential "Middle Americans." No longer politically insignificant as Mills had deemed them, ordinary/average/middle-class Americans were now "politically reactionary." In the image of the popular television character Archie Bunker, the "average American" was racist and suspicious of political and economic elites—much like the Italian and Irish Catholics who violently opposed school integration in Boston, or New York Jews who turned against racial minorities and the "liberal establishment" in Canarsie, Brooklyn. Like the construction workers who "reached their boiling point" and attacked antiwar protesters in 1970, or the main characters in films such as *Joe* or *The Deer Hunter*, these "white ethnics" were prone to violence; indeed, they had, according to sociologist Seymour Martin Lipset, an authoritarian, antidemocratic personality. Irrationally prejudiced and intolerant, antiliberal and populist, "the lower middle class" was at the center of what became known as the "white backlash."[2]

Since the 1970s, scholarly analysis has added both contextual and historical depth to this rejection of liberalism by white middle-class folks. Ronald Formisano and Jonathan Rieder have revealed the intricate combination of factors that led to such an explosion of racial hatred, including a strong ethnic and neighborhood identity and an acute sense of economic entrapment. Along similar lines, David Halle has argued that a concern for home and neighborhood is central to middle-class identity. Characterized by their lives away from the workplace, access to material possessions, and a residence and neighborhood of quality, the middle-class status embraced by the working men that he studied is closely associated with a sharp populist resentment of those with political and economic power, and a defense of racially exclusive neighborhood and schools. This combination of racist community politics and populism can also be found in the strong opposition to racial integration that Thomas Sugrue and Arnold Hirsch have documented in Detroit and Chicago in the 1940s and 1950s. Finally, this scholarship is congruent with Michael Kazin's contention that, in the postwar period, populism has been appropriated by antiliberal groups and politicians. Taken together, this body of work reinforces the image of a reactionary middle class already well established in the 1970s; it also directly links its reactionary politics to the populist defense of home and neighborhood. The white middle class, in other words, has become synonymous with reactionary populist politics.[3]

Yet the composite portrait that is drawn in this recent scholarship on middle-class politics is incomplete: the political experience in the postwar period of middle-class Americans—a group marked by a great diversity of ideological convictions—cannot be defined exclusively through their involvement in racist and antiliberal movements. The case of northeastern Queens, New York City, in the late 1940s and 1950s forces a reevaluation of the accepted paradigm. Here, in this rapidly developing area, we find many of the dynamics that have been noted by observers of middle-class life and politics. As in Sugrue's and Halle's works, concerns for the interests of the residential community were central to local politics and middle-class consciousness in Queens. Overcrowded public schools; lack of public transportation, public libraries, playgrounds and parks; changes to zoning restrictions and increases in property taxes—these were some of the main issues that mobilized an expanding network of homeowners', tenants', and parents' associations. Also, an unmistakable populist sensibility—reminiscent of that described by Kazin —permeated the area's political culture. Yet, unlike many other metropolitan areas at the time, northeastern Queens remained untouched by overt racial conflicts. Stripped of its association with racial antiliberalism, the attempt by middle-class citizens to defend the interests of their residential communities and the populist rhetoric that framed this political struggle appear in a new light.[4] A close look at these Queens citizens profoundly transforms the way we view the postwar middle class.

An examination of the area's political culture as well as some of the debates in which residents took part will illustrate the forces that shaped middle-class politics in Queens. In contrast to the focus on rights and privileges that, according to many scholars, has been at the center of postwar liberalism, we will see that a language of needs and responsibilities dominated Queens political culture.[5] In fact, a keen attention to the various (and at times competing) needs of the residential community shaped both the residents' definition of their role as "responsible" citizens and their expectations of the state. Turning next to a controversy over public housing and to the ongoing battle to obtain additional schools that mobilized Queens residents throughout the 1940s and 1950s, I analyze the dynamics that pitted many members of the white middle class against their government.

The role of conservative corporate interests in this story cannot be underestimated. As scholars have well documented, conservative business leaders developed sophisticated strategies to influence public opinion in the immediate postwar era, including the manipulation of populist rhetoric.[6] Attention to this form of corporate populism has to be put at the fore of local studies. Many middle-class citizens in Queens were strongly influenced, for example, by the real estate lobby's attempt to limit the scope of state intervention—in fact, many in the network of civic associations had professional and personal ties to the industry. But arguably more important in defining the relationship between citizens and their government was the absence of a consistent and balanced policy in matters of metropolitan development. In line with their belief in the state's responsibility toward its citizens and their communities, Queens residents expected policies that would assure that adequate public services be provided to match the rapid pace of residential construction. These demands were more often than not ignored by New York City politicians and bureaucrats. Yet, throughout the 1950s, civic leaders remained remarkably (perhaps even naively) confident that an informed and rational citizenry, presenting reasonable demands, could—or, at least, should—be heard by policy makers. It is this profoundly democratic impulse, overlooked in studies of the twentieth-century middle class, that needs to be rediscovered.

Queens was certainly not a suburb in the technical or commonly accepted sense of the word: administratively, it was located within the limits of New York City, and its built environment, which included an increasing number of large-scale garden apartment complexes, contrasted with the more familiar suburban setting dominated by detached, single-family dwellings.[7] Yet, the still undeveloped outer sections of the borough of Queens offered key "suburban" qualities prized by families with young children: a relatively pastoral environment located at easy commuting distance from the city center. Hence, in the context of the severe housing shortage of the immediate postwar period, the population of areas such as Flushing and Bayside increased by 46 percent from 1940 to 1948, and again by between 55 and 60 percent from 1950 to 1957.[8]

Although the residents of Queens usually spoke of their residential community in singular and unitary terms—as "the community"—their neighborhoods were, in fact, home to a diverse cross section of the postwar middle class. Not only did homeowners and tenants alike make up the population of this semisuburban environment, but as was typical of the new residential areas that developed after World War II, the neighborhoods of northeastern Queens were occupationally diverse, including families of unionized blue-collar workers, low-echelon white-collar workers, and professionals.[9] Culturally, the population of northeastern Queens was heterogeneous, with a majority of first- and second-generation immigrants. (In 1960, the census listed 15 percent of the population as foreign-born; they were, predominantly and in roughly equal proportions, from Eastern Europe, the U.S.S.R., Germany, and Italy; 38 percent of the population had foreign-born parents.)[10] The wide variety of Catholic, Protestant, and Jewish houses of worship also reflected the population's diversity.[11] Finally, reflecting the reality of postwar suburbia as a whole, northeastern Queens was, for the most part, racially segregated.

One exception to the rule was a small neighborhood known as Flushing Suburban, where a large number of African-American homeowners resided. This area saw its black population increase from 7.5 to 50 percent between 1950 and 1960. Although a partial white flight accompanied the arrival of African-American families in the area, its neighborhood and civic life remained racially mixed.[12] Along with a significant number of Jewish and politically progressive families that moved to neighboring areas of South Flushing in the late 1940s and early 1950s, Flushing Suburban residents were concerned with issues of racial justice and integrated these concerns in their civic life. The *Flushing Guide*, the Flushing Suburban Civic Association's newsletter, celebrated the desegregation of schools in the nation's capital and denounced the "barbarous" murder of Emmett Till in 1955. Julia Schreier, a resident of nearby Kew Hills and a columnist in the community newspaper *The Kew Hills News*, condemned the "frenzied mobs" of Little Rock, Arkansas, in 1957 and expressed her wishes that children in her predominantly white homeowning community would "feel a natural revulsion toward the goons who were violating basic human dignity." The same concern for racial justice—this time in their own neighborhoods —was expressed, for instance, through the 1952 Parkway Village rent strike, led by the young and radical Betty Friedan, and by the work of the "Neighbors for Brotherhood," a community organization that monitored local businesses to ensure nondiscrimination in employment in 1954. Throughout the 1950s and the early 1960s, South Flushing remained a bastion of progressive politics.[13]

Neighborhoods such as these were certainly not representative of northeastern Queens as a whole, let alone of postwar suburbs. But given the increasingly diverse nature of the postwar American middle class, and of Queens middle-class communities in particular, perhaps it is mistaken to search for a "representative" case study.[14] In fact, what is most striking, given the demographic heterogeneity of the population, is that whether they were homeowners or tenants, black or white, Jews or Gentiles, liberal or conservative, residents of Queens spoke the same language of community betterment and responsible citizenship. Contrary to what current scholarship suggests, the case of Queens reveals that the defense of home and residential communities in populist terms was neither restricted to a white, homeowning population, nor always centered on the defense of racially segregated neighborhoods. Rather, such populist domesticity was shared by a cross-section of the postwar middle class, including its most progressive elements.

Central to the expressed purpose of civic organizations in all of northeastern Queens was a dual commitment to securing the material needs of the community—to "improve," "better," or "protect" it, were the terms were often used—and to encourage what was known as "good citizenship," a term that referred to a citizen's involvement in, and responsibility for, his or her community. These needs varied according to the material circum-stances of different constituencies. For homeowners, the defense of their property investment was a central purpose of their civic involvement. As was unequivocally stated in the Bayside Hills Civic Association's monthly newsletter, the *Beacon*, in 1956: "Most of us have a good part of our life's savings invested in our home, and it is for our own benefit that we become deeply interested in our community."[15]

Tenants established a similar connection between their immediate mate-rial needs and an active civic life. A case in point is the Oakland Gardens Civic Association, which was formed as the first residents were confronted with their own particular problems. "Beset by ankle deep mud, unpaved and unmarked streets, pitch blackness because there were no street lights, a corner telephone booth their only outside means of communication," wrote the *Bayside Times*, "Oakland Gardens tenants came to a mass meeting that wintry evening determined to form an organization that would secure these services for them with a minimum of delay."[16] In addition to working to secure such basic services, the association joined its neighbors' struggle to improve public transportation and schools in the area. It also coordi-nated social and leisure activities for the tenants—"a softball league, . . . dra-matic society, book review club, photography club and even baby sitting listings."[17] Like their homeowners' counterparts, such tenants' organiza-tions were praised by local newspapers for their "spirit of community" and their contribution to "the civic life of the community."

Most explicit in articulating the political culture that permeated these neighborhoods were the weekly newspapers—and at the center of their edi-torial rhetoric was a glorification of the value of an active and politically engaged citizenry.[18] "Don't sit back and let the girl upstairs or the fellow down the block do all the work," wrote the *Pomonok News*, inviting the resi-dents of Pomonok Houses to attend the meeting of their tenants' council at the beginning of the fall season.[19] "If you have faith in your country and your form of government," declared a front-page article in the *Home Town News*, "you must take an active part in the operation of your community."[20]

Also explicit was the role of active citizens in keeping a close check on the actions of their elected representatives. Insisted the editor of the *Long Island Herald* after the inauguration of President Eisenhower in January 1953: "No matter how capable the men now in office are—and we believe they are extremely so—they cannot do the job alone. We, their con-stituents, must let them know our feelings on important subjects. We must believe in them, and obey the laws they write; but we must also offer our criticisms and suggestions as various issues arise."[21] Acting collectively to defend one's interests, and expressing one's "views, demands, and denunci-ations" to policy makers through appropriate channels such as public hear-ings were a crucial part of responsible citizenship.[22]

Intimately tied to this tradition of participatory democracy and to the politics of community needs, was a sharp populist sensibility. In the pages of community newspapers and in the documentation produced by civic associations, the community and its defenders, well-intentioned civic workers, consistently received high praise. These virtuous citizens compared favorably to a less noble breed, the inherently corrupt and selfish politicians, ruled by well-entrenched and undemocratic machines and generally distant from or disrespectful of their constituents. The opening of the fall season of community activities was always a good time for praising selfless, sincere civic leaders. Weekly newspapers never missed the occasion to point out "the debt of gratitude . . . due [to] these civic minded souls who give tirelessly and uncomplainingly of their time and effort on our behalf."[23] The common term civic "worker" also connoted honesty and uprightness.

The unselfish contribution of community volunteers was highlighted by an implicit contrast to those whose service stemmed from ulterior motives. As noted in the eulogy of a well-known civic leader, "He was always willing to do anything to help others without any thought of politics or fanfare."[24] A 1942 editorial of the *Bayside Times* conveyed a similar message: "We wish to congratulate the members of the civic units for their fine display of community spirit and interest. Most, if not all, of the organizations, are sincere in their requests and demands; and we are sure that none have any special axe to grind or personal gain to achieve."[25] Alongside this praise of civic workers came descriptions of civic activity as pleasurable—as a leisurely, yet constructive, activity. "Every resident could well become a member of one or the other of our several local civic organizations with great benefit to the community and with no small amount of interesting pleasure to themselves," wrote the editor of the *Bayside Times* in 1936. "When one takes part in civic matters . . . a person gets that satisfying feeling of really being a part of the community. It's a grand feeling. It's quite a natural one too. . . . Taking a real interest in community affairs . . . will fast become an enjoyable 'pastime.'"[26]

The very language that Queens citizens used to describe the purpose of community activism—service, benefits, improvements, betterment—conveyed this positive value. Civic leaders also constantly lobbied their government or themselves ran for office in order to secure their "vital needs," yet they took great pains to differentiate civic action from politics. Common in civic circles was an understanding that "Civics and politics don't mix"—that civic leaders should not "be politicians." "Politicians," in the eyes of civic leaders, were professional power brokers whose partisanship and loyalty to a corrupt political establishment kept them from a genuine devotion to the needs of grass-roots communities.[27] Highlighting the negative connotations of "politics" through this populist language reinforced the civic as worthy of involvement; it encouraged participation in civic activities and lent further legitimacy to the demands of civic leaders.

The citizens' sense of obligation toward their residential community was one of the key elements of Queens political culture. It was, if we follow David Halle's definition of middle-class consciousness as centered on issues related to the family and residential community, a political manifestation of their middle-class identity. This understanding of middle-class civic responsibility also went hand in hand with a populist disparagement of politics—only active civic workers who fulfilled their responsibility to the community through a participation in local organizations had the right to criticize policy makers and to hold them accountable. Moreover, the very corrupt nature of politicians demanded that citizens themselves play an active role as "watchdogs" for their interests. In this sense, their populist sensibility reinforced—and was reinforced by—a keen understanding of their civic duties. Seen in this light, populism appears as a political language that conveyed not only criticism of politicians, but also a more positive definition of the role and responsibilities of the citizen, one steeped in the long tradition of American participatory democracy.

Not only did Queens residents have a strong sense of their responsibility as citizens, but they also believed in the state's reciprocal responsibility toward its "responsible" citizens. As I have argued above, the citizen's responsibility was defined by his or her willingness to work on behalf of the residential community. The state's responsibility was defined in a similar fashion—by its ability to meet the concrete and immediate needs of its citizens. Their belief in the concept of government responsibility thus brought middle-class Queens citizens fully within the fold of the widely shared New Deal liberal consensus—and far from the resurgent conservatism of the postwar era.

Identifying Queens residents' stand on the issue of state intervention in matters of economic security requires careful distillation of political campaigns that were truly indigenous to middle-class communities and others that were shaped far more by forces external to "the people" themselves. As Elizabeth Fones-Wolf and Robert Griffith have shown, powerful corporate lobbies used a combination of anticommunist, racist, and selective anti-statist arguments to limit the scope of governmental intervention in the late 1940s and 1950s.[28] Their strength was based on an extensive system of communication between their Washington offices and local associations of Realtors and builders as well as chambers of commerce, newspapers, and civic and property owners' associations. The Washington-based "public relations" departments of the National Association of Real Estate Boards and the National Association of Home Builders were especially active in this regard, distributing thousands of leaflets, "suggested" news releases, canned editorials, letters to the editor, and even scripts for radio programs and speeches to be delivered before local clubs.[29] The strong opposition that rose in Queens over the construction of publicly assisted housing for middle-income families was part of this national campaign orchestrated by the real estate lobby.

Between 1948 and 1950, civic and homeowners' associations joined local builders and Realtors in pressing the municipal and state government to interrupt innovative attempts to assist in the construction of middle-income housing. The projects that became the center of a virulent controversy were sponsored by labor and veterans' organizations and, unlike other public housing projects, were aimed at the lower middle class: organized workers and veterans, most of them white, who at the peak of a severe housing shortage in the New York metropolitan area were unable to find affordable housing in the private market.

The decision by New York City and New York state to enter the middle-income market (a departure from the traditional focus on low-income families) and to use fast-disappearing vacant land (as opposed to slum clearance) stirred the real estate lobby into action, both nationally and locally. Undeterred by the fact that only an exemption from real estate tax, and no direct subsidy, was involved in the programs, the opponents stressed the injustice of the new policy. The homeowners and taxpayers who had the initiative and courage to invest in a property of their own, allegedly without governmental assistance, were now asked to pay for "free-riders" who benefited from government largesse without assuming any of its costs. Ultimately, the programs' foes were more effective than their supporters in shaping the terms of the debate and replacing the pressing question of access to affordable housing by the specter of an increased and unfairly distributed tax burden. The narrow definition of economic liberalism that prevailed as a result of this campaign—strictly defined, not to interfere with the private industry's dominance of the market—left many families inadequately housed.[30]

Taken on its own, the participation of Queens homeowners in the campaign to block the extension of state-assisted public housing confirms the image of antiliberalism associated with the postwar middle-class. When considered in light of the other political struggles in which Queens citizens participated, however, a more complex conclusion is in order. As reflected in their ongoing battle to obtain sufficient public schools—a battle that was, unlike the housing controversy, purely indigenous to Queens neighborhoods—Queens citizens fully expected that the state would provide their communities with what they considered their most basic needs. Rather than asking for a curbing of state intervention, they demanded a consistent policy to assist families with young children.

Although overlooked by scholars, the struggle of middle-class parents to ensure their children adequate educational facilities was at the center of a widespread neighborhood movement in the fifteen years following the end of the war. The curtailing of school construction during the war, the massive migration to suburban Queens since the 1930s, and the baby boom of the late 1940s and early 1950s all contributed to the school crisis that confronted local residents.³¹ The struggle to alleviate the overcrowding of schools involved the concerted action of parents', homeowners', civic, tenants', and community associations. The primary participants were women who, as mothers, embraced children's education as their primary responsibility and, as full-time housewives, were at the center of neighborhood networks.

Citizens who had taken opposite sides in the housing controversy only a year or two earlier rallied in a common effort to improve their schools. A case in point is the united action of Bayside homeowners, renters at Oakland Gardens, and the cooperative owners of Bell Park Gardens to secure the construction of a public school in 1950 and 1951. Previously, the homeowners and renters had opposed the granting of a tax exemption to Bell Park Gardens; yet, all three groups united when confronted with a shortage of school seats that affected them all.³² Weekly community newspapers and local state legislators also offered unwavering support. The means parents used to press their demands upon policy makers covered the full range of strategies available to grassroots movements, including large mass demonstrations in neighborhood streets, mass attendance at public hearings, and a volley of letters and briefs to policy makers.

Invariably, parents related their criticism of overburdened public schools to the rapid population increase brought on by continuing housing construction. This point was made, of course, during the controversy over public housing. As members of the Flushing Manor Civic Association argued, "We've fought hard for [the public] school [that] is scheduled to be built next year. But if Clearview Houses materialize, there won't be enough room in it for our children."³³ In December 1949, Edward Sharf, president of the Queens Valley Home Owners' Association, was most explicit about the need to balance residential development and adequate public services when he sponsored a resolution adopted by the United Civic Council. "Mammoth housing projects," it stated, "are responsible for a large portion of overcrowded conditions in Queens public schools." The municipal administration was asked "to allow for adequate school facilities before granting permits for multi-family developments."³⁴

The same demand for a balanced approach to metropolitan development was made repeatedly, albeit implicitly, in the numerous briefs submitted by groups of citizens to municipal authorities. Based on neighborhood surveys conducted by female volunteers, the figures they presented in the briefs highlighted the discrepancy between the number of available school seats in neighborhood schools and the population of school-age children, both actual and anticipated. Under the direction of the Oakland Area School Committee, for instance, "hordes and hordes" of volunteers polled the neighborhood, counting not only the current number of school-age children, but contacting builders of planned or unoccupied homes in the area in order to predict future additions to the current child population.[35] Clearly the parents understood that long-term planning was necessary, as reflected by the Kew Meadows Schools Committee's demand that the municipal government appropriate rapidly vanishing vacant land for the construction of future schools. They insisted, "since available land is being built up so rapidly by private builders, suitable sites for schools are fast disappearing, more schools will have to be built and *sites must be procured now!!!*"[36] This demand would have no doubt raised eyebrows in the real estate industry.

Queens residents' opposition to uneven metropolitan planning was framed in unmistakably populist terms. Their populism, however, had nothing of the emotionalism and irrationality that has been associated with the term. Most striking, indeed, is the determination with which they presented their painstakingly gathered "cold, hard statistics" to policy makers, convinced that such "objective" arguments would yield results.[37] Faithful to their populist sensibility, Queens parents refused to be intimidated by politicians who disregarded the needs of the people, or by bureaucrats who seemed to have only contempt for their demands. In a firm yet respectful manner, they brought to the attention of city officials (the board of education, board of estimate, city planning commission, and mayor) tables and graphs that proved the need for additional school seats. They insisted on their statistical mastery of the problem. As a representative of the Tyholland Civic Association wrote to the board of education vice president in 1951, ill-intentioned bureaucrats could not fool well-informed ordinary citizens:

> [Your letter] is filled with the gibberish that the board of Education continually engages in when replying to the average person. It is intended to confuse, confound and perplex the average person with unrelated purported facts. . . . We believe that this policy of confusion is a calculated one. However, we are well aware of the facts, we know what the terms "Cluster and Index of Utilization" mean and further, we know the capacities and areas which the schools you list are intended to serve.[38]

Explicit in this strategy was the belief that policy makers should give serious consideration to "responsible" citizens who were prepared to present thoroughly documented and rationally presented arguments. As "responsible" citizens, they had made the effort and taken the time to inform themselves about the situation at hand; they were presenting their "reasonable" claims in a rational, respectful manner, and they expected reciprocity on the part of their government.

Queens parents' struggle to secure adequate schools reflects, first, the expansive philosophy of government nurtured in postwar middle-class communities. Embracing the core principle of New Deal liberalism, they demanded that the state exercise responsibility toward its citizens. From their perspective, this was to be done by coordinating school and residential construction—by formulating consistent policies in support of balanced metropolitan development. Moreover, the struggles of Queens citizens betray their profound beliefs in participatory democracy. They firmly held to the conviction, reinforced by their populist suspicion of policy makers, that ordinary citizens should reach out to, and be heard by, political brokers. Students of the rise of the modern administrative state have assumed that the increased political authority gained by technical expertise since the Progressive Era has led to a decline of popular politics. That ordinary citizens have, in the words of Harry C. Boyte, "handed over to experts, technicians, and professionals the power to make the key decisions about our 'commonwealth.'"[39] Along similar lines, students of women's history have long assumed that women deferred to the authority of male experts in the years of the feminine mystique.[40] The example of Queens forces us to reconsider both interpretations. Rather than delegating to experts and professional politicians the responsibility to make decisions affecting their residential communities, ordinary citizens—male and female—consistently challenged policy makers, claiming their own local expertise as their source of authority.

The study of community politics in Queens invites us to reexamine some of our core assumptions about the postwar middle class and, more specifically, about the relationship between community politics, populism, and anti-liberalism. From the 1950s to the 1970s, "average" middle-class Americans, as represented by sociologists and popular culture, went through a profound metamorphosis: from private creatures completely devoid of political interests or significance (the archetypal man in the gray flannel suit and his domestic and passive wife), they became reactionary—steering the nation on a new conservative political course. To be sure, scholarship in the last twenty years (from Rieder to Sugrue) has added a great deal of ethnographic and historical depth to the postwar Archie Bunkers. But Bunker's middle-class Americans remain unapologetically antiliberal.

Central to this analysis of postwar anti-liberalism is the "defense" of residential neighborhoods. The virulence with which white middle-class Americans have sought to "protect" their community from the "intrusion" of African Americans and other minorities is well known, indeed indisputable (as the essay by Theresa Mah in this volume demonstrates). The proper questions then become: Is this all there is to the politics of white middle-class residential communities? Can middle-class politics and populism be *reduced* to racism and antiliberalism? I suggest not.

Home to a cross section of the American middle class, northeastern Queens presents a refreshing picture. Here, as elsewhere in the postwar era, defending the interests of the residential community, including the provision of public services such as schools, was a determinant concern for a large number of activists, both male and female. Moreover these were defended in populist terms: as legitimate concerns of "the people," or "the community," that corrupt politicians neglected at their peril. Yet these middle-class citizens were both profoundly liberal and democratic in their outlooks; "liberal" in the sense that they embraced the concept of governmental responsibility so central to New Deal liberalism. Their expectations regarding a balanced policy of metropolitan development and the provision of sufficient public services reflect this quality. Likewise, they were "democratic" in the sense that they believed in the crucial importance of an active citizenry who, through informed and rational arguments, could guide public policy. Unmuffled by racist politics, this is the message that echoes most clearly from these middle-class communities.

WHY CLASS
CONTINUES TO COUNT

Knights of Columbus. COURTESY OF STATE HISTORICAL SOCIETY OF WISCONSIN, CLASSIFIED FILE NO. 6795.

Linguistic conventions would seem to dictate that this should not be
a problem. The middle class, after all, is a class. Just look at the second
word. It says class.

Yet scholars of all kinds have insisted that what the middle class has
brought to the United States is, rather, classlessness. We all believe that we
are part of an "Imperial Middle," and that is why, according to Benjamin
DeMott, "Americans can't think straight about class." Or take the most
prominent historian of the American middle class, Stuart Blumin, who (following social theorist Anthony Giddens) argues, in what is likely his most-
quoted passage, that the "central paradox" of the middle class is the way
that it "binds itself together as a social group in part through the common
embrace of an ideology of social atomism" that is likely to lead to "a denial
of the significance of class."[1]

Yet class still does, and must, count in such an inegalitarian society as
ours, and middle-class folks have themselves long recognized this. Perhaps
The Imperial Middle hides class from those who would rather revel in a
genuine proletarian class struggle, but for those with a bit more patience
and curiosity the history of the American middle class reveals a tremendous
amount about class relations in our country's past. As Sven Beckert demonstrates in his essay, we simply need to know how to look. In European history it has long been customary to analyze social and political development
in terms of a petite bourgeoisie or lower middle class, and Beckert makes a
compelling case for how Americans historians must give up the exceptionalism that has kept these important theoretical categories—and the millions
of lives they represent—outside of our past. Beckert's interpretive essay
paves the way for historians to attempt to understand just how much being
middle class in American history has involved different—often vastly different—lifestyles, worldviews, and political commitments for a wide variety of
people. And Beckert helps us to recognize how the "bourgeoisie" is not the
same thing as the "middle class"—indeed, far from it.

Once we disassociate the bourgeoisie from the middle class, we can stop
using the epithet "bourgeois" so freely in our thinking about the American
middle class. As coeditor Robert Johnston argues in his concluding essay,
historians have been so intent on using words like these to abuse the middle
class that they have almost never stepped back to realize just how little
respect they have given to a class to which the vast majority of them belong.
Johnston traces the ways that historians and social scientists have demonized the American middle class and pleads for a more complex and more
balanced history that not only includes the stereotypical selfishness, racism,
and provincialism that is supposedly at the heart of middle-class culture
but, perhaps even more, the democratic contributions that members of the
American middle class have made to our culture.

These two essays thus close *The Middling Sorts* with a plea for historians
to abandon the path of bemoaning a monolithic middle class that has only

had a one-dimensional effect on American history. Even if not everyone will be persuaded to relish the middle class itself, we should begin to celebrate, really for the first time, the history of the American middle class as one that will continue to contain multitudes of stories, and interpretations, for many decades to come. Class still counts, and attention to the middle class is part of the solution, not part of the problem.

Propertied of a Different Kind: Bourgeoisie and Lower Middle Class in the Nineteenth-Century United States

SVEN BECKERT

There are few terms in American English that have been as often misused, poorly defined, and politically operationalized as the term "middle class." To historians, political scientists, and sociologists, as well as to those without academic credentials, the term has denoted so many different aggregations of Americans past and present that it has essentially lost any distinct meaning it may have had. Some, for example, see the middle class as a huge social group encompassing more or less all Americans, except for those who are extremely poor and those who are extremely rich.[1] Others have used the term as a rough equivalent to the term "bourgeoisie"; that is, they identified it as the modern group of owners of capital who did not work for wages, did not work manually, and employed others for wages.[2] For yet other scholars, middle class stands for a distinct, middling group between the older aristocracy and those who either worked on the land or owned no property whatsoever—a combination, in effect, of all owners of capitalist property, bourgeoisie and lower middle class.[3] Still others see in the middle class a group of people who are situated somewhat below the major industrialists, merchants, and bankers and clearly above the working class—a group of small artisan masters, shopkeepers, and white-collar employees of large corporations, the petite bourgeoisie or lower middle class.[4] Undoubtedly, if one digs hard enough, further shades of meaning could be found.

The confusion about the term middle class could hardly be more complete.[5] At least potentially, "middle class" can include any combination of major bankers such as J. P. Morgan, industrialists such as Andrew Carnegie, shopkeepers in rural Illinois, artisanal manufacturers in Providence, teachers in New Orleans, and even skilled workers in Pittsburgh. It is not surprising, then, that there are books on "middle-class formation" that speak of people entirely different from those in books on the "middle-class family," as well as studies of middle-class fashion and middle-class politics that have hardly the same kinds of people in mind.[6] What these works share, however, is an ill-advised commitment to uncovering a single, unifying set of ideas, cultural values, habits, and manners that bind together the "middle class," whatever its precise sociological definition.

This confusion arose to a significant degree out of the politics of the twentieth century, when policy makers and intellectuals were at great pains to demonstrate that the United States had overcome the kinds of class divisions characterizing other societies. The Cold War, in particular, was often fought in defense of a "middle-class society," a tent that was made so large as to include virtually all Americans. With the concept of "middle class" emerging as an ideological weapon, it became ever more difficult to use the term as an intelligible concept with a precise sociological meaning.

But, one might ask, why should we care? Defining and classifying people has always been a messy business, and definitions almost always have served ideological and political purposes. We should care, however, because the confused use of the term "middle class" has made it very difficult to come to terms with central issues in American history. Studies of Progressivism, for example, have suffered from an inflationary use of the concept of the "middle class."[7] We should also care because the specific beliefs, gender roles, and politics of the nation's bankers, industrialists, shopkeepers, artisans, and professionals have become so much harder to grasp since they were all subsumed into the great middle class. The unwillingness to come to terms with these issues is ironic, considering that we have made great progress in understanding the economics, social life, ideas, and politics of many other social groups outside of the great American middle. Our knowledge about nineteenth-century workers has increased tremendously; we also know much more about the peculiar worlds of southern slaveholders, yeoman farmers, and slaves. Yet this explosion in knowledge has had no correspondence in how we understand the different elements of the American middle class. Indeed, while the scholarship of the past three decades has effectively dismantled the consensus school notion of a classless society, the great middle class itself has remained, with important exceptions, outside the purview of historians.[8]

In order to successfully clarify the identity of the middle class, greater analytical precision is necessary. While it is fairly obvious that definitions of the middle class that include all but the poorest are only of limited use to historians, a more subtle and more pervasive problem is to distinguish between different groups of propertied Americans in the nineteenth century. After all, these propertied citizens had much in common: they did not work for wages, did not work on the land, did not own slaves, and were free. Yet there were also important differences that stood between them. Most important, I want to argue in this essay, was the distinction between the propertied bourgeoisie and the propertied lower middle class. Clarifying this distinction and disaggregating the middle class will not only allow historians to come to terms with the distinct life worlds of both the bourgeoisie and the lower middle class, but to come to a richer understanding of nineteenth-century culture and politics. It will also enable them to relate their findings to the burgeoning European historiography on these groups—a literature that initiated one of the most exciting historiographical debates during the 1980s and early 1990s.

In the following pages, I want to contribute a sharper, more refined focus to the debates on the bourgeoisie, as well as on the lower middle class. I will do so by trying to define the boundaries between these two groups. My main argument here is that we should not conflate the bourgeoisie and the lower middle class into one analytical category. Indeed, as Peter Stearns remarked a number of years ago, "the tendency to amalgamate upper class and middle class has been disastrous."[9] If we want to understand both the bourgeoisie and the lower middle class, we need to be aware of the differences between the two.

The discussion, however, needs to be prefaced by a disclaimer: It is the essence of modern societies that social groups are fluid—they are not "things" that exist outside of history. "Bourgeoisie" and "lower middle class" are historical categories, and the degree to which class identities were embraced, and the precise content of these identities, has shifted dramatically over time. Individuals, moreover, can leave one social group and move into another.[10] Social mobility is the characterizing element of bourgeois society, setting it sharply apart from societies in which social rank is defined by history and legal status. It is for this reason that we will never be able to categorize populations unproblematically, despite the efforts of historians and others. There is bound to be ambivalence; there is bound to be change. That does not mean, however, that we can not discern broad patterns of social difference.

Most useful in beginning our investigation is the delineation of the economic boundaries between the bourgeoisie and the lower middle class. From a structural point of view, they have much in common: both own capital and do not work for wages. That clearly sets them apart from members of the working class, who sell their labor power. Neither gained their wealth or status from feudal, inherited rights, which set them apart from the aristocracy. Neither worked the land, which set them apart from farmers. These are the boundaries that define the nineteenth-century bourgeoisie and lower middle class. They also make them, taken together, a relatively small social group, their importance varying greatly from place to place, with cities usually the centers of bourgeois and lower middle-class life.

But there were also crucial economic important differences; most important is that lower-middle-class Americans in the nineteenth century worked with their own hands in businesses that they owned. Some were masters of workshops or small factories. Others sold goods in retail stores. Yet no bourgeois would have ever exposed himself to the dirty world of the machine or stood next to her clerks at the counter of her store. Physical labor clearly drew a dividing line between bourgeoisie and lower middle class; as Edmond Goblot remarked in 1925, a bourgeois, by definition, does not "dirty his hands or his clothing."[11] Not only in the workplace was it a defining characteristic of bourgeois to distance themselves from manual labor; domestically, bourgeois women also kept a healthy distance from physical exertion, recruiting a staff of servants to attain the requisite level of cleanliness and orderliness in their often very substantial homes.

Differences in time horizons further sharpened these boundaries. A central characteristic of bourgeois life was its relative stability, predictability, and long-term security. Being bourgeois meant being fairly certain that a high standard of living and material security would continue throughout one's lifetime and could be passed on to one's children. Though large industrialists and bankers could go bankrupt and end up poor, most did not, not least because they had diversified investments, some of which would perform reasonably well, even during moments of deep economic crisis. This stability brought into bourgeois life a sense of security and an ability to plan that was entirely absent from the more precarious economic position of the lower middle class. Indeed, it was the essence of nineteenth-century lower-middle-class life that the smallest economic misfortunes—a deal gone bad, an extended illness, or a general economic crisis—threatened not only a specific business venture, but the whole social status of a person. This economic instability explains why so many small proprietors often were precariously close to joining the ranks of the working class, and why they so often took on wage work to bridge periods during which their businesses performed poorly.

Economically, moreover, lower-middle-class business ventures were often, if not always, clearly subordinated to the imperatives of larger businesses owned by substantial bourgeois. This subordination increased as the century went on. In some cases, such as with tailors and shoemakers, independence and autonomy were often imaginary, since their raw materials, credit, and work orders all came from substantial capitalists, who could dictate prices, profits, and working conditions. In other cases, merchants dominated the channels of distribution, making small producers clearly dependent on them for the sale of their products. And, in similar ways, shopkeepers were usually dependent on the credit of major merchants.[12]

While the economic dividing line between the bourgeoisie and the lower middle class was well defined, it was permeable. The lower middle class was probably the single most important reservoir of people who accumulated sufficient amounts of capital to liberate themselves and their families from physical labor and join the ranks of the bourgeoisie. Statistics on social mobility show that the small percentage of major industrialists who moved into the upper echelons of the bourgeoisie without being born into this class often came from lower-middle-class backgrounds. Successful owners of workshops and stores could similarly accumulate capital sufficient to increase the scale of their operations.[13] Others, however, fell into the working class. As the century progressed, the economic gulf between both small retailers and merchants, as well as between master artisans and industrialists increased considerably, as bourgeois Americans controlled amounts of capital that were all but unimaginable a hundred years earlier.

There were thus clear structural cleavages between the lower middle class and the bourgeoisie, but how important were these cleavages, and what was their meaning? After all, deep economic tensions existed within the economic elite itself, between merchants and manufacturers, between shippers and owners of railroads, and between domestic producers of raw materials and importers. Even more dramatically, market competition drove capital-owning Americans apart, including artisans, manufacturers, and shopkeepers. It is in this context that European historians have emphasized the importance of culture and social institutions in providing the glue that bonded people together across economic fault lines.[14] In their emphasis on culture, they have sympathized with Max Weber's concept of social class, and looked for moments in which classes and status groups corresponded.[15] But the most influential theoretical contributor to the debate among historians of the bourgeoisie and lower middle class has been Pierre Bourdieu, whose work emphasizes the transmission and reproduction of educational and cultural capital, and its importance to the production of collective social identities.[16] The question then arises: Did culture and social institutions replicate the structural economic divisions discussed earlier, or did they help overcome them?

There is no clear-cut answer to this question. Two points, though, are important: lower-middle-class Americans often strove to appropriate the outward trappings of bourgeois culture, sometimes with a greater vigor than the bourgeoisie itself. As Peter Gay observed, members of the lower middle class "could be more ostentatiously respectable than their betters, more severe with their family about table manners, just as calculating and manipulative to keep their children from marrying inappropriate suitors. Shabby gentility was a harsh taskmaster."[17] The appropriation of bourgeois culture was often the chief distinction that set small shopkeepers and master artisans apart from the working class, which was uncomfortably close to them materially. Culture was often the only ticket to distinction. Lower-middle-class Americans might form associations that replicated some forms of bourgeois sociability, such as the Masons; they might have set aside a room in their homes as a parlor for receiving visitors, a room that included some of the same points of reference that could be found in a bourgeois mansion; and they might have emphasized certain bourgeois values, such as orderliness, sobriety, and a devotion to the Protestant work ethic. Moreover, they might have had replicas of "high culture" art on their walls, they might have visited art museums or the Philharmonic, or they might have tried to familiarize their children with a canon of classical literature and the piano. The storied seriousness with which many lower-middle-class families embraced such cultural strategies derived directly from their desperate efforts at social distinction.[18]

While lower-middle-class Americans thus appropriated elements of bourgeois culture (something the "respectable" elements of the working class also tried to do), substantial differences between this culture and the culture of the bourgeoisie persisted. Lower-middle-class families might have had a parlor, just like their betters, but the parlor was sparsely furnished. It often lacked the symbols of leisure and continuity that were characteristic of genuinely bourgeois households, such as souvenirs of foreign travel and paintings of deceased forebears. Similarly, lower-middle-class families lacked the leisure hours that allowed bourgeois Americans to spend extensive time forging social networks, staging semipublic events in their homes, or embarking on a European grand tour. Thus while the cultural symbols might have been similar, their exact character was often dramatically different.

Further distinguishing the boundary between bourgeois and lower middle-class culture was each class's relationship to social institutions. It was above all here that bourgeois Americans created an insular world of their own, excluding capital-owning retail store owners and master artisans. Exclusive social clubs such as the Union Club in New York were accessible solely to owners of substantial amounts of capital. Membership in organizations such as the New York Chamber of Commerce also required real money. It was large merchants, bankers, and industrialists, not shop owners and artisans, who controlled institutions such as the Boston Museum of Fine Art or the manifold Philharmonic orchestras that emerged in major cities in the second half of the nineteenth century. While lower-middle-class Americans might have attended these institutions, they enjoyed no control over their financial dealings or their artistic repertoire.[19]

Last but not least, the lower middle class remained much more disorganized throughout the century then either the bourgeoisie or the working class. In great contrast to the lower middle classes of some European countries, especially Germany, shopkeepers and artisans in the United States did not create institutions that would have brought them together across sectional interests and space. This absence of organizations was also dramatically different from the associational life of bourgeois Americans, who, as the century went on, created ever more institutions that linked them across economic sectors and across the United States. These institutions ranged from Harvard University to the Metropolitan Museum of Art, from the National Municipal League to a host of employers' associations. Lower-middle-class Americans, in contrast, were probably more rooted in ethnic communities, and the organizations that came out of these communities. Indeed, shopkeepers and master artisans were often the leading figures in such organizations.[20] One can only speculate why this was so, but one reason was certainly the greater proximity of lower-middle-class Americans to ethnic working-class neighborhoods, which required them to focus most of their business dealings on other ethnics. Large merchants, industrialists, and bankers, in contrast, operated in national, or even international networks that transcended any one ethnic group, making ethnic identities much less central.

What about ideology? Did shopkeepers and master artisans embrace ideas different from those of major merchants, industrialists, and bankers? Was there a lower-middle-class way of looking at the world? Bourgeois and lower-middle-class Americans shared a number of assumptions: a belief in the importance of private property, a fundamental optimism about the opportunities of the United States, and a deeply held belief in the importance of work.

But throughout the nineteenth century, particularly during its latter half, important ideological fault lines opened. For one, master artisans and shopkeepers often articulated a theory of society that emphasized the importance of *productive* work, seeing profits earned from trade, financial transaction, or even the labor of others as fundamentally illegitimate. One expression of this hostility was the agitation, throughout the century, of lower-middle-class Americans against the monopolistic practices of major capitalists. These struggles were particularly pronounced in regions far removed from major metropolitan areas, regions that suffered from the real or perceived dominance and exploitation of those with access to large amounts of capital, especially the capitalists of New York City. Railroad companies, in particular, served as targets of such protest.

Lower-middle-class Americans indeed had a much greater propensity to hold on to notions of a "moral economy," notions they often shared with their working-class neighbors and customers, but that had decisively fallen out of favor with the upper echelons of the bourgeoisie. By late century, many shopkeepers and artisans still saw their businesses as a way to secure "independence" for their offspring, and not as a means of accumulating ever-larger amounts of capital—a trait that might explain why so many lower-middle-class citizens hung onto businesses that had lost their economic viability. As James Livingston has argued, the petite bourgeoisie, along with many farmers and workers, shared a belief in "dispersed assets, competitive markets, and control of the property in one's labor power as a condition of self-determination."[21]

In contrast, espousals of social Darwinism, a racialized view of social inequality, and the embrace of militaristic solutions to social conflict came increasingly from the ranks of the bourgeoisie. Widening the ideological divide, by late century, the propensity of some bourgeois Americans to advocate an expansion of the bureaucratic capacity of the state encountered hostility from those who had built their businesses without bureaucratic structures. What, in effect, happened in the course of the century was the emergence of different views on property and economic governance, views that directly related to the different kinds of property people controlled. At the same time, views on consumption also increasingly diverged. Nobody better described the embrace of conspicuous consumption by bourgeois Americans than Thorstein Veblen, and nobody better expressed a lower-middle-class critique of such practices.[22] The ideological gap between lower-middle class and bourgeois Americans at century's end therefore was considerable, with many of the economic and political arrangements that emerged during the 1880s and 1890s illegitimate in the eyes of the lower middle class. It was only after the turn of the century, when the sons and daughters of shopkeepers and master artisans joined the new corporations as managers, experts, and stockholders, that the new world forged in the late nineteenth century gained a more widespread legitimacy, although still a contested one.[23]

How much the differences or commonalities of these groups came to the fore depended very much on the specific context. We have many examples of lower middle-class citizens supporting strikers and trade unions, as well as examples of property owners, irrespective of the kind of property they owned, coming together to mobilize against working-class challengers.[24] In general, however, bourgeois Americans became much more concerned about the power of workers and, with their greater access to the resources of the state, played a much greater role in challenging the influence of trade unions and radical political parties than members of the often sympathetic lower middle class.[25]

During the course of the nineteenth century, the ideological divide between major merchants, industrialists, and bankers on one side, and shopkeepers and artisans on the other, deepened considerably. The question remains what political consequences this greater distance had. In a European context, the political proclivities of the lower middle class have stood at the center of historians' attention, with interest in both the pronounced radicalism of the petit bourgeoisie, as in the example of nineteenth-century France, and its affinity to fascist politics, as in the case of twentieth-century

Germany.[26] By century's end, lower-middle-class Europeans in general had become increasingly suspicious of liberalism. Most historians have seen the lower middle class as providing the foot soldiers for the Nazi ascendancy to power, and the petit bourgeois embrace of *völkisch* and anti-Semitic ideas have motivated historians to give them a central role in their research.

The general lack of attention to lower-middle-class Americans in the United States, in turn, testifies to the fact that United States historians give them a much less important and much less cohesive role in explaining American political development. Of course, issues of bourgeois and lower-middle-class politics are more difficult to grasp in the United States context because the American party system never splintered along class lines, and because both the Republican and Democratic parties always included bourgeois, lower-middle-class, as well as working-class, activists and voters. Sectoral and regional interests, as well as ethnic identities, often better explain political divisions than does class. Consequently, one might even argue that political parties were one of the most important meeting points between bourgeois Americans and those of lower-middle-class backgrounds. Ever since the 1840s, a division of labor had emerged that gave major merchants, industrialists, and bankers important roles in financing parties and steering their organizational and programmatic work, while allowing shopkeepers and artisans to fill a large share of party and state offices.[27] These coalitions testify to a correspondence of political interests. Equally significant, the European coalition of enfranchised property owners against a disenfranchised popular majority could not emerge in the United States because most white American men enjoyed the right to vote from the 1820s onward.

There were, however, important political splits between bourgeois and lower-middle-class Americans that articulated themselves outside the party system.[28] Indeed, as one historian remarked, "the middle class is as likely to struggle against the upper class as with it."[29] Lower-middle-class Americans frequently moved away from bourgeois political tutelage by mobilizing outside the established political parties. The Knights of Labor, for example, had a significant contingent of shopkeepers and artisans among its supporters.[30] Moreover, throughout the second half of the century, so-called reform movements worked to undermine the power of political parties. These movements were generally dominated by the highest echelons of the urban bourgeoisie, and often directed against the lower-middle-class holders of political offices. At the center of the conflict were accusations by the economic elite that lower-middle-class politicians made devious deals with the cities' working classes, buying their votes with expansive and expensive municipal programs. These movements constituted a clear political break between the two social groups. This break expressed itself most dramatically in efforts by the local economic elites to limit municipal democracy, even to restrict the suffrage, an effort firmly resisted by lower-middle-class

Americans.[31] In a telling twist, however, bourgeois Americans limited their efforts at disenfranchisement to the working class and poor, effectively symbolizing their effort to draw all property holders into a political coalition.

In conclusion, it seems that politically, as well as ideologically, culturally, and economically, for all their commonalities there were deep dividing lines between lower-middle-class and bourgeois citizens in the nineteenth-century United States. Perhaps what defined lower-middle-class citizens most decisively was the very ambivalence of their position; their embrace of both bourgeois and proletarian strategies and values. While both bourgeoisie and workers began, by the late nineteenth century, to build class networks and to see themselves as distinct social groups, lower middle-class Americans would not do so.[32]

Ultimately, however, it is important to explore both the relationship between the bourgeoisie and the lower middle class, as well as the history of these two social groups in specific settings, and to account for changes over time. After all, there were significant differences between small towns and cities, between the South, West, and Northeast and between the beginning and the end of the nineteenth century. In small towns, for example, lower-middle-class Americans continued to play a much more prominent role in cultural institutions and in politics than they did in major cities. In the countryside or in small towns, for obvious reasons, conflict between the lower middle class and the bourgeoisie often expressed itself in regional terms, with capitalists in cities such as New York or Chicago symbolizing the imagined or real enemy.[33] Another political division between lower-middle-class Americans and the bourgeoisie, based on regional animosities, emerged after the Civil War. Lower-middle-class southerners often saw themselves as dominated by northern interests in general and northern capital in particular.[34] Their class passion and their regional identity could merge to oppose the interests of northern merchants, industrialists, and bankers. Similarly, there were differences between towns dominated by agriculture and those dominated by industry, between manufacturing cities dominated by local capital and manufacturing cities dominated by national capital. And, over time, the distance between lower middle class and bourgeois Americans increased tremendously, first in major cities (noticeably so around the time of the Civil War) and later in smaller cities and towns.[35] To complicate matters even further, toward the end of the century a substantial new lower middle class of white-collar workers began to emerge.[36]

Much of the story is still so abstract because the histories of both the American lower middle class and of the bourgeoisie remain to be written. In this project, United States historians would do well to consult the observations of their Europeanist colleagues.[37] Not only have they outlined a method for studying both the bourgeoisie and the lower middle class, they have also defined important variables that need investigation. These historians have, for example, emphasized the varied impact of industrialization and urbanization on different segments of the lower middle class. They have detailed the impact of the presence or absence of guilds. They have argued that culture was extremely important in creating a sense of collective identity. And last but not least, they have found the structure of political systems to be an important variable in explaining the trajectory of lower-middle-class and bourgeois politics.[38] In this comparative frame, the United States—with its absence of an aristocratic elite, its fundamentally capitalist nature, its early democratization, and its late industrialization—can serve as an important and exceptional case that might well be uniquely rewarding for historians to explore. Considering the deeply bourgeois nature of nineteenth-century American society, there should be no place in the world that better lends itself to studies of the bourgeoisie and lower middle class than the United States. What we can learn from even a cursory discussion of the problem, however, is that we should refrain from using "middle class" as an all-purpose category, to be employed casually. Indeed, "middle class" might, in the end, be a term just too poisoned by ideology and too devoid of real meaning to be of use to historians. This, however, does not mean we should ignore the history of the people who have been described as middle class; to the contrary, they are in desperate search of their historians.

Conclusion: Historians and the American Middle Class

ROBERT D. JOHNSTON

There is [a] less worthy reason for the neglect of explicit writing about the middle classes. It is less exciting. There is less moral satisfaction to be gained. The moral meaning of writing about the middle classes is not clear cut. There can be no rescuing of stockingers in these histories. It is possible to stand outside the middle classes and condemn them, "the scheming classes," or to chuckle as they twist and turn in the moral dilemmas which respectability, status, and insecurity provided for them. It is possible to celebrate the middle classes or to examine them in a dull and clinical way, but this brings little understanding — none of their triumph, achievements, courage, cunning, oppressions, half knowledge of the world around them, their fears, anxieties and contempts. In terms of moral rhetoric the historians of the middle classes face a messy task.

—R. J. Morris[1]

In many ways it is remarkable how infrequently the American middle class has received scholarly attention. Arguably no class in human history has received so much comment, but so little systematic study, as this collection of tens of millions of people. Still, a considerable tradition of historical study of the American middle class has developed in postwar America. In this concluding essay I hope to put the contributions—and even some of the limitations—of this anthology into intellectual perspective by surveying that tradition and offering some ideas about where we might next proceed in our studies of that great beast that so defines the United States. This is largely a critical survey, but I hope one that criticizes both out of a sense of respect as well as a call to our higher democratic selves. For as I will show, among historians the American middle class still gets no—or, to be more accurate, little—respect.

Although the great multitude of ordinary Americans have been favorably disposed toward the solid and upstanding middle class, intellectuals have by and large held a different view. In scholarly circles, the middle class has, to put it mildly, an image problem. We cannot, therefore, even begin to think straight about—much less systematically to rethink—the middle class without first coming to grips with the one-dimensional vision that has served as the faulty tradition of American intellectuals. We can start by looking at two authors who have more than any intellectuals defined our vision of the American middle class. Drawing on a set of prewar studies of the middle class by writers ranging from the caustic Sinclair Lewis to the communist Louis Corey, it was two sociologists—C. Wright Mills and E. Franklin Frazier—who pioneered the historical study of the American middle class. Mills and Frazier also provided much of the tone for the caricature of the middle class that has been such a prominent part of the intellectuals' tool kit ever since nineteenth-century avant-garde denunciations of bourgeois philistinism.[2]

Indeed, C. Wright Mills crystallized and codified what we might call this demonization of the American middle class in his 1951 masterpiece *White Collar*, which after nearly a half-century is still the most important book we have about the American middle classes. Mills correctly argued that the most significant defining quality of twentieth-century American society was not its power elite, or its comfortable and business-oriented labor leaders, but rather the condition of the country's middle classes. He carefully charted the fall of a nineteenth-century society of small rural and urban property holders and the rise of a heterogeneous mass of salaried employees in the nation's modern offices and salesrooms.[3]

Yet *White Collar* quickly turned from balanced—if passionate—social analysis to a jeremiad that became what Cornel West has called a "brazen condemnation of the middle classes." Mills's middle-class subjects were essentially hopeless: alienated, confused, dependent, full of illusions and misery; in the best light, they were "cheerful robots." The white-collar worker, according to Mills, "has no culture to lean upon except the contents of a mass society that has shaped him and seeks to manipulate him to its alien ends." The American tradition of individual independence functioning in a viable communal setting died with this new middle class; buried simultaneously was the prospect for any meaningful American politics.[4]

An equally astute book from the same era unfortunately no longer shares the stature of the work of Mills, perhaps because "white" has almost always seemed to be the naturalized adjective for "middle class." Yet E. Franklin Frazier's 1955 *Black Bourgeoisie*, although a first-rate historical and sociological study of a section of the middle class to which mainstream academics had been blind, fits neatly into the trashing genre. As Frazier wrote, his book "reveals in an acute form many of the characteristics of modern bourgeois society, especially in the United States." The explanatory structure of *Black Bourgeoisie* emphasized oppression, but Frazier nonetheless remained pitiless toward his subjects. Frazier's white-collar workers had no values higher than money, adultery, and poker. The book's thesis admitted no complexity: the black middle class lived in a "world of make believe," identifying totally with white middle-class values and serving as pawns for the "white propertied classes." Its religion was an artifice, its "contempt for the Negro masses" boundless, and its politics often to the right of white reactionaries. Overall, Frazier wrote—in the grand year of the Montgomery bus boycott—the black middle class was "in the process of becoming NOBODY."[5]

Unfortunately, American historians have no more been able to transcend the demonization of the middle class than have other intellectuals. Although generally hidden behind a thick wall of empirical evidence, the assumptions that historians have made about American middling folks both reflect and have shaped the dominant intellectual outlook. For example, in the post–World War II heyday of consensus history most scholars took for granted the middle-class character of American society. The petty squabbles of American politics played themselves out upon this solid bedrock. Reading postwar suburban harmony back into America's past, intellectuals as talented as Louis Hartz recognized such a complete hegemony to middle-class values that they felt it unnecessary to examine the middle class itself. After all, as Hartz put it, "A triumphant middle class . . . can take itself for granted."[6]

The consensus historians in turn bequeathed a complex legacy to the new historians of the 1960s and 1970s. Despite the reorientation of historical studies to matters of race, class, and gender, power and diversity, at least one significant constituent of American life remained trapped in the 1950s—the middle class. Historians wielded a yardstick of condescension when measuring the impact of middling folks on America's past. In two influential studies of white-collar families in late nineteenth-century Chicago published in 1969 and 1970, for example, Richard Sennett exposed the attitude of many of his generation when he castigated the "slavery," "emotional poverty," "disaster," "counterfeit-nurturance" and "self-instituted defeat" of his subjects.[7] Unfortunately, more recent works have not decisively broken from Sennett's method of chastisement, even though the language employed has become milder. For example, the first self-conscious historical study of the American middle class, Burton Bledstein's pioneering *The Culture of Professionalism* (1976), concludes that "social idealism in middle-class America has existed only at the edge of personal cynicism and duplicity."[8]

Furthermore, the three most significant books that then marked a genuine renaissance of the study of the American middle class always retreated back to the old pieties after making significant attempts to move away from them. The first, Paul Johnson's *A Shopkeeper's Millennium,* skillfully analyzed the social context of the Second Great Awakening in Rochester, New York. Johnson argued that religious revivals and antebellum politics functioned as critical forces in the creation and legitimation of antebellum free-labor ideology. The revivals in many ways originated in cultural concerns over individual free will and moral perfection, even if in the end they served the economic needs of new entrepreneurial employers. Johnson's discussion of the middle class is brief and largely unsystematic, however, perhaps because his analysis resonates so well with the larger intellectual tradition from which it springs. "To put it simply," pronounced Johnson, "the middle class became resolutely bourgeois between 1825 and 1835." The implication: it has never been anything but. The sensitivity of Johnson's analysis to matters of religion correspondingly fades as being "bourgeois" means, unproblematically, an interest above all in the social control of the proletarian workforce.[9]

Mary Ryan, on the other hand, set out self-consciously to avoid the one-dimensional equation of the middle class with social control in her path-breaking *Cradle of the Middle Class.* Also writing a study of a medium-size antebellum New York community, Ryan explicitly directed her attention to the "problem" of the middle class, and the family in particular. In Ryan's hands, Utica's middle class is publicly active, full of energetic reform activity, creative in its cultural uses of evangelical religion, and nearly self-conscious at its creation. Ryan succeeded above all in treating her middle class with respect, realizing its complexity, and understanding that we cannot neatly assimilate middle-class hopes and desires into entrepreneurial ambitions. That is, her analysis proceeds in this manner until she reaches the mid-1800s. By the 1850s a stereotypical middle class comes to the fore, having abruptly realized the fulfillment of its historical mission and cozied up to the quiet, intensely privatized existence that Mills described—there to slumber until the 1960s. Ryan's post–Civil War middle class packed up and moved to a "darkened corner of history," she proclaimed without irony or sense of complexity (much less evidence).[10]

The other work crucial to renewed historiographical interest in the American middle class also dealt primarily with the antebellum period. In common with almost all other scholarship, Karen Halttunen's 1982 *Confidence Men and Painted Women* sought to capture a nearly timeless *essence* of the American middle class. As is standard practice for historians, Halttunen's middle class had its origins in her period of study; her inquiry into mid-nineteenth-century canons of sincerity, theatricality, and domestic parlor rituals more generally served an analysis of "the self-conscious self-definition of middle-class culture during the most critical period of its development." Halttunen's depiction of the creation of these middle-class rituals and their relationship to the growing imperatives of the market in American culture did sensitively demonstrate how such private performances could serve to subvert as well as to reinforce the entrepreneurial orientation of the middle class. In the end, though, in a familiar refrain, the complexities of nineteenth-century middle-class culture disappear. By the late 1800s, according to Halttunen, middle-class sincerity became little more than anxious deception of self and manipulation of others in the modern age of rigid class structure, mass immigration, and corporate capitalism.[11]

The works of Johnson, Ryan, and Halttunen launched a new era in the historical study of the American middle class, bringing to bear intriguing and complex theoretical considerations in matters of work, religion, family, and culture. Yet just as these historians launched their subject off the ground of condescension, their trial balloons fell back down to earth. The old demonization model maintained its grip after all. The middle class common to these social and cultural historians remains concerned above all with its own status, greatly fears outsiders, and generally lives a privatized existence with an increasingly tenuous relationship to the larger community or world. We can therefore tell that as the New Left generation has ascended to power in the historical profession, it looks back upon its roots in (professional) middle-class culture largely with fear and self-loathing. Few historians today would dare to be so naive as Kevin Mattson and argue that "I believe middle-class people can be committed to democratic activity and leadership. Privilege need not lead to domination." And only an exceptional scholar has the self-conscious willingness to "celebrate" her middle-class subjects, as Glenda Gilmore does in her eloquent portrayal of the democratic politics of middle-class African Americans in North Carolina during the early years of Jim Crow.[12]

The ground has thus remained open for scholars to castigate the middle class almost without cost or controversy. For example, Carroll Smith-Rosenberg helped to revolutionize American history in her path-breaking 1975 article on "The Female World of Love and Ritual." Her achievement was to show that in the nineteenth century white women from "a broad range of the middle class" enjoyed a liberating sense of gender and sexuality through same-sex relationships. Yet when Smith-Rosenberg collected her pioneering essays a decade later, her fluid and even admirable "middle class" had been swept up into a hegemonic (and often horrifying) "bourgeoisie," upon whose male members she unloosed a fusillade of abuse—with the help of advanced French thinkers such as Roland Barthes.[13]

Charles Sellers has followed Smith-Rosenberg's analytical path in his synthesis of Jacksonian history. His middle class/bourgeoisie is consistently anti-democratic, sexually repressed, and grossly entrepreneurial. At the same time, it is powerful enough to impose a "cultural imperialism of the bourgeoisie" and "the most pervasive hegemony of any modern ruling class."[14] Or consider what is almost certainly a relatively unconscious, but far from uncommon, illustration. Jennifer Scanlon remarks in her study of gender and *The Ladies' Home Journal* that the magazine promoted "a way of life that was overwhelmingly middle class and decidedly conservative." The two terms—"middle class" and "conservative"—apparently function, with no further comment necessary, as synonyms within the groves of academe.[15]

In the last decade, though, two books have again attempted to reopen most of the old questions about the middle class, the process of its creation during the nineteenth and early twentieth centuries, and its overall social role. Furthermore, they have done so on a much broader base than previous works, using evidence from metropolitan and national sources and consciously tying their arguments into larger interdisciplinary debates about the social role of the middle class in modern societies. The first, Stuart Blumin's *The Emergence of the Middle Class*, in many ways attempts to do for the middle class what the new labor history of the 1970s and 1980s sought to do for "the" working class—simply establish its existence for the tribe of doubting historians. Primarily drawing on evidence from Philadelphia and, secondarily, from Boston and New York, Blumin traces the fall of the eighteenth-century artisanal middling orders and the rise of a self-conscious, tightly bound class of white collars—clerks, merchants, and small manufacturers. Blumin seeks to show that the antebellum period witnessed an increasingly strong social distinction between nonmanual and manual workers. The former carved out lives in city and suburb that revolved around segregated neighborhoods, closed voluntary associations, and tightly guarded domestic interiors. Blumin provides evidence of a general loosening of these boundaries after the Civil War with the expansion in low-level white-collar work (particularly among non-Anglo ethnic groups), but he does not speculate much about the social consequences of that development.

Blumin's claims in the book are, however, much grander. Far from being a mere celebrant of the claim that all Americans were in a great middle class, he promises to be the first historian to locate the middle class within a coherently examined three-class structure. He takes good advantage of recent scholarship in working-class history to make his contrasting empirical claims about everyday middle-class social life. Yet beyond that Blumin falls, if not directly into the demonization trap, at least smack dab into an embrace of a suburbanization trope. His middle class is, culturally, little different from the 1950s garden variety. Blumin's middling folks remain above all intensely private, with the men worried most about getting ahead at work and the women with keeping order in the home. Members of the middle class are totally cut off from those below them, a complete transformation from the eighteenth century; they look only up in admiration of capitalist elites. •

No complex contests over politics, morality, or the social order intrude into Blumin's middle class. It is comfortably "individualistic"—an insight that he derives *not* from contemporary evidence but from a modern social theorist, Anthony Giddens, and a very problematic social theory of the 1950s. Middle-class ideology is no more than "social atomism." In this regard it is instructive to compare Blumin's book to the historiography of the working class. Historians once depicted working-class values as almost totally assimilated to individualism and other supposed aspects of the exceptional American consensus, but now a generation of work has completely problematized that assumption. Given his lack of actual evidence concerning middle-class ideology, it thus becomes clear that *The Emergence of the Middle Class* suffers from the same conceptual problems as the old labor history. Blumin's depiction of concrete social arrangements may be one step forward in the historical study of the American middle class, but in terms of overall questions of cultural and ideological developments Blumin's middle-class people remain close to stick figures.[16]

In turn, Olivier Zunz's *Making America Corporate, 1870–1920* represents the fullest break by a historian away from prevailing conceptualizations of the middle class. Through an imaginative use of a range of corporate archives, Zunz examines the role of a new class of white-collar executives, managers, and clerks in the creation of large corporations. According to Zunz, members of this middle class were not merely subservient slaves to impersonal entities. Rather, they independently—and creatively—built the new corporations. Through a sensitive portrayal of the work lives of corporate employees, ranging from top-level male railroad executives to female secretaries, Zunz effectively depicts the career opportunities as well as the office environments that the new corporate world provided for different segments of the new middle class. In the process, Zunz challengingly argues that corporations reached their dominance in the social life of the United States not because of their monolithic power, but rather largely because of the varied responses they evoked from members of the new middle class as well as a divided working class, which also participated in their staffing.

What makes *Making America Corporate* so refreshing is Zunz's insistence on the relative autonomy of white-collar people, not their passivity and degradation. Zunz consciously resists the tendency of historians to read the ideas of C. Wright Mills back into the past unmediated; a bit overenthusiastically, he states that "the privilege of hindsight turns out to be no privilege at all." Unfortunately, however, Zunz does not successfully break out of old stereotypes. His analysis turns out to be a fairly deterministic reduction of social to economic experience. Zunz's corporate executives almost heroically respond to the market imperatives driving them to build, very self-confidently, the new continental corporate economy. With few exceptions, "they bypassed larger ideological debates"; all segments of the middle class unproblematically "continued to take their cues from business values." In the end, Zunz's middle class is just as intensely privatized as those of Ryan and Blumin.[17]

We can sum up the crucial missing element in the works of both Zunz and Blumin, as well as almost all other historians, in one word: *politics*. Blumin and Zunz both make crucial claims about the nearly universal acceptance of a capitalist, and then a corporate, consensus by members of the middle class. Yet it is simply not possible to make this argument without a sustained analysis of the many ways in which the multitude of middle-class citizens participated in the making of the American political order.[18] For example, Blumin, with his equation of middle-class consciousness and individualism, raises the problem of politics as a major issue and then allots only three pages to his discussion of the subject. Likewise, Zunz ignores electoral politics and has only one section on explicitly political matters. That part of the book is about labor conflict, and Zunz notes there that many members of the middle class supported *workers* rather than the new corporate managers who are the main protagonists of his book. Yet his analysis of such matters stops in the 1880s. After that decade Zunz notes only in passing middle-class opposition to corporations, characterizing it as an anachronistic and vague struggle against "bigness."[19]

Interestingly, we need to go back more than forty years for the most sustained historical exploration of middle-class politics. As with so many questions on which historians have deserted him, Richard Hofstadter recognized the complexity of these issues. Although correctly located in the consensus camp, and a firm believer that members of an unproblematically defined middle class above all sought conservative respectability, Hofstadter realized (as do Bruce Laurie and Elizabeth White in their essays in this volume) that the relationship between the developing capitalist order and the middle class was profoundly ambivalent. Historians often use the sections of Hofstadter's classic *The Age of Reform* dealing with the Progressive Era as evidence of the futile politics of a declining middle class desperately trying to maintain its status. Yet Hofstadter actually presented significantly more complicated insights. Foremost, he showed that the middle class lived in an intensely public and politicized world. Middle-class politics derived from moral conceptions of character and justice in a manner substantively different from—and, Hofstadter strongly implies, better than—the technocratic politics that came to the fore in the New Deal. Even when the middle class did eventually accept the social dominance of corporations, it hardly embraced them. According to Hofstadter, weaknesses abounded in the realm of the middle-class political imagination, such as its frequent disdain for workers and its secret admiration for self-made robber barons. Nevertheless Hofstadter's message, albeit detached and ironic, was that middle-class Progressive Era politics contained within it the last opportunity for Americans to transcend the sterile liberalism he so abhorred.[20]

A handful of books that focus on the twentieth-century American middle class have revealed the fine intellectual fruits that we can harvest by extending Hofstadter's insights. Most ambitious in its theorizing is Jurgen Kocka's *White Collar Workers in America*. Kocka conducts a systematic comparison between German white-collar workers, with their alleged predisposition to Nazism, and the new class of American salaried workers. Using a comparative perspective, Kocka convincingly places middling people in the leftward portion of the political spectrum. The primary contribution of Kocka's work is his demonstration of the highly contingent nature of lower-middle-class political action and affiliation. Using a wide variety of evidence, Kocka persuasively establishes that white-collar workers in the United States were not susceptible to fascist appeals. He also shows that their ideology and political behavior did not substantially differ from those of blue-collar workers. "Insofar as the political stance of the American new middle class before the first world war can be determined," Kocka states, "it appears to have been part of the mass base for a heterogeneous but on the whole liberal-social democratic social reform movement." Nor did the Depression turn middle-class folks toward reaction. As Kocka contends, "American white collar workers did not respond to the economic crisis in specifically middle class or lower middle class ways that clearly distinguished their attitudes and behavior from the working class; they revealed no greater susceptibility to right-wing extremism than blue collar workers or other social groups."[21]

In turn, Alan Brinkley has explored the worlds of the two mass insurgencies that would most easily qualify as quasi-fascist, the movements of Huey Long and Father Coughlin. Brinkley has not himself reconceptualized the idea of the middle class and thus at times misinterprets the two movements' goals as "bourgeois" (on this, see the essays for this anthology by Andrew Wender Cohen and Sven Beckert). Still, Brinkley recognizes that the foundation of these two crusades lay not among "men and women who lived in neat suburban bungalows or who worked at comfortable, white-collar jobs." Instead, "the essentially middle-class nature of both movements" arose from the hopes and fears of "realtors, barbers, department-store saleswomen, grocers, bank clerks, chiropractors, [and] professionals of modest means." These people had "acquired a stake, however modest, in their community [and] were protecting hard-won badges of status and carefully guarded, if modest, financial achievements." About them, the *New Republic* explicitly spoke of the "militant and honorable protest" of the "lower middle class." Proletarians closest to the middle of the social order, often homeowners who worked in small businesses, effectively allied with those a step ahead of them in the class structure. And although Brinkley contends that Long's and Coughlin's populist ideology represented, by the time of the Depression, a futile protest against centralization, he makes it clear that the two movements were fundamentally democratic. They directed their anger at genuine economic problems while eschewing xenophobia and intolerance.[22]

If Brinkley presents a last honest and even valiant—but ultimately ineffectual—stand by those in the middle, Catherine Stock shows how the same kind of middling folks actually did come to grips with "modern" life. In *Main Street in Crisis*, Stock demonstrates how an "old middle class" in the Dakotas neither disappeared under the weight of the twentieth century nor acted out of panic and anxiety as corporations and big government threatened its traditional way of life. Her small business owners, family farmers, independent professionals, and skilled workers instead survived the economic and political crisis by balancing "fundamentally contradictory, but equally heartfelt, impulses: loyalties to individualism and community, to profit and cooperation, to progress and tradition." Perhaps most critically, the "moral economy" that these old middle-class Americans had constructed from roots in producerism came through the Depression battered and transformed, but still enduring in powerful ways. Middle-class Dakotans built a society that celebrated both the striving for individual success and "a cooperative vision of community life." Profit, competition, and growth were good, but only within limits that prevented the cultural honoring of too much accumulated wealth.[23]

Through a focus on politics, therefore, Kocka, Brinkley, and Stock have reinvigorated fundamental questions about the relationship between "the" American middle class, capitalism, and democracy—questions that should have been of interest to historians all along. The historian who has, in turn, most forcefully extended this line of argument is the late Christopher Lasch. In *The True and Only Heaven,* Lasch brilliantly analyzed intellectual, religious, and labor history to argue that the most distinctive form of opposition to capitalism in America has been what he characterized as "lower middle class populism." Such anticapitalism had roots in late eighteenth-century revolutionary radicalism and flourished from a material base in nineteenth-century artisanal craft production and small farming. Lasch forcefully contended that a political ideology based on such "petty bourgeois" small property—not on supposed proletarian virtues—has represented the most expansive of democratic hopes in American history. Within this rich tradition of hostility toward an elite-inspired emphasis on cosmopolitanism and material "progress," Lasch insists, Americans can discover a solution to our current cultural and political crisis. Despite his one-dimensional valorization of middling folk, *The True and Only Heaven* should help to ensure that a new politicized reconceptualization of the middle class will become a part of the debates of both historians and cultural critics.[24]

Significantly, historians like Kocka, Brinkley, Stock, and Lasch, who have done the most important work in undercutting the demonization tradition, have not attempted to analyze "the" middle class. Instead, they have pointed to critical *divisions* within that beast—above all, considering its "lower" segment as something of an autonomous actor. In other words, they have taken a decisive step away from considering "the middle class" as one monolithic entity. Analytically, as the essays of Laurie, Cohen, and Beckert in this volume demonstrate, this very well might be the most important lesson that we are currently learning—that study of *the* American middle class can proceed only by denying the essence and unity of the very subject under consideration.[25]

In the end, future studies might well not confirm my vision of a vigorously political—and, indeed, often democratic—set of middle classes. And we have plenty of other intellectual horizons ahead of us. We need to know, for example, how far chronologically we can push the roots of American middle-class traditions. Can we go further back than does Joyce Appleby's essay in this volume, and even longer ago than C. Dallett Hemphill's recent excavation of the eighteenth-century middling order? We would also greatly benefit from knowing just how genuinely different the "new" middle class of salaried workers has been from the "old" middle class of small business owners and farmers, as well as how truly distinct "the middle class" has been from "the working class." We might well find many more cultural and political continuities than we expect. Or perhaps we can re-open the question of the supposedly solid capitalist allegiances of middling folks, an issue allegedly solved by Alexis de Tocqueville more than 150 years ago but compellingly reopened by Bruce Laurie and Elizabeth White in these pages. Finally, we should begin to recognize that as the twenty-first-century middling sorts constitute an increasingly visible Rainbow Middle Class, we need to explore the historical origins of the process not just of racial exclusivity but inclusivity, as well.[26]

Right now, however, we should perhaps most simply take heart when we see from the essays in this volume that, in at least one crucial way, historians are finally moving in the right direction. For, above all, previous intellectuals have far too often simply failed to provide middle-class Americans with the *respect* they deserve. In some ways, middle-class Americans have proven the perfect Other, on whom scholars can freely project their own worst cultural and political fears. And, up until now, historians have been able to get away with this because of the sense almost all of us have that we are part of the middle class—and thus that we know all about the subject. Without a doubt, there are a multitude of unattractive parts of the middle-class tradition in America. How could this not be so in a mass of people so large and varied? Yet we may finally be at the point where The Middle Class need not be The Enemy. We have more than an intellectual world to gain from such a recognition. We have a democratic country, with millions and millions of our fellow citizens, to embrace as we seek to find out—together—just how much of the promise of American life lies in the middle class.[27]

Notes

Introduction

1 In the early period of polling see, for example, "The Fortune Survey: XXIII, 'The People of the U.S.A.—a Self-Portrait,'" *Fortune* 21 (February 1940), 20, 14. In more recent years, see Kevin Phillips, *The Politics of Rich and Poor: Wealth and the American Electorate in the Reagan Aftermath* (New York: Random House, 1990); Kevin Phillips, *Boiling Point: Democrats, Republicans and the Decline of Middle-Class Prosperity* (New York: Random House, 1993). For recent works addressing the larger theme, see Herbert J. Gans, *Middle American Individualism: Political Participation and Liberal Democracy* (New York: Oxford University Press, 1988); Katherine S. Newman, *Falling from Grace: The Experience of Downward Mobility in the American Middle Class* (New York: Vintage Books, 1989); Barbara Ehrenreich, *Fear of Falling: The Inner Life of the Middle Class* (New York: Harper Perennial, 1990).

2 See Maris A. Vinovskis, "Stalking the Elusive Middle Class in Nineteenth-Century America. A Review Article," *Comparative Studies in Society and History* 33 (July 1991), 582–587; G. D. H. Cole, "The Conception of the Middle Class," in *Studies in Class Structure* (London: Routledge & Kegan Paul, 1955), 93.

3 Interpreting the "American Dream" is controversial. For more positive assessments: Ely Chinoy, *Automobile Workers and the American Dream* (New York: Doubleday, 1955); Barbara Kelley, *Expanding the American Dream: Building and Rebuilding Levittown* (Albany: State University of New York, 1993); Stanley B. Greenberg, *Middle Class Dreams* (New York: Times Books, 1995). More critical assessments: Mike Davis, *Prisoners of the American Dream: Politics and Economy in the History of the U.S. Working Class* (London: Verso, 1986); Loren Baritz, *The Good Life: The Meaning of Success for the American Middle Class* (New York: Knopf, 1989); Katherine S. Newman, *Declining Fortunes: The Withering of the American Dream* (New York: Basic Books, 1993); Roland Marchand, *Advertising the American Dream: Making Way for Modernity 1920–1940* (Berkeley: University of California Press, 1985).

4 For the developing historiography on dimensions of the African-American middle-class experience, see Bart Landry, *The New Black Middle Class* (Berkeley: University of California Press, 1987); Michael C. Dawson, *Behind the Mule: Race and Class in African-American Politics* (Princeton, NJ: Princeton University Press, 1994); Jennifer L. Hochschild, *Facing Up to the American Dream: Race, Class, and the Soul of a Nation* (Princeton, NJ: Princeton University Press, 1995); Thomas J. Sugrue, *The Origins of the Urban Crisis: Race and Inequality in Postwar Detroit* (Princeton, NJ: Princeton University Press, 1996); Christopher Robert Reed, *The Chicago NAACP and the Rise of Black Professional Leadership, 1910–1966* (Bloomington: Indiana University Press, 1997); Charles T. Banner-Haley, *The Fruits of Integration: Black Middle-Class Ideology and Culture, 1960–1990* (Jackson: University Press of Mississippi, 1994). See also the essay in this volume by Adam Green, "The Rising Tide of Youth: Chicago's Wonder Books and the 'New' Black Middle Class."

On Mexican-Americans: Richard A. Garcia, *Rise of the Mexican-American Middle Class: San Antonio, 1929–1941* (San Antonio: Texas A&M University Press, 1991); George J. Sanchez, *Becoming Mexican-American: Ethnicity, Culture, and Identity in Chicano Los Angeles, 1900-1945* (New York: Oxford University Press, 1993).

On ethnic identification: Mary C. Waters, *Ethnic Options: Choosing Identity in America* (Berkeley: University of California Press, 1990). See the essays in this volume by Theresa Mah, "The Limits of Democracy in the Suburbs: Constructing the Middle Class through Residential Exclusion" and by Sylvie Murray, "Rethinking Middle-Class Populism and Politics in the Postwar Era: Community Activism in Queens."

On "whiteness": David R. Roediger, *The Wages of Whiteness: Race and the Making of the American Working Class* (London: Verso, 1991); Noel Ignatiev, *How the Irish Became White* (New York: Routledge, 1995).

5 Contemporary dictionaries and historical dictionaries are a primary source for naming: Samuel Johnson, *A Dictionary of the English Language* (London: W. Strahan, 1755); Noah Webster, *An American Dictionary of the English Language* (New York: S. Converse, 1828); John Russell Bartlett, *Dictionary of Americanisms: A Glossary of Words and Phrases Usually Regarded as Peculiar to the United States*, 4th ed. (Boston: Little, Brown & Co., 1896), editions appeared earlier in 1849, 1859, 1877; William A. Craigie and John R. Hilbert, *A Dictionary of American English: On Historical Principles* (Chicago: University of Chicago Press, 1938–1942); Milford M. Mathews, *A Dictionary of Americanisms* (Chicago: University of Chicago Press, 1951); *Oxford English Dictionary* (Oxford: Clarendon Press, 1993–1997); Daniel Defoe, *Robinson Crusoe* (New York: W. W. Norton, 1975), 32. See Keith Wrightson, "Estates, Degrees, and Sorts: Changing Perceptions of Society in Tudor and Stuart England," and Penelope J. Corfield, "Class by Name and Number in Eighteenth-Century Britain," in Corfield, ed., *Language, History, and Class* (Oxford: Basil Blackwell, 1991), 30–52, 101–130.

6 Elaine Forman Crane, *The Diary of Elizabeth Drinker: The Life Cycle of an Eighteenth-Century Woman* (Boston: Northeastern University Press, 1994), 179. Bartlett, *Dictionary of Americanisms*, 135–136. See C. Dallett Hemphill, *Bowing to Necessities: A History of Manners in America, 1620–1860* (New York: Oxford University Press, 1999).

7 Defoe, *A Review of the State of the British Nation*, Vol. 6, no. 36 (25 June 1709).

8 On the British scene in this period, see: Margaret R. Hunt, *The Middling Sort: Commerce, Gender, and the Family in England, 1680–1870* (Berkeley: University of California Press, 1996); Jonathan Berry and Christopher Brooks, eds., *The Middling Sort of People: Culture, Society and Politics in England 1550–1800* (New York: St. Martin's Press, 1994); John Smail, *The Origins of Middle-Class Culture: Halifax, Yorkshire, 1660–1780* (Ithaca, NY: Cornell University Press, 1994); Dror Wahrman, *Imagining the Middle Class: The Political Representation of Class in Britain, c. 1780–1840* (Cambridge: Cambridge University Press, 1995); Leonore Davidoff and Catherine Hall, *Family Fortunes: Men and Women of the English Middle Class, 1780–1850* (Chicago: University of Chicago Press, 1987).

9 See the essay in this volume by Joyce Appleby, "The Social Consequences of American Revolutionary Ideals in the Early Republic." Also Appleby, ed., *Recollections of the Early Republic: Selected Autobiographies* (Boston: Northeastern University Press, 1997); Appleby, *Inheriting the Revolution: The First Generation of Americans* (Cambridge, MA: Harvard University Press, 2000). See also, David W. Galenson, "'Middling People or 'Common Sort': The Social Origins of Some Early Americans," *William and Mary Quarterly* 35 (July 1978): 499–524; Billy G. Smith, *The "Lower Sort": Philadelphia's Laboring People, 1750–1800* (Ithaca, NY: Cornell University Press, 1990); Jackson Turner Main, "Contemporary Views of Class," in *The Social Structure of Revolutionary America* (Princeton, NJ: Princeton University Press, 1965), 221–239.

10 "From Tunbridge, Vermont, to London, England, The Journal of James Guild, Peddler, Tinker, Schoolmaster, Portrait Painter, from 1818 to 1824," *Proceedings of the Vermont Historical Society,* new series, Vol. 5 (1937), 279.

11 Hector St. John de Crevecoeur, *Letters from an American Farmer and Sketches of Eighteenth-Century America* (New York: New American Library, 1963), 75; *The Papers of Alexander Hamilton,* Vol. 4: January 1787–May 1788, ed. Harold C. Syrett (New York: Columbia University Press, 1962), 480.

12 Regarding the tensions represented in this paragraph and the next, see the essays in this volume by Elizabeth White, "Charitable Calculations: Fancywork, Charity, and the Culture of the Sentimental Market, 1830–1880," and by Edward James Kilsdonk, "Scientific Church Music and the Making of the American Middle Class." For the United States, see: Anne C. Rose, *Victorian America and the Civil War* (New York: Cambridge University Press, 1992). For Britain, see: Geoffrey Crossick, "From Gentlemen to the Residuum: Languages of Social Description in Victorian Britain," in Corfield, ed., *Language, History, and Class*, 150–178.

13 In this context for the second half of the nineteenth century, see the essays in this volume by Andrea

Volpe, "Cartes De Visite Portrait Photographs and the Culture of Class Formation," and by Marina Moskowitz, "Public Exposure: Middle-Class Material Culture at the Turn of the Twentieth Century."

14 Bartlett, *Dictionary of Americanisms*, 391. The Middling Interest was politically articulate from the outset: see the pamphlets at The American Antiquarian Society, *An Exposition of the Principles and Views of the Middling Interest* (Boston, May 1822); *Defense of the Exposition of the Middling Interest, on the Right of Constituents to give Instructions to their Representatives, and the Obligation of These to Obey Them* (Boston, July 1822). See also Matthew H. Crocker, *The Magic of the Many: Josiah Quincy and the Rise of Mass Politics in Boston, 1800–1830* (Amherst: University of Massachusetts Press, 1999); and the essay in this volume by Bruce Laurie, "'We Are Not Afraid to Work': Master Mechanics and the Market Revolution in the Antebellum North."

15 Ralph L. Rusk, ed., *The Letters of Ralph Waldo Emerson*, Vol. 1 (New York: Columbia University Press, 1939), 112, 110–111. On Emerson's career, Mary Kupieck Cayton, *Emerson's Emergence: Self and Society in the Transformation of New England, 1800–1845* (Chapel Hill: University of North Carolina Press, 1989).

16 On teaching values to children, see the essay in this volume by James Marten, "Bringing Up Yankees: The Civil War and the Moral Education of Middle-Class Children." See also, James Alan Marten, *The Children's Civil War* (Chapel Hill: University of North Carolina Press, 1998); Marten, ed., *Lessons of War: The Civil War in Children's Magazines* (Wilmington, DE: Scholarly Resources, 1999).

17 For a contemporary account of these relationships: "Preamble of the Mechanic's Union of Trade Associations," *A Documentary History of American Industrial Society*, ed. John R. Commons et al. (Cleveland: Arthur H. Clark Company, 1910), 94–90. See Bruce Laurie, *Artisans into Workers: Labor in Nineteenth-Century America* (New York: Hill & Wang, 1989); Howard Rock, Paul Gilje, and Robert Asher, eds., *American Artisans: Crafting Social Identity, 1750–1850* (Baltimore: Johns Hopkins University Press, 1995); Richard B. Stott, *Workers in the Metropolis: Class, Ethnicity, and Youth in Antebellum New York City* (Ithaca, NY: Cornell University Press, 1990). For the British scene: Gareth Stedman Jones, *Languages of Class: Studies in English Working-Class History 1832–1982* (Cambridge: Cambridge University Press, 1983).

18 On the manual vs. nonmanual occupational divide, see, Stuart M. Blumin, *The Emergence of the Middle Class: Social Experience in the American City, 1760–1900* (New York: Cambridge University Press, 1989); Nicholas K. Bromell, *By the Sweat of the Brow: Literature and Labor in Antebellum America* (Chicago: University of Chicago Press, 1993).

19 On contemporary accounts of Beecher's career, Mark Twain, "Sunday Amusements" and "Henry Ward Beecher," *Travels with Mr. Brown* (New York: Russell & Russell, 1971), 91–94; James Parton, "Henry Ward Beecher's Church," *Atlantic Monthly* 19 (January 1867), 38–51. See the essay in this volume by Debby Applegate, "Henry Ward Beecher and the 'Great Middle Class': Mass-Marketed Intimacy and Middle-Class Identity."

20 Mrs. Child, *The Mother's Book* (Boston: Carter & Hence, 1831), v. On the publication history of Child, *The American Frugal Housewife*, see Eleanor Lowenstein, *American Cookery Books 1742–1860* (Worcester: American Antiquarian Society, 1972).

21 Milton Meltzer and Patricia G. Holland, eds., *Lydia Maria Child: Selected Letters 1817–1880* (Amherst: University of Massachusetts Press, 1982), 544.

22 On the reading audience: William J. Gilmore, *Reading Becomes a Necessity of Life: Material and Cultural Life in Rural New England, 1780–1835* (Knoxville: University of Tennessee Press, 1989); Ronald J. Zboray, *A Fictive People: Antebellum Economic Development and the American Reading Public* (New York: Oxford University Press, 1993). On the distribution of popular manuals see: Judy Hilkey, *Character Is Capital: Success Manuals and Manhood in Gilded Age America* (Chapel Hill: University of North Carolina Press, 1987).

23 James Larson, *Sergeant Larson, 4th Cav.* (San Antonio, TX: Southern Literary Institute, 1935), 24, 71.

24 The trail guide was: Lansford W. Hastings, *The Emigrants' Guide to Oregon and California … and all Necessary Information Relative to the Equipment, Supplies, and the Method of Traveling* (Cincinnati: George Conclin, 1845). On the emigrants' reaction to the Hastings guide: Kristin Johnson, *"Unfortunate Immigrants": Narratives of the Donner Party* (Logan: Utah State University Press, 1996).

25 The sources for the Twain narrative include the Mark Twain Papers Project at the Bancroft Library, University of California, Berkeley; *Mark Twain's Letters* (Berkeley: University of California Press) Vol. 1: 1853–1866 (1988), Vol. 2: 1867–1868 (1990), Vol. 3: 1869 (1992), Vol. 4: 1870–1871 (1995), Vol. 5: 1872–1873 (1997); *Mark Twain's Notebooks & Journals* (Berkeley: University of California Press, 1975).

26 On this seminal period of his life: Paul Fatout, *Mark Twain on the Lecture Circuit* (Bloomington: Indiana University Press, 1960); Susan K. Harris, *The Courtship of Olivia Langdon and Mark Twain* (New York: Cambridge University Press, 1996); Jeffrey Steinbrink, *Getting to Be Mark Twain* (Berkeley: University of California Press, 1991).

27 See the meticulous reconstruction of the people of Hannibal: Mark Twain, "Villagers of 1840–3," *Huck Finn and Tom Sawyer among the Indians* (Berkeley: University of California Press, 1989), 93–108, 299–351.

28 On Twain's relationship to subscription publishing: Hamlin Hill, *Mark Twain and Elisha Bliss* (Columbia: University of Missouri Press, 1964). Among Twain's papers is a guide of helpful hints— "The Successful Agent"—issued for selling Grant's autobiography, which Twain's company published. On the reach of the network of agents canvassing the nation, see: Michael Hackenberg, "The Subscription Publishing Network in Nineteenth-Century America," *Getting the Books Out*, ed. Michael Hackenberg (Washington, DC: The Center for the Book, Library of Congress, 1987), 45–75; Nancy Cook, "Finding His Mark: Twain's *The Innocents Abroad* as a Subscription Book," in Michele Moylan and Lane Stiles, eds., *Reading Books: Essays on the Material Text and Literature in America* (Amherst: University of Massachusetts Press, 19), 151–178. On Twain's making of his public image: Louis J. Budd, *Our Mark Twain: The Making of His Public Personality* (Philadelphia: University of Pennsylvania Press, 1983).

29 *The Gilded Age Letters of E. L. Godkin*, ed. William M. Armstrong (Albany: State University of New York Press, 1974), 88. *The Letters of William James* (Boston: Atlantic Monthly Press, 1920), Vol. 2, 44, 43, 43–44.

30 William James, "What Makes a Life Significant," in *Talks to Teachers: On Psychology and to Students of Some of Life's Ideals* (New York: W. W. Norton, 1958), 173. See the essay in this volume by Andrew Chamberlin Rieser, "Secularization Reconsidered: Chautauqua and the De-Christianization of Middle-Class Authority, 1880–1920."

31 Theodore Dreiser, *Sister Carrie* (Philadelphia: University of Pennsylvania Press, 1981), 4.

32 George Ade, "The Advantage of Being 'Middle Class,'" in *Stories of the Streets and of the Town: From the Chicago Record 1893–1900*, ed. Franklin J. Meine (Chicago: The Caxton Club, 1941), 75. Ade speaking about Twain in letters, November 22, 1905, and July 6, 1938, in Mark Twain Papers, Bancroft Library, University of California, Berkeley.

33 Ade, "Advantage of Being 'Middle Class,'" 75.

34 Ibid., 75–79.

35 George Ade, *Artie: The Story of the Streets and Towns* (Chicago: Herbert & Stone, 1896). Ade, "The Fable of Sister May Who Did As Well As Could Be Expected," in Jean Shepherd, ed., *The America of George Ade* (New York: G. P. Putnam's Sons, 1961), 103–105. Ade, "The One or Two Points of Difference between Learning and Learning How," in *People You Know* (New York: Harper & Brothers, 1903), 26–36. Ade, in "The Married Couple That Went to Housekeeping and Began to Find Out Things," in *People You Know*, 168. Ade, "The Fable of the Caddy Who Hurt His Head While Thinking," Shepherd, *America of George Ade*, 106–107.

36 W. D. Howells, "Certain of the Chicago School of Fiction," *North American Review* 176 (1903), 740–743.

37 Ade, "Sidewalk Merchants and Their Wares," in *Stories of the Streets*, 111.

38 Joseph Jacobs, "The Middle American," *American Magazine* 65 (1907), 522–526. John Spargo, "The Influence of Karl Marx on Contemporary Socialism," *American Journal of Sociology* 216 (July 1910), 21–40.

39 For a bibliographic essay on recent historiography, see the essay in this volume by Robert D. Johnston, "Conclusion: Historians and the American Middle Class."

40 Vachel Lindsay, *The Art of the Moving Picture* (New York: Macmillan, 1922 [1915]), 291.

41 On home ownership in working-class neighborhoods in Chicago: Edith Abbott, *The Tenements of Chicago, 1908–1935* (Chicago: University of Chicago Press, 1936), 363–400; James R. Barrett, *Work and Community in the Jungle: Chicago's Packinghouse Workers, 1894–1922* (Urbana: University of Illinois Press, 1990), 104–107; Thomas J. Jablonsky, *Pride in the Jungle: Community and Everyday Life in Back of the Yards Chicago* (Baltimore: Johns Hopkins University Press, 1993), 53–55; Richard Harris, "Working-Class Home Ownership in the American Metropolis," *Journal of Urban History* 17 (November 1990), 46–69. See the essays in this volume by Andrew Wender Cohen, "Obstacles to History: Modernization and the Lower Middle Class in Chicago, 1900–1940" and Jeffrey M. Horn-

stein, "The Rise of the Realtor: Professionalism, Gender, and Middle-Class Identity, 1908–1950."

42 On the trend to professionalization and white-collar work: Burton J. Bledstein, *The Culture of Professionalism: The Middle Class and the Development of Higher Education in America* (New York: W. W. Norton, 1976); Oliver Zunz, *Making America Corporate, 1870–1920* (Chicago: University of Chicago Press, 1990); Margo Anderson, *The American Census: A Social History* (New Haven, CT: Yale University Press, 1988). See the essay in this volume by Clark Davis, "The Corporate Reconstruction of Middle-Class Manhood."

43 Suellen Hoy, *Chasing Dirt: The American Search for Cleanliness* (New York: Oxford University Press, 1995), 3–28.

44 On early statements, see: Lewis Corey, *The Crisis of the Middle Class* (New York: Covici, Friedl, 1935); Franklin Charles Palm, *The Middle Classes Then and Now* (New York: Macmillan, 1936). A generation later, see Robert Wiebe, *The Search for Order, 1877–1920* (New York: Hill & Wang, 1967). A seminal work under the rubric of the "organizational hypothesis" is Stephen Skowronek, *Building a New American State: The Expansion of National Administrative Capacities, 1877–1920* (New York: Cambridge University Press, 1982). Also see Robert Zussman, *Mechanics of the Middle Class: Work and Politics among American Engineers* (Berkeley: University of California Press, 1985); Arthur J. Vidich, ed., *The New Middle Classes: Life-Styles, Status Claims, and Political Orientations* (New York: New York University Press, 1995). For a sensitivity to historical transitions, see: Catherine McNicol Stock, *Main Street in Crisis: The Great Depression and the Old Middle Class on the Northern Plains* (Chapel Hill: University of North Carolina, 1992); John S. Gilkeson, Jr., *Middle-Class Providence, 1820–1940* (Princeton, NJ: Princeton University Press, 1986); Paul Axelrod, *Making a Middle Class: Student Life in English Canada During the Thirties* (Toronto: McGill-Queen's University Press, 1990).

45 See: Susan E. Gray, *The Yankee West: Community Life on the Michigan Frontier* (Chapel Hill: University of North Carolina Press, 1996); Carol Sheriff, *The Artificial River: The Erie Canal and the Paradox of Progress, 1817–1862* (New York: Hill & Wang, 1996); Timothy R. Mahoney, *Provincial Lives: Middle-Class Experience in the Antebellum Middle West* (New York: Cambridge University Press, 1999); John C. Hudson, *Plains Country Towns* (Minneapolis: University of Minnesota Press, 1985); Royden K. Loewen, *Family, Church, and Market: A Mennonite Community in the Old and the New Worlds, 1850–1930* (Urbana: University of Illinois Press, 1993); William Cronon, *Nature's Metropolis: Chicago and the Great West* (New York: W. W. Norton, 1991). Mary Ryan, *Cradle of the Middle Class: Family in Oneida County, New York 1790–1865* (New York: Cambridge University Press, 1981), is a classic on the domestic front.

46 David Riesman, *The Lonely Crowd: A Study of the Changing American Character* (New Haven, CT: Yale University Press, 1950); C. Wright Mills, *White Collar: The American Middle Classes* (New York: Oxford University Press, 1951); William H. Whyte, Jr., *The Organization Man* (New York: Simon & Schuster, 1956); Will Herberg, *Protestant, Catholic, Jew: An Essay in American Religious Sociology* (Garden City, NY: Anchor Books, 1960); Jacques Ellul, *The Technological Society* (New York: Alfred A. Knopf, 1964); Herbert Marcuse, *One-Dimensional Man: Studies in the Ideology of Advanced Industrial Society* (Boston: Beacon Press, 1964); Philip Rieff, *The Triumph of the Therapeutic; Uses of Faith After Freud* (New York: Harper & Row, 1966); Peter Berger, Brigitte Berger, and Hansfried Kellner, *The Homeless Mind: Modernization and Consciousness* (New York: Random House, 1973); Christopher Lasch, *The Culture of Narcissism: American Life in an Age of Diminishing Expectations* (New York: W. W. Norton, 1979).

47 See Wendy Kozol, *Life's America: Family and Nation in Postwar Photojournalism* (Philadelphia: Temple University Press, 1994).

48 Hofstadter to Mills, January 19, 1952. Cited in Irving Louis Horowitz, *C. Wright Mills: An American Utopian* (New York: The Free Press, 1983), 251. For a different contrasting representation, see: Christopher P. Wilson, *White Collar Fictions: Class and Social Representation in American Literature 1885–1925* (Athens: University of Georgia Press, 1992).

49 On recent efforts to "bring class back in": Scott G. McNall, Rhonda F. Levine, and Rick Fantasia, eds., *Bringing Class Back In: Contemporary and Historical Perspectives* (Boulder, CO: Westview Press, 1991); John R. Hall, ed., *Reworking Class* (Ithaca, NY: Cornell University Press, 1997); Martin J. Burke, *The Conundrum of Class: Public Discourse on the Social Order in America* (Chicago: University of Chicago Press, 1995).

50 Examples of the Refinement-Rough model: Richard L. Bushman, *The Refinement of America,*

1830–1870 (New Haven, CT: Yale University Press, 1982); Katherine C. Grier, *Culture and Comfort: Parlor Making and Middle-Class Identity, 1850–1930* (Rochester, NY: Strong Museum, 1988); John F. Kasson, *Rudeness & Civility: Manners in Nineteenth-Century Urban America* (New York: Hill & Wang, 1990); Lawrence W. Levine, *Highbrow/Lowbrow: The Emergence of Cultural Hierarchy in America* (Cambridge, MA: Harvard University Press, 1988); Ann Fabian, *Card Sharps, Dream Books, & Bucket Shops: Gambling in 19th-Century America* (Ithaca, NY: Cornell University Press, 1990); Michael Isenberg, *John L. Sullivan and His America* (Urbana: University of Illinois Press, 1988); Elliott J. Gorn, *The Manly Art: Bare-Knuckle Prize Fighting in America* (Ithaca, NY: Cornell University Press, 1986); David T. Courtwright, *Violent Land: Single Men and Social Disorder from the Frontier to the Inner City* (Cambridge, MA: Harvard University Press, 1996).

51 For examples, see Malcolm Rohrbough, *Days of Gold: The California Gold Rush and the American Nation* (Berkeley: University of California Press, 1997); Warren Goldstein, *Playing for Keeps: A History of Early Baseball* (Ithaca, NY: Cornell University Press, 1989); Amy S. Greenberg, *Cause for Alarm, The Volunteer Fire Department in the Nineteenth-Century City* (Princeton, NJ: Princeton University Press, 1988); Polly Welts Kaufman, *Women Teachers on the Frontier* (New Haven, CT: Yale University Press, 1984); Lynn A. Bonfield and Mary C. Morrison, *Roxana's Children: The Biography of a Nineteenth-Century Vermont Family* (Amherst: University of Massachusetts Press, 1995).

52 For a handy definition to consult in a large literature: Raymond Williams, "Class," in *Keywords: A Vocabulary of Culture and Society* (New York: Oxford University Press, 1983), 60–69. For reflections and studies from a historical perspective: E. J. Hobsbaum, "Notes on Class Consciousness," in *Workers: Worlds of Labor* (New York: Pantheon Books, 1984), 15–32; Patrick Joyce, "Narratives of Class," in *Class* (New York: Oxford, 1995), 322–332; Richard F. Hamilton, *The Bourgeois Epic: Marx and Engels on Britain, France, and Germany* (Chapel Hill: University of North Carolina Press, 1991).

53 See G. D. H. Cole, "Conception of the Middle Class," in *Studies in Class Structure*, and Arno Mayer, "The Lower Middle Class as Historical Problem," *Journal of Modern History* 47 (1975), 409–436. See the essay in this volume by Sven Beckert, "Propertied of a Different Kind: Bourgeoisie and Lower Middle Class in the Nineteenth-Century United States."

54 Karl Marx, "Communist Manifesto," in Robert Tucker, ed., *The Marx-Engels Reader* (New York: W. W. Norton, 1972), 341–342. Marx, cited in Harold Perkin, *The Rise of Professional Society: England since 1880* (London: Routledge, 1989), 83.

55 Marx, "Eighteenth Brumaire," *Marx-Engels Reader*, 515–516.

56 On recent discussions of "exceptionalism" in U.S. history: Brian Lloyd, *Left Out: Pragmatism, Exceptionalism, and the Poverty of American Marxism, 1890–1922* (Baltimore: Johns Hopkins University Press, 1997); Dorothy Ross, *The Origins of American Social Science* (New York: Cambridge University Press, 1991); Larry G. Gerber, "Shifting Perspectives on American Exceptionalism: Recent Literature on American Labor Relations and Labor Politics," *Journal of American Studies* 32 (1997), 253–274; Robert Middlekauff, "The Sources of American Exceptionalism," *Reviews in American History* 22 (1994): 387–392; Michael Kammen, "The Problem of American Exceptionalism: A Reconsideration," *American Quarterly* 45 (1993): 1–43.

57 See Erik Olin Wright, "Rethinking, Once Again, the Concept of Class Structure," in *Reworking Class*, 41–72. William M. Reddy, "The Concept of Class," in M. L. Bush, *Social Orders and Social Classes in Europe since 1500: Studies in Social Stratification* (London: Longmans, 1992), 13–25.

58 This generalization arguably extends to the focus by Max Weber on the mental structures of social status in studies of class and the focus by Antonio Gramsci on the hegemonic structures of culture.

59 Consult accounts by information from contemporary working-class neighborhoods: Marie Hall Ets, *Rosa: The Life of an Italian Immigrant* (Minneapolis: University of Minnesota Press, 1970); Thomas Bell, *Out of This Furnace* (Boston: Little, Brown, 1941); David Steven Cohen, ed., *America the Dream of My Life: Selections from the Federal Writers' Project's New Jersey Ethnic Survey* (New Brunswick, NJ: Rutgers University Press, 1990); Hilda Satt Polacheck, *I Came a Stranger: The Story of a Hull-House Girl*, ed. Dena J. Polacheck Epstein (Urbana: University of Illinois Press, 1991). Also see: Ira Katznelson, *Urban Trenches: Urban Politics and the Patterning of Class in the United States* (New York: Pantheon Books, 1981); Michael Kazin, "Struggling with the Class Struggle: Marxism and the Search for a Synthesis of U.S. Labor History," *Labor History* 28 (1898): 497–514; *Workers Speak, Self Portraits*, eds. Leon Stein and Philip Taft (New York: Arno Press, 1971).

60 E. P. Thompson, *The Making of the English Working Class* (New York: Alfred A. Knopf, 1963), 12. See Thompson's most important essays collected in E. P. Thompson, *Customs in Common: Studies in Traditional Popular Culture* (New York: New Press, 1993).

Middling Sorts for the New Nation

1   George Wilson Pierson, *Tocqueville and Beaumont in America* (New York: Oxford University Press, 1938), 548.

The Social Consquences of American Revolutionary Ideals in the Early Republic

1   Samuel Gilman, *Memoirs of a New England Village Choir* (Boston: S. G. Goodrich, 1829), 2.

2   Ibid., 17, 24–25, 64.

3   Ibid., 68–78.

4   Ibid., 68, 86, 112.

5   Ibid., 123–124, 128–130.

6   Ibid., 58–62.

7   Lee Soltow, *Distribution of Wealth and Income in the United States in 1798* (Pittsburgh: University of Pittsburgh Press, 1989), 232–248. Property ownership in Sweden was 29%; in England, 10%; and in Scotland, 3%.

8   "The Autobiography of Martin Van Buren," John C. Fitzpatrick, ed., 2:19.

9   Zoltan Haraszti, *John Adams and the Prophets of Progress* (New York: Grosset & Dunlop, 1964), 201.

10 John Pickering, *A Vocabulary or Collection of Words and Phrases...peculiar to the United States of America* (Boston: Hilliard & Metcalf, 1816), 14–15; William C. Dowling, *Literary Federalism in the Age of Jefferson: Joseph Dennie and the Port Folio* (Columbia: University of South Carolina Press, 1999), 24.

11 Eliza Lee, *Sketches of a New England Village* (Boston: J. Munroe, 1838), 6–7; Catharine M. Sedgwick, *Life and Letters of Catharine M. Sedgwick* (New York: Harper, 1871), 60.

12 Edith Wharton, *A Backward Glance* (New York: D. Appleton-Century, 1934), 7–25, lists the Schermehorns, Ledyards, Rhinelanders, Pendletons, Gallatins, Stevens, Van Rensselaers, Cadwaladers, Renshaws, Duers, Rutherfurds, Livingstons, and De Grasses.

13 James Flint, *Letters from America* (Edinburgh: W. & C. Tait, 1822), repr. in Reuben Gold Twaites, ed., *Early Western Travels, 1748–1846* (Cleveland: A. H. Clark, l904), 292–293, 62–63. "Pennslyvania through a German's Eyes: The Travels of Ludwig Gall, 1819–1820," *Pennsylvania Magazine of History and Biography* 105 (1981), ed. and trans. Frederic Trautmann, 54.

14 Morris Birkbeck, *Notes on a Journey in America, from the Coast of Virginia to the Territory of Illinois*, 2nd ed. (London: Severn & Co., 1818), 35–36.

15 Malcolm Rohrbough, *The Land Office Business: The Settlement and Administration of American Public Lands, 1789–1837* (New York: Oxford University Press, 1968), 48. See also Arthur H. Cole, "Cyclical and Sectional Variations in the Sale of Public Land," *Review of Economics and Statistics* 9 (1927): 50.

16 John Chambers, *Autobiography*, John Carl Parish, ed. (Iowa City: State Historical Society of Iowa, 1908), 30–31.

17 E. S. Thomas, *Reminiscences of the Last Sixty-Five Years* (Hartford, 1840), 45; Alan Taylor, *William Cooper's Town: A Story of Power and Persuasion on the Frontier of the Early American Republic* (New York: Knopf, 1995), 371–372.

18 Richard Gabriel Stone, *Hezekiah Niles as an Economist* (Baltimore: Johns Hopkins University Press, 1933, 54. J. H. B. Latrobe, ed., *The Journal of Benjamin Latrobe: Being the Notes and Sketches of an Architect, Naturalist and Traveler in the United States from 1796 to 1820* (New York: D. Appleton, l905), 51.

19 *The Treasury of Knowledge and Library of Reference*, 3rd ed. (New York: Conner & Cooke, 1833) published a seven-page list of Old Testament names from Aalar to Zuzima and one page devoted to names derived from the New Testament.

20 Birkbeck, *Notes on a Journey in America*, 37, 108, 98; "Pennsylvania through a German's Eyes," 41; Flint, *Letters from America*, 42.

21 James Guild, "From Tunbridge, Vermont to London, England: The Journal of James Guild: Peddler, Tinker, Schoolmaster, Portrait Painter from 1818 to 1824," *Proceedings of the Vermont Historical Society*, new series, Vol. 5 (1937): 307.

22 (Lydia Sigourney), *Letters to Young Ladies* (Hartford: P. Canfield, 1833), 28–31; *New England and Her Institutions* (Boston: J. Allan & Co., 1835), 28–29, as quoted in Nancy Cott, *The Bonds of Womanhood: 'Women's Sphere' in New England, 1780–1835* (New Haven, CT: Yale University Press, 1977), 51; Taylor, *William Cooper's Town*, 379.

23 Nora Pat Small, "The Search for a New Rural Order: Farmhouses in Sutton, Massachusetts, 1790–1830," *William and Mary Quarterly* 43 (1996): 85–96.

24 Jonathan Prude, *The Coming of Industrial Order: Town and Factory in Rural Massachusetts* (Cambridge: Harvard University Press, 1983), 156.

25 Julia Tevis, *Sixty Years in a School Room* (Cincinnati: Western Methodist Book Concern, 1878), 252.

26 Arthur Singleton, *Letters from the South and West* (Boston: Richardson & Lord, 1824), 96–99; Christiana Holmes Tillson, *Reminiscences of Early Life in Illinois* (Amherst, MA: private printing, 1873), 78–81.

27 Timothy Flint, *A Condensed Geography and History of the Western States* (Cincinnati: E.H. Flint, 1828), 207–208.

28 Carole Shammas, "Anglo-American Household Government in Comparative Perspective," *William and Mary Quarterly* 52 (1995): 137–141.

29 Elihu H. Shepard, *The Autobiography of Elihu H. Shepard* (St. Louis: G. Knapp, 1869), 19; Diana de Marly, *Dress in North America, The New World*, Vol. 1 (New York: Holmes & Meier, 1990), 169–173.

30 Guild, "From Tunbridge, Vermont," 300.

31 Rebecca Burton Burlend, *A True Picture of Emigration*, ed. Milo Milton Quaife (Chicago: Lakeside Press, 1936), 46; Birkbeck, *Notes on a Journey in America*, 134.

32 Chambers, *Autobiography*, 30–31; Latrobe, *Journal*, 15, 24, 26.

33 Benjamin Lease and Hans-Joachim Lang, *The Genius of John Neal: Selections from His Writings* (Frankfurt am Main: Lang, 1978), 241–249.

34 (Mary Hunt Tyler), *The Maternal Physician; A Treatise on the Nurture and Management of Infants* (New York: Isaac Riley, 1811), 280.

35 Elizabeth W. Levick, *Recollections of Early Days* (Philadelphia: Chesterfield S.N., 1881), 23; Olive Cleaveland Clarke, *Things that I Remember at Ninety-Five* (1881), 3; and John E. Murray, "Generation(s) of Human Capital: Literacy in American Families, 1830–1875," *Journal of Interdisciplinary History* 27 (1997): 427.

36 Frederick Marryat, *A Diary in America, with Remarks on Its Institutions*, ed. Sydney Jackman ([1839] New York: Knopf, 1962, 366.

37 Sigourney, *Letters to Young Ladies*, 29–30.

38 Timothy Dwight, *Travels in New England and New York*, ed. Barbara Solomon (Cambridge, MA: Harvard University Press, 1969), I: xxxiv, as quoted in Jane Tompkins, *Sensational Designs: The Cultural Work of American Fiction, 1790–1860* (New York: Oxford University Press, 1985), 107–108; Barry O'Connell, ed., *On Our Own Ground: The Complete Writings of William Apess, a Pequot* (Amherst: University of Massachusetts Press, 1994); Henry Highland Garnet, *Walker's Appeal, with a Brief Sketch of His Life* (New York: J.H. Tobitt, 1848); William Jenks, *Memoir of the Northern Kingdom* by Rev. William Jahnsenykss (Boston: Ferrard & Mallory, 1808), 28.

39 I have discussed these themes in my *Inheriting the Revolution: The First Generation of Americans* (Cambridge, MA: Harvard University Press, 2000).

"We Are Not Afraid to Work"

The research for this paper was supported by a grant from the National Endowment for the Humanities in cooperation with the American Antiquarian Society, Worcester, Massachusetts.

1 See, for instance, Richard Hofstadter, *The American Political Tradition and the Men Who Made It* (New York: Alfred A. Knopf, 1948), and Louis Hartz, *The Liberal Tradition in America: An Interpretation of American Political Thought since the Revolution* (New York: Harcourt, Brace, 1955). For recent work in this spirit, focused on mechanics and small businessmen, that reflects the recent fascination with the category of republicanism, see Rowland Berthoff, "Independence and Attachment, Virtue and Interest: From Republican Citizen to Free Enterpriser," in Richard Bushman, ed., *Uprooted Americans: Essays in Honor of Oscar Handlin* (Boston: Little, Brown; 1979), 97–124. Also see Mansel G. Blackford, *A History of Small Business in America* (New York: Twayne, 1991), and Stuart Bruchey, ed., *Small Business in American Life* (New York: Columbia University Press, 1980).

2 Alan Dawley, *Class and Community: The Industrial Revolution in Lynn* (Cambridge, MA: Harvard University Press, 1976), 11–41; here, 25. For the rural version of this argument see Allan Kulikoff, *The Agrarian Origins of American Capitalism* (Charlottesville: University of Virginia Press, 1992). For Marx's clearest treatment of petty producers as a historical and political force, see his *Eighteenth Brumaire of Louis Bonaparte* (New York: International Publishers, 1963, repr. of 1852 ed.).

3 See, for instance, Susan E. Hirsch, *Roots of the American Working Class: The Industrialization of the Crafts in Newark, 1800–1860* (Philadelphia: University of Pennsylvania Press, 1978), 15–51; Bruce Laurie, *Working People of Philadelphia, 1800–1850* (Philadelphia: Temple University Press, 1980),

3–30; and Sean Wilentz, *Chants Democratic: New York City and the Rise of the Working Class* (New York: Oxford University Press, 1984), 3–19 and 61–141.

4   Wilentz, *Chants Democratic,* 315–325.

5   Gary Kornblith, "From Artisans to Businessmen: Master Mechanics in New England, 1790–1850" (Ph.D. diss., Princeton University, 1983), vi.

6   Bruce Laurie et al., "Immigrants and Industry: The Philadelphia Experience, 1850–1880," *Journal of Social History* 9 (winter 1975): 219–248, esp. table 4. For a similar landscape of shops in Indianapolis, see Robert Richardson, "Industrial Employment and the Wages of Men, Women and Children in the Nineteenth-Century City: Indianapolis, 1850–1880," *American Sociological Review* 55 (December 1990): 912–928.

7   Joyce Appleby, "The Popular Sources of American Capitalism," *Studies in American Political Development* 9 (fall 1995): 437–457; here, 440.

8   See, for example, Stuart Blumin, "Mobility in a Nineteenth Century American City: Philadelphia, 1820–1860," (Ph.D. diss., University of Pennsylvania, 1968); Michael B. Katz, *The People of Hamilton, Canada West: Family and Class in a Mid-Nineteenth Century City* (Cambridge, MA: Harvard University Press, 1975); and Clyde and Sally Griffen, *Natives and Newcomers: The Ordering of Opportunity in Mid-Nineteenth-Century Poughkeepsie* (Cambridge, MA: Harvard University Press, 1979).

9   Harriet Weed, ed., *Autobiography of Thurlow Weed* (Boston: Houghton Mifflin, 1883), 76–78; Joseph Tinker Buckingham, *Personal Memoirs and Recollections of Editorial Life,* 2 vols. (Boston: Ticknor, Reed and Fields, 1852) Vol. 1: 63–64; and Philip Scranton, *Proprietary Capitalism: The Textile Manufacture at Philadelphia, 1800–1885* (New York: Cambridge University Press, 1983), esp. 49–121.

10   See, for instance, Lansford Wood, Account Book, 1833–1841, ms., American Antiquarian Society. Hereafter AAS.

11   See, for instance, Richard Stott, *Workers in the Metropolis: Class, Ethnicity, and Youth in New York City* (Ithaca, NY: Cornell University Press, 1990), and Elizabeth Blackmar, *Manhattan for Rent, 1785–1850* (Ithaca, NY: Cornell University Press, 1989).

12   See Stott, *Workers in the Metropolis,* 34–67, for the best study of early shop migration we have.

13   The seminal statement of this is John R. Commons, "American Shoemakers, 1648–1895: A Sketch of Industrial Evolution," *Quarterly Journal of Economics* 24 (November 1909): 39–84.

14   See, for instance, Daniel Vickers, *Farmers and Fishermen: Two Centuries of Work in Essex County, Massachusetts, 1630–1850* (Chapel Hill: University of North Carolina Press, 1994), esp. 11, 195–203, 247ff.

15   Merle Curti, ed., *The Learned Blacksmith: The Letters and Journals of Elihu Burritt* (New York: Winston-Erickson, 1937), 129.

16   Robert Goodell, "Matthias Zahn's Diary," *Papers of the Lancaster County Historical Society* 47 (1943): 61–91.

17   Isaac Whiting, Journals, 1809–1855, mss., AAS. Also see Jacob Emerson, Account Book, 1820–1842, ms., AAS.

18   Wood, Journal, esp. 22–23, 29.

19   Lyman H. Wilson, Account Book, 1849–1855, AAS.

20   See, for instance, Mark Voss Hubbard, "The Amesbury-Salisbury Strike and the Social Origins of Political Nativism in Antebellum Massachusetts," *Journal of Social History* 29 (spring 1996): 565–590; For more on dual or bi-employment, see Curti, *Learned Blacksmith,* 127 and passim; Goodell, "Matthias Zahn's Diary"; Whiting, Journals, 1809–1855; and Wilson, Account Book. The best modern account is Vickers, Farmers and Fishermen.

21   See Gary J. Kornblith, "Becoming Joseph T. Buckingham: The Struggle for Artisanal Independence in Early Nineteenth-Century Boston," in Howard Rock et al., eds., *American Artisans: Crafting Social Identity, 1750–1850* (Baltimore: Johns Hopkins University Press, 1995), 123–134.

22   See, for instance, Blumin, "Mobility in a Nineteenth Century American City." Also Katz, *People of Hamilton, Canada West,* esp. 176–189.

23   Weed, *Autobiography,* 23–57.

24   On seasonality see Alexander Keyssar, *Out of Work: The First Century of Unemployment in Massachusetts* (Cambridge, MA: Harvard University Press, 1986). Also Hirsch, *Roots of the Working Class,* 81ff; and Stott, *Workers in the Metropolis,* 110–119 and 161–162.

25   While these downturns figure in all standard economic histories, we still do not have systematic studies of their social impact. See, for instance, W. Eliot Brownlee, *Dynamics of Ascent: A History of the*

American Economy (New York: Knopf, 1979), esp. 139–149. Also Douglass North, *The Economic Growth of the United States* (Englewood Cliffs, NJ: Prentice Hall, 1961), esp. 177–215; and Samuel Reznick, *Business Depressions and Financial Panics* (Westport, CT: Greenwood Press, 1968), a series of essays with a social slant that marked an important departure in the history of recession, but is now dated.

26 This was a chronic complaint, and not just against bankers of master craftsmen throughout the period under analysis. Contractors and customers of masters sometimes discounted their bills, as well. See (New England) *Artisan* Jan. 5, 1832. Hereafter NEA. Also Joseph T. Buckingham, comp., *Annals of the Massachusetts Charitable Association* (Boston: Crocker & Brewster, 1853), 45.

27 Goodell, "Matthias Zahn's Diary," 75. On friction between mechanics and bankers over discounting and the like, see Samuel N. Dickinson Papers, 1841–1849, mss., AAS, especially Dickinson to Elihu Geer, March 25, 1847. Hereafter S. N. D. to E. G.

28 Buckingham, *Memoir* II, 98–101.

29 "Petition to the legislature. . . for incorporation of a bank," ms. in John and Sidney Babcock Papers, 1800–1871, mss., AAS.

30 Christopher Clark, *The Roots of Rural Capitalism: Western Massachusetts, 1780–1860* (Ithaca, NY: Cornell University Press, 1990), 236–239.

31 Jonathan Prude, *The Coming of Industrial Order: Town and Factory Life in Rural Massachusetts, 1810–1860* (New York: Cambridge University Press, 1983), 105–106 and 238–263.

32 Buckingham, *Memoir,* II, 1–10.

33 Weed, *Autobiography,* 85ff.

34 See (Boston) *Courier,* June 2, 1832. See also June 5 and 7, 1832. Hereafter BC.

35 S. N. D. to E. G., Dickinson Papers, AAS, passim.

36 See esp. Clark, *Roots of Rural Capitalism,* 31–33, 214–220, and 222–223.

37 Ibid., 122–128. Also Dickinson Papers, passim.

38 He was, after all, the largest typefounder in Boston and one of the city's largest printers, with about 100 employees in the early 1840s. On his business career, see Rollo Silver, "'The Flash of the Comet': The Typographical Career of Samuel N. Dickinson," *Papers of the Biographical Society of the University of Virginia,* 31 (1978): 68–89.

39 See S. N. D. to E. G., passim., Dickinson Papers, AAS.

40 Ibid., S. N. D. to E. G., Nov. 30, 1846. See also (Boston) *Mechanics' Journal,* May 31, 1823, for a plaintive call to subscribers to pay their bills.

41 Ibid., S. N. D to E. G., July 10, 1848. Also Jan. 26, 1847, and Silver, "Flash of the Comet," 83–84.

42 Ibid., S. N. D. to E. G., March 27, 1843.

43 Kornblith, "Artisans to Businessmen," esp. 94–114. See also (Worcester) *Daily Spy,* April 14, 1854, for master printers' organization, whose rules included a prohibition on raiding apprentices. Hereafter WDS.

44 This turf or territorial aspect of artisanship is implied in Carl Bridenbaugh, *The Colonial Craftsman* (Chicago: University of Chicago Press, 1950), esp. 144ff., but needs firmer confirmation in colonial times and later.

45 Buckingham, *Memoir,* I, 81.

46 For a description of these firms, see WDS, May 9, 1851. Also, U.S. Census Office, Seventh Census of the United States, Industrial Schedule, ms. (Washington, DC, 1850). Also, Eighth Census, ms (l860). It is likely that simpler parts were made in farmsteads by yeomen under the putting-out system, then returned to central shops for assembly.

47 BC, June 2, 1832.

48 Kornblith, "Artisans to Businessmen." See also Bruce Sinclair, *Philadelphia's Philosopher Mechanics, 1824–1865: A History of the Franklin Institute* (Baltimore: Johns Hopkins University Press, 1974); and John S. Gilkeson, Jr., *Middle-Class Providence, 1820–1940* (Princeton, NJ: Princeton University Press, 1986).

49 Boston Association of Booksellers Papers, Record Book, 1800–1814, ms. 1, AAS. Hereafter BAB Papers.

50 Ibid., 1–6.

51 Ibid., 7ff.

52 Ibid., 20.

53 Ibid., 38–40.

54 The committee report, signed by Thomas Wells, William Fowle, James Loring, David Francis, and

Samuel Armstrong, survives as a loose letter in BAB Papers; emphasis in original.

55 Melvin Lord, "Boston Booksellers," ms. in BAB Papers, AAS.

56 Carpenters' Company, Reminiscences of Carpenters' Hall in the City of Philadelphia, and . . . Extracts from the Ancient Minutes (Philadelphia: Crissy & Markley, 1858). See also Roger W. Moss, "The Origins of the Carpenters' Company of Philadelphia," in Charles E. Peterson, ed., *Building Early America* (Radnor, PA: Chilton Book Co., 1976). Charles E. Peterson, Jr., ed., *The Carpenters' Company of the City and County of Philadelphia 1786 Rule Book* (Princeton, NJ: The Pyne Press, 1971).

57 Copies of the masons' and plasterers' price lists are included in John Haviland, *The Practical Builders' Assistant.* . . . 4 vols. (2nd ed., Baltimore: Fielding Lucas, Jr., n.d.), Vol. 3: appendices.

58 Scranton, *Proprietary Capitalism,* does not refer to such a code, but it is difficult to see how his weavers sustained solidarity without written rules, or at least formal association of some kind.

59 For evidence of a trade agreement in clothing in Philadelphia, see Marcus T. C. Gould, recorder, *Trial of Twenty-Four Journeymen Tailors, Charged with Conspiracy* . . . (Philadelphia: n.p., 1827), 133–134, and 142. See also letters of shoemakers, and saddlers/harness makers (Philadelphia) *Pennsylvanian,* April 25 and July 30, 1835.

60 On baking, see (Philadelphia) *Public Ledger,* June 27, 1839, and Arthur W. Brayley, *Bakers and Baking of Massachusetts* (Boston: Master Bakers' Association of Massachusetts, 1909), which reports no trade organization in the first half of the nineteenth century, but apparently overlooks several groups.

61 Carpenters' Company, *Reminiscences,* p. 4.

62 Haviland, *Builders' Assistant,* Vol. 3: appendix 2, 48.

63 WDS, April 14, 1854.

64 See letter signed "An Old Painter," ibid., Feb. 21, 1854.

65 Ibid.

66 See, for instance, W. R. Rorabaugh, *The Craft Apprentice: From Franklin to the Machine Age in America* (New York: Oxford University Press, 1986), 32–56.

67 E. G. to Mr. Ely, Aug. 15, 1844, Dickinson Papers, AAS. Also Sidney Babcock letter of Aug. 2, 1825, Babcock Papers, AAS.

68 James Lloyd Homer, *Address Delivered before the Massachusetts Charitable Mechanic Association, on the Celebration of their Triennial Celebration, Delivered October 1836* (Boston: Homer & Palmer and Joseph Adams, 1836), 17.

69 See, for instance, Bruce Laurie, *Artisans into Workers: Labor in Nineteenth-Century America* (New York: Noonday Press, 1989), 36–39. For a different interpretation that stresses the discipline of the work routine and the industriousness of labor, see Stott, *Workers in the Metropolis,* 148–161.

70 See, for example, Philip Scranton, "Varieties of Paternalism: Industrial Structures and the Social Relations of Production in American Textiles," *American Quarterly* 36 (summer 1984): 235–258. Also Wilentz, *Chants Democratic,* 316–323, and Willam S. Pretzer, "From Artisan to Alderman: The Career of William W. Moore, 1803–1886," in Rock, ed., *American Artisans,* 135–152.

71 Buckingham, *Memoir,* Vol. 1: 63–64.

72 Ibid., 61–63. Also, Kornblith, "Becoming Joseph T. Buckingham."

73 Loring to John Babcock, Sept. 10, 1823, Babcock Papers, AAS.

74 Homer, *Address,* 17.

75 Voss Hubbard, "The Amesbury-Salisbury Strike." For an intriguing treatment of the economic squeeze of the 1850s, see Robert Fogel, *Without Consent or Contract: The Rise and Fall of American Slavery* (New York: W. W. Norton, 1989), 354–362.

76 See my forthcoming "'To Establish an Equilibrium of Power': Social Relations in the American Printing Industry, 1830–1880," in Stephen Nissenbaum and Michael Winship, eds., *The Industrial Book* (working title of book-in-progress, Cambridge University Press).

77 See Philip Scranton, "Varieties of Paternalism."

78 Norman Ware, *The Industrial Worker, 1840–1860* (Chicago: Quadrangle, 1964, repr. of 1924 ed.), 185–192. See also Carl J. Guarani, *The Utopian Alternative: Fourierism in Nineteenth-Century America* (Ithaca, NY: Cornell University Press, 1991); and Edwin C. Rozwenc, *Cooperatives Come to America: The History of the Protective Union Movement, 1845–1867* (Mt. Vernon, IA: Hawkeye-Record Press, 1941).

79 Wilentz, *Chants Democratic,* 346–349; and Laurie, *Working People of Philadelphia, 1800–1850,* 174–176.

80 Quoted in Laurie, *Working People,* 123.

81 Stuart M. Blumin, *The Emergence of the Middle Class: Social Experience in the American City, 1760–1900* (New York: Cambridge University Press, 1989). Also see Martin J. Burke, *The Conundrum of Class: Public Discourse on the Social Order in America* (Chicago: University of Chicago Press, 1995).

82 Homer, *Address,* 25; emphasis in original.

83 Buckingham, *Memoir,* Vol. 2: 121.

84 Kornblith, "Artisans to Businessmen," 338; emphasis in original.

85 Christopher Clark, "The Diary of an Apprentice Cabinetmaker: Edward Jenner Carpenter's 'Journal,'" *Proceedings of the American Antiquarian Society* 98 (1988): 303–394.

86 Ibid., 327–338.

87 Ibid., 356.

88 Blumin, *Emergence of the Middle Class,* 10–11.

89 Ibid., 135–136. Here 136.

90 Bruce Laurie, "'Spavined Ministers, Lying Toothpullers, and Buggering Priests': Third Partyism and the Search for Security in the Antebellum North," in Howard B. Rock et al., eds., *American Artisans: Crafting Social Identity, 1750–1850* (Baltimore: Johns Hopkins University Press, 1994), 98–119.

91 Michael Kazin, *The Populist Persuasion: An American History* (New York: Basic Books, 1995), esp. 1–25 and 165–286.

92 Scranton, *Proprietary Capitalism,* 70.

Morality and Markets in the Nineteenth Century

1 Alexis de Tocqueville, *Democracy in America* (New York: Alfred A. Knopf, 1963), Vol. 2: 129, 133.

Charitable Calculations

I would like to thank Steven Schwartzberg, Jean-Christophe Agnew, Ann Fabian, and Ethan Nelson for their comments, encouragement, and support.

1 Kathleen D. McCarthy, *Women's Culture: American Philanthropy and Art, 1830–1930* (Chicago: University of Chicago Press, 1991), 47.

2 Beverly Gordon, "Victorian Fancywork in the American Home: Fantasy and Accommodation," in Marilyn Ferris Motz and Pat Browne, eds., *Making the American Home: Middle Class Women & Material Culture, 1840–1940* (Bowling Green, OH: Bowling Green State University Popular Press, 1988), 53–55.

3 Nancy Bercaw, "Solid Objects/Mutable Meanings: Victorian Fancywork and the Construction of Bourgeois Culture," *Winterthur Portfolio* (winter 1991): 231–232, 240.

4 Ibid., 231.

5 Mrs. C. S. Jones and Henry T. Williams, *Beautiful Homes, or Hints in House Furnishing* (New York: Henry T. Williams, 1878), 3–4.

6 Gordon, "Victorian Fancywork," 49.

7 Ann Douglas, *The Feminization of American Culture* ([1977]; New York: Anchor Books, 1988)

8 See Colin Campbell, *The Romantic Ethic and the Spirit of Modern Consumerism* (Oxford: Basil Blackwell, 1987); Albert O. Hirschman, *The Passions and the Interests: Political Arguments for Capitalism before Its Triumph* (Princeton, NJ: Princeton University Press, 1977); and Jean-Christophe Agnew, *Worlds Apart: The Market and the Theater in Anglo-American Thought, 1550–1750* (New York: Cambridge University Press, 1986) for discussions of the ties of sentimentalism to the rise of capitalism and market culture.

9 See Raymond Williams, *The Sociology of Culture* (New York: Schocken Books, 1981), for an interesting discussion of the relationship of these categories.

10 On middle-class identity, see Burton J. Bledstein, *The Culture of Professionalism: The Middle Class and the Development of Higher Education in America* (New York: Norton, 1976); Mary P. Ryan, *The Cradle of the Middle Class: The Family in Oneida County, New York, 1790–1865* (New York: Cambridge University Press, 1981); and Stuart M. Blumin, *The Emergence of the Middle Class: Social Experience in the American City, 1760–1900* (New York: Cambridge University Press, 1989).

11 Arjun Appadurai, ed., *The Social Life of Things: Commodities in Cultural Perspective* (Cambridge: Cambridge University Press, 1986), 11.

12 See Marcel Mauss, *The Gift: Forms and Functions of Exchange in Archaic Societies,* trans. Ian Cunnison, introduction by E. E. Evans Prichard (Glencoe, IL: Free Press, 1954), 18, 22.

13 See Christopher Clark, *The Roots of Rural Capitalism: Western Massachusetts, 1780–1860* (Ithaca, NY:

Cornell University Press, 1990), for a discussion of the evolution of market exchange in rural communities.

14 Virginia Penny, *The Employments of Women: A Cyclopedia of Woman's Work* (Boston: Walker, Wise, & Company, 1863), 105.

15 *Ladies' Magazine* (February 1828): 96. Quoted in Margaret Vincent, *The Ladies Work Table: Domestic Needlework in Nineteenth-Century America* (Hanover, NH: University of New England Press, 1988), 47.

16 From Frances Trollope, *Domestic Manners of the Americans* (1832). Quoted in Felice Hodges, *Period Pastimes: A Practical Guide to Four Centuries of Decorative Crafts* (New York: Weidenfeld and Nicolson, 1989), 47.

17 Vincent, *Ladies Work Table,* 47–48.

18 Lori D. Ginzberg, *Women and the Work of Benevolence: Morality, Politics and Class in the 19th-Century United States* (New Haven, CT: Yale University Press, 1990), 36, 43.

19 Ibid., 57–59.

20 See Jeanne Boydston, *Home & Work: Housework, Wages, and the Ideology of Labor in the Early Republic* (New York: Oxford University Press, 1990).

21 Ginzberg, *Women and Work,* 46.

22 Salem *Gazette*, May 17, 1833. I am grateful to Cassandra Cleghorn for bringing this fair to my attention.

23 Ibid.

24 Ibid.

25 In Sarah Josepha Hale, *Traits of American Life* (Philadelphia: E. L. Carey & A. Hart, 1835), 259–267.

26 Ibid.

27 Ibid.

28 Ibid.

29 Mauss, *Gift: Forms,* 18. See also Lewis Hyde, *The Gift: Imagination and the Erotic Life of Property* (New York: Vintage Books, 1983), 56.

30 Louisa May Alcott, *Little Women* ([1868] New York: Penguin Books, 1989), 306.

31 Hale, *Traits of American Life,* 261–262.

32 Ibid., 264.

33 Virginia Penny, *The Employments of Women* (Boston: Walker, Wise, & Co.,1863); Caroline H. Dall, *The College, The Market and The Court, or, Woman's Relation To Education, Labor and Law* ([1859] Boston: Memorial Edition, 1914); (Dinah Maria Mulock), *A Woman's Thoughts About Women* (New York: John Bradburn, 1866).

34 Hale, *Traits of American Life,* 265.

35 Hyde, *Gift: Imagination,* xiv.

36 Hale, *Traits of American Life,* 260–261.

37 Hyde, *Gift: Imagination,* 138.

38 Ginzberg, *Women and Work,* 46.

39 George M. Frederickson, *The Inner Civil War: Northern Intellectuals and the Crisis of the Union* ([1965] Chicago: University of Illinois Press, 1993), 103–108.

40 (Elisha Harris), *The United States Sanitary Commission* (Boston: Crosby & Nichols, 1864), 48–49. Reprinted from an article in the *North American Review* 203 (April 1864).

41 Philadelphia Sanitary Fair Catalogue, 1864, in Vincent, *Ladies Work Table,* 24.

42 Mary Livermore, *My Story of the War: A Woman's Narrative of Four Years Personal Experience* (Hartford, CT: A. D. Worthington, 1888), 455.

43 Ibid., 412.

44 Katharine Wormley, *The Cruel Side of the War* (Boston: Roberts Brothers, 1898), 11.

45 *Godey's Lady's Book* (January 1862): 100, Juvenile Dept., "Articles that Children can make for Fancy Fairs or Holiday Presents"; *Peterson's* (January 1863): 76; *Peterson's* (June 1863): 476–477, "Fancy Articles For Fairs." See also Lucretia P. Hale and Margaret E. White, *Decorative and Fancy Articles for Presents and Fairs* (Boston: S. W. Tilton & Co., 1885).

46 Marjorie Barstow Greenbie, *Lincoln's Daughters of Mercy* (New York: G. P. Putnam's Sons, 1944), 206.

47 Ginzberg, *Women and Work,* 152.

48 See also Kathleen Waters Sander, "'Not a Lady among Us!': Entrepreneurial Philanthropy and Economic Independence as Expressed through the Women's Exchange Movement, 1832–1900." (Ph.D.

diss., University of Maryland, College Park, 1994) for further discussion of the Women's Exchange movement.

49 McCarthy, *Women's Culture,* 61.

50 Ibid., 40.

51 Ibid., 43.

52 *Nonprofit entrepreneurship* is Kathleen McCarthy's term, 62.

53 McCarthy, *Women's Culture,* 62, 63; Lucy M. Salmon, "The Women's Exchange: Charity or Business?" *Forum* 13 (May 1892): 394–340.

Bringing Up Yankees

1 J. T. Trowbridge, "The Turning of the Leaf," *Our Young Folks* 1 (June 1865), 398–399; Lydia Maria Child, "The Two Christmas Evenings," *Our Young Folks* 2 (January 1866), 10.

2 Stuart M. Blumin, *The Emergence of the Middle Class: Social Experience in the American City, 1760–1900* (New York: Cambridge University Press, 1989), 13; Anne C. Rose, *Victorian America and the Civil War* (New York: Cambridge University Press, 1992), 12.

3 Rose, *Victorian America and the Civil War,* 5, 237.

4 Blumin, *The Emergence of the Middle Class,* 192–229; Mary P. Ryan, *Cradle of the Middle Class: The Family in Oneida County, New York, 1790–1865* (New York: Cambridge University Press, 1981), 105–144, 237–238; Clifford E. Clark, Jr., *Henry Ward Beecher: Spokesman for Middle-Class America* (Urbana: University of Illinois Press, 1978), 3–4; John S. Gilkerson, Jr., *Middle-Class Providence, 1820–1940* (Princeton, NJ: Princeton University Press, 1986), 9–10, 23–28, 36–53, 55–94; Marilyn Dell Brady, "The New Model Middle-Class Family (1815–1930)," in Joseph M. Hawes and Elizabeth I. Nybakken, eds., *American Families: A Research Guide and Historical Handbook* (Westport, CT: Greenwood, 1991), 82–124; Gilkerson, *Middle-Class Providence,* 13.

5 Joel Cook, *The Siege of Richmond: A Narrative of the Military Operations of Major-General George B. McClellan during the Months of May and June, 1862* (Philadelphia: George W. Childs, 1862), 151–154.

6 Randall C. Jimerson, *The Private Civil War: Popular Thought during the Sectional Conflict* (Baton Rouge: Louisiana State University Press, 1988), 81–83; James H. Moorhead, *American Apocalypse: Yankee Protestants and the Civil War, 1860–1869* (New Haven, CT: Yale University Press, 1978), 205–207; Reid Mitchell, *Civil War Soldiers: Their Expectations and Their Experiences* (New York: Viking, 1988), 121–123; Nina Silber, *The Romance of Reunion: Northerners and the South, 1865–1900* (Chapel Hill: University of North Carolina Press, 1995), 81–83.

7 Mitchell, *Civil War Soldiers,* 91–117; Mitchell, *The Vacant Chair: The Northern Soldier Leaves Home* (New York: Oxford University Press, 1993), 91–103; Mitchell, *Civil War Soldiers,* 91.

8 Karen Halttunen, *Confidence Men and Painted Women: A Study of Middle-Class Culture in America, 1830–1870* (New Haven, CT: Yale University Press, 1982), 96–97, 104–105; Randall C. Jimerson, *The Private Civil War: Popular Thought during the Sectional Conflict* (Baton Rouge: Louisiana State University Press, 1988), 35–38, 132–135; here, 135, 33.

9 William R. Taylor, *Cavalier & Yankee: The Old South and American National Character* (New York: Harper & Row, 1957).

10 Bertram Wyatt-Brown, *Yankee Saints and Southern Sinners* (Baton Rouge: Louisiana State University Press, 1985), 4–5, 8–10: here, 4; Steven V. Ash, *When the Yankees Came: Conflict & Chaos in the Occupied South, 1861–1865* (Chapel Hill: University of North Carolina Press, 1995), 24–25, 34–35, 53, 171–177. See also Michael C. C. Adams, *Fighting for Defeat: Union Military Failure in the East, 1861–1865* (Lincoln: University of Nebraska Press, 1992), 1–47.

11 Rose, *Victorian America and the Civil War,* 236; Moorhead, *American Apocalypse,* 65–72.

12 For two examples among a large literature, see Steven Mintz, *A Prison of Expectations: The Family in Victorian Culture* (New York: New York University Press, 1983), 20, 28, 37, 67; and Michael Grossberg, *Governing the Hearth: Law and Family in Nineteenth-Century America* (Chapel Hill: University of North Carolina Press, 1985), 9–11.

13 James Marten, *The Children's Civil War* (Chapel Hill: University of North Carolina Press, 1998), ch. 3; David Coon to Emma Coon, June 5, 1864, transcript, David Coon Letters, Library of Congress.

14 Marten, *The Children's Civil War,* especially ch. 5.

15 Ryan, *Cradle of the Middle Class,* 161, 184–185; Brady, "The New Model Middle-Class Family," 87; Kirk Jeffrey, "Family History: The Middle Class American Family in the Urban Context, 1830–1870" (Ph.D. diss., Stanford University, 1972), 56–67; here, 57.

16 Ann Scott MacLeod, *American Childhood: Essays on Children's Literature of the Nineteenth and Twentieth Centuries* (Athens: University of Georgia Press, 1994), 87–98; J. Merton England, "The Democratic Faith in American Schoolbooks 1783–1860," *American Quarterly* 15 (summer 1963): 191–199; Carol Billman, "McGuffey's Readers and Alger's Fiction: The Gospel of Virtue According to Popular Children's Literature," *Journal of Popular Culture* 11 (winter 1977): 614–619; Carolyn L. Karcher, "Lydia Maria Child and the Juvenile Miscellany: The Creation of an American Children's Literature," in *Periodical Literature in Nineteenth-Century America*, ed. Kenneth M. Price and Susan Belasco Smith (Charlottesville: University Press of Virginia, 1995), 90–114; John H. Westerhoff III, *McGuffey and His Readers: Piety, Morality, and Education in Nineteenth-Century America* (Nashville: Abingdon, 1978); John G. Cawelti, *Apostles of the Self-Made Man* (Chicago: University of Chicago Press 1965), 104–108; MacLeod, *American Childhood*, 90. See also Robert Franklin Berman, "The Naive Child and the Competent Child: American Literature for Children and American Culture, 1830–1930" (Ph.D. diss., Harvard University, 1978), esp. chapters 2 and 3.

17 James Marten, *Lessons of War: The Civil War in Children's Magazines* (Wilmington: SR Books, 1998), xi–xviii; John B. Boles, "Jacob Abbott and the Rollo Books: New England Culture for Children," *Journal of Popular Culture* 6 (spring 1972): 507–528.

18 Oliver Optic, "Teacher's Desk," *The Student and Schoolmate* 15 (May 1865): 158–159; Ann Scott MacLeod, *A Moral Tale: Children's Fiction and American Culture, 1820–1860* (Hamden, CT: Archon Books, 1975), 104–116; Anne M. Boylan, *Sunday School: The Formation of an American Institution, 1790–1880* (New Haven, CT: Yale University Press, 1988), 80–85; Mary E. Quinlaven, "Race Relations in the Antebellum Children's Literature of Jacob Abbott," *Journal of Popular Culture* 16 (summer 1982): 27–36; John C. Crandall, "Patriotism and Humanitarian Reform in Children's Literature, 1825–1860," *American Quarterly* 21 (spring 1969): 3–22; John B. Crume, "Children's Magazines, 1826–1857," *Journal of Popular Culture* 6 (spring 1973): 698–707.

19 G. N. Coan, "Dear Pilgrim," *The Little Pilgrim* 11 (June 1864), 81–82.

20 Oliver Optic, "Teacher's Desk," *The Student and Schoolmate* 11 (December 1862): 428–429; Christie Pearl, "The Fort and How It Was Taken," *The Student and Schoolmate* 11 (August 1862): 273–274; "Union Boys in Kentucky," *The Student and Schoolmate* 12 (May 1863): 151–156; Louisa May Alcott, "Nelly's Hospital," *Our Young Folks* 1 (April 1865): 267–277; Mrs. Phebe H. Phelps, "A Box for the Soldier," *The Student and Schoolmate* 13 (March 1864): 71–74.

21 Optic's books, all published by the Boston house of Lee & Shepard, were *The Soldier Boy* (1863), *The Young Lieutenant* (1865), *Fighting Joe* (1866), *The Sailor Boy* (1863), *The Yankee Middy* (1866), and *The Brave Old Salt* (1867).

22 Horatio Alger, Jr., *Frank's Campaign; or, What Boys can do on the Farm for the Camp* (Boston: Loring, 1864).

23 Child, "The Two Christmas Evenings," 2–13; "The Cloud With the Silver Lining," *Our Young Folks* 1 (December 1865): 557–561; "The Discontented Girl," *The Little Pilgrim* 9 (November 1862): 150–151.

24 Christie Pearl, "The Contraband," *The Student and Schoolmate* 11 (February 1862): 45–48.

25 Amanda M. Douglas, *Kathie's Soldiers* (Boston: Lee & Shepard, 1870); Mary G. Darling, *Battles at Home* (Boston: Horace B. Fuller, 1870), 246–247.

26 Gail Hamilton, "Small Fighting," *The Student and Schoolmate* 11 (January 1862): 7–11.

27 Sophie May, *Captain Horace* (Boston: Lee & Shepard, 1864); *Kate Morgan and Her Soldiers* (Philadelphia: American Sunday School Union, 1862), 121–122; Caroline E. Kelly, *Andy Hall: The Mission Scholar in the Army* (Boston; Henry Hoyt, 1863); Sarah S. Baker, *Charlie the Drummer Boy* (New York; American Tract Society, n.d.); Sarah Town Smith, "The Drummer-Boy of the Twenty-Sixth," in *Our Village in War-Time* (New York: American Tract Society, 1864), 50–79.

28 Robert C. Morris, *Reading, 'Riting, and Reconstruction: The Education of Freedmen in the South, 1861–1870* (Chicago: University of Chicago Press, 1981), 198–201; Ronald E. Butchart, *Northern Schools, Southern Blacks, and Reconstruction: Freedmen's Education, 1862–1875* (Westport, CT: Greenwood, 1980), 135–139, 155–159.

29 *The Freedman* 1 (January 1864): 1.

30 Ibid., 1 (April 1865): 15; 2 (June 1865): 23; 2 (January 1865): 2; 1 (August 1864): 30; 1 (June 1864): 23; 1 (March 1864): 11.

31 Ibid., 1 (November 1864): 41.

32 The classic history of the USSC is William Quentin Maxwell, *Lincoln's Fifth Wheel: The Political History of the United States Sanitary Commission* (New York: Longmans, Green, 1956). For the middle-

class background of most of the organizers of the Great Central Fair in Philadelphia, see J. Matthew Gallman, *Mastering Wartime: A Social History of Philadelphia during the Civil War* (New York: Cambridge University Press, 1990), 146–169.

33 William Y. Thompson, "Sanitary Fairs of the Civil War," *Civil War History* 4 (March 1958): 51–67; Beverly Gordon, "A Furor of Benevolence," *Chicago History* 15 (winter 1986–1987): 48–65.

34 *Chicago Tribune,* October 25, 1863, and May 30, 1865; *Philadelphia Public Ledger and Transcript,* June 15, 1864; *Frank Leslie's Illustrated Newspaper*, June 25 and April 23, 1864; The Canteen (Albany), February 20, 27, and 29, and March 4, 1864; *The Drumbeat* (Brooklyn and Long Island), March 1, 1864.

35 *Spirit of the Fair*, April 4, 16, 6, 7, 18, 22, and 15, 1864.

36 *Chicago Tribune,* October 1864; Kingsbury, *In Old Waterbury*, n.p; Frank B. Goodrich, *The Tribute Book: A Record of the Munificence, Self-Sacrifice and Patriotism of the American People during the War for the Union* (New York: Derby & Miller, 1865), 116, 193–194, 166, 190; John Y. Simon, ed., *Personal Memoirs of Julia Dent Grant*, 131; Noah Brooks, *Washington in Lincoln's Time* (New York: Century Co., 1895), 280–281.

37 Goodrich, *Tribute Book*, 219–222, 258; *Ladies Knapsack*, December 29, 1863; Thomas Jean Walters, "Music of the Great Sanitary Fairs: Culture and Charity in the American Civil War" (Ph.D. diss., University of Pittsburgh, 1989), 237, 278–279, 249, 287, 119.

38 "Officer's Commission," Army of the American Eagle, Emily J. Crouch File, Wisconsin State Historical Society; *Chicago Tribune,* May 31, 1865; "How I Came to Print the *Little Corporal,*" and "The Army of the American Eagle," *The Little Corporal* 1 (July 1865), 1–2, 3; "The Veteran Eagle, and What the Children Did," *The Little Corporal* 3 (December 1866), 88–90.

39 Phillip Shaw Paludan, *"A People's Contest": The Union and Civil War, 1861–1865* (New York: Harper & Row, 1988), 354–355; Jeanie Attie, "Warwork and the Crisis of Domesticity in the North," in Clinton and Silber, eds., *Divided Houses*, 247–259.

40 Edmund Kirke, "The Boy of Chancellorsville," *Our Young Folks* 1 (September 1865): 600–608.

41 Ibid., 601.

The Cultural Uses of the Spirit

1 S. G. Goodrich, *Recollections of a Lifetime, Men and Things Have Seen* (New York: Miller, Orton, & Mulligan, 1856), Vol. 1: 63, 182, 63–64.

2 R. Laurence Moore, *Selling God: American Religion in the Marketplace of Culture* (New York: Oxford University Press, 1994); Stephen Nissenbaum, *The Battle for Christmas* (New York: Knopf, 1997); William Leach, "Wanamaker's Simple Life and the Moral Failure of Established Religion," *Land of Desire: Merchants, Power, and the Rise of a New American Culture* (New York: Random House, 1993), 191–224; Roland Marchand, *Advertising the American Dream: Making Way for Modernity, 1920–1940* (Berkeley: University of California Press, 1985); Jackson Lears, *Fables of Abundance: A Cultural History of Advertising in America* (New York: Basic Books, 1994).

Henry Ward Beecher and the "Great Middle Class"

1 Löic J. D. Wacquant, "Making Class: The Middle Class(es) in Social Theory and Social Structure," in *Bringing Class Back In: Contemporary and Historical Perspectives*, ed. Scott G. McNall, Rhonda F. Levine, Rick Fantasia (Boulder, CO: Westview, 1991), 39.

2 *The Collected Works of Abraham Lincoln*, ed. Roy F. Basler, 9 vols. (New Brunswick, NJ: Rutgers University Press, 1953–55), Vol. 2: 364.

3 Stuart Blumin, *The Emergence of the Middle Class: Social Experience in the American City, 1760–1900* (New York: Cambridge University Press, 1989), 9–10. On this paradox, see also Martin Burke, *The Conundrum of Class: Public Discourse on the Social Order in America* (Chicago: University of Chicago Press, 1995).

4 Anthony Giddens, *The Class Structure of Advanced Societies* (New York: 1975), 11. Indeed, Blumin suggests that the shared "denial of the significance of class" could be the defining characteristic of middle-class awareness.

5 Melanie Archer and Judith R. Blau, "Class Formation in the Nineteenth Century: The Case of the Middle Class," *Annual Review of Sociology* 19 (1993): 28.

6 Blumin, *Emergence of the Middle Class,* 13.

7 *New York Tribune*, March 10, 1855, quoted by Blumin, *Emergence of the Middle Class,* 247.

8 Archer and Blau, "Class Formation," 21.

9   Secondary sources on Henry Ward Beecher include Clifford E. Clark, Jr., *Henry Ward Beecher: Spokesman for a Middle-Class America* (Urbana: University of Illinois Press, 1978); Altina Waller, *The Rev. Beecher and Mrs. Tilton: Sex and Class in Victorian America* (Amherst: University of Massachusetts Press, 1982); William McLoughlin, *The Meaning of Henry Ward Beecher: An Essay on the Shifting Values of Mid-Victorian America* (New York: Alfred Knopf, 1970); Paxton Hibben, *Henry Ward Beecher: An American Portrait* (New York: George H. Doran Co., 1927).

10 For more detailed references to the arguments contained in this essay, see Debby Applegate, "The Culture of the Novel and the Consolidation of Middle-Class Consciousness: Henry Ward Beecher and the Uses of Sympathy, 1830–1880," (Ph.D. diss., Yale University, 1997).

11 On the Beecher family, see Milton Rugoff, *The Beechers* (New York: Harper & Row, 1981); Marie Caskey, *Chariot of Fire: Religion and the Beecher Family* (New Haven, CT: Yale University Press, 1978); Constance Rourke, *Trumpets of Jubilee* (New York: Harcourt, Brace, 1927); Lyman Beecher, *The Autobiography of Lyman Beecher*, ed. Barbara M. Cross, 2 vols. (Cambridge, MA: Belknap Press of Harvard University Press, 1961); Kathryn Kish Sklar, *Catharine Beecher: A Study in American Domesticity* (New Haven, CT: Yale University Press, 1973); Joan Hedrick, *Harriet Beecher Stowe* (New York: Oxford University Press, 1994); Jeanne Boydston, Mary Kelley, and Anne Margolis, *The Limits of Sisterhood: The Beecher Sisters on Women's Rights and Woman's Sphere* (Chapel Hill: University of North Carolina Press, 1988); Gillian Brown, *Domestic Individualism: Imagining Self in Nineteenth-Century America* (Berkeley: University of California Press, 1990).

12 Henry Ward Beecher, *Life Thoughts* (Boston: Phillips, Sampson & Company, 1858), 31.

13 Robert Bonner to H. W. B., March 27, 1867; Beecher Papers, Yale University Manuscripts and Archives (YUMA).

14 Gordon Hutner, *Secrets and Sympathy: Forms of Disclosure in Hawthorne's Novels* (Athens: University of Georgia Press, 1988), 11.

15 William C. Beecher and Samuel Scoville, *A Biography of Henry Ward Beecher* (New York: Charles L. Webster & Co., 1888), 164.

16 Henry Ward Beecher, *Patriotic Addresses*, ed. John Raymond Howard (New York: Fords, Howard, & Hulbert, 1887), 96–97.

17 David Montgomery, *Beyond Equality: Labor and the Radical Republicans, 1862–1962* (New York: Vintage Books, 1967), 204.

18 Henry Ward Beecher, "Honor Your Business," *New York Ledger*, Oct. 22, 1859, 4. On economic insecurity and class identity, see Bruce Laurie, "'Spavined Ministers, Lying Toothpullers, and Buggering Priests': Third-Partyism and the Search for Security in the Antebellum North," *American Artisans: Crafting Social Identity, 1750–1850*, ed. Howard B. Rock, Paul A. Gilje, Robert Asher (Baltimore: Johns Hopkins University Press, 1995), 98–119.

19 Henry Ward Beecher, *Christian Union*, Oct. 9, 1872, 306. Waller, *Rev. Beecher*, makes the alternative argument that affinity was a rationalization for new, exclusive standards of gentility and the breaking of old ties as one moved up the economic ladder.

20 William T. Craig to H. W. B., July 19, 1875, Oct. 5, 1875; Beecher Papers, YUMA. On the rise of "begging letters" to famous figures, see Scott Sandage, "The Gaze of Success: Failed Men and the Sentimental Marketplace, 1873–1893," in *Sentimental Men: Masculinity and the Politics of Affect in American Culture*, ed. Mary Chapman and Glenn Hedler (Berkeley: University of California Press, 1999), 181–201.

21 Eric Foner, *Free Soil, Free Labor, Free Men* (New York: Oxford University Press, 1995), xi, xvi.

22 Michael Denning, *Mechanic Accents: Dime Novels and Working Class Culture* (New York: Verso, 1987), 173.

23 Henry Ward Beecher, *Life Thoughts*, 116; "Phases of the Times," *New Star Papers, or Views and Experiences of Religious Subjects* (New York: Derby & Jackson, 1859), 116.

24 Henry Ward Beecher, *Life Thoughts*, 149; "My Property," in *Eyes and Ears* (Boston: Ticknor & Fields, 1863), 246.

25 Henry Ward Beecher, *Life Thoughts*, 218.

26 Ibid., 195.

27 J. W. Tripp to H. W. B., Aug. 9, 1875; Beecher Papers, YUMA.

28 John Browning to H. W. B., March 22, 1869; Beecher Papers, YUMA.

29 Adam Badeau, *The Vagabond* (New York: Rudd & Carleton, 1859), 283.

30 Henry Ward Beecher, *Yale Lectures on Preaching* (New York: J. B. Ford & Co., 1872–73), I: 91.

31 Henry Ward Beecher, *Yale*, I: 113.

32 Matthew Hale Smith, *Sunshine and Shadow in New York* (Hartford, CT: J. B. Burr & Co., 1868), 92.

33 On Bonner and the *Ledger,* see Mary Noel, *Villains Galore: The Heyday of the Popular Story Weekly* (New York: Macmillan Co., 1954); James L. Crouthamel, "The Newspaper Revolution in New York, 1830–1860," *New York History* 45 (April 1964): 91–113; Ralph Adamari, "Bonner and the Ledger," *American Book Collector* 6 (Jan. –June 1935): 176–193.

34 *Vanity Fair*, October 25, 1862, front page.

35 Lester Hills to H. W. B., March 2, 1876; John Henry Barrows to H. W. B., Nov. 6, 1875; Crammond Kennedy to H. W. B., March 26, 1870, Beecher Papers, YUMA; Oliver Wendell Holmes, "The Minister Plenipotentiary," *The Atlantic Monthly*, January 1864, 108.

36 F. A. Burnum to H. W. B., n.d.; Beecher Papers, YUMA.

Scientific Church Music and the Making of the American Middle Class

This essay is part of a larger work that examines notions of denominational identity in Jacksonian America.

1 Andrew Fletcher, "Letter to the Marquis of Montrose," *Bartlett's Familiar Quotations*, web edition, cited December 8, 1998 from http://www.columbia.edu/acis/bartelby/bartlett/199.html. The line was often referred to in reference to church music; see quote attributed to the "ancient philosopher" in "Thoughts on Singing," *Methodist Magazine*, Vol. 3 (1820), 145, and to the "distinguished statesman" in "A Collection of Psalms and Hymns," *Christian Examiner*, Vol. 10 (1831), 31.

2 See, for example, Ronald Walters, *The Antislavery Appeal* (Baltimore: Johns Hopkins University Press, 1976); and Richard Bushman, *The Refinement of America: Persons, Houses, Cities* (New York: Knopf, 1992).

3 An important overview is Gilbert Chase, *America's Music: From the Pilgrims to the Present,* rev. 3rd edition (Urbana: University of Illinois Press, 1987); for an excellent monograph, see Michael Broyles, *Music of the Highest Class: Elitism and Populism in Antebellum Boston* (New Haven, CT: Yale University Press, 1992).

4 Myra Glenn, *Thomas Beecher: Minister to a Changing America* (Westport, CT: Greenwood Press, 1996), 24. See also James Freeman Clarke, "Church Music," *Western Messenger devoted to Religion and Literature*, Vol. 1 (1836), 136.

5 When Lowell Mason and his brother, Timothy Batelle Mason, put together *The Sacred Harp or Electric Harmony* (Cincinnati: Truman & Smith, 1834), the publisher chose against their wishes to print the tunes in shape notes. Thus, for example, "Wayfaring Stranger" first appeared in print in Benjamin White's 1844 *Sacred Harp.*

6 "Sacred Harmony," *Methodist Quarterly Review*, Vol. 30, 287–288.

7 "Spiritual Songs for Social Worship," *Quarterly Christian Spectator*, Vol. 6 (1834), 213.

8 Lawrence W. Levine, *Highbrow/Lowbrow: The Emergence of Cultural Hierarchy in America* (Cambridge, MA: Harvard University Press, 1988).

9 The ideas of scientific musicians begin to appear soon after Lowell Mason's 1828 Boston Address, Thomas Hastings's 1822 *Dissertation on Musical Taste*, and the strongly worded introduction to their 1832 *Spiritual Songs for Social Worship*. (Thomas Hastings, *Dissertation on Musical Taste; or, General Principles of Taste applied to the Art of Music* (Albany: Websters & Skinners, 1822); Hastings published a revised edition in 1853.) They continued to appear and re-appear, showing up in the major periodicals of all the major denominations, first among cultured Bostonians in the late 1820s, then in the New Haven theology, and from there in mainstream Congregationalists and Old-School Presbyterian services in the early 1840s, and last, but most powerfully, among the Methodists by the end of the 1840s. See, for example, the [Unitarian] *Christian Examiner and Theological Review*, Vol. 3 (1826), 489–498; the [New Haven Theology] *Quarterly Christian Spectator*, Vol. 6 (1834), 208–226; the Trinitarian Congregationalist *American Biblical Repository*, 2nd ser., Vol. 14 (1842), 361–375; the Old-School Presbyterian *Biblical Repertory and Princeton Review,* Vol. 15 (1843), 88–110; and *The Methodist Quarterly Review*, Vol. 30 (1848), 283–293. The ordering of periodicals and dates here is a reasonable approximation of the progress of the rhetoric of scientific music through the major denominations.

10 The music of the scientific musicians was the biggest seller of the antebellum years, with Lowell Mason leading all. His *Carmina Sacra* may have sold more than 500,000 copies in its various printings over its long commercial life. For comparison, consider that Stephen Foster's most successful song, "Old Folks at Home," sold only about 130,000 copies. Michael Broyles, ed., *A Yankee Musician in Europe: The 1837 Journals of Lowell Mason* (Ann Arbor, MI: UMI Research Press, 1990), 219.

11 Carol A. Pemberton, *Lowell Mason: His Life and Work* (Ann Arbor, MI: UMI Research Press, 1985); and Arthur Lowndes Rich, *Lowell Mason: "The Father of Singing Among the Children,"* (Chapel Hill: University of North Carolina Press, 1946).

12 Anna Campbell, Diary, April 14, 1851; Charles Campbell papers, College of William and Mary. Cited from Suzanne Lebsock, *Free Women of Petersburg* (New York: Norton, 1984), 30.

13 "Review of the Christian Lyre," *Christian Spectator,* Vol. 3 (1831), 664–672.

14 Lyman Beecher, *The Autobiography of Lyman Beecher,* ed. Barbara M. Cross, 2 vols. (Cambridge, MA: Belknap Press of Harvard University Press, 1961), Vol. 2, 112–116.

15 "Review of Jackson's Sacred Harmony," *The Methodist Quarterly Review*, 3rd ser., Vol. 8 (1848), 285.

16 *The Reformer* (Philadelphia, PA), Vol. 9, 101 (May 1828), 74.

17 "Congregational Singing," *Christian Examiner*, Vol. 65 (1858), 234.

18 "Church Music," *The Western Messenger; Devoted to Religion and Literature*, Vol. 1 (1836), 134–135.

19 For Clarke's background, see Edward Everett Hale, ed., *Autobiography, Diary and Correspondence of James Freeman Clarke* (Boston, MA: Houghton Mifflin, 1891).

20 Explicit contrast between the godly and the profane was a central part of evangelical identity. As Francis Trollope observed, "It is in the churches and chapels of the town that the ladies are to be seen in full costume ... all dressed with care, and sometimes with great pretension; it is there that all display is made, and all fashionable distinction sought." Francis Trollope, *Domestic Manners of the Americans* ([1832] New York: Penguin, 1997), 59. See also A. Gregory Schneider, *The Way of the Cross Leads to Home* (Bloomington: Indiana University Press, 1993); and Christine Leigh Heyrman, *Southern Cross: The Beginnings of the Bible Belt* (New York: Knopf, 1997).

Secularization Reconsidered

1 David Hollinger, "Jewish Intellectuals and the De-Christianization of American Public Culture in the Twentieth Century," Harry S. Stout and D. G. Hart, eds., *New Directions in American Religious History* (New York: Oxford University Press, 1997), 462–486, 465. By stressing the role of Social Gospel theology in promoting exchange among American, British, and Continental reformers at the turn of the century, Daniel Rodgers offers an implicit critique of the professionalization thesis of Thomas Haskell and others. Daniel T. Rodgers, *Atlantic Crossings: Social Politics in a Progressive Age* (Cambridge, MA: Harvard University Press, 1998), 63.

2 See Donald D. Meyer, *The Positive Thinkers: A Study of the American Quest for Health, Wealth, and Personal Power from Mary Baker Eddy to Norman Vincent Peale* (Garden City, NY: Doubleday, 1965); Philip Rieff, *The Triumph of the Therapeutic: Uses of Faith after Freud* (New York: Harper & Row, 1966); Daniel J. Boorstin, *The Americans: The Democratic Experience* (New York: Random House, 1973).

3 George E. Mowry, "The California Progressive and His Rationale: A Study in Middle Class Politics," *Mississippi Valley Historical Review* 36 (1949): 241–250 and *The California Progressives* (Berkeley: University of California Press, 1957); Richard Hofstadter, *The Age of Reform* (New York: Knopf, 1955), 55; Samuel P. Hays, "The Politics of Reform in Municipal Government in the Progressive Era," *Pacific Northwest Quarterly* 55 (1964): 159–169.

4 Robert H. Wiebe, *The Search for Order, 1877–1920* (New York: Hill & Wang, 1967), 166; Kenneth Cmiel, "Destiny and Amnesia: The Vision of Modernity in Robert Wiebe's *The Search for Order,"* *Reviews in American History* 21 (1993): 352–368.

5 Ferdinand Tönnies, *Community and Society* (New York: Harper Torchbooks, 1963), 231; Max Weber, *The Theory of Social and Economic Organization* (New York: Free Press, 1947) and *The Protestant Ethic and the Spirit of Capitalism*, trans. Talcott Parsons (New York: Charles Scribner's Sons, 1958); Emile Durkheim, *The Division of Labor in Society* (Glencoe, IL: Free Press, 1949).

6 Walter Lippmann, *Drift and Mastery* (New York: M. Kennerley, 1914), 94, 100; Thorstein Veblen, *The Theory of the Leisure Class* ([1899] New York: Penguin Books, 1994), 330. See esp. ch. 12, "Devout Observances."

7 Talcott Parsons, "Christianity and Modern Industrial Society," in Edward Tirayakian, ed., *Sociological Theory, Values, and Sociocultural Change* (New York: Free Press, 1963), 385–421; Thomas Luckmann, *The Invisible Religion: The Transformation of Symbols in Industrial Society* (New York: Macmillan, 1967); Peter L. Berger, *The Sacred Canopy: Elements of a Sociological Theory of Religion* (Garden City, NY: Anchor, 1969). Dissenting viewpoints include David Martin, "Towards Eliminating the Concept of Secularization," in J. Gould, ed., *Penguin Survey of the Social Sciences* (Baltimore: Penguin Books, 1965); Andrew M. Greeley, *Unsecular Man: The Persistence of Religion* (New York: Schocken

Books, 1972); R. Stephen Warner, "Work in Progress toward a New Paradigm for the Sociological Study of Religion in the United States," *American Journal of Sociology* 98, no. 5 (March 1993): 1044–1093.

8   Warren I. Susman, "'Personality' and the Making of Twentieth-Century Culture" (1979) in Susman, *Culture as History: The Transformation of American Society in the Twentieth Century* (New York: Pantheon Books, 1984), 271–285, 276.

9   T. J. Jackson Lears, *No Place of Grace: Antimodernism and the Transformation of American Culture* (Chicago: University of Chicago Press, 1981).

10 Lears, *No Place of Grace*, 9, xvii; Lears, "From Salvation to Self-Realization: Advertising and the Therapeutic Roots of the Consumer Culture, 1880–1930," in Lears and Richard Wightman Fox, eds., *The Culture of Consumption: Critical Essays in American History, 1880–1980* (New York: Pantheon Books, 1983), 3–38, 4.

11 Lears, *No Place of Grace*, 41–47, 41.

12 Note, though, Christopher Lasch's criticism that his colleagues were using modernization to make conclusions beyond their evidence. Christopher Lasch, "Experiment and Resistance," *Times Literary Supplement*, May 25, 1984, 574.

13 William Leach, *Land of Desire: Merchants, Power, and the Rise of a New American Culture* (New York: Vintage Books, 1993), 5, 3, 211, 195. See also Pamela Walker Laird, *Advertising Progress: American Business and the Rise of Consumer Marketing* (Baltimore: Johns Hopkins University Press, 1998).

14 *Dictionary of American History*, Vol. 4 (New York: Charles Scribner's Sons, 1976), s.v. "Middle Class," by Paul J. Hoffmann.

15 R. Laurence Moore, *Selling God: American Religion in the Marketplace of Culture* (New York: Oxford University Press, 1994), 148. Works on the continuing vitality of American religion in the first half of the twentieth century include Kevin J. Christiano, *Religious Diversity and Social Change: American Cities, 1890–1906* (Cambridge: Cambridge University Press, 1987); and Roger Fink and Rodney Stark, *The Churching of America* (New Brunswick, NJ: Rutgers University Press, 1992).

16 Jon Butler, "Protestant Success in the New American City, 1870–1920: The Anxious Secrets of Rev. Walter Laidlaw, Ph.D.," in Harry S. Stout and D. G. Hart, eds., *New Directions in American Religious History* (New York: Oxford University Press, 1997), 296–333, 313. On the Social Gospel generally, see Ronald White, *The Social Gospel: Religion and Reform in Changing America* (Philadelphia: Temple University Press, 1976); Paul Boyer, *Urban Masses and Moral Order in America, 1820–1920* (Cambridge, MA: Harvard University Press, 1978); Susan Curtis, *A Consuming Faith: The Social Gospel and Modern American Culture* (Baltimore: Johns Hopkins University Press, 1991); Paul T. Phillips, *Kingdom on Earth: Anglo-American Social Christianity, 1880–1940* (University Park: Pennsylvania State University Press, 1996).

17 Diane H. Winston, "Boozers, Brass Bands, and Hallelujah Lassies: The Salvation Army and American Commercial Culture, 1880–1918," (Ph.D. diss., Princeton University, 1996), 5. See also Nina Mjagkij and Margaret Spratt, eds., *Men and Women Adrift: The YMCA and the YWCA in the City* (New York: New York University Press, 1997); Judith Weisenfeld, *African American Women and Christian Activism: New York's Black YWCA, 1905–1945* (Cambridge, MA: Harvard University Press, 1997).

18 Richard T. Ely, *Ground under Our Feet: An Autobiography* (New York: Macmillan, 1938), 79; Frank Bohn, "America Revealed in Chautauqua," *New York Times Magazine*, October 10, 1926, 3. My analysis here was shaped by Alan Trachtenberg's concise article "'We Study the Word and Works of God': Chautauqua and the Sacralization of Culture in America," *Henry Ford and Greenfield Village Herald* 13:2 (1984): 3–11.

19 Herbert B. Adams, "Summer Schools in England, Scotland, France, and Switzerland," *United States Bureau of Education, Report of the Commissioner of Education, 1896–97*, Vol. 1 (Washington, DC: Government Printing Office, 1897), 318.

20 John Heyl Vincent, *The Chautauqua Movement* (Boston: Chautauqua Press, 1886), 4, 31, 20; John Heyl Vincent, *A History of the Wesleyan Grove, Martha's Vineyard, Camp Meeting* (Boston: Geo. C. Rand & Avery, 1858), 10, 11.

21 General histories of the Chautauqua Institution include Charles Robert Knicker, "The Chautauqua Literary and Scientific Circle, 1878–1914: A Historical Interpretation of an Educational Piety in Industrial America" (EED diss., Columbia University, 1969); Theodore Morrison, *Chautauqua: A Center for Education, Religion and the Arts in America* (Chicago: University of Chicago Press, 1974); Alan Trachtenberg, *The Incorporation of America: Culture and Society in the Gilded Age* (New York: Hill

& Wang, 1982), 140–144; Trachtenberg, "'We Study the Word and Works of God'"; Thomas J. Schlereth, "Chautauqua: A Middle Landscape of the Middle Class," *Henry Ford and Greenfield Village Herald* 13:2 (1984): 22–31; Alfreda M. Irwin, *Three Taps of the Gavel* (Chautauqua, NY: Chautauqua Press, 1987); Joseph F. Kett, *The Pursuit of Knowledge Under Difficulties: From Self-Improvement to Adult Education in America, 1750–1990* (Stanford, CA: Stanford University Press, 1994), esp. ch. 5: "The Homely Renaissance, 1870–1900," 143–179; Moore, *Selling God*, esp. ch. 6: "Chautauqua and Its Protective Canopy: Religion, Entertainment, and Small-Town Protestants," 147–171; Jeffrey Simpson, *Chautauqua: An American Utopia* (New York: Harry N. Abrams in association with Chautauqua Institution, 1999); Andrew C. Rieser, "Canopy of Culture: Chautauqua and the Renegotiation of Middle-Class Authority, 1874–1919," (Ph.D. diss., University of Wisconsin-Madison, 1999).

22 Willard F. Mallalieu, "The March of the Anglo-Saxon" *Chautauqua Assembly Herald* 8:13 (August 18, 1883), 2–3, quoted in Robert Louis Utlaut, "The Role of the Chautauqua Movement in the Shaping of Progressive Thought in America" (Ph.D. diss., University of Minnesota, 1972), 89–90; Josiah Strong, "An Address," *Chautauqua Assembly Herald* 13:5 (August 9, 1888): 4, quoted in Utlaut, 90; John R. Commons, "Race and Democracy," *The Chautauquan* 38:1 (September 1903): 33–42; William Graham Sumner, "The Social Revolution," *Chautauqua Assembly Herald* 11:13 (August 14, 1886): 2, in Utlaut, 131; Albion Tourgee, "The Christian Citizen" *The Chautauquan* 2:3 (December 1881), see Utlaut, 86–90. Richard T. Ely's special affection for the Chautauqua idea is evident throughout his autobiography *Ground under Our Feet* (1938).

23 "Georgetown CLSC," *Williamson County Sun* (Georgetown, Texas), January 30, 1890, Newspaper Collection, Center for American History, University of Texas at Austin.

24 Rexford Tugwell, *The Light of Other Days* (Garden City, NJ: Doubleday, 1962), 61.

25 Vincent, *The Chautauqua Movement*, vii.

26 Rev. Jasper L. Douthit, *Jasper Douthit's Story: The Autobiography of a Pioneer* (Boston: American Unitarian Association, 1905), 167.

27 See Howard M. Jones, *The Age of Energy: Varieties of American Experience, 1865–1915* (New York: Viking Press, 1971); John G. Sproat, *"The Best Men": Liberal Reformers in the Gilded Age* (New York: Oxford University Press, 1968); George Cotkin, *Reluctant Modernism: American Thought and Culture, 1880–1900* (New York: Twayne Publishers, 1992); David D. Hall, "The Victorian Connection," *American Quarterly* 27, no. 5 (December 1975): 561–574.

28 Vincent, *The Chautauqua Movement*, 114; Vincent, "Chancellor Vincent's Lecture," *Chautauqua Assembly Herald* 9:18 (August 22, 1884): 1.

29 See Peggy K. Pearlstein, "Understanding through Education: One Hundred Years of the Jewish Chautauqua Society, 1893–1993," (Ph.D. diss., George Washington University, 1993); "The Columbian Reading Union," *The Catholic World* 55:327 (June 1892): 466; "A Catholic Chautauqua," *Chautauqua Assembly Herald* 13:15 (August 5, 1892), 1.

30 Ida Husted Harper, *The Life and Work of Susan B. Anthony* (Indianapolis: Bowen-Merrill Company, 1898), 708; Anna Howard Shaw, *Story of a Pioneer* (New York: Harper & Brothers Publishers, 1915), 256–259. Carrie Chapman Catt portrayed Vincent's decision to publish an article in a 1898 anti-suffrage publication "the last struggle of the opposition." "Woman's Day. Addresses by Three Noted Woman Suffragists," *Chautauqua Assembly Herald* 25:5 (July 14, 1900), 1, 5–6. Vincent's opposition to suffrage is most fully laid out in his "Letter to Rev. J. M. Buckley—1894," reprinted in *Why Women Do Not Want the Ballot* (Boston, 1903), Rare Books, Bancroft Library, University of California at Berkeley.

31 The composite figures here are based on the conclusions of four statistical analyses of the CLSC roll books located at the Chautauqua Archives. See Charles Knicker, "The Chautauqua Literary and Scientific Circle, 1878–1914: A Historical Interpretation of an Educational Piety in Industrial America," (Ph.D. diss., Columbia University, 1969); Catherine Kleiner, "Chautauqua and Women: Ladies, Learners, and Leaders, 1874–1920," (M.A. thesis, Duke University, 1989); Stephanie Rath, "Through the Golden Gate: Women and the Chautauqua Movement in Nineteenth-Century America," (B.A. thesis, Yale University, 1995); Mary Lee Talbot, "A School at Home: The Contribution of the Chautauqua Literary and Scientific Circle to Women's Educational Opportunities in the Gilded Age, 1874–1900" (Ph.D. diss., Columbia University, 1997), 133–153. In addition, I have conducted my own analysis of the 1893 CLSC roll books at the Chautauqua Archives, Chautauqua, N.Y.

32 Vincent, *The Chautauqua Movement*, 7; between 1882 and 1893, a total of 27,141 women received CLSC diplomas while 32,684 women graduated from U.S. colleges. Compiled from census statistics and CLSC records by Talbot, 152–153; Zona Gale, "Katytown in the Eighties," *Harper's Magazine*

157 (August 1928), 288–294, reprinted in *Portage, Wisconsin and Other Essays* (New York: Alfred A. Knopf, 1929), 25–42, 27.

33 Virginia Scharff, "Beyond the Narrow Circle: Women and Chautauqua, 1874–1898," (1983) unpub. ms., p. 4. I am indebted to Professor Scharff for providing me with a copy of this essay. See also Jeanne Halgren Kilde, "The 'Predominance of the Feminine' at Chautauqua: Rethinking the Gender-Space Relationship in Victorian America," *Signs* 24, no. 2 (winter 1999): 449–486.

34 Challenging the secularization thesis implies a challenge to the underlying assumptions relied on by women's historians to highlight the politicization of gender in the nineteenth and early twentieth centuries. See Ann Braude, "Women's History Is American Religious History," in Thomas A. Tweed, ed., *ReTelling U.S. Religious History* (Berkeley: University of California Press, 1997), 75–94.

35 Rudyard Kipling, "Chautauquaed," *Pioneer Mail* (1890), repr. in *Abaft the Funnel* (New York: B. W. Dodge & Company, 1909), 180–203, 203; William James to Mrs. James, July 31, 1896, in Henry James, ed., *Letters of William James* (London: Longmans, Green & Co., Ltd., 1926), 43–44; William James, "What Makes a Life Significant" in his *Talks to Teachers on Psychology* ([1899] Cambridge, MA: Harvard University Press, 1983), 150–167, 155, 152, 155, 154. See Trachtenberg, *The Incorporation of America*, 144.

36 Vincent, *The Chautauqua Movement*, 172.

37 See Cindy S. Aron, *Working at Play: A History of Vacations in the United States* (New York: Oxford University Press, 1999).

38 Moore, *Selling God*, 148.

39 Christopher H. Evans, Review of Phillips, *A Kingdom on Earth*, H-Net Book Review, published by H-SHGAPE (February 1999), 3.

40 Jane Addams, "The Subjective Necessity of Social Settlements," (1910). Kevin Mattson defends the progressives on similar grounds in *Creating a Democratic Public: The Struggle for Urban Participatory Democracy during the Progressive Era* (University Park: Pennsylvania State University Press, 1998), 1–13.

41 Emily Raymond, *About Chautauqua: As an Idea, as a Power, and as a Place* (Toledo, OH: Blade Printing & Paper Co., 1886), 1; Millard Fillmore Owen, History of Orange Township (Rome City, IN: American Legion Post 381, n.d.), 59–65.

42 See Paula Baker, *The Moral Frameworks of Public Life: Gender, Politics, and the State in Rural New York, 1870–1930* (New York: Oxford University Press, 1991).

43 On the circuit Chautauquas, see John S. Noffsinger, *Correspondence Schools, Lyceums, Chautauquas* (New York: The Macmillan Company, 1926); David Mead, "1914: The Chautauqua and American Innocence," *Journal of Popular Culture* 1, no. 4 (spring 1968): 339–356; R. Alan Hedges, "Actors under Canvas: A Study of the Theatre of the Circuit Chautauqua, 1910–1933," (Ph.D. diss., Ohio State University, 1976); Janice P. Dawson, "Chautauqua and the Utah Performing Arts," *Utah Historical Quarterly* 58, no. 2 (spring 1990): 131–144; Greg Alan Phelps, "Popular Culture in Crisis: Circuit Chautauqua during the First World War" (Ph.D. diss., University of Iowa, 1994).

44 Quoted in Stephen Schlosnagle, *Garrett County: A History of Maryland's Tableland* (Parsons, W.V.: Garrett County Bicentennial Committee, 1978), 290–307, 297; S. D. Chaney to George E. Vincent, March 27, 1900, Folder 1, George Vincent's Letters 1890–1900, Chautauqua Archives, Chautauqua, N.Y.

45 See Kenneth T. Jackson, *Crabgrass Frontier: The Suburbanization of the United States* (New York: Oxford University Press, 1985), 20–156; Marc A. Weiss, *The Rise of the Community Builders: The American Real Estate Industry and Urban Land Planning* (New York: Columbia University Press, 1987), 40–48; Mary Corbin Sies, "The City Transformed: Nature, Technology, and the Suburban Ideal, 1877–1917," *Journal of Urban History* 14, no. 1 (November 1987): 81–111, 83.

46 Shailer Mathews, *The Individual and the Social Gospel* (New York: Missionary Education Movement of the United States and Canada, 1914), 67, 4.

47 As Nell Irvin Painter argues, "there were working classes and middle classes, not only agricultural and industrial, but also of many ethnicities and races." Painter, *Standing at Armageddon: The United States, 1877–1919* (New York: W. W. Norton & Co., 1987), xxiv.

The Middle Is Material

1   C. Dallett Hemphill, *Bowing to Necessities: a History of Manners in America, 1620–1860* (New York: Oxford University Press, 1999); Richard L. Bushman, *The Refinement of America: Persons, Houses, Cities* (New York: Alfred A. Knopf, 1992); Carole Shammas, *The Pre-Industrial Consumer in England*

and America (Oxford: Clarendon Press, 1990); *American Economic Growth and Standards of Living before the Civil War*, ed. Robert E. Gallman and John Joseph Wallis (Chicago: University of Chicago Press, 1992).

2   *A Philadelpha Perspective; the Diary of Sidney George Fisher Covering the Years 1834–1871*, ed. Nicholas B. Wainwright (Philadelphia: Historical Society of Pennsylvania, 1967), 218.

3   Walt Whitman, *Notebooks and Unpublished Prose Manuscripts*, ed. Edward F. Grier (New York: New York University Press, 1984), II: Washington, 540; III: Camden, 1078.

Cartes de Visite Portrait Photographs and the Culture of Class Formation

A previous version of this essay won the 1996 Wise-Susman Prize awarded by the American Studies Association. Thanks to Wendy Kozol, Angela L. Miller, Jennifer Ratner-Rosenhagen, and the 1999–2000 Pembroke Seminar at Brown University for their comments. This essay is dedicated to my husband, Sam Walker.

1   Herman Melville, *Pierre, or the Ambiguities*, quoted in Robert Sobieszek and Odette M. Appel, *Spirit of Fact: the Daguerreotypes of Southworth and Hawes* (Rochester and Boston: D. R. Godine, 1976), xxi.

2   "Photographic Eminence," *Humphrey's Journal*, July 15, 1864: 93–94.

3   "The Photographic Art a Blessing to the World—Cartes de Visite," *American Journal of Photography*, August 15, 1862: 77.

4   On nineteenth-century photography, see William Darrah, *Cartes de Visite in Nin[e]teenth-Century Photography* (Gettysburg, PA: W. C. Darrah, 1981); Elizabeth Edwards, ed., *Anthropology and Photography* (New Haven, CT: Yale University Press, 1992); Mary Panzer, *Mathew Brady and the Image of History* (Washington, DC: Smithsonian Institution Press, 1997); Robert Taft, *Photography and the American Scene* (New York: Dover, 1964); John Tagg, *The Burden of Representation: Essays on Photographies and Histories* (Amherst: University of Massachusetts, 1988); Alan Trachtenberg, "Photography: The Emergence of a Key Word," in *Photography in Nineteenth-Century America*, ed. Martha Sandweiss (New York and Ft. Worth: Harry N. Abrams, 1991), 17–47; Laura Wexler, "Tender Violence: Literary Eavesdropping, Domestic Fiction and Educational Reform," in Shirley Samuels, ed., *The Culture of Sentiment: Race, Gender and Sentimentality in Nineteenth-Century America* (New York: Oxford University Press, 1992), 9–38; Susan S. Williams, *Confounding Images: Photography and Portraiture in Antebellum American Fiction* (Philadelphia: University of Pennsylvania Press, 1997).

5   Jane Tompkins, *Sensational Designs: The Cultural Work of American Fiction, 1790–1860* (New York: Oxford University Press, 1985), xi and xvi.

6   David Jaffee, "'One of the Primitive Sort': Portrait Makers of the Rural North, 1790–1860," in *The Countryside in the Age of Capitalist Transformation*, ed. Steven Hahn and Jonathan Prude (Chapel Hill: University of Chapel Hill Press, 1985), 130 and 104, respectively.

7   Michel Foucault, *The History of Sexuality*, Vol. 1, trans. Robert Hurley (New York: Pantheon Books, 1978), 126.

8   Patricia O'Brien, "Michel Foucault's History of Culture," in *The New Cultural History*, ed. Lynn Hunt (Berkeley: University of California Press, 1989), 25.

9   Wai Chee Dimock and Michael Gilmore, eds., *Rethinking Class: Literary Studies of Social Formation* (New York: Columbia University Press, 1994), 2.

10   Foucault, *History of Sexuality*, 102.

11   Michel Foucault, *Discipline and Punish*, trans. Alan Sheridan (New York: Pantheon Books, 1979), 112.

12   Edward L. Wilson, "Trouble in the Studio," *Photographic Mosaics* (Philadelphia, 1869), 131.

13   "Sitting for a Picture," *American Journal of Photography*, Feb. 15, 1863: 367.

14   "Having Your Photograph Taken," *American Journal of Photography*, Jan. 1, 1863: 292.

15   M. De Valincourt, "Photographic Portraiture, Continued; On Likeness in Photographic Portraits," *Humphrey's Journal*, March 15, 1862.

16   H. Garbanati, "The Influence of the Operator on the Sitter," *American Journal of Photography*, Oct. 1, 1858: 134–136; F. Welch, "A Few Hints on the Best Means of Obtaining Good Cartes de Visite," *Humphrey's Journal*, June 15, 1865: 59–60.

17   A. K. P. Trask, *Trask's Practical Ferrotyper* (Philadelphia 1872, repr. in Robert A. Sobieszek, *The Collodion Process and the Ferrotype, Three Accounts, 1854–1872* [New York: Benerman and Wilson, 1973]), 49–50.

18   Disderi, "The Aesthetics of Photography, Continued," *Humphrey's Journal*, Sept. 15, 1863: 155.

19   "Troubles of a Photographer," *Humphrey's Journal*, Jan. 1, 1865: 265.

20 Morton, "Photography Indoors," *Philadelphia Photographer*, July 1864: 105.

21 John Towler, *The Silver Sunbeam* (New York: J. H. Ladd, 1864; repr. Hastings-on-Hudson, NY: Morgan & Morgan,), 31.

22 Edward L. Wilson, "Trouble in the Studio," *Photographic Mosaics* (Philadelphia, 1869), 131.

23 Cynthia Eagle Russett, *Sexual Science: The Victorian Construction of Womanhood* (Cambridge, MA: Harvard University Press, 1989), 7.

24 For the pervasive and general influence of phrenology and physiognomy on nineteenth-century life, see Allan Sekula, "The Body and the Archive," *October* 39 (winter 1986): 3–64; John Davies, *Phrenology, Fad and Science: A 19th-Century American Crusade* (New Haven, CT: Yale University Press, 1955); Madeleine B. Stern, *Heads and Headlines: The Phrenological Fowlers* (Norman: University of Oklahoma Press, 1971), 214; John F. Kasson, *Rudeness and Civility: Manners in Nineteenth-Century Urban America* (New York: Hill and Wang, 1990), 96–97.

25 "Photography and Truth," *Philadelphia Photographer*, November 1876: 323.

26 The editor of *Humphrey's Journal*, Dr. John Towler, was professor of mathematics, natural philosophy, and modern languages at Hobart College, as well as professor of chemistry, pharmacy, and dean of the medical faculty at the Geneva Medical College in New York state. Towler published his photographic manual, *The Silver Sunbeam*, in 1864; the book went through four editions within the next ten months. "Important Editorial Change," *Humphrey's Journal*, July 1, 1862: 17. Beaumont Newhall, introduction to *The Silver Sunbeam* (New York: J. H. Ladd, 1864; repr. Hastings-on-Hudson, NY: Morgan & Morgan); and Stanley H. Burns, "Early Medical Photographs in America, 1839–1883, part II," *New York State Journal of Medicine* 79 (May 1979): 943–944. Charles A. Seely, founder of the *American Journal of Photography* in 1855, was a chemist by training and had worked at *Scientific American* and served as professor of chemistry at New York Medical College. While working as a chemist, book dealer, and publisher of photographic titles, Seely edited the photography journal until 1867.

27 Disderi, "The Aesthetics of Photography, Continued," *Humphrey's Journal*, Aug. 15, 1863: 127.

28 "Anatomy, Phrenology, and Physiognomy, and Their Relation to Photography, No. 2," *Philadelphia Photographer*, April 1876: 103; E. D. Ormsby, "Defects in Our Sitters," *Photographic Mosaics*, 1875: 31; "A Hint for Posing the Sitter," *Photographic Mosaics*, 1866: 59–60; W. H. Lipton, "Anatomy, Phrenology and Physiognomy, and Their Relation to Photography, No. 1," *Philadelphia Photographer*, February 1876: 53–54; "How to Sit for a Photograph," *Photographic Mosaics*, 1866: 46–50.

29 Oliver Wendell Holmes, "Doings of the Sunbeam," *Atlantic Monthly*, July 1863: 9.

30 See Root, "Some Items, Relating to the Process of Sitting for a Heliographic Portrait," *Photographic and Fine Arts Journal*, September 1858: 263.

31 "The Treatment of the Sitter," *Anthony's Photographic Bulletin*, December 1873: 377.

32 "Position and Composition," *Photographic World*, June 1871: 25.

33 Rev. A. A. E. Taylor, "The Photographer's Study of Character," *Philadelphia Photographer*, October 1864: 151.

34 Root, *Camera and the Pencil*, 253.

35 "A Few Words on Portraiture," *American Journal of Photography*, Aug. 1, 1863: 50.

36 "The Aesthetics of Photography," *Humphrey's Journal*, September 15, 1863: 154.

37 H. J. Rodgers, *Twenty-three Years Under a Skylight, or Life and Experiences of a Photographer* (Hartford, CT: H. J. Rogers, 1872; repr., New York: Hill and Wang, 1973), 148–157.

38 Sekula, "The Body and the Archive"; Brian Wallis, "White Science, Black Bodies: Louis Agassiz's Slave Daguerreotypes," *American Art* 9 (summer 1995): 39–61.

39 Mary Kupiec Cayton, "The Making of an American Prophet: Emerson, His Audiences and the Rise of Cultural Industry in Nineteenth-Century America," *American Historical Review* 92 (1987): 615.

40 Foucault, *Discipline and Punish*, 104.

41 Richard Brodhead, "Sparing the Rod: Discipline and Fiction in Antebellum America," *Representations* 21 (winter 1988): 144.

Public Exposure

1 Matlack Price, "Great Modern Hotels of America," *Arts and Decoration*, Vol. 21, July 1924: 39.

2 Reed & Barton Collection, Harvard Business School, Box B. A-10, File: Reed & Barton Letters — Correspondence with agents, domestic and foreign, 1866–1875; subsequent references to this collection will be designated "R&B Coll." with the appropriate box or volume references.

3 Oscar Lewis and Carroll D. Hall, *Bonanza Inn: America's First Luxury Hotel* (New York: Alfred A. Knopf, 1939), passim, especially chapter 1, "Show Place."

4   While I will focus in this essay on the examples of silverplate flatware and bathroom fixtures, Katherine Grier has advanced a similar argument about upholstered furniture in *Culture and Comfort: Parlor
Making and Middle-Class Identity, 1850–1930* (Washington, DC: Smithsonian Institution Press,
1997).

5   Norman S. Hayner, *Hotel Life* (Chapel Hill: University of North Carolina Press, 1936), 22, 79; J.
Anthony Lukas, *Big Trouble: A Murder in a Small Western Town Sets Off a Struggle for the Soul of America* (New York: Simon & Schuster, 1997), 511–512.

6   Edmund P. Hogan, *An American Heritage: A Book about the International Silver Company* (Dallas:
Taylor Publishing Co., 1977), 65; George Sweet Gibb, *The Whitesmiths of Taunton: A History of Reed
and Barton, 1824–1943* (Cambridge, MA: Harvard University Press, 1943), 187–188, 254–255.

7   Mark Twain and Charles Dudley Warner, *The Gilded Age: A Tale of To-Day* (New York: Harper &
Bros., 1903, repr. 1873); John F. Kasson, *Civilizing the Machine: Technology and Republican Values in
America, 1776–1900* (New York: Penguin, 1977), 161–165.

8   In fact, the country was not always prosperous in this generation; in both the early 1870s and the
early 1890s, widespread financial distress settled on the country. But even then, those who could
masked those financial conditions with the abundant production, and consumption, of material culture.

9   For background on the Gilded Age and Progressive Era, see Steven J. Diner, *A Very Different Age:
Americans of the Progressive Era* (New York: Hill & Wang, 1998); Richard Hofstadter, *The Age of
Reform* (New York: Vintage, 1955); Nell Irvin Painter, *Standing at Armageddon: The United States,
1877–1919* (New York: W. W. Norton, 1987); Alan Trachtenberg, *The Incorporation of America: Culture and Society in the Gilded Age* (New York: Hill & Wang, 1982); Gwendolyn Wright, *Moralism and
the Model Home: Domestic Architecture and Cultural Conflict in Chicago 1873–1913* (Chicago: University of Chicago Press, 1980).

10 Price, "Great Modern Hotels of America," 40.

11 R&B Coll., Box B. A-10, File: Reed & Barton Letters—Correspondence with agents, domestic and
foreign, 1866–1875; Gibb, 189.

12 I am using the term "flatware" to encompass fork, spoon, and knife, though originally, and still sometimes today, knives are separately classed as cutlery, while flatware meant the fork and spoon only.

13 Gibb, *The Whitesmiths,* 217–218; Hogan, *American Heritage,* 65; Susan Williams, *Savory Suppers &
Fashionable Feasts: Dining in Victorian America* (New York: Pantheon Books in association with the
Strong Museum, 1985), 8.

14 R&B Coll., Fiske letter books, Vol. 148, 24, January 18, 1877.

15 On magazines, consumer culture, and gender, see Richard Ohmann, *Selling Culture: Magazines,
Markets, and Class at the Turn of the Century* (London: Verso, 1996); Eleen Gruber Garvey, *The
Adman in the Parlor: Magazines and the Gendering of Consumer Culture, 1880s to 1910s* (New York:
Oxford University Press, 1996); Jennifer Scanlon, *Inarticulate Longings: The Ladies' Home Journal,
Gender, and the Promises of Consumer Culture* (New York: Routledge, 1995).

16 "How Delmonico Sets a Table," *Ladies' Home Journal,* November 1891, as cited in Charles Venable,
Silver in America, 1840–1940: A Century of Splendor (Dallas: Dallas Museum of Art, 1995), 127–128.

17 R&B Coll., Vol. 188, 1878–1882.

18 R&B Coll., Volume D-1, *Electro Gold and Silver Plate Catalogue,* 1882.

19 *Jeweler's Circular and Horological Review,* Vol. 16 (November 1885): 314; (January 1886): 389–390.

20 Gibb, *The Whitesmiths,* 217–218, 256; R&B Coll., Vol. 206, Scrapbook; Box A-4, File 2: Payrolls,
1829, 1903–15, Payroll Expense 5/1/1905–5/1/1906.

21 R&B Coll., Vol. 181, Letter book of Philadelphia branch office, 2–4, 7, 10, 23–24, 33.

22 Clifford E. Clark, Jr., "The Vision of the Dining Room: Plan Book Dreams and Middle-Class Realities," in *Dining in America, 1850–1900,* ed. Kathryn Grover (Amherst: University of Massachusetts
Press, 1987) 142–171; Williams, *Savory Suppers,* 51–90; Venable, *Silver in America,* 124–125.

23 Christopher J. Berry, *The Idea of Luxury: A Conceptual and Historical Investigation* (New York: Cambridge University Press, 1994).

24 Theodore Dreiser, *Jennie Gerhardt* ([1911] Cleveland: World Publishing Co., 1954), 199.

25 John F. Kasson, "Rituals of Dining: Table Manners in Victorian America," in *Dining in America,
1850–1900,* ed. Kathryn Grover (Amherst: University of Massachusetts Press, 1987), 119–139;
Williams, *Savory Suppers,* ix, 21–22, 75–78; Venable, *Silver in America,* 137–139; Arthur M.
Schlesinger, *Learning How to Behave: An Historical Study of American Etiquette Books* (New York:
Macmillan, 1946), passim.

26 Kohler Company Archives, Kohler, Wisconsin, *Catalogue "K,"* 1914. All subsequent references to this archive will be designated "KCA," with the appropriate volume or box listing. See also, William Leach, *Land of Desire: From the Department Store to the Department of Commerce: The Rise of America's Commercial Culture* (New York: Pantheon, 1993), 151–154.

27 Jefferson Williamson, *The American Hotel: An Anecdotal History* (New York: Alfred A. Knopf, 1930), 23, 36, 55.

28 Frederick Hammill, "Great Modern Hotels of America," *Arts and Decoration*, Vol. 23, August 1925, 46.

29 KCA, *Kohler of Kohler News*, Vol. 1, November 1916: 4; March 1917: 7; Vol. 2, April 1918: 10; Vol. 3, January 1919: 9.

30 Sinclair Lewis, *Babbitt* ([1922] New York: Penguin Books, 1996), 131.

31 KCA, 2–100: 658.84: Kohler Company: Plumbing, Sales Action Manual, Kohler Sales Helps, 1, 28, and passim.

32 KCA, 2–100: 659.13 Kohler Company: Plumbing, Consumer Ads, 1920–24.

33 Hayner, *Hotel Life*, 179–180.

34 Robert Schweitzer and Michael W. R. Davis, *America's Favorite Homes: Mail-Order Catalogues as a Guide to Popular Early Twentieth-Century Houses* (Detroit: Wayne State University Press, 1990).

35 Aladdin Company Archive, Clarke Historical Library, Central Michigan University, Mt. Pleasant, Michigan, Catalog #30, 1918, 86. Subsequent references to this collection will be designated "ACA," with the appropriate volume or box reference.

36 Lewis, *Babbitt*, 12.

37 ACA, *The Wedge*, Vol. 1, April 1913: 9.

38 Matlack Price, "Great Modern Hotels of America," *Arts and Decoration*, Vol. 21, June 1924: 27.

39 ACA, *The Wedge*, Vol. 6, February 1916: 3–4.

40 ACA, Box 7, Folder: 1920: "Low Cost Homes Designed Especially For Industrial Purposes."

41 Lukas, *Big Trouble*, 511.

42 Jessica B. Peixotto, *Getting and Spending at the Professional Standard of Living: A Study of the Costs of Living and Academic Life* (New York: Macmillan Co., 1927); Robert S. Lynd and Helen Merrell Lynd, *Middletown: A Study in Modern American Culture* (New York: Harcourt, Brace, & Co., 1929).

Obstacles to History

I wish to thank George Chauncey, Kathleen Conzen, Robert Johnston, William Novak, Susan Radomsky, Mark Schmeller, David Tanenhaus, Michael Willrich, and my colleagues at Syracuse for their support and helpful readings of the text.

1 A number of labor historians have defended nineteenth-century craft workers. See Sean Wilentz, *Chants Democratic: New York and the Rise of the American Working Class, 1788–1850* (New York: Oxford University Press, 1984). But scholars tend to chide twentieth-century craft workers who refused to abandon protocapitalist identities. See for example, Dana Frank, *Purchasing Power: Consumer Organizing, Gender, and the Seattle Labor Movement, 1919–1929* (New York: Cambridge University Press, 1994), 167, 200–204, 224–227; Daniel Ernst, *Lawyers against Labor: From Individual Rights to Corporate Liberalism* (Chicago: University of Illinois, 1995); Robert H. Wiebe, *Businessmen and Reform: A Study of the Progressive Movement* (Chicago: Ivan R. Dee, 1962), 167. Mansel Blackford notes the paucity of scholarship on the small businessperson in "Small Business in America: A Historiographic Survey," *Business History Review* 65 (spring 1991): 1–26, esp. 10–11. Arthur M. Schlesinger, Jr., *The Politics of Upheaval* (Boston: Houghton Mifflin, 1960), 69; Seymour Martin Lipset, *The Politics of Unreason: Right Wing Extremism in America, 1790–1970* (Evanston, IL: Harper Torchbooks, 1970), 178.

2 Anthony Giddens, *Capitalism and Modern Social Theory* (New York: Cambridge University Press, 1971), 163. In his clarion call for historians to analyze the lower middle class, Arno Mayer argues that Marxists are not alone in presupposing that the petite bourgeoisie disappeared in the twentieth century. See "The Lower Middle Class as a Historical Problem," *Journal of Modern History* 47, no. 3 (September 1975): 409; Giddens, 165. For Weber's view of class formation, see Max Weber, "Class, Status, Party" in *From Max Weber: Essays in Sociology*, ed. H. H. Gerth and C. Wright Mills (New York: Oxford University Press, 1946), 181–196. Marx's most notable description of the role of craft workers and small businessmen in the revolution is in the *Communist Manifesto*. See *The Marx-Engels Reader*, ed. Robert C. Tucker, 2nd ed. (New York: Norton, 1978), 479–480, 182, 267–271.

3 C. Wright Mills, *White Collar: The American Middle Classes* (New York: Oxford University Press,

1951); Daniel Bell, *The Coming of Post-Industrial Society: A Venture in Social Forecasting* (New York: Basic Books, 1973). Lenin called craft workers a "labour aristocracy," a term indicating both privilege and a feudal heritage. Lenin, *"Left Wing" Communism: An Infantile Disorder* (New York: International, 1940). Similarly, Antonio Gramsci condemned American skilled workers for engaging in a "defence [sic] of craft rights against 'industrial liberty'," fighting a war "similar to the struggle that took place in Europe in the eighteenth century." Antonio Gramsci, "Americanism and Fordism," in *Selections from the Prison Notebooks*, ed. Quintin Hoare and Geoffrey Nowell Smith (New York: International Publishers, 1992), 286. Ernest Mandel, *Maxistische Wirtschaftstheorie*, in George Steinmetz and Erik Olin Wright, "The Fall and Rise of the Petty Bourgeoisie: Changing Patterns of Self-Employment in the Postwar United States," *American Journal of Sociology* 94, no. 5 (March 1989): 982.

4 Dorothy Sue Cobble, *Dishing It Out: Waitresses and the Unions in the Twentieth Century* (Urbana, IL: University of Illinois Press, 1991), 7; Michael Kazin, *Barons of Labor: The San Francisco Building Trades and Union Power in the Progressive Era* (Chicago: University of Illinois Press, 1989); Georg Leidenberger, "'The Public is the Labor Union': Working-Class Progressivism in Turn-of-the-Century Chicago," *Labor History* 36, no. 2 (spring 1995): 187–210; Philip Scranton, *Proprietary Capitalists: Textile Manufacture at Philadelphia, 1800–1885* (New York: Cambridge, 1983) and *Figured Tapestry: Production, Markets and Power in Philadelphia Textiles, 1885–1941* (New York: Cambridge, 1989); Mansel G. Blackford, *A History of Small Business in America* (New York: Twayne Publishers, 1991), esp. 53–57; Olivier Zunz, *The Changing Face of Inequality: Urbanization, Industrial Development, and Immigrants in Detroit, 1880–1920* (Chicago: University of Chicago, 1982), 5, 200–217; Alan Brinkley, *Voices of Protest: Huey Long, Father Coughlin, and the Great Depression* (New York: Vintage, 1983), 194–215, esp. 198, 201; Mayer, "The Lower Middle Class as a Historical Problem," 434–436; Jonathan Wiener, "Marxism and the Lower Middle Class: A Response to Arno Mayer," *Journal of Modern History* 48, no. 4 (December 1976): 666–671.

5 Dipesh Chakrabarty, *Rethinking Working-Class History: Bengal, 1890–1940* (Princeton, NJ: Princeton University Press, 1989), 226; Alice Kessler-Harris, "Treating the Male as 'Other': Redefining the Parameters of Labor History," *Labor History* 34 (1993): 192; Christopher Tomlins, "Why Wait for Industrialism? Work, Legal Culture, and the Example of Early America—An Historiographical Argument," *Labor History* 40, no. 1 (February 1999): 5–34.

6 Hugo S. Grosser, *Chicago: A Review of its Governmental History from 1837 to 1906* (Chicago: Municipal Information Bureau, 1906), 74. Richard Hofstadter noted the effects of urbanization on small-scale enterprise in the city's service sector in *The Age of Reform: From Bryan to F.D.R.* (New York: Vintage, 1951), 220.

7 In the category "building trades," I count carpenters, electricians, masons, painters, plumbers, roofers, stonecutters, brick makers, paperhangers, cabinetmakers, and plasterers. For male "service trades," I count barbers, bartenders, bootblacks, janitors, launderers, servants, waiters, watchmen, police, and firemen. For women, I count barbers, housekeepers, janitors, laundresses, servants, and waitresses. Bureau of the Census, Special Reports, *Occupations at the Twelfth Census* (Washington, DC: Government Printing Office, 1904), 516–523.

8 Because the census groups retail and wholesale bakers together, it is difficult to determine the extent of retail baking in the city. A quick inspection of the city directory shows that only thirty-two were wholesalers. *Census of Manufactures*, 1905, 232; *Lakeside Directory*, 1902, 2235. The two most common occupations were "Laborers (not specified)" and "Clerks and copyists." Included in the category "retail dealer" are managers and superintendents of stores. Also, I shift here to 1910 because the categories are clearer as to whether a dressmaker worked inside or outside a factory. Bureau of the Census, Special Reports, *Occupations at the Twelfth Census* (Washington, DC: Government Printing Office, 1904), 516–23; Bureau of the Census, *Thirteenth Census of the United States taken in the year 1910, v. IV, Population, 1910: Occupations* (Washington, DC: Government Printing Office, 1914), 544–547.

9 *Occupations at the Twelfth Census*, 516–523. In certain crafts, such as baking, painting, woodworking, butchering, hod carrying, printing, and tailoring, Polish, Bohemian, Jewish, and Italian workers were populous enough to demand separate union locals. *Lakeside Directory*, 1906, 72–73. The proportion of each nationality in different occupations changed as immigration continued and manufacturing employment grew. It is difficult, however, to estimate these changes, as the census abandoned the ethnic breakdowns in 1910.

10 Ursula B. Stone, "The Baking Industry with Special Reference to the Bread Baking Industry of

Chicago" (Ph.D. diss., University of Chicago, School of Commerce, 1929), 124; John Commons, "Types of American Labor Organization—The Teamsters of Chicago," *Quarterly Journal of Economics* 19 (1905): 414–420; Robert A. Christie, *Empire in Wood: A History of the Carpenters Union* (Ithaca, NY: Cornell University, 1956), 19–28, 79–82.

11 *Lakeside Directory*, 1902, 2651–2652. These figures are from accounts of the teamsters' strike of 1905. Luke Grant, "Rights and Wrongs of the Chicago Strike," *Public Opinion* 38, no. 23 (June 10, 1905): 888–889; Commons, "Types of American Labor Organizations," 403–406; *Census of Manufactures*, 1905, v. II, 232–233. Generally speaking, the *Census of Manufactures* gives a misleading portrait of the scale of business enterprise because it omits construction, service, and retail in its estimates of firm size, effectively cutting out the city's smallest employers. *Census of Manufactures*, 1914, v. I, (Washington, DC: Government Printing Office, 1918), 338–340.

12 For Kidd's comment, see Hutchins Hapgood, *The Spirit of Labor* (New York: Duffield & Company, 1907), 361. Montgomery estimated that over half the city's subcontractors had once been journeymen. Royal E. Montgomery, *Industrial Relations in the Chicago Building Trades* (Chicago: University of Chicago, 1927), 7, 30. For Robinson's comments, see Testimony before Master of Chancery, 6 July 1899, *Union Pressed Brick v. Chicago Hydraulic Press Brick et al.*, case no. 196935 in the Circuit Court of Cook County (1899), 27–28.

13 *Industrial Chicago: The Building Interests*, Vol. 1 (Chicago: Goodspeed Publishing, 1891), 670. Daniel T. Rogers, *The Work Ethic in Industrial America: 1850–1920* (Chicago: University of Chicago Press, 1978), 35–39.

14 The same day, five hundred northside grocery clerks staged a parade down North Avenue, seeking to encourage shopkeepers to close at 6 P.M. on Wednesdays and Fridays. All but one complied with the request. "Disorder Marks Barbers Fight for Early Closing," *Chicago Daily Tribune*, May 28, 1903, 3.

15 "The Teaming Contractor: A Glimpse into the Future," *Chicago Team Owners' Journal*—Special Edition, May 1910, 1.

16 *The Book of Chicagoans* (Chicago: A. N. Marquis, 1905), 341.

17 Christie, *Empire in Wood*, 19–28; George E. Barrett, "The Stonecutters' Union and the Stone-Planer." *Journal of Political Economy* 25, no. 5 (May 1916): 417–420.

18 George W. Jackson, "Freight Tunnels in Chicago," *Independent* 57:3 (1904): 1018–1022; William Hard, "Building the Chicago Subway," *Public Opinion* 38, no. 20 (May 20, 1905): 769; Glenn A. Bishop, *Chicago's Accomplishments and Leaders* (Chicago: Bishop Publishing, 1932), 482–488. These tunnels flooded spectacularly in 1992. "Maze Down Under Opened in '04," *Chicago Sun-Times*, April 14, 1992, 18.

19 "Old King Coal," *Chicago Tribune*, May 18, 1994, Sec. C, 1–2.

20 "SHARKEY," typescript in Howard Levansellaer Willett Papers, Chicago Historical Society, 3.

21 Carroll Lawrence Christensen, *Collective Bargaining in Chicago: 1929–30: A Study of the Economic Significance of the Industrial Location of Trade-Unionism* (Chicago: University of Chicago Press, 1933), 8, 11, 13, 15, 17, 27.

22 "Indict Leaders of the Strikers," *Chicago Daily Tribune*, May 30, 1905, 2; *Lakeside Directory*, 1917, 157; *James B. Barry v. Thomas C. Platt*, Case File #244201 in the Superior Court of Cook County (1905).

23 Industrial Commission, *Report of the Industrial Commission on the Chicago Labor Disputes of 1900 with Especial reference to the Disputes in the Building and Machinery Trades*, v. 8 (Washington, DC: Government Printing Office, 1901), v. 8, 479; *Industrial Chicago: The Building Interests*, v. 1, 579, 673, 786; *Lakeside Directory*, 1906, 63; Industrial Commission *Reports*, v. 8, 233; *Lakeside Directory*, 1912, 564.

24 Ernest Bogart, "Chicago Building Trades Dispute. II," *Political Science Quarterly* 16:2 (1901): 227–228; Industrial Commission, *Reports*, v. 8, 6, 395, 244; Luke Grant, "Rise and Fall of Skinny," *Chicago Record-Herald*, May 30, 1909, 3; Eugene Staley, *History of the Illinois State Federation of Labor* (Chicago: University of Chicago Press, 1930), 185; Jane Addams, "The Present Crisis in Trades-Union Morals," *North American Review* 179 (August 1904): 188; Hoyt King, *Citizen Cole of Chicago* (Chicago: Holders, 1931), 60.

25 "Tips on Aldermen By Voters' League," *Chicago Record-Herald*, April 1, 1905, 3; "Council Chosen is Republican," *Chicago Tribune*, April 5, 1905, 4; Carter H. Harrison II, *Growing Up with Chicago* (Chicago: Bobbs-Merrill, 1944), 233–234; Irving Dillard, "William Lorimer," *Dictionary of American Biography*, v. 11 (New York: Scribners & Sons, 1931), 511–512; Joel A. Tarr, *A Study in Boss Politics: William Lorimer of Chicago* (Urbana: University of Illinois, 1971).

26 "Tips on Aldermen by Voters' League," *Chicago Record-Herald*, April 1, 1905, 3; *Lakeside Directory*,

1902, 519; *Lakeside Directory*, 1910, 335; *Lakeside Directory*, 1917, 420; Montgomery, 286–287; "Thomas Curran Dies in Auto Crash," *Chicago Daily Tribune*, November 13, 1928, 1; Harrison, *Growing Up*, 225; "Bullies Aid his Plans," *Chicago Times-Herald*, August 19, 1900, 3; John Landesco, *Organized Crime in Chicago*, part 3 of the Illinois Crime Survey, 1929 (Chicago: University of Chicago Press, 1968), 121–124.

27 John Mangan, *History of the Steam Fitters Protective Association of Chicago* (Chicago: Steam Fitters Protective Association, 1930), 38, 24; "The Object of the Parade for Owners and Drivers," *Chicago Team Owners' Journal*—Special Edition, May 1910, 2; Bill, September 12, 1904, *Doehne v. Chicago Federation of Musicians*, case #255329 in the Circuit Court of Cook County (1904).

28 Ray Stannard Baker, "Capital and Labor Hunt Together," *McClure's Magazine* 21 (1903): 453, 451.

29 The Chicago Commission on Race Relations, *The Negro in Chicago* (Chicago: University of Chicago Press, 1922), 414–420; Oscar D. Hutton, Jr., "The Negro Worker and the Labor Unions in Chicago" (M.A. thesis, University of Chicago, 1939), 25–37; Bureau of the Census, Special Reports, *Occupations at the Twelfth Census* (Washington, DC: Government Printing Office, 1904), 516–523. For the experience of black replacement workers between 1902 and 1905, see William M. Tuttle, *Race Riot: Chicago in the Red Summer of 1919* (New York: Atheneum, 1970), 120–123. For women as strikebreakers during this period, see Emily Clark Brown, *Book and Job Printing in Chicago* (Chicago: University of Chicago Press, 1931), 83–87.

30 The author of this quote was a steamfitter. Not coincidentally, between 1902 and 1912, the steamfitters and the plumbers—both skilled white male unions—fought one of history's bloodiest jurisdictional battles. This bitter feud suggests that these organizations excluded not only black and female workers from the labor market, but also white male craft unionists who threatened their governing authority. Mangan, *History of the Steam-fitters*, 13; Nathaniel Ruggles Whitney, *Jurisdiction in American Building-Trades Unions* (Baltimore: Johns Hopkins University Press, 1914), 135. For the economic function of racial exclusion, see Eric Arnesen, "Like Banquo's Ghost, It Will Not Down": The Race Question and the American Railroad Brotherhoods, 1880–1920," *American Historical Review* 99, no. 5 (December 1994): 1601–1633.

31 Commons, "Types of American Labor Organization," 406; Baker, "Capital and Labor Hunt Together," 455; Ernest Poole, "How a Labor Machine Held Up Chicago, and How the Teamsters Union Smashed the Machine," *The World To-Day* 7, no. 1 (July 1904): 898.

32 For the view of corporations as progressive advocates of the trade agreement, see Ernst, *Lawyers against Labor*, 7–8. For the opposing view, see David Montgomery, *Workers' Control in America* (New York: Cambridge University Press, 1992), 82; Alfred H. Kelly, "A History of the Illinois Manufacturers' Association" (Ph.D. diss., University of Chicago, 1938), 33–34, 21. For a discussion of the business elite and the teamsters, see Andrew Wender Cohen, "The Struggle for Order: Law, Labor, and Resistance to the Corporate Ideal in Chicago, 1900–1940" (Ph.D. diss., University of Chicago, 1999), 127–132, 170–182.

33 Some historians argue that corporate associations influenced New Deal policy. Others see industrial workers as the progenitors of the New Deal. In my larger work, I contend that the lower middle class controlled the political organizations that elected Roosevelt. I also suggest that urban trade agreements inspired New Deal architects like Raymond Moley. Robert Himmelberg, *The Origins of the National Recovery Administration* (New York: Fordham University Press, 1993); Colin Gordon, *New Deals: Business, Labor, and Politics in America, 1920–1935* (New York: Cambridge University Press, 1994); Lizabeth Cohen, *Making a New Deal: Industrial Workers in Chicago, 1919–1939* (New York: Cambridge University Press, 1990), 251–289; Cohen, "The Struggle for Order," 268–280. For the occupational composition of the Kelly-Nash machine, see Harold F. Gosnell, *Machine Politics: Chicago Model* (Chicago: University of Chicago Press, 1937), 47.

The Corporate Reconstruction of Middle-Class Manhood

1 Victor Willard, "Making $5 grow to Millions: How the Pepperdines, with Team Work and Courage, Have Built a Chain of Stores," *Sunset Magazine* (August 1925): 30–31, 56.

2 Thomas C. Cochran, *Challenges to American Values: Society, Business, and Religion* (New York: Oxford University Press, 1985), 64–65.

3 I explore the social and cultural dynamics of corporate emergence more broadly in *Company Men: White-Collar Life and Corporate Cultures in Los Angeles* (Baltimore: Johns Hopkins University Press, 2000). See also: Sharon Hartman Strom, *Beyond the Typewriter: Gender, Class, and the Origins of Modern American Office Work, 1900–1930* (Urbana: University of Illinois Press, 1992); Oliver Zunz,

Making America Corporate, 1870–1920 (Chicago: University of Chicago Press, 1990); Angel Kwolek-Folland, *Engendering Business: Men and Women in the Corporate Office, 1870–1930* (Baltimore: Johns Hopkins University Press, 1994).

4   The best general study of the construction of masculinity in American history is E. Anthony Rotundo, *American Manhood: Transformations in Masculinity from the Revolution to the Modern Era* (New York: Basic Books, 1993). George Chauncey offers an excellent synthesis and analysis of these issues in *Gay New York: Gender, Urban Culture, and the Making of the Gay Male World, 1890–1940* (New York: Basic Books, 1994), 111–114. See also: Peter Filene, *Him/Her/Self: Sex Roles in Modern America*, 2nd ed. (Baltimore: Johns Hopkins University Press, 1986); Peter N. Stearns, *Be a Man! Males in Modern Society*, 2nd ed. (New York: Holmes & Meier, 1990); Harry Brod, ed., *The Making of Masculinities: The New Men's Studies* (Boston: Unwin Hyman, 1987); Elliott J. Gorn, *The Manly Art: Bare-Knuckle Prize Fighting in America* (Ithaca, NY: Cornell University Press, 1986); Mark C. Carnes, *Secret Ritual and Manhood in Victorian America* (New Haven, CT: Yale University Press, 1989); Michael C. C. Adams, *The Great Adventure: Male Desire and the Coming of World War I* (Bloomington: Indiana University Press, 1990).

5   For broad discussions of corporate attempts to create occupational cultures conducive to corporate operations, see Charles Delheim, "The Creation of a Company Culture: Cadbury's, 1861–1931," *American Historical Review* (February 1987): 13–44; Zunz, *Making America Corporate*; Stephen Meyer II, *The Five Dollar Day: Labor Management and Social Control in the Ford Motor Company, 1908–1921* (Albany: State University of New York Press, 1981); David Vrooman, *Daniel Willard and the Progressive Management on the Baltimore & Ohio Railroad* (Columbus: Ohio State University Press, 1991); Francis X. Sutton et al., *The American Business Creed* (Cambridge, MA: Harvard University Press, 1956); Edward Chase Kirkland, *Dream and Thought in the Business Community, 1860–1900* (Ithaca, NY: Cornell University Press, 1956); Walter Licht, "Studying Work: Personnel Policies in Philadelphia Firms, 1850–1950," in *Masters to Managers: Historical and Comparative Perspectives on American Employers* (New York: Columbia University Press, 1991); and JoAnne Yates, *Control through Communication: The Rise of System in American Management* (Baltimore: Johns Hopkins University Press, 1989).

6   For a fuller explanation of the arguments presented here, see: Davis, *Company Men*, chapter 6.

7   For widely varying treatments of the history of Los Angeles, see Robert Fogelson, *The Fragmented Metropolis: Los Angeles, 1850–1930* (Cambridge, MA: Harvard University Press, 1967); Kevin Starr, *Material Dreams: Southern California through the 1920s* (New York: Oxford University Press, 1990); and Mike Davis, *City of Quartz: Excavating the Future in Los Angeles* (New York: Verso, 1990).

8   James Findley Clifford, "The Economic Boom of the 'Twenties in Los Angeles," (Ph.D. diss., Claremont Graduate School, 1958), 29; Margaret S. Gordon, *Employment Expansion and Population Growth: The California Experience, 1900–1950* (Los Angeles: University of California Press, 1954). A variety of factors have been put forward to explain the unusually high proportion of service-sector employment in California, including the presence of the entertainment industry; the presence of the regional offices of many federal government agencies; and a heavy volume of immigration, which creates needs for expanded services.

9   Rotundo, *American Manhood*, 168, 176; see also Filene, *Him/Her/Self*, 70. For an excellent study of corporate response to the emasculating qualities of factory work, see Wayne A. Lewchuk, "Men and Monotony: Fraternalism as a Managerial Strategy at the Ford Motor Company," *Journal of Economic History* 53 (December 1993): 824–856.

10 Cindy Sondik Aron, *Ladies and Gentlemen of the Civil Service: Middle-Class Workers in Victorian America* (New York: Oxford University Press, 1987), 34–35; C. Wright Mills discusses the degrading nature of white-collar work in *White Collar: The American Middle Classes* (New York: Oxford University Press, 1956), 227; Stuart Blumin, *The Emergence of the Middle Class: Social Experience in the American City, 1760–1900* (New York: Cambridge University Press, 1989). See also: Harry Braverman, *Labor and Monopoly Capital: The Degradation of Work in the Twentieth Century* (New York: Monthly Review Press, 1974).

11 Even accepting this sort of compromise was not easy. Historians have traced a heightened celebration of individualistic accomplishment in the late nineteenth century as American men increasingly idealized those who stood out in the emerging organizational order. For example, a cult of Napoleon flourished among American men in the 1890s, as did the celebration of many business magnates and other "celebrities." See Carnes, *Secret Ritual*; Michael Messener, "The Meaning of Success: The Ath-

letic Experience and the Development of Male Identity," in Brod, ed., *Masculinities,* 193–210; Filene, *Him/Her/Self,* 72, 138–142; Rotundo, *Manhood,* 238–239.

12 For works tracing the emergence of the modern corporate business enterprise, see Alfred Chandler, Jr., *The Visible Hand: The Managerial Revolution in American Business* (Cambridge, MA: Harvard University Press, 1977); Alfred Chandler, Jr., and Louis Galambos, "The Development of Large-Scale Economic Organizations in Modern America," *Journal of Economic History* 30 (1970): 201–217; Louis Galambos and Joseph Pratt, *The Rise of the Corporate Commonwealth: U.S. Business and Public Policy in the Twentieth Century* (New York: Basic Books, 1988), 73–75; Edward S. Herman, *Corporate Control, Corporate Power* (New York: Cambridge University Press, 1981); Martin J. Sklar, *The Corporate Reconstruction of American Capitalism, 1890–1960; The Market, Law, and Politics* (Cambridge: Cambridge University Press, 1988); Naomi Lamoreaux, *The Great Merger Movement in American Business, 1895–1904* (Cambridge: Cambridge University Press, 1985); Glenn Porter, *The Rise of Big Business, 1860–1910* (New York: Thomas Y. Crowell Company, 1973).

13 Bureau of the Census, United States Department of Commerce, *Historical Statistics of the United States from Colonial Times to the Present, Part 1* (Washington, DC: United States Government Printing Office, 1975), 139–140; Jurgen Kocka, *White-Collar Workers in America, 1890–1940: A Social-Political History in International Perspective* (London: Sage Publications, 1980), 94–95.

14 For general studies of the development of white-collar employment in this period, see C. Wright Mills, *White Collar: The American Middle Classes* (New York: Oxford University Press, 1951); and Kocka, *White Collar Workers in America, 1890–1940.*

15 Gail B. Johnson, "Side Talks to The Agents," *Pacific Mutual News* 12 (August 1913): 170; "How the Pacific Mutual Is Helping the Agent to Organize His Time," *Pacific Mutual News* 25 (September 1926): 328.

16 Eugene C. Walsh, personnel file, PMSC collection, Box 30; PMSS Co. letter to Mr. Clifton S. Wardell, February 27, 1926, PMSC collection, Box 30. Huntington Library (HL). The notices send to junior employees read: "Owing to the discontinuance of shipping board operations it is necessary to reduce forces and therefore advise you that effective immediately you will be released." Daulton Mann letter to Mr. Albert Walker, freight clerk, June 1925, PMSC collection, Box 30, HL.

17 See Ileen A. DeVault's excellent *Sons and Daughters of Labor: Class and Clerical Work in Turn-of-the-Century Pittsburgh* (Ithaca, NY: Cornell University Press, 1990); Lisa Fine, *The Souls of the Skyscraper; Female Clerical Workers in Chicago, 1870–1930* (Philadelphia: Temple University Press, 1990); Margery Davies, *Woman's Place Is at the Typewriter: Office Work and Office Workers, 1870–1930* (Philadelphia: Temple University Press, 1982); Zunz, *Making America Corporate,* 147–148; Sharon Hartman Strom, *Beyond the Typewriter: Gender, Class, and the Origins of Modern American Office Work, 1900–1930* (Urbana: University of Illinois Press, 1992).

18 "President's Report to the Board of Directors of the Alfred Dolge Felt Company for the Year 1908," Henry E. Huntington Personal and Corporate Papers, Box 3, HL; Kocka, *White-Collar Workers,* 100–101, 291; Kwolek-Folland, *Engendering Business,* 30, 42; *Clerical Salaries in the United States, 1926* (New York: National Industrial Conference Board, Inc., 1926), 32.

19 Strom, *Beyond the Typewriter,* 192; Kwolek-Folland, *Engendering Business,* 11, 42–69.

20 See Gail Bederman, *Manliness and Civilization: A Cultural History of Gender and Race in the United States, 1880–1917* (Chicago: University of Chicago Press, 1995).

21 Fogelson, *The Fragmented Metropolis,* 75–84.

22 The 1910 and 1920 census samples used in this research comprise 588 and 651 gainfully employed men, respectively, and come from Steven Ruggles and Matthew Sobek, *Integrated Public Use Microdata Series: Version 1.0* (Minneapolis: Social History Research Laboratory, University of Minnesota, 1995). This hereafter will be referred to as IPUMS–95.

23 Bederman, *Manliness and Civilization,* 10.

24 Ibid.; Kwolek-Folland, *Engendering Business,* 51–52.

25 For an argument on the centrality of promotions in managerial theory, see William Lazonick, "Strategy, Structure, and Management Development in the United States and Britain," in Kesaji Kobayashi and Hidemasa Morikawa, eds., *Development of Managerial Enterprise* (Tokyo: University of Tokyo Press, 1986), 104, 115.

26 "The Edison Organization," *Edison Facts* 2 (February 1924): 1.

27 Joseph French Johnson, *Modern Business, Volume 1: Business and The Man* (New York: Alexander Hamilton Institute, 1917), 216, 234; Joseph French Johnson et al., *Modern Business, Volume 19: Office Management* (New York: Alexander Hamilton Institute, 1919), 126, 146.

28 Lyman Stewart to Mr. H. P. Lane, February 5, 1918, Biola University Archives.

29 T. W. Johnson, "All the Worlds a Stage," *News of the Los Angeles First National* 5 (November 1927): 2; Ira B. Cross, *Financing an Empire: History of Banking in California* (Los Angeles: S. J. Clarke Publishing Company, 1927). The practice of promoting from within continues in recent times as Security Pacific National Bank (now merged with Bank of America) boasted as recently as 1989 that all its presidents had climbed the corporate ladder.

30 Paul Shoup Letter to Mulford Wade, June 16, 1924, Los Angeles Railway Collection; "Method of Filling Station Vacancies Is Announced," *Pacific Electric Magazine* 12 (June 10, 1927): 12.

31 *Proceedings of the First Annual Convention of the California Bankers Association, San Francisco, October 14–16, 1891* (Los Angeles: Times-Mirror, 1891), 38–40, 42–44; "Smock establishes personnel department: Cashier creates new and much needed division," *Security First News Bulletin* 1(July 1, 1929): 3; "New Personnel Program Outlined," *Security First News Bulletin* 1 (November 1, 1929): 1; "Making Good a Promise," *Security First News Bulletin* 1(November 15, 1929): 2; A. H. Nieter, "Personnel," *The Pacific Southwest* 5 (July 1927): 2; Lynne P. Doti and Larry Schweikart, *Banking in the American West: From the Gold Rush to Deregulation* (Norman: University of Oklahoma Press, 1991), 4.

32 "Promotion," *Union Oil Bulletin* 3 (December 1923): 25.

33 "Ready for Promotion," *Pacific Electric Magazine* 10 (December 10, 1925): 8; "Employees up Ladder Chosen from Ranks," *Pacific Electric Magazine* 10 (October 10, 1925): 18; "What Are Your Chances to Get Ahead Here?" *Two Bells* 6 (September 14, 1925): 21; "Our New Year's Resolution," *Pacific Electric Magazine* 6 (January 1922): 1.

34 Clipping from D. W. Pontius Scrapbook, General Scrapbook Collection #55, Huntington Library.

35 J. M. Mills, "A Wail 'bout the Frail," *Pacific Electric Magazine* 9 (July 10, 1924): 13; "The Feminine in Engineering," *Pacific Electric Magazine* 10 (March 10, 1926): 15.

36 "Women Forced into Employment by Increased Responsibilities," *Pacific Mutual News* 29 (March 1930): 95.

37 Mansel G. Blackford, *A History of Small Business in America* (New York: Twayne Publishers, 1991), chapter 2.

38 Aron, *Ladies and Gentlemen of the Civil Service* 3; Charles Heston Peirson, "More than Service," *Edison Current Topics* 5 (August 1916): 159.

39 Adams's career can be pieced together from a series of service awards chronicles appearing sporadically throughout the publication of the *Union Oil Bulletin* during the late 1920s.

40 Howard P. Chudacoff, "Success and Security: The Meaning of Social Mobility in America," *Reviews in American History* 10 (December 1982): 101–111; See also James Henretta, "The Study of Social Mobility: Ideological Assumptions and Conceptual Bias," *Labor History* 18 (1977): 165–178.

41 Oral History of Lloyd McCampbell by Evelyn F. Scott, April 18, 1980. Ventura County Historical Society.

42 Oliver Palmer Personnel File, PMSC collection, box #30, HL.

43 Kocka, *White Collar Workers in America, 1890–1940*, 184.

44 "Salaried and Registered Expenses, 1904–1909," Pacific Mail Steamship Company, PMSC Collection, Box 30, HL.

45 The ability of many firms to screen out numerous people at the lower levels often reflects that they encountered vast pools of applicants. SCE, for instance, in 1922 received 24,769 applicants for "ordinary positions," in technical and clerical areas and 1,500 applicants for "better" positions (defined as jobs with an income of over $150 per month). Of these applicants, 2,282 were hired for "ordinary positions," and 121 were hired for "better" positions. "Statement of the Southern California Edison Company of its Claims for the Charles A. Coffin Medical Effort for the Year 1922," unpublished manuscript, 1923, Southern California Edison Archives.

46 H. E. A. Railton memo to Mr. Graham, January 20, 1922, PMSC Collection, Box 4, H. L.; Moore, *Pacific Mutual Life,* 163–165; Superintendent of Dispatching, "Yearly Report, 1927; SCE Annual Operating Report, 1927," SCE Archives.

47 Grinsfelder, "J. E. Brick Elliot," *Transcribed Interviews Collected*, 298.

48 For an interesting reference to this, see Melissa Dabakis, "Douglas Tilden's *Mechanics Fountain*: Labor and the 'Crisis of Masculinity' in the 1890s," *American Quarterly* 47 (June 1985): 204–205. For other examples of what I call "Corporate Noir," see: King Vidor's The *Crowd* (MGM, 1928) and *If I Had a Million* (Paramount Pictures, 1932)

49 See Judy Hilkey, *Character Is Capital: Success Manuals and Manhood in Gilded Age America* (Chapel Hill: University of North Carolina Press, 1997); Theodore P. Green, *America's Heroes: Changing*

Models of Success in American Magazines (New York, 1970); Daniel T. Rodgers, *The Work Ethic in Industrial America: 1850–1920* (Chicago: University of Chicago Press), 38–39; Kocka, *White Collar Workers*, 150; Morrell Heald, *The Social Responsibilities of Business: Company and Community, 1900–1960* (Cleveland, OH: Press of Case Western Reserve University, 1970), 69; Jay Cohn, "The Business Ethic for Boys: The Saturday Evening Post and the Post Boys," *Business History Review* 61 (1987): 185–215.

50 Christopher P. Wilson, *White Collar Fictions: Class and Social Representation in American Literature, 1885–1925* (Athens: University of Georgia Press, 1992).

51 "Prominent Personalities," *The Graphic* 53 (October 10, 1918): 8; Harold J. Fitzgerald, "Room at the Top: What the Retail Business Has to Offer the Ambitious Young Man," *Sunset* 48 (January 1922): 43–45; Lyle M. Spencer, "Going Up! Traffic Rules for Those Who Want to Get Where There's Abundant Room—The Top," *Sunset* 49 (December 1922): 24–26, 68–70; Eddy Elford "Has Your Job a Future? The Story of a Musical Youth Who Abandoned Harmonics for the Gas Business," *Sunset* (July 1923): 40, 81.

52 "Chance to Climb," *Southern California Business* 1 (November 1922): 18; "Business Review—Thomas Is Promoted," *Saturday Night* (January 7, 1922): 5.

53 Helen Ormsbee, "The Man Who Failed," *The Atlantic Monthly* 109 (April 1912): 508–517; "The Executive Looks for a Job; and What He Encounters in the Search," *The Century Magazine* 117 (1928–29): 484–490.

54 "The End of the Trail: Why Does a Woman Leave Home and Faithful Mate after Twenty Years?" *Sunset* 50 (March 1923): 30–33; Part II, 50 (April 1923): 40–43.

55 King Vidor, *The Crowd* (MGM, 1928)

The Rise of the Realtor®

The author thanks James B. Gilbert, Robyn Muncy, David Sicilia, Adriane Kinnane, Nancy K. Berlage, and the participants in the University of Maryland History Department's Graduate Colloquium for excellent suggestions on earlier drafts of this essay. I am indebted to the staff at the Urban Archives at Temple University; Mary Martinez and John Krukoff of the National Association of Realtors; Gary Krysler of the Women's Council of Realtors; and Mary Ann Herzig of the Realtors Association of Metropolitan Pittsburgh for invaluable research assistance; and to the William Randolph Hearst Fund at the University of Maryland for financial support.

1 Webster's *International Dictionary* (1917), addendum, 88.

2 *Minneapolis Real Estate Board v. Northwestern Telephone Exchange Co.*, Sept. 13, 1920. District Court of Hennepin County, Minnesota. Case cited in Pearl Janet Davies, *Real Estate Achievement in the United States: A history*, Archives of the National Association of Realtors (hereafter, NAR Archives), mss., n.d. (1955?), vol. 2, chap. 5, part 6, 42.

3 Frank Ward O'Malley, "Thence by Seagoing Hack," *Saturday Evening Post*, November 27, 1920, 8–9, 89–98.

4 "Apology to Realtors," *Saturday Evening Post*, February 13, 1921, 14.

5 Henry Louis Mencken, *The American Language: An Inquiry into the Development of English in the United States*, Supplement I (New York: Knopf, 1975 [1945]), 565–566.

6 There is a growing literature on this topic. I am indebted to Daniel Clark of Purdue University for sharing portions of his forthcoming dissertation, "Why the Businessman Needs a College Education."

7 I use the term "professionalization project" after Magali S. Larson, *The Rise of Professionalism: A Sociological Analysis* (Berkeley: University of California Press, 1977).

8 One of the few recent books to entertain this problematic is Daniel Walkowitz's outstanding *Working With Class: The Politics of Middle Class Identity* (Chapel Hill: University of North Carolina Press, 1999). Cf. also Burton Bledstein's classic, *The Culture of Professionalism: Higher Education and the American Middle Classes* (New York: Norton, 1976). For polling data on Americans and their middle classness, cf. *The Gallup Poll, 1936–1971* (New York, 1971), 148; "The Fortune Survey," *Fortune Magazine* 21, no. 2 (February 1940), 14.

9 The index of residential construction rose from 44 in 1921 to 124 in 1925, dropped slightly in 1926–27, and rose to its peak of 126 in 1928. Cf. George Soule, *The Prosperity Decade: A Chapter from American Economic History, 1917–1929* (London: Pilot Press, 1962), 113–114.

10 Other than its role in institutionalizing racial redlining in the policies of the Federal Housing Administration, documented by Kenneth Jackson, the National Association of Real Estate Boards has not

received due credit for shaping American housing policy. The work of Marc Weiss and William Worley are exceptions. Cf. Jackson, *Crabgrass Frontiers: The Suburbanization of the United States* (New York: Columbia University Press, 1985), chap. 6; Gail Radford, *Modern Housing for America: Policy Struggles in the New Deal Era* (Chicago: University of Chicago Press, 1996), chap. 2; Marc A. Weiss, *The Rise of the Community Builders: The American Real Estate Industry and Urban Land Planning* (New York: Columbia University Press, 1987); William S. Worley, *J. C. Nichols and the Shaping of Kansas City* (New York: Columbia: University of Missouri Press, 1991). On associationalism generally, cf. Ellis Hawley, "Herbert Hoover, the Commerce Secretariat, and Visions of an 'Associative State,' 1921–1928" *Journal of American History* 61 (June 1974): 125–144.

11 On heterosociality, cf. Cindy S. Aron, *Ladies and Gentlemen of the Civil Service* (New York: Oxford University Press, 1981), and *Working at Play* (New York: Oxford University Press, 1999). The term "female dominion" comes from Robyn Muncy, *Creating a Female Dominion in American Reform, 1890–1935* (New York: Oxford University Press, 1991).

12 Cf. Catharine Beecher and Harriet Beecher Stowe, *The American Woman's Home, or The Principles of Domestic Science, Being a Guide to the Formation and Maintenance of Economical, Healthful, Beautiful, and Christian Homes* ([1869] Hartford, CT: Stowe-Day Foundation, 1975); Kathryn Kish Sklar, *Catharine Beecher: A Study in American Domesticity* (New York: Norton, 1976). On the home as a symbol, cf. Clifford Edward Clark, *The American Family Home, 1820–1960* (Chapel Hill: University of North Carolina Press, 1981), xv; Dolores Hayden, *The Grand Domestic Revolution: A History of Feminist Designs for American Homes, Neighborhoods, and Cities* (Cambridge: MIT Press, 1981); Gwendolyn Wright, *Moralism and the Model Home* (Chicago: University of Chicago Press, 1980). On urban planning, cf. M. Christine Boyer, *Dreaming the Rational City: The Myth of American City Planning* (Cambridge: MIT Press, 1983). On housing reformers, cf. Roy Lubove, *The Progressives and the Slums: Tenement House Reform in New York City, 1890–1917* (Westport, CT: Greenwood Press, 1974). On home economists, cf. Nancy K. Berlage, "The Establishment of an Applied Social Science: Home Economists, Science, and Reform at Cornell University, 1870–1930," in Helene Silverberg, ed. *Gender and American Social Science: The Formative Years* (Princeton, NJ: Princeton University Press, 1998), 185–231. On social workers, cf. Daniel Walkowitz, "The Making of a Feminine Professional Identity: Social Workers in the 1920s," *American Historical Review* 95, no. 4 (October 1990): 1051–1075 and Daniel J. Walkowitz, *Working with Class: Social Workers and the Politics of Middle-Class Identity* (Chapel Hill: University of North Carolina Press, 1999).

13 See note 10 above.

14 On the frontier as a mythical construct, cf. Henry Nash Smith, *Virgin Land: The American West as Symbol and Myth* ([1950] Cambridge, MA: Harvard University Press, 1970).

15 J. D. House, *Contemporary Entrepreneurs* (Toronto, 1977).

16 Davies, *Real Estate Achievement in the United States*, chap. 3, 5.

17 Folder 150, Box 59, Series VIII, Membership Applications, Records of the Philadelphia Board of Realtors, Urban Archives, Philadelphia, PA (hereafter, PBR).

18 Alexander S. Taylor, "Benefits of the National Association," *National Real Estate Journal* (hereafter *NREJ*), Vol. 11, no. 6 (June 1915), 79.

19 See note 11, above.

20 Pearl Janet Davies, *Real Estate Achievement in the United States*, chap. 3, 5.

21 Edward Mott Woolley, "Inner Secrets of a Real Estate Broker's Rise," *NREJ* 5, no. 3 (May 15, 1912), 192.

22 Ibid., "Inner Secrets," 193.

23 Ibid. Space does not permit discussion of the implicit counternarrative, that white-collar work was nonheroic and emasculating, a ubiquitous theme in magazines in the early twentieth century. An early example is H. Stimpson, "Small Business as a School of Manhood," *Scribners* 93, no. 557 (May 1904): 337–340.

24 The most coherent statement of the "business professionalism" argument is made by Louis D. Brandeis in a speech at Brown University's commencement in 1912, published as *Business: A Profession* ([1914] New York: Augustus M. Kelley, 1971).

25 For a full discussion of the curbstone broker, see Weiss, *Rise of the Community Builders*, ch. 2.

26 Frank S. Craven, "The Real Estate Profession and Ethics," *NREJ* 3, no. 4 (July 15, 1912), 166.

27 "Code of Ethics National Association of Real Estate Exchanges," adopted at NAREB convention at Los Angeles, June 24, 1915, *NREJ* (July 1915) (italics added).

28 Clifford Siskin, "Wordsworth's Prescriptions: Romanticism and Professional Power," in Gene W.

Ruoff, ed., *The Romantics and Us: Essays on Literature and Culture* (New Brunswick, NJ: Rutgers University Press, 1990), 308–311.

29 J. J. Kenna, "Opposes Licenses for Brokers," *NREJ* 11, no. 1 (January 1915): 50.

30 Kenna, "Opposes Licenses for Brokers," 51.

31 Brandeis, *Business: A Profession*, 1–3.

32 Isman, "The Accountings of a Real Estate Man," 58.

33 The notion of women as natural "home managers" grew out of the earlier "domestic science" movement. A representative text is Lilian Gilbreth, *Management in the Home* (1923).

34 Isman, "The Accountings of a Real Estate Man—Buying a House? Or Making a Home?" *Saturday Evening Post*, October 13, 1923, 58.

35 Ibid.

36 Glenn Frank, "The Realtor as the New Pioneer," *Annals of Real Estate Practice* (Chicago: National Association of Real Estate Boards, 1928): 1–11.

37 Cf. Aaron Morton Sakolski, *The Great Land Bubble: The Amazing Story of Land-Grabbing, Speculations, and Booms from Colonial Days to the Present Time* (New York and London: Harper & Brothers, 1932).

38 For an excellent analysis of the "crisis of masculinity" in the early 1900s, see Gail Bederman, *Manliness and Civilization: A Cultural History of Gender and Race in the United States, 1880–1917* (Chicago: University of Chicago Press, 1995).

39 The concepts of *bricolage* and the *bricoleur* are, of course, poached from Claude Levi-Strauss's classic text, *The Savage Mind* ([1962] Chicago: 1966), 16–36.

40 Berlage, "Establishment of an Applied Social Science"; Walkowitz, "Making of a Feminine Professional Identity."

41 Gladys Irene Hiestand, "Real Estate as a Profession for Women," *NREJ* 7, no. 1 (January 1913): 20–21. G. Louise Slocomb, "Women in the Real Estate Profession," *NREJ* 22, no. 11 (November 21, 1921): 34–35.

42 Slocomb, "Women in the Real Estate Profession," 35; Slocomb, "The Realty Woman as Broker," *NREJ* 22, no. 12 (December 5, 1921): 26–27.

43 Figures derived from US Census.

44 "In What Type of Real Estate Activity Are Women Succeeding Best?" Conference of Women Realtors, National Association of Real Estate Boards, Twentieth Annual Convention, Seattle, Washington, August 10–13, 1927, typescript, vertical file, archives of the Women's Council of Realtors, Chicago, IL (hereafter WCR).

45 On the "women question," cf. "Women as Board Members," *Annals of Real Estate Practice: Administrative Problems of Real Estate Boards: Proceedings and Reports of the Realtor Secretaries Division*, Vol. 9, 1925 (Chicago, 1925), 41–51. As official NAREB historian, Pearl Janet Davies, noted, there are few records as to how many women belonged to the National Association prior to the formation of the Women's Council in the late 1930s. I have attempted to estimate numbers by examination of published annual rosters, but unless a person is listed as "Mrs." or "Miss," or by an unambiguously feminine name, it is impossible to make reliable gender distinctions. The numbers appear to be quite small, proportionately smaller than the number of licensed female brokers given in the census of licensed brokers and salespersons. Several boards, mostly in the West, such as Long Beach, California, accepted women as active members in the 1920s, and their membership rosters demonstrate near-parity with census figures. Cf. Pearl Janet Davies, *Women in Real Estate: A History of the Women's Council of the National Association of Real Estate Boards* (Chicago, 1963).

46 "Women in Business," *Fortune Magazine*, July and August 1935. Cf. Angel Kwolek-Folland, *Engendering Business: Men and Women in the Corporate Office, 1870–1930* (Baltimore: Johns Hopkins University Press, 1994).

47 Figures derived from *15th Census of the US: 1930, Population, Vol. V: General Report on Occupations*, Table 5. Cf. D. G. Baird, "Is Woman's Place in the Home?" *How to Sell* (May 1920); Edwin Stoll, "Women Make Good Realtors," *Lifetime Living* (December 1952), 32–34, 68.

48 On the association of sales with masculinity, cf. Kwolek-Folland, *Engendering Business*. Note that only 5 percent of Kwolek-Folland's insurance brokers were women in 1930, and less than 10 percent in 1960, versus 13 percent and 24 percent, respectively, in real estate.

49 Pearl Janet Davies, *Women in Real Estate*, 36.

50 Sally Ross Chapralis, *Progress of Women in Real Estate: 50th Anniversary, Women's Council of Realtors* (Chicago, 1988), 28.

51 For a variety of reasons, probably having to do with the lack of a settled tradition and a generally more fluid social structure, women were accepted into membership from the beginning in most of the newer boards that were proliferating in the West during the 1920s. In fact, members of West Coast boards, Long Beach's in particular, often hurled gentle barbs at their "effete" East Coast brethren regarding their ostensible fear of feminization.

52 Mary Amelia Warren, "Home Selling for Women," Minutes of Breakfast Meeting, Women's Council, NAREB, Detroit, Michigan, November 5, 1941, 4, WCR.

53 For lively anecdotal accounts of enormously successful women Realtors, see Robert Shook, *The Real Estate People: Top Salespersons, Brokers, and Realtors Share the Secrets of Their Success* (New York: Harper & Row, 1980), and Chapralis-Ross, *Women's Progress in Real Estate*.

54 Mary Ann Herzig, Executive Secretary, Realtors' Association of Metropolitan Pittsburgh, conversation with author, January 22, 1998.

55 It is as yet unclear why Columbus, so intransigent for so long, succumbed to heterosociality only in 1962.

56 Derived from *17th Census of the US: 1950, Population, United States Summary*, Table 125, 1–267; *Statistical Abstract of the United States: 1995*, Section 13: Labor Force, Employment, and Earnings, Table 649, 412.

57 Mary Shern, *Real Estate, A Woman's World: The Saga of Suzy Soldsine, Super Salesperson* (Chicago, 1977), ix.

58 Cf. *Fortune* 21, no. 2 (February 1940), 14, 20, 28.

59 I am implicitly taking issue with Peter Stearns's call for precision in defining the middle class. Cf. Stearns, "The Middle Class: Toward a Precise Definition," *Comparative Studies in Society and History* 21 (July 1979): 177–196.

The Politics of Race and Community

1 Mike Davis, *Prisoners of the American Dream: Politics and Economy in the History of the U.S. Working Class* (London: Verso, 1986), 303–306. See also Davis's more sophisticated, but ultimately unconvincing portrayal of the "tendential degeneration of [Los Angeles's] middle strata" in *City of Quartz: Excavating the Future in Los Angeles* (London: Verso, 1990), esp. 151–219 (quote, 18). Robin D. G. Kelley, *Race Rebels: Culture, Politics, and the Black Working Class* (New York: Free Press, 1994), 36.

The Rising Tide of Youth

While researching and writing this essay, I was supported through a postdoctoral fellowship at the Center for African American Studies at UCLA; my thanks to the students, staff, and faculty there. Many thanks to Michael Flug, archivist for the Harsh Research Collection at the Woodson Branch of the Chicago Public Library, who first brought the Wonder Books to my attention. Copies of the Wonder Books are there, as well as in a handful of collections elsewhere. I am indebted to Michael Flug, Robert Johnston, Tessie Liu, and Carolyn Rouse for comments and suggestions through earlier drafts. All conclusions and errors are, of course, my responsibility.

1 Frederic H. Robb, ed., *1927 Intercollegian Wonder Book, or, The Negro in Chicago, 1779–1927*, (Chicago: Washington Intercollegiate Club of Chicago, 1927), 4. Jones's review appeared in the Chicago *Defender*, October 1, 1927, part 2, 2.

2 For scholarly citation of the Wonder Books, see Willard B. Gatewood, *Aristocrats of Color: The Black Elite, 1880–1920* (Bloomington: Indiana University Press, 1990), 410 n. 21; James R. Grossman, *Land of Hope: Chicago, Black Southerners and the Great Migration* (Chicago: University of Chicago Press, 1989), 320 n. 53, and 350 n. 24; and Allan H. Spear, *Black Chicago: The Making of a Negro Ghetto, 1890–1920* (Chicago: University of Chicago Press, 1967), 236.

3 On racial uplift, see Kevin K. Gaines, *Uplifting the Race: Black Leadership, Politics and Culture in the Twentieth Century* (Chapel Hill: University of North Carolina Press, 1996); Gatewood, *Black Aristocrats*; Tera W. Hunter, *To 'Joy My Freedom: Southern Black Women's Lives and Labors after the Civil War* (Cambridge, MA: Harvard University Press, 1997), chapters 6–10; and Stephanie Shaw, *What a Woman Ought to Be and to Do: Black Professional Women Workers in the Age of Jim Crow* (Chicago: University of Chicago Press, 1996). Quotes are from Gaines, *Uplifting the Race*, 2, 4, 5.

4 Robb, *1927 Intercollegian Wonder Book*, 8, 9, 21, 24; David Levering Lewis, *When Harlem Was in Vogue* (New York: Oxford University Press, 1979), 157–158; U.S. Department of Commerce, Bureau of the Census, *Fourteenth Census of the United States* (Washington, DC: U.S. Government Printing Office, 1921), Vol. 2, "Population: General Report and Analytical Tables," 1044; U.S.

Department of Commerce, Bureau of the Census, *Fifteenth Census of the United States: 1930* (Washington, DC: U.S. Government Printing Office, 1933), Vol. 2, "General Report: Statistics by Subjects," 1094; U.S. Department of Commerce, Bureau of the Census, *Negroes in the United States, 1920–1932* (Washington, DC: U.S. Government Printing Office, 1935), 221.

5 Robb, *1927 Intercollegian Wonder Book*, 13.

6 Yergan's talk was titled "Five Years of Study in Africa," while Shachtman presented on the "Imperialistic Attitude of the U.S. towards Central [and] South American Republics and China." Robb, ed., *1927 Intercollegian Wonder Book*, 26–27. Both figures went on to become controversial figures in the history of the American Left. For material on Yergan, see Brenda Gayle Plummer, *Rising Wind: Black Americans and U.S. Foreign Affairs, 1935–1960* (Chapel Hill: University of North Carolina Press, 1996), and Penny Von Eschen, *Race against Empire: Blacks and Anti-Colonialism, 1937–1957*, (Ithaca, NY: Cornell University Press, 1997). On Shachtman, see Maurice Isserman, *If I Had a Hammer: The Death of the Old Left and the Birth of the New Left* (New York: Basic Books, 1987), especially chapter 2.

7 Frederic H. Robb, ed., *The Wonder Book: The Negro in Chicago, 1779–1929* (Chicago: Washington Intercollegiate Club of Chicago, 1929), 105, 172; Robb, *1927 Intercollegian Wonder Book*, 26–27.

8 Robb, *1927 Intercollegian Wonder Book*, 4.

9 E. Franklin Frazier, *Black Bourgeoisie: The Rise of a New Middle Class* (New York: Free Press, 1957), 84; Robb, *1927 Intercollegian Wonder Book*, 4. On anticolonial thinking among African-Americans at this time, see Plummer, *Rising Wind*, chapter 2. On support for birth control, see Jessie M. Rodrique, "The Black Community and the Birth Control Movement," in Darlene Clark Hine, Wilma Reed, and Linda King, eds., *"We Specialize in the Wholly Impossible": A Reader in Black Women's History* (Brooklyn: Carlson, 1995), 505–520; and Dorothy Roberts, *Killing the Black Body: Race, Reproduction, and the Meaning of Liberty* (New York: Vintage, 1997), 56–103.

10 Robb, *1927 Intercollegian Wonder Book*, 47. The Wonder Books are among a handful of texts featuring Wendell Phillips High School, among the most storied black high schools nationally at the time. Closer examination of material on Phillips in the Wonder Books might well suggest further study of black public education in the urban North, a crucial and underresearched topic. For discussion of Phillips and its community role, see Grossman, *Land of Hope*, chapter 9; Spear, *Black Chicago*; and Michael Homel, *Down From Equality: Black Chicagoans and Public Schools, 1920–1941* (Urbana: University of Illinois Press, 1984).

11 James D. Anderson, *The Education of Blacks in the South, 1860–1935* (Chapel Hill: University of North Carolina Press, 1988), chapter 6. Figures are from pages 204 and 236.

12 Robb, *The Wonder Book*, 161; Stuart Hall and Tony Jefferson, eds., *Resistance through Rituals: Youth Subcultures in Post-War Britain*, (London: Unwin Hyman, 1976), 51, 69. For sample discussions of youth subculture in the United States, see Joe Austin and Michael Nevin Willard, eds., *Generations of Youth: Youth Culture and History in Twentieth Century America* (New York: New York University Press, 1997); Paula S. Fass, *The Damned and the Beautiful: American Youth in the 1920s* (New York: Oxford University Press, 1977); and William Graebner, *Coming of Age in Buffalo: Youth and Authority in the Postwar Era* (Philadelphia: Temple University Press, 1990).

13 Robb, *1927 Intercollegian Wonder Book*, 16.

14 Ibid., 82–88; Robb, *The Wonder Book*, 17–30, 33–37; Alain Locke, "The New Negro" and "Negro Youth Speaks," in *The New Negro* (New York: Atheneum, 1968), 7. On campus unrest at black colleges, see Anderson, *The Education of Blacks in the South, 1860–1935*, chapter 7; and Raymond Wolters, *The New Negro on Campus: Black College Rebellions of the 1920s* (Princeton, NJ: Princeton University Press, 1975). For discussion of "generational consciousness" within the Negro Renaissance, see Nathan Huggins, *Harlem Renaissance* (London: Oxford University Press, 1971); Langston Hughes, *The Big Sea* (New York: Thunder's Mouth Press, 1940); and Arnold Rampersad, *The Life of Langston Hughes, Volume 1: 1902–1941: I, Too, Sing America* (New York: Oxford University Press, 1986).

15 Lewis, *When Harlem Was in Vogue*, 305–307; Frazier, "The New Negro Middle Class," in G. Franklin Edwards, ed., *E. Franklin Frazier on Race Relations* (Chicago: University of Chicago Press, 1968), 262; Harold Cruse, *The Crisis of the Negro Intellectual: A Historical Analysis of the Failure of Black Leadership* (New York: Quill, 1984), 38.

16 Gatewood, *Aristocrats of Color*; Frazier, "Durham: Capital of the Black Middle Class," in Locke, *The New Negro*, 333–340. For other accounts of the "new" black middle class in the 1920s, see Gaines, *Uplifting the Race*, 246–247; and Spear, *Black Chicago*, especially chapter 5. For a useful account drawn from Chicago at this time, see Claude A. Barnett, "We Win a Place in Industry," *Opportunity* 7,

no. 3 (March 1929): 82–86, repr. in Joe W. Trotter and Earl Lewis, eds., *African Americans in the Industrial Age: A Documentary History, 1915–1945* (Boston: Northeastern University Press, 1996), 126–135.

17 St. Clair Drake and Horace R. Cayton, *Black Metropolis: A Study of Negro Life in a Northern City* (New York: Harcourt, Brace, and Company, 1945), 669; Robb, *1927 Intercollegian Wonder Book*, 53–69, 93, 95, 122, 123, 139–180; Robb, *The Wonder Book*, 67, 129–160, 261–272.

18 Robb, *The Wonder Book*, 14, 90, 94, 186–187, 199. Robb, *1927 Intercollegian Wonder Book*, 92. In their portrayal of Wells-Barnett, the editors maintained that she was "still an example of courage, industry, zeal, and determination for the Negro youth of today." The tribute paid Wells as her life neared its end challenges the judgment of historians that, following her epic battle against lynching and her early efforts as a club woman and dissident black voice, she proved too iconoclastic and embittered to remain an effective force for social change. For such an account of Wells-Barnett's later career, see Thomas Holt, "The Lonely Warrior: Ida B. Wells-Barnett and the Struggle for Black Leadership," in John Hope Franklin and August Meier (eds.), *Black Leaders of the Twentieth Century* (Urbana, IL: University of Illinois Press, 1982), 39–62.

19 The "Who's Who" sections can be found in Robb, *1927 Intercollegian Wonder Book*, 89–124; and in Robb, *The Wonder Book*, 110–128. On "socially responsible individualism," see Shaw, *What a Woman Ought to Be and to Do*, 5.

20 Spear, *Black Chicago*, 91; Robb, *1927 Intercollegiate Wonder Books*, 110, 219, 222. Spinning the 1919 Riot as a cautionary tale of interracial patronage gone awry, editors would recount the role played by black voters in the election of Mayor William Hale Thompson earlier in 1919, noting that the "factional struggle aroused resentment against the race that had so conspicuously allied itself with the Thompson side."

21 Spear, *Black Chicago*, 228–229.

22 Robb, *The Wonder Book*, 33–37. On the National Association of Negro Musicians, see Willis Charles Patterson, "A History of the National Association of Negro Musicians (NANM): The First Quarter Century, 1919–1943" (Ph.D. diss., Wayne State University, 1993). On local jazz artists like Armstrong and Barnes, see William Howland Kenney, *Chicago Jazz: A Cultural History, 1904–1930* (New York: Oxford University Press, 1993).

23 Robb, *The 1927 Intercollegian Wonder Book*, 35–37, 96, 209; Robb, *The Wonder Book*, 34, 81, 109, 113. I am indebted to Victor Margolin for sharing this point about Dawson, both in conversation and through his paper "African American Designers in Chicago: Themes and Issues," presented at "African American Designers: The Chicago Experience Then and Now" (DuSable Museum of African American History, Chicago), February 5, 2000.

24 Robb, *The Wonder Book, 1779–1929*, 101, 104, 106, 305, 310. On London and the African diaspora, see Folarin Shyllon, "Blacks in Britain: A Historical and Analytic Overview," in Joseph E. Harris ed., *Global Dimensions of the African Diaspora* (Washington, DC: Howard University Press, 1993), 236–240; and Kent Worcester, *C.L.R. James: A Political Biography*, (Albany: State University of New York Press, 1996), 30–33.

25 Irene McCoy Gaines, "The Negro Woman in Politics," in *The Wonder Book*, 88.

26 Edith Sampson, "Are Our Women Holding Their Own?" in *The Wonder Book*, 78–79.

27 Robb, *1927 Intercollegian Wonder Book*, 92, 93, 107; Robb, *The Wonder Book*, 119. On the idea of "womanism," see Elsa Barkley Brown, "Womanist Consciousness: Maggie Lena Walker and the Independent Order of Saint Luke," in Vicki L. Ruiz and Ellen Carol DuBois, eds., *Unequal Sisters: A Multicultural Reader in U.S. Women's History* (New York: Routledge, 1994), 268–283.

28 Darlene Clark Hine, *Hinesight: Black Women and the Reconstruction of American History* (Bloomington: Indiana University Press, 1994), xxii. See also Brown, "Womanist Consciousness," Evelyn Brooks Higginbotham, *Righteous Discontent: The Women's Movement in the Black Baptist Church, 1880–1920* (Cambridge, MA: Harvard University Press, 1993); Hunter, *To Joy My Freedom*; Shaw, *What A Woman Ought to Be and to Do*; and Carol Stack, *All Our Kin: Strategies for Survival in a Black Community* (New York: Harper & Row, 1974).

29 Robb, *1927 Intercollegian Wonder Book*, 8. In the 1929 book, only fourteen of forty-three editors were women. Yet virtually all of them, including Sampson, Gaines, Beulah Hill, Vivian Garth, and Frankie Adams, contributed major articles to the book. Robb, *The Wonder Book*, 8, 13.

30 Of course, this sentiment is amply documented in the historical record, as obligation to white benefactors, along with cynicism concerning the prospects for cross-class solidarity, has time and again moved privileged blacks to subvert attempts by black labor to improve their leverage. On this subject,

see Robin D. G. Kelley, "We Are Not What We Seem: Re-thinking Black Working Class Opposition in the Jim Crow South," *Journal of American History* 80, no. 1 (June 1993): 75–112; Daniel Letwin, *The Challenge of Interracial Unionism: Alabama Coal Miners, 1878–1921* (Chapel Hill: University of North Carolina Press, 1998); and Earl Lewis, *In Their Own Interests: Race, Class and Power in Twentieth Century Norfolk, Virginia* (Berkeley: University of California Press, 1991).

31 Grossman, *Land of Hope*, chapter 8; William H. Harris, *Keeping the Faith: A. Philip Randolph, Milton P. Webster, and the Brotherhood of Sleeping Car Porters, 1925–1937* (Urbana: University of Illinois Press, 1977), chapter 2; Spear, *Black Chicago*, chapters 9 and 10.

32 Lewis, *In Their Own Interests*, 1–7.

33 Robb, *1927 Intercollegian Wonder Book*, 160–161, 180, 189.

34 Robb, *The Wonder Book*, 66–67, 174, 193, 194–195, 196–197, 304.

35 A sample of those participating in the four-day event include: Edith Sampson, Robert Abbott, Pastor Harold M. Kingsley of Good Shepard Church, Pastor W. D. Cook of Metropolitan Community Church, Frankie Adams, Frederic Robb, Bennie Smith, Milton Webster, and A. Philip Randolph from the Brotherhood of Sleeping Car Porters. All of the speech digests and resolutions can be found in "National Negro Labor Conference." See Robb, *The Wonder Book*, 68–74, 198–199.

36 Harris, *Keeping the Faith*, chapters 2–5. Extensive records of Barnett's work opposing the Brotherhood, which included regular communication with Pullman Company management, can be found in the Claude A. Barnett Papers, Box 278, Folders 4 and 5, at the Chicago Historical Society.

37 "Irene McCoy Gaines," and "Edith Sampson," in Darlene Clark Hine, Elsa Barkley Brown, and Rosalyn Terborg-Penn, eds., *Black Women in America: An Historical Encyclopedia* (Bloomington: Indiana University Press, 1994), Vol. 1, 476; Vol. 2, 1002–1003; Mark Newman, *Entrepreneurs of Profit and Pride: From Black-Appeal to Radio Soul* (New York: Praeger Publishers, 1988), chapters 3 and 4.

38 As yet no systematic study of Hammurabi has been done: indeed, few observers link him to his earlier life as Frederic Robb. See "Fidepe H. Hammurabi—African Elder: A Mind from the Past, An Eye Into the Future," *History, The Bible, and the Black Man* (April 1978): 5–8, available in the Harsh Collection, Carter G. Woodson Branch, Chicago Public Library. Material on his work at the American Negro Exposition is in Box 368, Folder #3 of the Barnett Papers, Chicago Historical Society.

39 Cruse, *The Crisis of the Negro Intellectual*, 26. If anything, work on the black middle class must catch up to revisionist accounts of black working-class life in terms of grasping the unique relationship of race and class in black history. See for instance Hunter, *To 'Joy My Freedom*; and Robin Kelley, *Hammer and Hoe: Alabama Communists during the Great Depression* (Chapel Hill: University of North Carolina Press, 1990). For work treating the black middle class in the manner recommended here, see Shaw, *What a Woman Ought to Be and to Do*; Glenda Elizabeth Gilmore, *Gender and Jim Crow: Women and the Politics of White Supremacy in North Carolina, 1896–1920* (Chapel Hill: University of North Carolina Press, 1996); and Higgenbotham, *Righteous Discontent*, especially chapter 2. On local political history as a case study in racial clientage, see Charles R. Branham, "The Transformation of Black Political Leadership, 1864–1942" (Ph.D. diss., University of Chicago, 1981); William J. Grimshaw, *Bitter Fruit: Black Politics and the Chicago Machine, 1931–1991* (Chicago: University of Chicago Press, 1992); and James Q. Wilson, *Negro Politics: The Search for Leadership* (New York: Free Press, 1960), especially chapters 1, 3, and 4.

40 C. Wright Mills, *White Collar: The American Middle Classes* (New York: Oxford University Press, 1951). On working-class history's engagement with the question of race privilege, see David R. Roediger, *The Wages of Whiteness: Race and the Making of the American Working Class* (London: Verso, 1991); for suggestions of the direction such inquiry might take in relation to the study of white American middle classes, see Mike Davis, *City of Quartz: Excavating the Future in Los Angeles* (London: Verso, 1990); Douglas S. Massey and Nancy A. Denton, *American Apartheid: Segregation and the Making of the Underclass* (Cambridge, MA: Harvard University Press, 1993); and Thomas J. Sugrue, *The Origins of the Urban Crisis: Race and Inequality in Postwar Detroit* (Princeton, NJ: Princeton University Press, 1996).

The Limits of Democracy in the Suburbs

1 "America Plus Drive," *San Francisco Chronicle*, December 1, 1951; "Measure Would Permit Bias, Lawyers Contend," *San Francisco Chronicle*, December 3, 1951; also see "Fact Sheets" on America Plus, copies in C.L. Dellums Papers, Bancroft Library, carton 25, "America Plus" folder; and CFCU Papers, Bancroft Library, carton 1, untitled folder; *Shelley v. Kramer*, 334 U.S. 1 (1948).

2 *San Francisco Chronicle*, December 3, 1951. Its second incarnation was in the form of a bill proposed in the California State Senate. The bill was known variously as the "Freedom of Choice" Bill, the "Tenney Bill," after its author, or simply, "SCA 21." See *San Francisco News*, February 12, 1952.

3 Arnold Hirsch, "With or Without Jim Crow: Black Residential Segregation in the United States," in Arnold R. Hirsch and Raymond A. Mohl, eds., *Urban Policy in Twentieth Century America* (New Brunswick, NJ: Rutgers University Press, 1993), 65–99; Douglas Massey and Nancy Denton, *American Apartheid: Segregation and the Making of the Underclass* (Cambridge, MA: Harvard University Press, 1993).

4 Character in the 1950 novel *My Kind! My Country!* Aldrich Blake, chairman of America Plus, Inc., quoted in "America Plus Fact Sheet #1," January 21, 1952.

5 A narrative of the events in Southwood can be found in Robert Lee, "Christian Ethics and Race Relations: A Community Case Study" (M.A. thesis, Department of Christian Ethics, Pacific School of Religion, 1952). Also see Robert Lee, "Community Exclusion: A Case Study," *Phylon* 15, no. 2 (1954): 15:2, 202–205; and Robert Lee, "The Church in a Case of Neighborhood Exclusion," *Phylon* 13, no. 4 (1952): 338–340. See also *San Francisco Chronicle*, "South S.F. Votes to Exclude a Chinese Family," February 17, 1952.

6 "South S.F. Area Votes to Exclude a Chinese Family," *San Francisco Chronicle*, February 17, 1952. Lee's master's thesis mentions that there were headlines in almost all Bay Area newspapers as well as in the *New York Times*, the *Chicago Tribune*, and reports "in newspapers throughout the world, and on television, on the newsreel, and in many leading magazines in the nation" (p. 14).

7 "South S.F. Area Votes to Exclude a Chinese Family," *San Francisco Chronicle*, February 17, 1952.

8 Ibid.; in Lee, "Christian Ethics and Race Relations," 69. Emphasis mine.

9 Lee, "Christian Ethics and Race Relations," 9; Kenneth Jackson, *Crabgrass Frontier* (New York: Oxford University Press, 1985), 196–206.

10 Thomas J. Sugrue, "Crabgrass-Roots Politics: Race, Rights, and the Reaction against Liberalism in the Urban North, 1940–64," *Journal of American History* (September 1995): 557. Also see Thomas Sugrue, *The Origins of the Urban Crisis* (Princeton, NJ: Princeton University Press, 1996).

11 "War Brought Segregated Housing to the East Bay," *Oakland Tribune*, August 21, 1994; Elaine D. Johnson, "Survey of Peninsula Realtors," November 6, 1957. NAACP Papers, Bancroft Library, carton 39, "housing-surveys" file, 5, 6, 8.

12 Lee, "Christian Ethics and Race Relations," 20; all details are included in chapter 2 of Lee's dissertation: "Chronological Documentation of Proceedings," 19–35.

13 Survey of state office candidates on civil rights, 1950. California Federation for Civic Unity Papers, Bancroft Library, carton 2, "FEPC" folder #3; in Lee, "Christian Ethics and Race Relations," 31.

14 Reginald R. Isaacs, "Are Urban Neighborhoods Possible?" *Journal of Housing* (July 1948): 177; Successful Subdivisions, Federal Housing Administration, 1941. Cited in Isaacs, "Are Urban Neighborhoods Possible?" 177. The predominant notion of the ideal neighborhood during this midcentury period seemed to emphasize homogeneity in dwelling types as well as residents. *Time Magazine*, "The Country Clubber," December 1, 1947, in Isaacs, "Are Urban Neighborhoods Possible?" 178.

15 *Among These Rights,* newsletter of the Council for Civic Unity, San Francisco, double issue, April-June 1959. Copy in San Francisco Labor Council Records, Bancroft Library, carton 89, "C-1959" folder.

16 Lee, "Christian Ethics and Race Relations," 11.

17 Ibid., 10–11; 59.

18 For a fascinating examination of the way in which increasing consciousness about class position was coupled with growing insistence on outward adherence to principles of egalitarianism and classlessness, see William Dobriner, *Class in Suburbia* (New York: Prentice Hall, 1963), 34–36; Reginald R. Isaacs, "The Neighborhood Theory—A Basis for Social Disorganization," preliminary draft, April 20, 1947. Copy in C.B. Wurster Collection, Bancroft Library, carton 23, "Neighborhoods" folder, 3.

19 Lee, "Christian Ethics and Race Relations," 54–56; quote, 53.

20 The development of this argument owes much to David Roediger's influential work *The Wages of Whiteness* and other recent literature that has emphasized the ways in which the exercise of domination can be based on fundamental social insecurities. David Roediger, *The Wages of Whiteness* (New York: Verso, 1991).

21 Lee, "Christian Ethics and Race Relations," 68, 70; Elaine Tyler May argues in *Homeward Bound: American Families in the Cold War Era* (New York: Basic Books, 1988) that the dangerous potential of female sexuality found safe expression in motherhood. Yet in the postwar suburb, unless the family

could be completely protected from outside threats, female sexuality would remain a dangerous potential.

22 Elsie Smith Parker, "Both Sides of the Color Line," *Appraisal Journal* 11, no. 1 (January 1943): 31.

23 Lee, "Christian Ethics and Race Relations," 68; quotes, 31, 38; *San Francisco Chronicle*, February 20, 1952.

24 Friedrich Engels, *The Origin of the Family, Private Property and the State* ([1884]; repr., New York: Penguin, 1985).

25 Lee, "Christian Ethics and Race Relations," 68–70.

26 Aldrich Blake to Mr. Milton Senn, April 18, 1952, 2. California Federation for Civic Unity Papers, Box 4, incoming correspondence file: "A—Anti-defamation League," Bancroft Library.

27 Ibid., 3.

28 See Lee, "Christian Ethics and Race Relations," 70, 74; see also Aldrich Blake to Mr. Milton Senn, April 18, 1952; Lee, "Christian Ethics and Race Relations," 69.

29 Lee, "Christian Ethics and Race Relations," 21, 67, 69.

30 William Issel and Robert Cherney, *San Francisco, 1865–1932: Politics, Power, and Urban Development* (Berkeley: University of California Press, 1986), 58–79; 66–68; Douglas Henry Daniels, *Pioneer Urbanites: A Social and Cultural History of Black San Francisco* (Berkeley: University of California Press, 1990), 162–175; Albert Broussard, *Black San Francisco: The Struggle for Racial Equality in the West, 1900–1954* (Lawrence: University Press of Kansas, 1993); Brian J. Godfrey, *Neighborhoods in Transition: The Making of San Francisco's Ethnic and Nonconformist Communities* (Berkeley: University of California Press, 1988), 94–113; Kenneth L. Kusmer, *A Ghetto Takes Shape: Black Cleveland, 1870–1930* (Urbana: University of Illinois Press, 1976); Massey and Denton, *American Apartheid*, 17; James Borchert, *Alley Life in Washington: Family, Community, Religion, and Folklife in the City, 1850–1970* (Urbana: University of Illinois Press, 1980); Arnold R. Hirsch, *Making the Second Ghetto: Race and Housing in Chicago, 1940–1960* (New York: Cambridge University Press, 1983).

Rethinking Middle-Class Populism and Politics in the Postwar Era

1 C. Wright Mills, *White Collar: The American Middle Classes* (New York: Oxford University Press, 1951), xviii, 328.

2 Barbara Ehrenreich well describes the popular and academic representation of the white backlash in the 1970s in *Fear of Falling: The Inner Life of the Middle Class* (New York: HarperCollins, 1989), chapter 3. Richard Rogin's *New York Times* article is a good example of the journalistic portrayal of "Middle America." See "Joe Kelly Has Reached His Boiling Point," reprinted in Murray Freedman, *Overcoming Middle-Class Rage* (Philadelphia: Westminster, 1971).

3 David Halle, *America's Working Man: Work, Home, and Politics among Blue-Collar Property Owners* (Chicago: Chicago University Press, 1984); Jonathan Rieder, *Canarsie: The Jews and Italians of Brooklyn against Liberalism* (Cambridge, MA: Harvard University Press, 1985); Ronald P. Formisano, *Boston against Busing: Race, Class, and Ethnicity in the 1960s and 1970s* (Chapel Hill: University of North Carolina Press, 1991); Thomas J. Sugrue, "Crabgrass-Roots Politics: Race, Rights, and the Reaction against Liberalism in the Urban North, 1940–1964," *Journal of American History* 82, 2 (September 1995): 551–578, and *The Origins of the Urban Crisis: Race and Inequality in Postwar Detroit* (Princeton, NJ: Princeton University Press, 1996); Arnold Hirsch, *Making the Second Ghetto: Race and Housing in Chicago, 1940–1960* (New York: Cambridge University Press, 1983) and "Massive Resistance in the Urban North: Trumbull Park, Chicago, 1953–1966," *Journal of American History* 82, 2 (September 1995): 522–550; for an older study of the same topic, see Charles Abrams *Forbidden Neighbors: A Study of Prejudice in Housing* (New York: Harper & Brothers, 1955); Michael Kazin, *The Populist Persuasion: An American History* (New York: Basic Books, 1995). Robert Johnston has questioned the automatic association of populism with reactionary, antiliberal views in "American Populism and American Language of Class," a paper presented at the 1997 meeting of the Organization of American Historians, see esp. 15–16. Andrew Hurley's analysis of environmentalist activism in Gary, Indiana, presents a refreshing exception to this association of postwar middle-class politics with antiliberalism. See *Environmental Inequalities: Class, Race, and Industrial Pollution in Gary, Indiana, 1945–1980* (Chapel Hill: University of North Carolina Press, 1995).

4 A detailed analysis of the political culture and struggles of northeastern Queens communities between 1945 and 1960 can be found in my own "Suburban Citizens: Domesticity and Community

Politics in Queens, New York, 1945–1960" (Ph.D. diss., Yale University, 1994) and my forthcoming book from Cornell University Press.

5 I am not arguing that "rights" and "privileges" were unimportant to Queens residents; simply that "needs" and "responsibilities" were the concepts that dominated their political rhetoric, both in their public comments (as printed and editorialized in community newspapers, for instance) and in their private correspondence with city officials. On the primacy of rights talk in postwar liberalism, see Sugrue, "Crabgrass-Roots Politics," 564, especially note 24; and Alan Brinkley, *The End of Reform: New Deal Liberalism in Recession and War* (New York: Vintage, 1995), 10, 167.

6 Fones-Wolf, *Selling Free Enterprise: The Business Assault on Labor and Liberalism, 1945–60* (Urbana: University of Illinois Press, 1994) and Griffith, "Forging America's Postwar Order: Domestic Politics and Political Economy in the Age of Truman," in *The Truman Presidency*, ed. Michael J. Lacey (Cambridge: Cambridge University Press, 1989), 57–88.

7 Levittown, with its detached, single-family, and privately owned dwellings, is the model most often associated with American postwar suburbs. See, for instance, Kenneth T. Jackson, *Crabgrass Frontier: The Suburbanization of the United States* (New York: Oxford University Press, 1985), chapter 13. Garden apartment complexes built in Queens in the late 1940s and 1950s were commonly referred to as "suburban apartments" (see, in the case of Glen Oaks Village, *Journal of Housing*, February 1948, 29, and the *New York Times*, November 14, 1948, VIII, 1). Lewis Mumford also praised the suburban qualities of the New York Life Insurance Company's Fresh Meadows, in "The Sky Line," *The New Yorker*, October 22, 1949, 102–106. Tenants represented 39 percent of the population of northeastern Queens in 1950, a figure that was on the rise thanks to the construction of several large-scale garden apartment complexes in the early 1950s. Figures compiled from U.S. Census of population: 1950 (hereafter *1950 Census*), Table 3, "Characteristics of Dwelling Units, by Census Tracts."

8 This demographic growth is documented in Queens Community Council of Greater New York, *Queens Communities: Population Characteristics and Neighborhood Social Resources* (New York: Bureau of Community Statistical Services, Research Department, 1958). Hereafter *Queens Communities*. See also a survey compiled by the Consolidated Edison Company from the records of gas and electricity consumption. Letter to Maurice Fitzgerald, Queens Borough President, from Robert W. Dasey, Gladstone-Dasey Associates Realtors, May 4, 1950, folder "Parking #1313," box 125, Subject Files, Mayor William O'Dwyer Papers, New York City Municipal Archives (hereafter O'Dwyer Papers).

9 See *1950 Census*, Table 2, "Age, Marital Status, and Economic Characteristics, by Sex, by Census Tracts" and *U.S. Census of Population: 1960* (hereafter *1960 Census*), Table P-3, "Labor Force Characteristics of the Population, by Census Tracts." As Halle has convincingly argued, income overlap between better-paid blue-collar workers and lower-echelon white-collar workers (including clerical workers, accountants, retail managers, and teachers) and the widespread availability of cars ensured the formation of occupationally mixed residential neighborhoods after World War II (*America's Working Man*, see esp. 16–22). He takes issue here with scholars like Bennet Berger and Richard F. Hamilton who have argued that postwar residential developments were strictly separated by occupation into working-class and middle-class suburbs. See Berger, *Working-Class Suburb: A Study of Auto Workers in Suburbia* (Berkeley: University of California Press, 1960), and Hamilton, *Class and Politics in the United States* (New York: Wiley, 1972).

10 Compiled from *1950 Census*, Table 1, "Characteristics of the Population, by Census Tracts" and *1960 Census*, Table P-1, "General Characteristics of the Population, by Census Tracts."

11 See *Queens Communities*.

12 For the change in the racial composition of Flushing Suburban from 7.5 to 50 percent between 1950 and 1960, see census tract 1257 in *1950 Census*, Table 1, and *1960 Census*, Table P-1. According to Marilyn Mossop, a black professional who moved to the area in 1950 from Harlem and became actively involved in its civic and political life, the partial white flight involved "low class" white families. Her personal papers (which include papers of the Flushing Suburban Civic Association and home movies of civic activities) documented a racially integrated civic life. Interview with M. Mossop, March 13, 1992, in the author's possession; documents in Mossop's possession.

13 See "Desegregation in Washington," *Flushing Guide*, September 1955, 2; "School News," *Kew Hills News*, October 1957, 6; for another of Schreier's denunciations of southern racist violence, this time the killing of four children in the bombing of the Birmingham Sixteenth Street Baptist Church in 1963, see "Oh, Promised Land!" *Kew Hills News*, October 1963. Friedan's involvement in radical politics in the 1940s and early 1950s is described in Daniel Horowitz, *Betty Friedan and the Making of the Feminine Mystique: The American Left, the Cold War, and Modern Feminism* (Amherst: University

of Massachusetts Press, 1998); I also examine the Parkway Village rent strike in "Suburban Citizens." For the activities of "Neighbors for Brotherhood," see *Kew Hills News*, September 1954, 2.

14 Although Queens was known prior to the New Deal as a bastion of conservatism, this changed with the tremendous population boom of the 1930s and 1940s. Debates raging over public housing, or Cold War issues, reflected the ideological diversity of the population. Electorally, as well, the area was divided between Republicans, Democrats and, to a lesser extent, progressive third parties such as the American Labor Party and, at the state level, the Liberal Party. I discuss these debates and the electoral makeup of specific neighborhoods in "Suburban Citizens."

15 *Beacon*, June 1956, BHCA Papers. Similar statements were found in "Constitution and By-Laws of the Bayside Hills Civic Association, Inc.," September 1953. I am grateful to the Bayside Hills Civic Association, and especially to William Caulfield, for allowing me to consult their papers.

16 "Salute Oakland Gardens" and "The Toughest Year," editorial, *The Bayside Times*, February 2, 1950, 1, 8.

17 On the OGCA's cooperation with the Greater Bayside Citizen's Association to improve bus service in the area, see "Citizen's Meeting at Legion Hall Probes Bus Problem Tonight," March 10, 1949, 1, and "OGCA to Hear Bus, Community House Talks," November 3, 1949, 1. On its leisure activities, see "Form Oakland Garden Civic-Social Group," February 10, 1949, 1; all in *Bayside Times*.

18 The *Bayside Times* was first published in 1935, just as the county embarked on its modern era of expansion. After the war, four additional weeklies—the *Pomonok News* (founded in 1952 and renamed the *Kew Hills News* the following year), the *Meadow Lark* (founded in 1949 and renamed the *Long Island Herald* in 1951), the *Glen Oaks News* (founded in 1948 and bought by the owners of the *Bayside Times* in July 1954), and the *Home Town News* (founded in 1948)— were published in northeastern Queens. These newspapers offered a wealth of information on the area's community and political life. They are available on microfilms at the Queens Borough Public Library, Long Island Division.

19 "Pomonok Tenants' Council To Hold First '52–'53 Meeting," *Pomonok News*, September 10, 1952, 1.

20 "Which One Are You?," *Home Town News*, July 15, 1958, 1.

21 "Good Luck!" *Long Island Herald*, January 22, 1953, 4.

22 "Protecting Your Interests," editorial, *Glen Oaks News*, August 21, 1952, 1.

23 "Support Your Civic Groups," editorial, *Bayside Times*, September 4, 1952, 20. See also "It's Your Job, Too!" *Long Island Herald*, September 11, 1952, 4, and "Join Now!" *Meadow Lark*, August 4, 1949, 1.

24 "Heart Fells Osterman," *Long Island Herald*, February 21, 1952, 2.

25 "Our Civic Groups," *Bayside Times*, January 22, 1942, 6.

26 "Civic Workers," editorial, *Bayside Times*, September 17, 1936, 6.

27 This is reflected, for instance, in the popularity of the "anti-machine" liberal Democrats in the area, and the numerous "independent" candidates who stemmed from civic ranks.

28 Fones-Wolf, *Selling Free Enterprise* and Griffith, "Forging America's Postwar Order."

29 Details about the formation and the strategies of the real-estate lobby can be found in the report of a congressional committee formed in March 1950 to study "the role of lobbying in representative self-government." See U.S. Congress, *Hearings before the House Select Committee on Lobbying Activities*, 81st Congress, 2nd Session (Washington, DC: U.S. Government Printing Office, 1950). What became known as "the lobby" is also described in Leonard Freedman, *Public Housing: The Politics of Poverty* (New York: Holt, Rinehart & Winston, 1969), 4–7, and Gwendolyn Wright, *Building the Dream: A Social History of Housing in America* (Cambridge: MIT Press, 1981), 220–222. For critical assessment of the lobby's practices, see "Housing: A 1950 Tragedy," by Lee F. Johnson, executive vice president of the National Housing Conference, in *Survey* (December 1950): 551–555 and "What Makes the Real Estate Lobby Tick?" by Leo Goodman, director of the CIO National Housing Committee, in *Journal of Housing* (December 1950): 423–427. The "grass-roots" campaigns in various localities were described at length in a series of articles published in the *Journal of Housing*: January 1950, 8–10; May 1950, 158–159; July 1950, 226–227; August 1950, 265–268; January 1951, 9–10, 24–26; February 1951, 49–50; March 1951, 90, 94; May 1951, 153–154.

30 This controversy can be followed in the pages of the *Long Island Daily Press* and the *Long Island Star Journal*, two daily newspapers that played a major role in fueling the public outrage that followed the announcement of these programs by the New York City and State governments. Many homeowners' and civic associations joined the protest, as reflected by their letters to city officials (in particular, letters to the New York City Housing Authority and to Mayor O'Dwyer). Community newspapers—

although they took no editorial position on this issue—reported the controversy, as well. I discuss this issue at length in "Suburban Citizens."

31 In *The Great School Wars: A History of the New York City Public Schools* ([1974] New York: Basic Books, 1988), Diane Ravitch argued that by 1940 the New York City school system had solved its chronic overcrowding problem (239). Her analysis does not take into account the factors mentioned above. The only "great school war" of the postwar period that she analyzed is that over racial integration. The voluminous correspondence found in the Mayors' Papers from New York parents belie her assertion.

32 The joint effort of the Oakland Gardens Civic Association, the Bell Park Community Council, and the area's homeowners' associations to secure additional school seats is documented in *The Bayside Times* ("P.S. 46 in Mind, OGCA Supports P.S. 31 Wing Drive," January 12, 1950, 12 and "Bell Park Backs Hills Wing Drive," February 2, 1950, 6).

33 "Home Owner Groups Oppose Housing Plan," *Star*, December 13, 1949, 1:5.

34 "Civics Propose Housing Limits," *Meadow Lark*, December 1, 1949, 1. See copy of proposal, January 27, 1950, folder "Zoning #1872," box 174, Subject Files, O'Dwyer Papers.

35 "Survey Area School Kids," *Bayside Times*, May 4, 1950, 18.

36 Emphasis in the original. Memorandum, "Kew Meadows School Committee, P.S. 201, Queens," folder "Schools—Queens, 1950–1951 #1274," box 115, Subject Files, Impellitteri Papers.

37 "Hundreds of Parents Set for School 'Zero Hour'," *Meadow Lark*, November 16, 1950, 1.

38 Letter to the Editor, *Bayside Times*, June 14, 1951, 20.

39 Brian Balogh offers a good review of the scholarship on the twentieth-century managerial state, and an incisive critique of the false dichotomy established between claims to technical expertise and mass-based political movements. See his *Chain Reaction: Expert Debate and Public Participation in American Commercial Nuclear Power, 1945–1975* (New York: Cambridge University Press, 1991), 1–18. For Boyte, see his *Commonwealth: A Return to Citizen Politics* (New York: Free Press, 1989), 10.

40 See, among others, Elaine Tyler May, *Homeward Bound: American Families in the Cold War Era* (New York: Basic Books, 1988). For a more complex view, see Joanne Meyerowitz, ed., *Not June Cleaver: Women and Gender in Postwar America, 1945–1960* (Philadelphia: Temple University Press, 1994).

Why Class Continues to Count

1 Benjamin DeMott, *The Imperial Middle: Why Americans Can't Think Straight about Class* (New York: William Morrow, 1990); Stuart M. Blumin, *The Emergence of the Middle Class: Social Experience in the American City, 1760–1900* (New York: Cambridge University Press, 1989), 9–10. The most recent statements of "middle-class classlessness" are C. Dallett Hemphill, *Bowing to Necessities: A History of Manners in America, 1620–1860* (New York: Oxford University Press, 1999); and Brian Roberts, *American Alchemy: The California Gold Rush and Middle-Class Culture* (Chapel Hill: University of North Carolina Press, 2000).

Propertied of a Different Kind

Thanks to Robert Johnston and Joan Roe for their helpful comments on an earlier draft of this article. The author also thanks the Center for Scholars and Writers at the New York Public Library for its support.

1 Louis Hartz, *The Liberal Tradition in America: An Interpretation of American Political Thought since the Revolution* (New York: Harcourt, Brace, & Company, 1955); Seymour Martin Lipset, *Continental Divide: The Values and Institutions of the United States and Canada* (London: Routledge, 1990), 25.

2 Paul E. Johnson, *A Shopkeeper's Millennium: Society and Revivals in Rochester, New York, 1815–1837* (New York: Hill & Wang, 1978), 5–6.

3 Among many, many others, see Stephen M. Frank, *Life with Father: Parenthood and Masculinity in the Nineteenth-Century American North* (Baltimore: Johns Hopkins University Press, 1998), 81; George Chauncey, *Gay New York: Gender, Urban Culture, and the Making of the Gay Male World, 1890–1940* (New York: Basic Books, 1994), 106–107.

4 The most sustained and promising effort at exploring the history of the middle class defined in this way is Stuart Blumin, *The Emergence of the Middle Class: Social Experience in the American City, 1760–1900* (Ithaca, NY: Cornell University Press, 1989). See also John S. Gilkeson, Jr., *Middle Class Providence, 1820–1940* (Princeton, NJ: Princeton University Press, 1986).

5 However, for a thoughtful definition of middle class that draws a clear distinction between middle class and bourgeoisie, see the *Encyclopedia of the Social Sciences*, Vol. 10 (New York: The Macmillan

Company, 1933), 407–415. For a very similar definition of bourgeoisie, see also Jürgen Kocka, "Bürgertum und bürgerliche Gesellschaft im 19. Jahrhundert: Europäische Entwicklungen und deutsche Eigenarten," in Jürgen Kocka, ed., *Bürgertum im Neunzehnten Jahrhundert* (München: dtv, 1988), 60.

6 Karen Halttunen, *Confidence Men and Painted Women: A Study of Middle-Class Culture in America, 1830–1870* (New Haven, CT: Yale University Press, 1982); Nancy Cott, *The Bonds of Womanhood: "Woman's Sphere" in New England, 1780–1835* (New Haven, CT: Yale University Press, 1977); Bruce Eugene Curtis, *The Middle Class Progressivism of William Graham Sumner* (Boston: Twayne, 1981).

7 Richard Hofstadter, *The Age of Reform* (New York: Random House, Vintage Books, 1955); Gabriel Kolko, *The Triumph of Conservatism: A Re-Interpretation of American History, 1900–1916* (New York: Free Press, 1963); James Weinstein, *The Corporate Ideal in the Liberal State, 1900–1918* (Boston: Beacon, 1968); Daniel Aaron, *Men of Good Hope: A Story of American Progressives* (New York: Oxford University Press, 1970); Robert H. Wiebe, *The Search for Order, 1877–1920* (Westport, CT: Greenwood Press, 1980, 1967); Curtis, *Middle Class Progressivism*.

8 Ernest Labrousse bemoaned already in 1955 the absence of such studies. See his "Voies Nouvelles Vers une Histoire de la Bourgeoisie Occidentale aux XVIIIème et XIXème Siècles," in *Relazioni del X. Congresso Internazionale di Scienze Storiche*, Vol. 4, *Storia Moderna* (Firenze: G. C. Sansoni, 1955). See also Peter N. Stearns, "The Middle Class: Toward a Precise Definition," *Comparative Studies in Society and History* 21 (July 1979): 378. This point also has been made by Olivier Zunz, *Why the American Century?* (Chicago: University of Chicago Press, 1998), xv.

9 Stearns, "The Middle Class," 393. For a similar argument, see Bruce Laurie, "Spavined Ministers, Lying Toothpullers, and Buggering Priests: Third-Partyism and the Search for Security in the Antebellum North," in Howard B. Rock, Paul A. Gilje, and Robert Asher, eds., *American Artisans: Crafting Social Identity, 1750–1850* (Baltimore: Johns Hopkins University Press, 1994), 98–119.

10 E. P. Thompson, *The Making of the English Working Class* (London: V. Gollancz, 1963); Stearns, "The Middle Class," 380.

11 Edmond Goblot, *La Barrière et le Niveau* (Paris: Librarie Félix Alcan, 1925), 27.

12 Philip Scranton, *Endless Novelty: Specialty Production and American Industrialization, 1865–1925* (Princeton, NJ: Princeton University Press, 1997); Mary H. Blewett, *Men, Women, and Work: Class, Gender, and Protest in the New England Shoe Industry, 1780–1910* (Urbana: University of Illinois Press, 1988).

13 Frances W. Gregory and Irene D. Neu, "The American Industrial Elite in the 1870s: Their Social Origins," in William Miller, ed., *Men in Business: Essays in the History of Entrepreneurship* (Cambridge, MA: Harvard University Press, 1952), 202.

14 Jürgen Kocka, "Bürgertum und bürgerliche Gesellschaft im 19. Jahrhundert;" Pierre Bourdieu, *Distinction: A Social Critique of the Judgment of Taste* (Cambridge, MA: Harvard University Press, 1984).

15 Max Weber, *Wirtschaft und Gesellschaft: Grundriss der Verstehenden Soziologie* ([ca. 1922] Tübingen: J. C. B. Mohr, 1985), 177–180; 531–540.

16 Bourdieu, *Distinction*; Norbert Elias, *Über den Prozeß der Zivilisation: Soziogenetische und Pychogenetische Untersuchungen* (Frankfurt: Suhrkamp Verlag, 1976); Goblot, *La Barrière et le Niveau*.

17 Peter Gay, *Pleasure Wars: The Bourgeois Experience: Victoria to Freud* (New York: Norton, 1998), 7.

18 Most important in this context is the five-volume study of bourgeois culture by Peter Gay. See Peter Gay, *The Bourgeois Experience: Victoria to Freud* (New York: Norton, 1984–1998). See also Heinz-Gerhard Haupt and Geoffrey Crossick, *Die Kleinbürger: Eine Europäische Sozialgeschichte des 19.Jahrhunderts* (München: C.H. Beck, 1998); Paul DiMaggio, "Cultural Entrepreneurship in Nineteenth-Century Boston: The Creation of an Organizational Base of High Culture in America," in *Media, Culture, and Society* 4 (1982): 33–50; Lawrence W. Levine, *Highbrow/Lowbrow: The Emergence of Cultural Hierarchy in America* (Cambridge, MA: Harvard University Press, 1988); Sven Beckert, *The Monied Metropolis: New York City and the Consolidation of the American Bourgeoisie* (New York: Cambridge University Press, forthcoming); Thomas Bender, *New York Intellect: A History of Intellectual Life in New York City, From 1750 to the Beginnings of Our Own Time* (New York: Knopf, 1987); Roy Rosenzweig and Elizabeth Blackmar, *The Park and the People: A History of Central Park* (Ithaca, NY: Cornell University Press, 1992); Nicola Beisel, *Imperiled Innocents: Anthony Comstock and Family Reproduction in Victorian America* (Princeton, NJ: Princeton University Press, 1997); Leora Auslander, *Taste and Power: Furnishing Modern France* (Berkeley: University of California Press, 1996).

19 DiMaggio, "Cultural Entrepreneurship in Nineteenth-Century Boston", 33–50.

20 Sven Beckert, "Migration, Ethnicity, and Working-Class Formation, Passaic, 1889–1926," in Dirk Hoerder and Jörg Nagler, eds., *People in Transit, German Migrations in Comparative Perspective* (New York: Cambridge University Press, 1995), 347–377.

21 James Livingston, *Origins of the Federal Reserve System* (Ithaca, NJ: Cornell University Press, 1986), 42.

22 Thorstein Veblen, *The Theory of the Leisure Class: An Economic Study in the Evolution of Institutions* (New York: The Macmillan Company, 1899).

23 See especially Robert Johnston, "Middle-Class Political Ideology in a Corporate Society: The Persistence of Small-Propertied Radicalism in Portland, Oregon, 1883–1926" (Ph.D. diss., Rutgers University, 1993).

24 Sklar, *Corporate Reconstruction*, 21.

25 Stearns, "The Middle Class," 391; Robert G. Gutman, "Class, Status and Community Power in Nineteenth-Century American Industrial Cities: Paterson, New Jersey, A Case Study," in Frederic Cople Jaher, *The Age of Industrialism in America* (New York: Free Press, 1968), 263–288; Livingston, *Federal Reserve*, 42.

26 See Geoffrey Crossick and Heinz-Gerhard Haupt, eds., *Shopkeepers and Master Artisans in the Nineteenth-Century* (New York: Methuen, 1984), especially the essays by David Blackbourn and Philip Nord. The sociological character of Nazi Party supporters has recently been subject to controversies, as Richard Hamilton has challenged the long-standing assertion that NSDAP membership was heavily lower middle class. However, I still agree with scholars such as Thomas Childers and Barrington Moore who have empirically demonstrated the overrepresentation of lower-middle-class Germans in the Nazi Party. Obviously, other social groups also supported the Nazis. See Thomas Childers, *The Nazi Voter: The Social Foundations of Fascism in Germany, 1919–1933* (Chapel Hill: University of North Carolina Press, 1983); Barrington Moore, *Injustice: The Social Bases of Obedience and Revolt* (White Plains, NY: M. E. Sharpe, 1978); Richard Hamilton, *Who Voted for Hitler?* (Princeton, NJ: Princeton University Press, 1982).

27 Amy Bridges, *A City in the Republic, Antebellum New York and the Origins of Machine Politics* (New York: Cambridge University Press, 1984).

28 A point also made by Stearns, "The Middle Class," 391; Richard F. Hamilton, *Class and Politics in the United States* (New York: John Wiley & Sons, 1972).

29 Stearns, "The Middle Class," 390.

30 Leon Fink, *Workingmen's Democracy: The Knights of Labor and American Politics* (Urbana: University of Illinois Press, 1983), 223.

31 Sven Beckert, "It Is Not Safe to Place the Execution of the Laws in the Hands of the Classes against Which They Are Principally to Be Enforced: Democracy in the Age of Capital" (manuscript, in author's possession, 2000).

32 On workers see Sean Wilentz, *Chants Democratic: New York City and the Rise of the American Working-Class, 1788–1850* (New York: Oxford University Press, 1984); Alan Dawley, *Class and Community: The Industrial Revolution in Lynn* (Cambridge, MA: Harvard University Press, 1976). On the bourgeoisie, see Livingston, *Federal Reserve*; Lears, *No Place of Grace*; Beckert, *The Monied Metropolis*.

33 William Cronon, *Nature's Metropolis: Chicago and the Great West* (New York: W.W. Norton, 1991).

34 Steven Hahn, *The Roots of Southern Populism: Yeoman Farmers and the Transformation of the Georgia Upcountry, 1850–1890* (New York: Oxford University Press, 1983), 169; Edward Ayers, *The Promise of the New South: Life after Reconstruction* (New York: Oxford University Press, 1992).

35 Blumin, *The Emergence of the Middle Class*; Nick Salvatore, *Eugene V. Debs: Citizen and Socialist* (Urbana: University of Illinois Press, 1982).

36 Jürgen Kocka, *White Collar Workers in America, 1890-1940: A Social-Political History in International Perspective* (London: Sage Publications, 1980).

37 The best work on the European lower middle class is Haupt and Crossick, *Die Kleinbürger*. On the bourgeoisie, see, among many others, Ernest Labrousse, "Voies Nouvelles Vers une Histoire de la Bourgeoisie Occidentale aux XVIIIème et XIXème Siècles," in *Relazioni del X. Congresso Internazionale di Scienze Storiche*, Vol. 4, *Storia Moderna* (Firenze: G. C. Sansoni, 1955). By far the largest comprehensive research effort was accomplished in the context of the University of Bielefeld's project on the German bourgeoisie in European perspective. For the results, see Kocka, *Bürgertum im Neunzehnten Jahrhundert*; Kocka, ed., *Bürger und Bürgerlichkeit im 19. Jahrhundert*; Hans-Juergen Puhle, ed., *Bürger in der Gesellschaft der Neuzeit: Wirtschaft, Politik, Kultur* (Göttingen: Vandenhoeck & Ruprecht, 1991). For Germany, see also the innovative conceptualization in Hartmut Zwahr, *Prole-*

tariat und Bourgeoisie in Deutschland: Studien zur Klassendialektik (Köln: Pahl-Rugenstein-Verlag, 1980). David Blackbourn and Geoff Eley, *The Peculiarities of German History: Bourgeois Society and Politics in Nineteenth-Century Germany* (New York: Oxford University Press, 1984); Blackbourn and Evans, eds., *The German Bourgeoisie* (especially Blackbourn's introduction); Charles S. Maier, *Recasting Bourgeois Europe: Stabilization in France, Germany, and Italy in the Decade after World War 1* (Princeton, NJ: Princeton University Press, 1975); Marion Kaplan, *The Making of the Jewish Middle Class: Women, Family, and Identity in Imperial Germany* (New York : Oxford University Press, 1991); Thomas Mergel, *Zwischen Klasse und Konfession: Katholisches Bürgertum im Rheinland, 1794–1914* (Göttingen: Vandenhoeck & Ruprecht, 1994). On specifc cities see Thomas Weichsel, *Die Bürger von Wiesbaden* (München: R. Oldenbourg, 1997); Ralf Zerback, *München und sein Stadtbürgertum* (München: R. Oldenbourg, 1997); Birgit-Katharine Seeman, *Stadt, Bürgertum und Kultur: Kulturelle Entwicklung und Kulturpolitik in Hamburg von 1839 bis 1933 am Beispiel des Museumswesens* (Husum: Matthiesen Verlag, 1998); Ralf Roth, *Stadt und Bürgertum in Frankfurt am Main: Ein besonderer Weg von der ständischen zur modernen Bürgergesellschaft, 1760–1914* (München: R. Oldenbourg, 1996); Dolores L. Augustine, *Patricians and Parvenus: Wealth and High Society in Wilhelmine Germany* (Oxford and Providence: Berg, 1994).

For the Habsburg bourgeoisie, see Ernst Bruckmüller et al., eds., *Bürgertum in der Habsburgmonarchie*, Vol. 1 (Wien: Böhlau Verlag, 1992); Hannes Stekl et al., eds., *"Durch Arbeit, Besitz, Wissen und Gerichtigkeit": Bürgertum in der Habsbugmonarchie*, Vol. 2 (Wien: Böhlau Verlag, 1992).

For the French bourgeoisie, see the work of Adeline Daumard, for example Adeline Daumard, *Les Bourgeois et la Bourgeoisie en France depuis 1815* (Paris: Aubier, 1987). See also Theodore Zeitlin, *France, 1845–1945: Ambition & Love* (Oxford: Oxford University Press, 1973); Michael B. Miller, *The Bon Marche: Bourgeois Culture and the Department Store, 1869–1920* (Princeton, NJ: Princeton University Press, 1981); Bonnie G. Smith, *Ladies of the Leisure Class: The Bourgeoises of Northern France in the Nineteenth Century* (Princeton, NJ: Princeton University Press, 1981); Richard Holt, "Social History and Bourgeois Culture in Nineteenth-Century France," in *Comparative Studies in Society and History* 27 (October 1985): 713–726; David Garrioch, *The Formation of the Parisian Bourgeoisie, 1690–1830* (Cambridge, MA: Harvard University Press, 1996).

For Great Britain, see especially the work by W. D. Rubinstein, for example, W. D. Rubinstein, "Wealth, Elites, and the Class Structure of Modern Britain," *Past and Present* 76 (August 1977): 99–126. See also Leonore Davidoff and Catherine Hall, *Family Fortunes: Men and Women of the English Middle Class, 1780–1850* (London: Hutchinson, 1987); Peter Earle, *The Making of the English Middle Class: Business, Society, and Family Life in London, 1660–1730* (London: Methuen, 1989); R. J. Morris, *Class, Sect, and Party: The Making of the British Middle Class: Leeds, 1820–1850* (Manchester: Manchester University Press, 1990); G. R. Seale, *Entrepreneurial Politics in Mid-Victorian Britain* (Oxford: Oxford University Press, 1993); Hills, "Division and Cohesion in the Nineteenth-Century Middle Class"; Charles A. Jones, *International Business in the Nineteenth Century: The Rise and Fall of a Cosmopolitan Bourgeoisie* (Brighton: Wheatsheaf Books, 1987); Richard H. Trainor, *Black Country Élites: The Exercise of Authority in an Industrialized Area, 1830–1900* (Oxford: Clarendon Press, 1993); Eleanor Gordon and Richard Trainor, "Employers and Policymaking: Scotland and Northern Ireland, c. 1880–1939," in S. J. Connolly, R. A. Houston, and R. J. Morris, eds., *Conflict, Identity, and Economic Development: Ireland and Scotland, 1600–1939* (Preston: Carnegie Publishing, 1995), 254–267. For Italy, see Marco Meriggi, "Italienisches und deutsches Bürgertum im Vergleich," in Kocka, ed., *Bürgertum im 19. Jahrhundert*, 141–159; Francesco Volpe, *La Borghesia di Provincia Nell'Eta Borbonica* (Napoli: Edizioni Scientifiche Italiane, 1991). See also Daniela Luigia Caglioti, "Voluntary Societies and Urban Elites in Nineteenth-Century Naples," (paper presented at the Fourth International Conference on Urban History, Venice, 1998).

For the Netherlands, see Boudien de Vries, *Electoraat en Elite: Sociale Structuur en Sociale Mobiliteit in Amsterdam, 1850–1895* (Amsterdam: Bataafsche Leeuw, 1986). It is striking how similar the social and cultural conflicts between merchants and industrialists were in Amsterdam and New York.

For Switzerland, see the excellent study by Albert Tanner, *Arbeitsame Patrioten, Wohlanständige Damen: Bürgertum und Bürgerlichkeit in der Schweiz, 1830–1914* (Zürich: Orell Fussli, 1995).

For a perspective on less industrialized countries and a very different set of problems, see the essay collection by Enrique Florescano, ed., *Origenes y Desarrollo de la Burguesia en America Latina, 1700–1955* (Mexico: Editorial Nueva Imagen, 1985) and Marie-Claire Bergère, *The Golden Age of the Chinese Bourgeoisie, 1911–1937* (New York: Cambridge University Press, 1989).

38 Haupt, *Die Kleinbuerger*.

1   R. J. Morris, *Class, Sect and Party: The Making of the British Middle Class: Leeds, 1820–1850* (New York: Manchester University Press, 1990), 9.

2   Sinclair Lewis, *Babbitt* (New York: Harcourt, Brace, & World, 1922); Lewis Corey, *The Crisis of the Middle Class* (New York: Covici-Friede, 1935). For the depth of the tradition of antibourgeois sentiment in nineteenth-century Europe, see Peter Gay, *The Bourgeois Experience, Victoria to Freud: Education of the Senses* (New York: Oxford University Press, 1984), 17–44.

3   C. Wright Mills, *The Power Elite* (New York: Oxford University Press, 1956); Mills, with the assistance of Helen Schneider, *The New Men of Power: America's Labor Leaders* (New York: Harcourt, Brace, 1948).

4   Cornel West, *The American Evasion of Philosophy: A Genealogy of Pragmatism* (Madison: University of Wisconsin Press, 1989), 135; C. Wright Mills, *White Collar: The American Middle Classes* (New York: Oxford University Press, 1951); quotes on 233 and xvi.

5   E. Franklin Frazier, *Black Bourgeoisie: The Rise of a New Middle Class* (New York: Free Press, 1957), 233, section 2, 86 and passim, 217, 26. Frazier's shadow stands over studies of the African-American middle class as does Mills's over the white; for an overview, see Bart Landry, *The New Black Middle Class* (Berkeley: University of California Press, 1987).

    It is important to note here, as does Adam Green in his essay for this volume, that even though there is not yet much of a self-conscious historical literature about the African-American middle class, those scholars who have tackled the subject generally continue to follow Frazier in arguing that even when it is at its most radical, the black middle class (or petite bourgeoisie) is inherently incapable of forming alliances with the black masses. See, for example, Thomas Holt, *Black over White: Negro Political Leadership in South Carolina during Reconstruction* (Urbana: University of Illinois Press, 1977); Judith Stein, *The World of Marcus Garvey: Race and Class in Modern Society* (Baton Rouge: Louisiana State University Press, 1986); and Daniel Letwin, *The Challenge of Interracial Unionism: Alabama Coal Miners, 1878–1921* (Chapel Hill: University of North Carolina Press, 1997). A book that historicizes Frazier but still effectively follows in his footsteps is Kevin K. Gaines, *Uplifting the Race: Black Leadership, Politics, and Culture in the Twentieth Century* (Chapel Hill: University of North Carolina Press, 1996); one that much more effectively demonstrates the complex promise of black middle-class radicalism is Jonathan Scott Holloway, *Confronting the Veil: Black Intellectual Radicalism in the New Deal Era* (Chapel Hill: University of North Carolina Press, 2001).

    For more favorable views of the black middle class, see Eric Foner's disagreement with Holt, "Reconstruction and the Black Political Tradition," in Richard L. McCormick, ed., *Political Parties and the Modern State* (New Brunswick, NJ: Rutgers University Press, 1984); Joe William Trotter, *Black Milwaukee: The Making of an Industrial Proletariat* (Urbana: University of Illinois Press, 1985), esp. chapter 3; Trotter, *Coal, Class and Color: Blacks in Southern West Virginia, 1915–1932* (Urbana: University of Illinois Press, 1990), esp. chapter 6; Charles Pete T. Banner-Haley, *To Do Good and to Do Well: Middle-Class Blacks and the Depression, Philadelphia, 1929–1941* (New York: Garland, 1993); Nick Salvatore, *We All Got History: The Memory Books of Amos Webber* (New York: Random House, 1996); Stephanie J. Shaw, *What a Woman Ought to Be and to Do: Black Professional Women Workers During the Jim Crow Era* (Chicago: University of Chicago Press, 1996); Judith Weisenfeld, *African American Women and Christian Activism: New York's Black YWCA, 1905–1945* (Cambridge, MA: Harvard University Press, 1997); and Juliet E. K. Walker, *The History of Black Business in America: Capitalism, Race, and Entrepreneurship* (New York: Twayne, 1998).

6   Louis Hartz, *The Liberal Tradition in America: An Interpretation of American Political Thought since the Revolution* (New York: Harcourt, Brace, & Company, 1955), 52.

7   Richard Sennett, "Middle-Class Families and Urban Violence: The Experience of a Chicago Community in the Nineteenth Century," in *Nineteenth-Century Cities: Essays in the New Urban History*, ed. Stephan Thernstrom and Sennett (New Haven, CT: Yale University Press, 1969), 414 and 418; and Sennett, *Families against the City: Middle Class Homes of Industrial Chicago, 1872–1890* (Cambridge, MA: Harvard University Press, 1970), 207, 217, and 237. For a later work that follows in Sennett's footsteps, see Loren Baritz's *The Good Life: The Meaning of Success for the American Middle Class* (New York: Knopf, 1989).

8   Burton J. Bledstein, *The Culture of Professionalism: The Middle Class and the Development of Higher Education in America* (New York: Norton, 1976), 334.

9   Paul E. Johnson, *A Shopkeeper's Millennium: Society and Revivals in Rochester, New York, 1815–1837*

(New York: Hill & Wang, 1978), 8. Lori D. Ginzberg, *Women and the Work of Benevolence: Morality, Politics, and Class in the 19th-Century United States* (New Haven, CT: Yale University Press, 1990) is another book that ends with a middle class, which "cornered . . . in a defense of privilege" is interested above all in "social control" (211–212).

Although unfortunately undertheorized, Nancy Hewitt's companion book on women's activism in nineteenth-century Rochester is the most effective scholarship we have showing that divisions within the middle class and political struggles between different kinds of middling folks have been crucial to opening up American sexual and racial politics. See Nancy A. Hewitt, *Women's Activism and Social Change: Rochester, New York, 1822–1872* (Ithaca, NY: Cornell University Press, 1984).

10 Mary P. Ryan, *Cradle of the Middle Class: The Family in Oneida County, New York, 1790–1865* (New York: Cambridge University Press, 1981): here, 147. For another community study, see John S. Gilkeson, Jr., *Middle-Class Providence, 1820–1940* (Princeton, NJ: Princeton University Press, 1986).

11 Karen Halttunen, *Confidence Men and Painted Women: A Study of Middle-Class Culture in America, 1830–1870* (New Haven, CT: Yale University Press, 1982), 29. For a more complex view of middle-class culture, see Anne C. Rose, *Victorian America and the Civil War* (New York: Cambridge University Press, 1992).

12 Kevin Mattson, *Creating a Democratic Public: The Struggle for Urban Participatory Democracy during the Progressive Era* (University Park: Pennsylvania State University Press, 1998), 11; Glenda Elizabeth Gilmore, *Gender and Jim Crow: Women and the Politics of White Supremacy in North Carolina, 1896–1920* (Chapel Hill: University of North Carolina Press, 1996), xix.

13 Carroll Smith-Rosenberg, *Disorderly Conduct: Visions of Gender in Victorian America* (New York: Oxford University Press, 1985), 54. For Barthes, see especially 50. Smith-Rosenberg offers her most explicit condemnation of the bourgeoisie in "Davy Crockett as Trickster: Pornography, Liminality, and Symbolic Inversion in Victorian America," 90–108.

14 Charles Sellers, *The Market Revolution: Jacksonian America, 1815–1846* (New York: Oxford University Press, 1991), 239, 365. A firm exception to such denigration of the middle class is Gordon S. Wood's celebration of the democratic triumph of middling people in *The Radicalism of the American Revolution* (New York: Random House, 1991). Yet Wood's analysis simply mirrors that of Sellers; in both accounts "the middle class" is unproblematically the world-historical purveyor of market liberalism.

15 Jennifer Scanlon, *Inarticulate Longings: The Ladies' Home Journal, Gender, and the Promises of Consumer Culture* (New York: Routledge, 1995), 26. Gail Bederman's *Manliness and Civilization: A Cultural History of Gender and Race in the United States, 1880–1917* (Chicago: University of Chicago Press, 1995) is a prominent example of a work that simply assumes the conservatism of "the middle class" and its estrangement from the working class, even though the overwhelming bulk of her evidence comes from *elite* sources. For a grand theoretical treatise that attempts to argue for an ahistorical "cosy middle-class conservatism," see Michael Mann, *The Sources of Social Power, Volume II, The Rise of Classes and Nation-States, 1760–1914* (Cambridge: Cambridge University Press, 1993), 575 and passim.

16 Stuart M. Blumin, *The Emergence of the Middle Class: Social Experience in the American City, 1760–1900* (New York: Cambridge University Press, 1989); 9–10. For a perceptive critique of Blumin's analysis of the supposedly wide gap between workers and white-collar folks, see Maris A. Vinovskis, "Stalking the Elusive Middle Class in Nineteenth-Century America. A Review Article," *Comparative Studies in Society and History* 33 (July 1991): 582–587. For a book that closely follows Blumin's theoretical lead, albeit with more attention to politics, see Andrew C. Holman, *A Sense of Their Duty: Middle-Class Formation in Victorian Ontario Towns* (Montreal: McGill-Queens University Press, 2000).

17 Olivier Zunz, *Making America Corporate, 1870-1920* (Chicago: University of Chicago Press, 1990), 69, 201, 147.

18 For two recent studies that effectively highlight the complexities of middle-class politics, see Andrew Hurley, *Environmental Inequalities: Class, Race, and Industrial Pollution in Gary, Indiana, 1945–1980* (Chapel Hill: University of North Carolina Press, 1995) and Daniel J. Walkowitz's *Working with Class: Social Workers and the Politics of Middle-Class Identity* (Chapel Hill: University of North Carolina Press, 1999). See also, especially, the essays by Adam Green, Theresa Mah, and Sylvie Murray in this volume.

19 Blumin, *Emergence*, 255–257; Zunz, *Making*, 61–64, 123.

20 Richard Hofstadter, *Age of Reform: From Bryan to F.D.R.* (New York: Knopf, 1955).

21 Jurgen Kocka, *White Collar Workers in America, 1890–1940: A Social-Political History in International Perspective* (Beverly Hills: Sage, 1980), 255, 253.

22 Alan Brinkley, *Voices of Protest: Huey Long, Father Coughlin, and the Great Depression* (New York: Vintage, 1982), 197–198, 202–203, 144, 146.

23 Catherine McNicol Stock, *Main Street in Crisis: The Great Depression and the Old Middle Class on the Northern Plains* (Chapel Hill: University of North Carolina Press, 1992), 10, 1, 42, 53, 47.

24 Christopher Lasch, *The True and Only Heaven: Progress and Its Critics* (New York: W. W. Norton, 1991).

25 The only substantive study of the American lower middle class, Nancy MacLean's *Behind the Mask of Chivalry: The Making of the Second Ku Klux Klan* (New York: Oxford University Press, 1994), is an innovative attempt to force American historians to confront the lower middle class, or petite bourgeoisie. Yet by painting only a protofascist set of middling folks, MacLean fails to recognize any complexity to lower-middle-class politics.

26 C. Dallett Hemphill, *Bowing to Necessities: A History of Manners in America, 1620–1860* (New York: Oxford University Press, 1999). One of the burdens of my manuscript-in-progress, *The Radical Middle Class: Populist Democracy and the Question of Capitalism in Progressive Era Portland, Oregon*, is to renew the quest for middle-class anti-capitalism. For a study that explicitly goes beyond our ideas of a "white" middle class, see Richard A. Garcia, *Rise of the Mexican American Middle Class, San Antonio, 1929–1941* (College Station: Texas A & M Press, 1991); for one that implicitly does, see George J. Sanchez, *Becoming Mexican American: Ethnicity, Culture, and Identity in Chicano Los Angeles, 1900–1945* (New York: Oxford University Press, 1993).

27 The key text recognizing the connection between simple respect for the American middle class and the social theory about it is a brilliant letter from Richard Hofstadter to C. Wright Mills concerning the presuppositions of *White Collar*. Irving Louis Horowitz quotes the letter extensively in *C. Wright Mills: An American Utopian* (New York: Free Press, 1983), 250–252; Olivier Zunz also discusses it in *Making America Corporate*, 3–4. For an example of a book that gives members of the middle class the respect they deserve while hardly avoiding the warts, see Elaine S. Abelson, *When Ladies Go A-Thieving: Middle-Class Shoplifters in the Victorian Department Store* (New York: Oxford University Press, 1989).

Contributors

Joyce Appleby is Professor of history at UCLA and author of *Inheriting the Revolution: The First Generation of Americans* (2000).

Debby Applegate holds a doctorate in American studies from Yale University and is the author of a forthcoming biography of Henry Ward Beecher.

Sven Beckert is Associate Professor of history at Harvard University and recently a fellow at the Center for Scholars and Writers at the New York Public Library. His book *The Monied Metropolis: New York City and the Consolidation of the American Bourgeoisie* was recently published.

Burton J. Bledstein is Associate Professor of history at the University of Illinois, Chicago, and the author of *The Culture of Professionalism*.

Andrew Wender Cohen is Associate Professor of history at Syracuse University's Maxwell School of Citizenship and Public Affairs. He is currently working on a book tentatively titled *The Struggle for Order: Law, Labor, and Resistance to the Corporate Ideal in Chicago, 1900–1940*.

Clark Davis is Assistant Professor of history at California State University, Fullerton, and is the author of *Company Men: White-Collar Life and Corporate Cultures in Los Angeles, 1892–1941* (2000), which contains an expanded version of his essay in this volume.

Adam Green is Assistant Professor of history at Northwestern University, in Evanston, Illinois. His current project, *Selling Race: Culture and Community in Black Chicago, 1940–1955,* is forthcoming.

Jeffrey M. Hornstein is a Ph.D. candidate at the University of Maryland. His article is drawn from his dissertation, "Selling Home: The Rise of the Realtor® and the Transformation of the Twentieth-Century American Middle Class."

Robert D. Johnston is Associate Professor of history and American studies at Yale University, where he recently completed a three-year yerm as Director of Undergraduate Studies in the History Department. He received his bachelor's degree from Reed College, holds a doctorate from Rutgers University, and has also taught at Buena Vista

College, in Storm Lake, Iowa. He is completing *The Radical Middle Class: Populist Democracy and the Question of Capitalism in Progressive Era Portland, Oregon* and beginning work on *A Middle-Class Hero Is Something to Be: Radicals and Radicalism from Tom Paine to Tom Hayden*.

Edward James Kilsdonk is the Director of the Project for Technology in History Education at the University of Virginia. He is completing a Ph.D. in history.

Bruce Laurie is Professor of history at the University of Massachusetts at Amherst. His most recent work is "The 'Fair Field' of the 'Middle Ground': Abolitionism, Labor Reform, and the Making of an Antislavery Bloc in Antebellum Massachusetts," in Eric Arnesen, Julie Greene, and Bruce Laurie, eds., *Labor Histories: Class, Politics, and the Working-Class Experience* (1998).

Theresa Mah received her Ph.D. in history from the University of Chicago. Her dissertation, "Buying into the Middle Class: Residential Segregation and Racial Formation in the United States, 1920–1964," was completed in 1999. She is currently an Assistant Professor in the Department of Ethnic Studies at Bowling Green State University, in Ohio.

James Marten is Professor of history at Marquette University and author of *The Children's Civil War* (1998) and Director of the Children in Urban America Project: A Digital Archive.

Marina Moskowitz is a Lecturer in American history at the University of Glasgow, where she is also affiliated with the Andrew Hook Centre for American Studies. She recently completed her dissertation, "Standard Bearers: Material Culture and Middle-Class Communities at the Turn of the Century," in the American studies program at Yale.

Sylvie Murray teaches in the History Department at the University College of the Fraser Valley, British Columbia, Canada. Her book on community politics and citizenship in the post–World War II era will be published by Cornell University Press.

Andrew Chamberlin Rieser, an Assistant Professor of history at St. Cloud State University, received the Ph.D. in U.S. history from the University of Wisconsin–Madison in 1999. Recently a fellow in the Pew Program in Religion and American History at Yale University, he is presently serving as an editor of H-Ideas, H-Net's online forum for the discussion of intellectual history.

Andrea Volpe holds a Ph.D. from Rutgers University and was a postdoctoral fellow at the Pembroke Center for Teaching and Research on Women at Brown University during the 1999–2000 school year. She has taught at Colby College, the University of Southern Maine, and Rutgers. She is at work on *National Bodies: Cartes de Visite and the Politics of Visual Culture in the Nineteenth-Century United States*.

Elizabeth Alice White teaches at the University of Nevada, Las Vegas, in the History Department. Her research explores the role of sentimentality in the development of a market culture in nineteenth-century America. She is working on a book titled *Sentimental Enterprise: Sentiment and Profit in Nineteenth-Century American Market Culture*.

Index